Intimacy on the Internet

Lauren Rosewarne is among our most daring and adroit explorers of the sexual scene, always poking at the edges, the margins, to reveal how mass media have constructed our experiences. By ranging across a variety of media representations, from online dating to cyberporn, *Intimacy on the Internet* tells a new story of the Internet's impact on love and sex. Neither exclusively brave new world nor solely a haven for lonely and dangerous perverts, it's all of that, and a lot more.

Professor Michael Kimmel, Stony Brook University, Author of *Angry White Men: American Masculinity at the End of an Era*

Simply put, this is the best book I've read in some time! I couldn't put it down when I started reading it. This work addresses an exceptionally timely topic in an extremely comprehensive, yet parsimonious fashion. It is meticulously researched, and Rosewarne artfully succeeds in placing numerous depictions of the subject matter from popular culture into a tremendously solid scholarly framework. This book is destined to make a substantial contribution to professional literature in a number of fields including sociology, psychology, and cultural studies. However, the best feature of this book is that it is well-written and enjoyable! The writing style makes it accessible to a variety of audiences. Not only will advanced scholars in a number of social and behavioural sciences find it useful, I strongly believe that undergraduate students would benefit from reading the book. Additionally, the non-academic reader with an interest in this topic would find the book just as enjoyable.

Professor Keith F. Durkin, Ohio Northern University, Co-Author of *Sociology: Beyond Common Sense*

This book masterfully explores one of the most fascinating and controversial issues about digital lifestyles. By providing important insights into how contemporary media portrays intimacy in cyberspace, it reveals not just our underlying fears about the Internet, but also our hidden anxieties about connecting deeply to others. This book is a must-read for anyone who seeks to understand intimate relationships in the age of technology.

Professor John Suler, Rider University, Author of *Psychology of the Digital Age: Humans Become Electric*

The focus of this book is on the media representations of the use of the Internet in seeking intimate connections—be it a committed relationship, a hook-up, or a community in which to dabble in fringe sexual practices. Popular culture (film, narrative television, the news media, and advertising) present two very distinct pictures of the use of the Internet as related to intimacy. From news reports about victims of online dating, to the presentation of the desperate and dateless, the perverts and the deviants, a distinct frame for the intimacy/Internet connection is negativity. In some examples however, a changing picture is emerging. The ubiquitousness of Internet use today has meant a slow increase in comparatively more positive representations of successful online romances in the news, resulting in more positive-spin advertising and a more even-handed presence of such liaisons in narrative television and film. Both the positive and the negative media representations are categorized and analysed in this book to explore what they reveal about the intersection of gender, sexuality, technology, and the changing mores regarding intimacy.

Lauren Rosewarne is a Senior Lecturer at the University of Melbourne, Australia. She is the author of seven books, most recently *Cyberbullies, Cyberactivists, Cyberpredators: Film, TV, and Internet Stereotypes*, and specializes in gender, sexuality, and popular culture.

Routledge Research in Cultural and Media Studies

For a full list of titles in this series, please visit www.routledge.com.

Intimacy on the Internet
Media Representation of
Online Connections

Lauren Rosewarne

Routledge
Taylor & Francis Group

NEW YORK AND LONDON

First published 2016
by Routledge
711 Third Avenue, New York, NY 10017

and by Routledge
2 Park Square, Milton Park, Abingdon, Oxon OX14 4RN

Routledge is an imprint of the Taylor & Francis Group, an informa business

Library of Congress Cataloging-in-Publication Data

Names: Rosewarne, Lauren, author.
Title: Intimacy on the Internet: media representations of online connections /
by Lauren Rosewarne.
Description: New York, NY: Routledge, 2016. |
Series: Routledge research in cultural and media studies; 86 | Includes
bibliographical references and index.
Identifiers: LCCN 2015050143
Subjects: LCSH: Online dating. | Love in mass media. |
Mass media—Social aspects.
Classification: LCC HQ801.82 .R67 2016 | DDC 306.730285—dc23LC
record available at http://lccn.loc.gov/2015050143

ISBN: 978-1-138-82417-1 (hbk)
ISBN: 978-1-315-74085-0 (ebk)

Typeset in Sabon
by codeMantra

To Dr. C.
In happy recognition of an abundance of on-topic
conversations.

Contents

Acknowledgments

With thanks to Felisa Salvago-Keyes and Allie Simmons at Routledge. Thanks also to Professor Nancy Naples and Coleen Spurlock, both at the Women's, Gender, and Sexuality Studies Program at the University of Connecticut, Storrs, who kindly hosted me during the completion of this manuscript.

Introduction

Having previously written about, and participated in interviews on topics like love, infidelity, perversion and friendship, it seemed inevitable that I would be asked to comment on the Internet's role; about how social media, online dating and hook-up apps have impacted on human connectedness. Each interview my thoughts returned to the same idea: that the Internet gives us new and often more efficient ways to do the things—finding love, making friends, having sex, as well as documenting, bragging about and mourning their loss—that we have been doing offline for time immemorial; that the methods may have changed but that the desires remain the same. The search, therefore, for intimacy[1] online, is less about the *technology*, and more so about the simple human desire to connect; the Internet just offers a new set of tools to do it. *Connect* in this discussion centers on love, on sex, and expands the definition of intimacy to include *self*-intimacy through masturbation.

Technology however, is certainly not irrelevant to this discussion. While the Internet has replaced the other methods—like matchmaking, video-dating, escort agencies or pornography on VHS or in magazines—used in previous eras to satisfy yens for connection and pleasure, the Internet creates its own medium-specific attributes that shape intimacy quests. Akin to personal columns in decades past, for example, anonymity plays a unique and significant role; people online are invariably introduced using screen names, sometimes without photos, and can postpone or entirely *prevent* any kind of physical relationship altogether, thus allowing the entirety of a liaison to play out via the written word. Something that distinguishes an activity like online dating from introductory methods like classifieds however, is numbers: *millions* of people date online, something that wasn't the case for other market-based matchmaking methods in years prior. The relevance of scale extends to pornography, escort services and other online intimacy offerings: indeed, there were professional and amateur marriage brokers and professional and amateur pornographers before the World Wide Web but the Internet created—and notably *legitimized*—markets, made access effortless, and expanded the consumer base.

The expanded, and now highly lucrative, markets for online dating and netporn highlight another unique aspect of the Internet's role in intimacy: commerce. Whereas people meeting on networked bulletin boards in a pre-Web era ushered in online socializing, it wasn't until the mid-1990s with the launch of companies like Match.com that Internet dating became a market—and, eventually, a large and lucrative one—that suddenly the role of money in the quest for intimacy became a consideration with relevance to many. Suddenly, *paying* for an introduction, of being faced with a deluge of possible matches and having to actively market oneself in this busy marketplace spawned a range of debates about just how romantic this caper is, or whether in fact, going online suddenly made the quest for intimacy a little cold, a little sterile and a whole lot unserendipitous.

Another unique aspect of the Internet's role here is the computer, not merely as an efficiency tool, but rather as the incarnation of the long-feared harbinger of dehumanization. While "science" was indeed involved in the early computer-aided dating of the 1960s[2] and the video-dating of the 1980s, again, not only were those earlier methods largely unpopular, but the use today of the Internet—of *computers*—on such a large scale has revolutionized the entire dating landscape and raised some very specific issues about modern intimacy. While technophobia has long plagued the use of machines and any new means of doing things once done manually—by humans—the Internet creates its own unique set of anxieties. Technophobia and, more recently, the emergence of *cyberphobia*, have led to questions about just how "real" interactions are online given the role of computers, of money and of carefully constructed and curated profiles, if not outright *deceit*; about just how *romantic* matches are when made through a machine.

While much has been written elsewhere about topics like online dating and cybersex—and while a great deal of this research is indeed examined throughout this book—*Intimacy on the Internet: Media Representations of Online Connections* focuses specifically on how the topics introduced thus far—the role of the market in love, issues of authenticity and rampant techno- and cyberphobia—play out in screen fiction. Since the mid-1990s the Internet has come to have a distinct presence in film and television; thus, it is no surprise that just as topics like hacking and cyberbullying have featured prominently,[3] so too have online dating, cybersex and the emerging social dilemma of cyberinfidelity.

Immediately prior to this volume, my research centered on analyzing the denizens of the Internet—cyberpredators, cyberbullies and cyberperverts— as depicted in popular media.[4] *Intimacy on the Internet* continues this project of examining the Internet in pop culture but focuses more specifically on the messages delivered about the technology's role in love and sex. Such a focus allows me to return to topics that I have held a long-standing academic interest in—infidelity,[5] perversion[6] and masturbation[7]—and examine how such experiences are impacted by new modes of participation and, ultimately, how they get fictionalized and served up as an entertainment product. While many of the themes that I examined in my previous book—the tropes of the Internet as a Wild West and cyberspace as a hunting grounds—are relevant to this discussion, *Intimacy on the Internet* also introduces a range of new themes that further our understandings of how intimacy has been changed in the Internet age and how this change has been portrayed. In this volume, for example, I examine how some of the screen stereotypes of online daters—as losers, as desperate, as gullible—mirror, as well as potentially *feed*, our off-screen perceptions about those who go online for love, for sex. Despite enormous participation in online dating in real life, on screen the act continues to not only be depicted as niche, but one associated with society's unlovable and notably *unfuckable*: it is the dating market for those who have failed at intimacy in "real life."

More than just undesirable daters, popular media presents a strong link between the Internet and characters with nefarious intent; something illustrated through a range of examples where online daters are portrayed as duplicitous, dangerous and where the Internet is used to prey on those seeking connection. The capacity for anonymity means that screen representations are invariably haunted by the theme of "stranger danger" and the presumption that anyone met online is likely to be a villain. There is, of course, also a significant gender element here, whereby it is *men* who are portrayed as hunting for female prey online and it is *women* who are invariably punished for using a machine to find love, sex.

Through an analysis of over 300 film and television examples—spanning genres from thrillers through to Christian-drama—depictions of characters seeking love and sex have been probed for narrative themes; those that confirm my assumption that the Internet's role in intimacy is framed largely as problematic, as well as those rare occasions when a neutral or even positive portrayal is proffered.

From narrative themes of commerce and authenticity through to (un)fuckability, duplicity and sex of the vanilla and not-so kind, these presentations are used to illustrate, as well as provide opportunities for academic inquiry into the place of the Internet in the popular imaginary and its presentation in entertainment media. These screen portrayals are then analyzed to determine what they reveal about our complicated offline relationship with subjects like technology, gender, sexuality and love, and how the screen reflects, and also impacts, upon these perceptions.

Intimacy on the Internet is an extension of my academic interest in popular culture. My work is conducted to gain an insight into the complicated ways that the body, sex and gender get discussed, portrayed, consumed, and enjoyed in real life. This volume contributes to the discussion of the ever-evolving role of technology in our private lives and spotlights the increasingly fluid nature of terms like *intimacy* and *connectedness* in the Internet age.

Notes

1. I use social scientist Jo Barraket and Millsom Henry-Waring's definition of intimacy as presented in their work on e-dating: "We use the term 'intimacy' to describe emotional/romantic and/or sexual relations between adults, ranging from one-off interactions to sustained offline relationships" (Jo Barraket and

Millsom S. Henry-Waring, "Getting It On[line] Sociological Perspectives on e-Dating," *Journal of Sociology*, 44 [2008]): 149–65, 150). As becomes apparent in Chapters 5 and 6, I extend this definition to include intimacy with the self, as relevant to behavior like netporn-aided masturbation and cybersex.

2. Ted Sutton, "Project Flame," *Slate*, March 4, 2014. Accessed June 25, 2015 from http://www.slate.com/articles/technology/technology/2014/03/before_okcupid_and_match_com_there_was_project_flame_what_happened_when.html.
3. Lauren Rosewarne, *Cyberbullies, Cyberactivists, Cyberpredators: Film, TV, and Internet Stereotypes* (Santa Barbara, CA: Praeger, 2016).
4. Lauren Rosewarne, *Cyberbullies, Cyberactivists, Cyberpredators: Film, TV, and Internet Stereotypes* (Santa Barbara, CA: Praeger, 2016).
5. Lauren Rosewarne, *Cheating on the Sisterhood: Infidelity and Feminism* (Santa Barbara, CA: Praeger, 2009).
6. Lauren Rosewarne, *Part-Time Perverts: Sex, Pop Culture and Kink Management* (Santa Barbara, CA: Praeger, 2011).
7. Lauren Rosewarne, *Masturbation in Pop Culture: Screen, Society, Self* (Lanham, MD: Lexington Books, 2014).

1 The Market Economy of Love

In a world of online shopping, electronic funds transfers and digital commerce, thinking of the Internet as a kind of marketplace—as its own economy—is nothing new. More than a generic place, and means, to conduct trade, this chapter focuses on the Internet's specific role in retailing love and sex: as a place aiding in the acquisition of relationships, the arrangement of hook-ups and a means to satisfy niche sexual interests. The use of the Internet in this fashion is, of course, easily identifiable on screen. Portrayals of online dating perfectly fit this bill, as do more recent depictions centered on location-based hook-up apps. Other, more explicitly sex-based products such as Internet pornography (netporn), erotic webcam sites and the online booking of sex workers are also part of this.

While the depiction of the Internet as a venue for intimacy commerce is a central theme in this chapter, the focus more specifically is on how the values of consumerism such as choice, customization and disposability have impacted on intimacy and its online acquisition. This chapter begins with the contentious idea of love as purchasable, and moves on to examine the role that the screen has in normalizing the Internet in intimacy quests and thus legitimizing the market. The economic drivers underpinning love in the Internet age are then analyzed.

The Purchase of Love

In a scene from the drama *Temptation: Confessions of a Marriage Counselor* (2013), the entrepreneur Harley (Robbie Jones)—within his critique of the online dating industry—remarked, "I prefer the old-fashioned way of meeting women." Later in the film, Judith (Jurnee Smollett-Bell), a dating company psychologist—and a woman about to have an affair with Harley—says to him, "I prefer the old-fashioned way of finding love." Both comments allude to the characters' belief—and an attitude widely detected both on screen and off—that use of the Internet to find love is fundamentally *different* to other methods; that it is somehow less authentic, less romantic. The fact that Harley and Judith first met in "real life" as opposed to online—most notably with the online dating industry existing in the background—subtly implies that true passion is spontaneous, is serendipitous and happens without the "sullying" influence of technology. This subtle condemnation, in fact, gets confirmed in every screen example where an online dating experiment not only ends badly, but notably gets contrasted with a better real-life introduction and love match. The television drama *The Husband She Met Online* (2013) illustrates this particularly well. Rachel (Meredith Monroe) met Craig (Jason Gray-Stanford) online; Craig turned out to be a violent, controlling murderer. In the final scene of the film—after Craig is killed— Rachel is walking in a park when she bumps into a central casting *nice guy*.[1] This accidental meet cute[2] is presented as the way a couple *should* meet and exists in sharp contrast to Rachel's ill-fated Internet-instigated relationship. Although in *The Husband She Met Online* the contrast between off- and online meetings is extreme, other examples convey the same message, albeit with more subtlety. In the comedy *Jack and Jill* (2011), lonely and homely Jill (Adam Sandler) signed up for online dating. Her foray was marred by rejection and disappointment. By the end of the film however, Jill does find love, albeit love she found *offline*. The romantic-comedy *Because I Said So* (2007) centers on Daphne's (Diane Keaton) attempts to find love online for her daughter Milly (Mandy Moore). Like Jill, Milly ends up finding love, but again, it happens with someone met offline. In the television holiday movie *A Very Merry Mix-Up* (2013), despite Alice's (Alicia Witt) engagement to Will (Scott Gibson)—whom she met on Mates.com with a 75% compatibility rating—her true love, *her destiny*, was with Matt (Mark Wiebe) who she met serendipitously at an airport. In the "Sweet Little Lies" episode of the drama series *Black Box* (2014), Lina (Ali Wong) posted an online dating profile. Lina's use of the website was scarcely mentioned again in the series; shortly after she posted her profile, she found love in the "normal way"[3]. A variation on this theme was apparent in the pilot episode of the sitcom *A to Z* (2014–15), where it turned out that Andrew's (Ben Feldman) love interest, Zelda (Cristin Milioti)—whose profile was on his online dating company's website—hadn't actually put it there herself, in turn quietly repeating the screen truism that real love comes *without* the assistance of the Internet; that Andrew and Zelda were a true match because neither were really dating online. Similarly, for Diana (Natasha Henstridge) and Ken (Gabriel Hogan) in the television holiday film *A Christmas Song* (2012), even though they were matched online—on *two* separate occasions—and while they ended up together, the couple already knew each other offline as teaching colleagues and thus, the Internet simply *validated* the serendipity of their offline match.

A different spin on this idea is fate and the Internet being framed as diametrically—if not *dangerously*—opposed. In *A Very Merry Mix-Up* for example, Alice ultimately saw it as her *destiny* to meet Matt, regardless of the on-paper perfection of her online match with Will. In an unnamed series 2 episode of the British comedy series *Starlings* (2012–13), destiny was similarly alluded to when Grandpa (Alan Williams) tried online dating. After his failed date—his match was in a vegetative state—he was riding the bus home, feeling dejected, and a fellow passenger counselled him, "if you're meant to find someone, you will." Grandpa found comfort in this remark, an idea that, again, taps into the idea of serendipity and real love arriving, *like magic*, rather than being worked for, paid for or found online.

In his book *Love Online*, the sociologist Jean-Claude Kaufmann bitingly remarked, "Welcome to the consumerist illusion which would have us believe that we can choose a man (or a woman) in the same way that we choose a yoghurt in the hypermarket."[4] The same shopping analogy was used in the documentary *Hooked* (2003), centered on the use of the Internet by gay men seeking sex: "It's like in the supermarket ... you go into the supermarket and look for a product that appeals to you." The journalist David Masciotra also used this analogy: "Online dating offers transactional romance, allowing users to browse for a partner as they would browse for a book, refrigerator, or lawnmower."[5] Not only do these remarks reference the capitalist edict of choice (discussed later in this chapter), but they present online dating as a thoroughly unromantic way to meet; that the transaction is cold, perfunctory and exists in strong opposition to Hollywood's idealized meet cutes. In several screen examples the apparent lack of romance in a Web meet actually gets verbalized. In the British drama *Birthday Girl* (2001), John (Ben Chaplin) used the FromRussiaWithLove.com site to find a bride, "Nadia" (Nicole Kidman). Nadia, in fact, turned out to be a con artist intent on scamming him. During an argument, John's new bride summarized perfectly his miserable situation which Nadia mocked was capped by his use of the Internet to find intimacy:

> So tell me, John, did you say, when I grow up, what I want is to still be in this town, in this job that I hate, in a house with ants and a big bag of pornography? And then I'm going to send off to Russia for a wife and she'll fall in love with me. What did you expect, John? What did you really expect to happen?

Harley and Judith's comments in *Temptation: Confessions of a Marriage Counselor*, and Nadia's comments in *Birthday Girl*, reflect the simple but commonly held screen belief that online dating is unromantic; that it's nobody's *ideal* way to meet, but rather, is something succumbed to after other methods are exhausted. The title character's foray into online dating in the drama series *Ally McBeal* (1997–2002) provides a perfect illustration of this: Ally (Calista Flockhart) went online in the "Do You Wanna Dance?" episode *only* after exhausting many other options in pursuit of love (worth noting, Ally's online dating efforts also failed dismally).

The supposed lack of romance in an online meet is, apparently, entrenched sufficiently in the zeitgeist for online dating companies to aggressively attempt to challenge it; an idea discussed by film theorist Michele Schreiber:

> Television advertisements for the two most successful American dating sites eharmony.com and match.com actively deflate the negative

connotations of online dating's unromantic nature by appropriating aesthetics reminiscent of postfeminist romance films. Eharmony's advertisements are particularly skilful at playing up the serendipitous possibilities available once the site matches you.[6]

The sociologist John Bridges made similar points in his discussion of eHarmony's advertising:

> [T]hose sappy, romantically oriented, overly simplistic, "I found the love of my life" and "I'm so happy" messages—which successfully plucked the heart strings of those "I want to believe" viewers in a way that left their critical faculties unengaged and their credulity unchallenged, were a major part of eHarmony's success.[7]

A 2015 Match.com commercial provides a good example of an explicit challenge to the unromantic idea: "If you're sitting at dinner with Mr. Right, does it matter where you met him?" This notion of the Internet as less romantic than other options is discussed in more detail in Chapter 2.

Noted earlier was the idea of online dating being imbued with stigma. In fact, such stigma has been steadily abating over the years and the use of the Internet in intimacy-seeking has undergone a progressive process of normalization, one admittedly slow to be replicated on screen.

Normalizing the Net

A key factor that has enabled the Internet to so substantially revolutionize the quest for intimacy is its mainstreaming: both the mainstreaming of use in general, but more specifically the mainstreaming of certain products associated with it. The most obvious example is high-level participation in online dating.

Dating in the Mainstream

Kaufmann identified how, over time, online dating has undergone a dramatic rebranding:

> Online dating, whose image was once little better than that of marriage agencies, has, in the space of only a few years, become a normal and legitimate way of finding a soulmate ... It has even become trendy, which is not something that can be said of marriage agencies.[8]

Bridges made a similar claim, noting how the online daters in his study now "accepted the dating sites as the new way to meet people, and some really do see it as the only game in town."[9] Whether we think of online dating as simply having lost its stigma as Kaufmann implies or embraced as enthusiastically as Bridges contends, in real life the Internet has become a key player in intimacy. While a variety of studies attempt to put a figure on just how many people have signed up, dated someone they met online or even gotten *married* as a result,[10] for the purposes of this discussion, statistics are much less important than the simple reality that the Internet is now a place—if not *the* place—turned to for human connection: that just as we go online to seek answers to every other life question, it has become the default way to answer *who's out there for me?*

Spouses, of course, are still met via well-established methods such as through friends, at school, university, work and church, but the Internet—specifically online dating and, more recently, hook-up apps—has ushered in the first truly new means of connecting that has been embraced so widely. This latter point is particularly important because it would be fraudulent to contend that online dating is the first *new* attempt to connect, nor the first depicted in film: in fact, the alternatives have a long history both off screen and on. The rabbi Sidney Markowitz, for example, traced professional matchmaking services back to the Torah,[11] and matchmaking on screen dates back as early as the American silent-short *Blind Marriage* (1914) and is a theme in narratives as diverse as the musical *Hello, Dolly!* (1969) and Hitchcock's thriller *Frenzy* (1972).[12] In fact, although there are a deluge of popular media examples centered on spontaneous meet cutes, there are also many examples where serendipity gets eschewed and a proactive, market-based approach is adopted. Dan Slater, in his book *Love in the Time of Algorithms*, traced use of newspaper classifieds in the quest for love back to Britain in the 1600s,[13] and unsurprisingly this method has a distinct screen history dating back to the beginning of the twentieth century in two American silent shorts: *Personal* (1904) and *How a French Nobleman Got a Wife Through the 'New York Herald' Personal Columns* (1904). The use of classifieds is also detected in a range of modern screen examples,[14] notably those exploiting their use as a hunting grounds for lonely hearts[15] (a storyline, in fact, with close parallels to online dating portrayals in modern cinema; see Chapter 4). In the 1960s, computers had their first role in dating in a pre-Web, eHarmony-precursor[16]—a "scientific" matchmaking method which made its way into a range of other screen narratives.[17] With the rise of video recorders in the 1970s, *video-dating*—a process whereby VHS cassettes of potential love matches got exchanged—came to hold a small place in the dating landscape and again, a small spot on screen: the short-lived television series *Lovespring International* (2006) was, in fact, centered on a video-aided matchmaking business, and this method has featured in a range of screen examples.[18] Such methods however, never reached anywhere near the levels of real-life use, nor acceptance, as online dating: a matchmaking mode that has completely overhauled relationship instigation.[19] While such popularity is partly explained by psychologist Al Cooper's Triple-A engine of the

Internet—affordability, accessibility and anonymity[20]—Slater presents some other, zeitgeist-specific rationales:

> An easily accessible, rationalized marketplace of relationships: This was the big, game-changing difference between online dating and other forms of relationship intermediation that came before. The online-dating industry sold choice and control at a time when choice and control were exactly what many people wanted and needed.[21]

Off screen the Internet has increasingly come to be viewed as a viable dating option, but on screen the picture is more complicated. As shown in my previous research on the Internet in pop culture, a barrage of negative stereotypes still haunt online activities such as dating.[22] That said, the very fact that use of the Internet to find love has such a strong screen presence is testimony to it having become normal—not necessarily without critique, but certainly normal. In film and television there are numerous ways this normalcy is depicted; the first, in line with Bridges' comments earlier, are those occasions when it is presented as *the only game in town*.

The Only Game in Town

In an unnamed episode of the lesbian-themed Scottish series *Lip Service* (2010–12), Frankie (Ruta Gedmintas) suggested online dating to her friend Tess (Fiona Button). Tess declined, and Frankie countered, "What's the alternative?" While Frankie wasn't championing online dating as a solution—in fact, there was resignation in her tone—she nonetheless alluded to the reality that the landscape has changed and that online dating is now the standard option, that other methods are simply not as effective or, as discussed later in this chapter, as *efficient*. While Frankie's comment alludes to slight regret that things have changed to such an extent—that perhaps, as discussed earlier, this method is not a particularly romantic way to meet a partner—other scenes portray the new dating landscape with much less concern. The "Good Crazy" episode of the sitcom *How I Met Your Mother* (2005–14), for example, frames the Internet as the modern replacement for the meet cute, something apparent in Barney's (Neil Patrick Harris) comments to his single friend Ted (Josh Radnor):

BARNEY: I'm thinking of something much more traditional. Online dating.
TED: Yeah, no thanks.
BARNEY: Come on, Ted. It's 2012. What do you expect? To meet some cute travel agent when you're reading a newspaper at a bookstore. None of those things exist anymore.
TED: Barney, I will never ever ever try online dating.

A similar, modern frame is offered in the "Newer Elements of Our Defense" episode of the Canadian sci-fi series *Orphan Black* (2013–), when Felix (Jordan Gavaris) touted the "Sapphire" hook-up app to Cosima (Tatiana Maslany): "Nobody meets anyone in person anymore, darling. It's the future." The same modern frame was apparent in the "Joey and the Holding Hands" episode of the sitcom *Joey* (2004–6), when Michael (Paulo Costanzo) countered his uncle's (Matt Le Blanc) concerns about online dating: "You can be as cynical as you want, Joey, this is how my generation meets people, okay?"

Tess in *Lip Service*, Ted in *How I Met Your Mother* and Cosima in *Orphan Black*—despite their initial reluctance—did actually try online dating, providing visual testimony to the idea that when carefully considered, online dating may not be the *only* game in town, but is certainly better than many others.

In Chapter 3 I discuss how online dating is routinely framed on screen as a last resort for the unfuckable. *Lip Service*, *How I Met Your Mother* and *Orphan Black* present a detour from this trope. This change can simply be explained by the democratizing of the Internet attributable to ease of use and affordability: that everyone is online now, not just the nerds who once dominated its use,[23] thus expanding the image of the typical user to include attractive and eligible people like Tess, Ted and Cosima. Social theorist Sophia DeMasi also suggests a range of demographic factors contributing to this changed landscape which have increased the dating pool and led to the embrace of online options out of necessity; for example the postponement of marriage, divorce rates, longevity and the rise in acceptability of homosexuality. DeMasi notes that the increased number of lovelorn have both fueled the demand for online dating and legitimized it as a means to cater to it.[24] (Diana Senechal in her book *Republic of Noise* makes a similar point in the context of the *lonely* driving the industry;[25] see Chapter 3). Many of these demographic changes exist as underpinnings of the online pursuit of intimacy on screen.

In screen narratives with divorce as a theme, online dating is routinely tried by characters seeking a new relationship, albeit most commonly in one-off television episodes where the activity is played for laughs. In the "Online Dating" episode of the sitcom *Hot Properties* (2005), for example, divorced Lola (Sofía Vergara) and two of her friends joined an online dating site; a narrative that is, in fact, relatively common on screen. Divorced, attractive, middle-aged women try online dating in the "California Girls" episode of the family-drama *Make It or Break It* (2009–12), the "Zero Dark Forties" episode of the sitcom *The Exes* (2011–), the "May the Best Friend Win" episode of the sitcom *Baby Daddy* (2012–), "The Tryst" episode of the sitcom *Trophy Wife* (2013–14), the "Internet Dating" episode of the sitcom *The Millers* (2013–15), and in the romantic-comedy *The Perfect Man* (2005). In *A Christmas Song*, mentioned earlier, Diana was also an eligible divorcee using online dating to restart her romantic life. The romantic-comedy *Must*

Love Dogs (2005) centered on the divorced Sarah (Diane Lane), who was convinced by friends and family to start dating online; she met Jake (John Cusack), a divorced man also looking for a new beginning. Jake, in fact, is indicative of a range of middle-aged, and older, *male* characters also restarting their romantic lives with the help of the Web. Sarah's father, Bill (Christopher Plummer), dates online in the same film. In the "New Kids on the Block" episode of the legal-drama *Boston Legal* (2004–8), Denny (William Shatner), an attorney in his 70s, begins online dating and is matched with a midget; the same thing that happens to middle-aged Moe in the "Eeny Teeny Maya Moe" episode of the animated series *The Simpsons* (1989–). In the aforementioned episode of *Starlings*, Grandpa tries online dating; Grandpa in the "Attack of the Killer Kung-Fu Wolf Bitch" episode of the animated series *The Boondocks* (2005–) does the same thing.

The "Generation of Vipers" episode of the British crime-drama *Lewis* (2006–) centered on the murder of a university professor who was dating online. During the episode, Detective Inspector Lewis (Kevin Whately) discussed the case with his middle-aged colleague, Dr. Laura Hobson (Clare Holman):

LEWIS: Going online. Exposing yourself to millions of strangers. I don't know.
HOBSON: Don't knock it until you've tried it.
LEWIS: You haven't.
HOBSON: Single woman, my age. Any age. What we supposed to do? Hang around in bars? Like—
LEWIS: Like lumberjacks?
HOBSON: Exactly. Online you can reveal yourself relatively painlessly.

Laura verbalizes a pivotal rationale for older single characters—or in fact, *any* single characters—going online: that methods like lingering in bars are unappealing (and even *inefficient*, as explored later in this chapter)[26] and thus alternatives are sought. Laura's comments aren't about online dating being some kind of *last resort*, but rather, the method serving as a logical option given the alternatives.

This *Lewis* scene also alludes to another means by which online dating has become normalized on screen: via reference to participation numbers. Although Lewis was referring to millions of *strangers* (a means by which the method gets framed as impersonal, unromantic and possibly even dangerous as discussed in Chapter 2), nonetheless the sheer magnitude of participation has helped the method to undergo a mainstreaming on screen.

Safety in Numbers

eHarmony's advertising frequently references success stories: their website, for example, boasts, "We've helped over one million people create successful relationships and understand what it takes to initiate harmony between two people." Match.com similarly run commercials boasting that 25,000 people join their site everyday; in 2015 the company aired an advertisement claiming that their matches lead to more second dates and marriages than any other. These tactics illustrate a point made by DeMasi about *broad appeal* which is another way that online dating has becoming normalized, and something advertising has had a key role in:

> Equally significant is the purposeful effort by marketeers to construct online dating as a legitimate way for ordinary people to meet partners. In order to increase revenues through paid customer subscriptions, marketeers of online dating sites have deployed strategies to increase their mass appeal.[27]

References made in advertising to success or to the quantity of participation is a mode of normalization that has been mirrored in screen fiction. The drama *In Search of a Midnight Kiss* (2007), for example, opened with a statement attributed to *The Los Angeles Gazette*: "Between December 25th and January 1st the number of people on Match.com, CraigsList and MySpace increased by three hundred percent." While this quote can be construed as insight into holiday-based loneliness (Chapter 3), it also presents the simple idea that lots of people participate—a safety-in-numbers plea widely detected. In the same film, a conversation between friends Jacob (Brian McGuire) and Wilson (Scoot McNairy) furthers this idea:

JACOB: Look, if you really want to meet somebody that's pretty and cool
    and interesting, you can do that. All you gotta do, my friend, is put up
    an ad on the CraigsList.
WILSON: No, I don't know, man. The whole online dating thing, I think is a
    little bit too, you know, pathetic for me.
JACOB: It's not pathetic. I mean, everybody does it. I have a Myspace, Facebook,
    Min [Kathleen Luong] does too. Everybody does.

While Wilson, like Tess in *Lip Service* and Ted in *How I Met Your Mother*—along with several of the naysayer characters discussed throughout this section—gives voice to possible audience scepticism about online dating, their views get challenged within narratives by other characters who posit that it is perfectly normal. In *Temptation: Confessions of a Marriage Counselor*, for example, Harley alleges that, "more than half of new relationships started online in this day and age." In the aforementioned *Lewis* episode, Laura made a similar point, telling Lewis, "Over twenty percent of all married couples now meet on the Internet." The same case is presented in the "Two Bodies in the Lab" episode of the crime-drama *Bones* (2005–), when Temperance (Emily Deschanel), started online dating. Although Temperance's colleague, Agent Booth (David Boreanaz), was skeptical, two others—Angela (Michaela Conlin) and Hodgins (T.J. Thyne)—argued that the activity is completely normal:

BOOTH: So what if your computer date's psycho?
ANGELA: Only about a billion people date online.
HODGINS: I have.

In "The Cinderella in the Cardboard" episode of the same series, a conversation between Booth, Hodgins and Angela about a location-based hook-up app again conveys normalization through reference to participation numbers:

HODGINS: Okay, this is embarrassing.
BOOTH: Yeah, it's worse than that because your picture just popped up on a
    dead woman's cell phone.
HODGINS: Because my phone was within one hundred yards of hers.
BOOTH: Hey, don't get all squinty on me, okay, Hodgins. I want an explanation.
HODGINS: It's a dating service.
ANGELA: You're using a dating service?
HODGINS: Yes, along with millions of other people.[28]

In political science, *legitimacy* is often defined as the popular acceptance of an authority. As related to this discussion, online dating gets legitimized via participation numbers; lots of participants means that it becomes perceived as mainstream rather than something utilized only by a small, unappealing subculture. Interestingly, and a topic addressed later in this chapter (and explored throughout this book), is that the modern perception of *so many* participants has a variety of market-based impacts on the online dating experience including the necessity for participants to actively self-promote in a competitive marketplace, through to the perception of the disposability and replaceability of dates. Equally, as discussed in Chapter 4, the sheer volume of participants—of, in Lewis's wording, *strangers*—also helps to further the idea of not merely danger, but *volume* of danger.

Normalization is also achieved on screen through the framing of online daters as normal people as opposed to distinctly unfuckable people.

Normal People Date Here

While there are a deluge of screen examples of online daters presented as freaks and perverts (Chapter 4), there are also some interesting exceptions. A common exception transpires in narratives where shock is exhibited about someone so normal (read: conventionally fuckable) dating online, in turn, subtly challenging preconceptions about the *who* of online dating and suggesting in fact, that normal people do it. In the aforementioned "Generation of Vipers" episode of *Lewis*, for example, the title character seemed shocked that someone like his attractive and respected colleague

Laura had tried it. Such shock and skepticism in fact, is widely identifiable.[29] In the "Two Bodies in the Lab" episode of *Bones*, this idea was apparent in a conversation between Temperance's online date, David (Coby Ryan McLaughlin), and Booth:

BOOTH: You're an investment banker, good-looking guy, but yet you find your women online.
DAVID: Excuse me?
BOOTH: Don't you find any women at work?
DAVID: [Gesturing to Temperance] She was online too and she's a great-looking doctor.

In *In Search of a Midnight Kiss*, on Vivian's (Sara Simmonds) first date with Stevie (Bruce Jay), she—like Booth—exhibited skepticism, "So you seem like a really nice guy. Why are you posting ads on CraigsList? I mean, don't you think that's a little pathetic?" In the Belgian sci-fi film *Thomas est amoureux* (*Thomas in Love*) (2000), the agoraphobic title character (Benoît Verhaert) met a woman on a dating site and commented, "You seem rather cute. Your face at least. What is your problem?" In the thriller *Hard Candy* (2005), on their first in-person date, Hayley (Ellen Page) remarked to Jeff (Patrick Wilson), "You just don't look like the kind of guy who has to meet girls over the Internet." In the "No Ordinary Mobster" episode of the superhero series *No Ordinary Family* (2010–11), on discovering that his tutor, Katie (Autumn Reeser), was dating online, teen JJ (Jimmy Bennett), expressed confusion: "That doesn't make any sense," he says, "I mean, why are you meeting guys online? You're, like, amazing." Such confusion is also apparent in the thriller *Perfect Stranger* (2007), in a conversation between Rowena (Halle Berry) and her boss Harrison (Bruce Willis):

ROWENA: Actually, I'm thinking about joining Match.com
HARRISON: No you're not. Are you kidding me?
ROWENA: Lots of people date online.
HARRISON: You're gorgeous.

In my book *Cyberbullies, Cyberactivists, Cyberpredators*, I contended that such scenes work to normalize the assumption that the Internet is populated by freaks and weirdos; that this idea gets bolstered when a character expresses surprise to have found someone *so normal*—so *outlier*—within the badlands of cyberspace and among the presumably cretinous population.[30] An alternate interpretation however, is that these scenes actually help to subtly normalize the idea that sane, attractive and intelligent people *do* use the Internet; that while surprise may be exhibited, nevertheless sane, attractive and intelligent daters *are* online. An extension of this idea is apparent when normal characters—characters who would likely be successful in *any* dating game—actively elect to date online; that doing so is construed as rational action rather than a last resort. A good illustration transpires in the "Red Lacquer Nail Polish" episode of the crime-drama series *The Mentalist* (2008–15). Detective colleagues Cho (Tim Kang) and Rigsby (Owain Yeoman) have a brief conversation about the latter's relentless pining for his colleague Grace (Amanda Righetti):

CHO: How long has it been since you've had relations with a woman?
RIGSBY: Recently.
CHO: Lying again. Find a woman.
RIGSBY: Yeah, you know what? You're right. I will. It's what I have to do.

Rigsby, an attractive police detective, then signs up with a dating site. Something similar transpired in the "I'm Moving On" episode of *Hart of Dixie* (2011–15), a drama series centered on Zoe (Rachel Bilson), a young, attractive doctor working in a small town in Alabama. The day after Zoe failed to seduce her neighbor, George (Scott Porter), she signed up for online dating: "Moving on. Fishing in a whole new pond," she chimed. While neither Rigsby nor Zoe actually successfully coupled with anyone they met online—the common fate, incidentally, for the online dater on screen—nonetheless, that these two attractive characters tried the method helps to normalize it by signaling to the audience that it is an option, even for the attractive. Another interpretation—and one again, connected to market values—is that going online enables characters to take control of their dating life. In signing up to a site, a person is (a) making a conscious effort to change his or her romantic fate and (b) is actively outing him- or herself as someone who is looking to connect (as opposed to passively waiting for a serendipitous meet cute). A dater in Slater's work, for example, had seemingly internalized these ideas: "My friends think I'm crazy for being on Match ... They tell me I don't need it. But quote unquote need isn't really the point, is it? It's about taking control."[31] This desire to *take control* gets verbalized in several screen examples. In "The Practice Around the Corner" episode of the British comedy-drama series *Doc Martin* (2004–), Al (Joe Absolom) began online dating because he wanted his life to be different; something made apparent in a conversation with his father, Bert (Ian McNeice):

AL: She's agreed to meet me. Tonight.
BERT: Nosferatu?
AL: Nefertari.
BERT: It's a bad idea ...
AL: It's my night off. It's only over in Wainbridge.
BERT: Yeah, but searching for love on the Internet, I mean that's for losers.
AL: Yeah, it's been ages since I've been out with anyone. I don't want to end up sitting on my tod in front of the TV every night. No offence, Dad.

The same proactivity played out in the "Furt" episode of the comedy-drama series *Glee* (2009–15). Sue (Jane Lynch) was told by a love rival, "Face it

Sue, you're never gonna find someone and you're gonna die alone." Via voiceover Sue revealed, "So I decided to try online dating." In the Australian comedy *Da Kath and Kim Code* (2005), a decision to change her life was similarly articulated by Sharon (Magda Szubanski): "I'm Internet dating. I've made a vow, I'm not going to spend Christmas on my own again." Control and changing-fate was also apparent in *Must Love Dogs* in comments made by Sarah's friend, Carol (Elizabeth Perkins), in her justification for why she posted a profile on Sarah's behalf: "You can't just sit back and passively answer other people's ads anymore. We are on offence."

These characters are framed as rational market actors, having identified a need and entered the market to satisfy it as efficiently as possible.

Mentioned earlier were the stories presented in dating company advertisements about success. This idea alludes to the final means I discuss in this chapter by which the normalization of online dating is facilitated: happy matches serving as testimony to legitimacy.[32]

Normal People Couple Here

While things going awry is the more common screen trajectory—due, of course, to screen narratives needing to be sufficiently entertaining and, notably, *dramatic*—examples of online dating successes do transpire, working to reinforce the idea that not only do normal people do it, but that the method can work as intended. In the "Two Bodies in the Lab" episode of *Bones*, for example, success is referenced in a conversation between David and Booth:

BOOTH: So, this whole you know, online thing, how long does it last? Because
    if it's just a way to, you know, hook up, I gotta tell you it's pretty low.
DAVID: Yeah, one of my partners met his wife online.
BOOTH: You're kidding?
DAVID: No. They've been married five years.
BOOTH: Doesn't mean it's not creepy.

Although in this example, success is merely anecdotal, a small number of other examples actually follow the online dating journey through to relationship success. In narratives such as the comedy *Napoleon Dynamite* (2004), and the British biopic *One Chance* (2013), relationships instigated online actually last. This similarly happens for Sheldon (Jim Parsons) and Amy (Mayim Bialik) in the sitcom *The Big Bang Theory* (2007–). Matched in "The Lunar Excitation" episode, Sheldon and Amy stay together across numerous seasons. These examples however, involved characters who are, in varying degrees, *nerdy* and not conventionally attractive; in turn, they comply with common (and negative) perceptions about the *who* of online dating (Chapter 3). Other examples however, do actually portray attractive and conventionally "eligible" characters successfully coupling. In the romantic-comedy *You've Got Mail* (1998), for example—a film often credited for helping to change real-life perceptions about online dating[33]—Joe (Tom Hanks) and Kathleen (Meg Ryan) met in a chatroom and ended up together. Sarah and Jake in *Must Love Dogs* also ended happily ever after. In the Canadian television drama *Perfect Romance* (2004), Tess (Kathleen Quinlan), who went online to find a man for her daughter, Jenny (Lori Heuring), met Peter (Henry Ian Cusick). Despite Peter attempting an in-person relationship with Jenny, it was Tess and Peter who had the true connection and ended up together. In the romantic-comedy *Meet Prince Charming* (2002), the two attractive leads—Samantha (Tia Carrere) and Jack (David Charvet)—met in a chatroom and were coupled by the end. This also happens for the teens Sam (Hilary Duff) and Austin (Chad Michael Murray) in the romantic-comedy *A Cinderella Story* (2004). In the Christian-drama *Christian Mingle* (2014), Paul (Jonathan Patrick Moore) and Gwyneth (Lacey Chabert)—both eligible and attractive—met on the titular site and also ended up together.

Most screen narratives don't offer a happy ending for a relationship instigated online, but those few that do—notably when the participants involved are normal, fuckable folk—help to normalize this tool for finding intimacy.

While the normalization of online dating has been focused on thus far, it is worth briefly mentioning other kinds of mainstreaming that have occurred in the realm of the Web and, more specifically, in intimacy quests. Many of the same explanations for mainstreaming—the presentation of normal people using the technology, for example, or via safety-in-numbers pleas—have also worked to normalize and mainstream *netporn*. I discuss netporn further in Chapter 5, but it should be noted that the idea of the Internet—both in real-life and on screen—contributing to normalizing the *gamut* of intimacy quests is worth noting.

The remainder of this chapter focuses on specific aspects of consumer culture that have both infiltrated our thinking about online dating but are also themes in screen depictions, whereby the dating landscape is presented as being substantially impacted on by market values.

Dating and Repeat Custom

Discussed thus far have been professional partner-seeking methods—matchmaking and matrimonial agencies, personals ads, computer and video-dating and ultimately online dating—that each exist as not merely departures from serendipity, but are notably *for-profit* ventures. *A to Z* for example, along with the aforementioned *Temptation: Confessions of a Marriage Counselor*, are both set around the business-side of online dating. The reality of online dating as a means to make money means that both in real life and on screen this method is often perceived as unromantic, as fundamentally different from offline dating and as potentially exploiting the lovelorn. There are several market drivers underpinning such perceptions; the first I explore is the need for companies to make a profit, to get repeat custom and to grow their market.

In the pilot episode of *A to Z*, the Wallflower dating company manager, Lydia (Christina Kirk), scrunches up a thank you letter from a satisfied client and presents to her employees an interesting conundrum about the business of online dating:

> We're getting way too many of these, people. The idea is to keep them paying the monthly fee—they won't do that if they get married. No! No! Keep pushing the new app, folks. They swipe, they click, they hook up. They swipe, they click, they hook up. They swipe, they click, they hook up.

Although Lydia is actively encouraging a kind of *planned obsolescence* in regard to relationships,[34] she also hints to the idea that online dating companies have a vested interest in matches *not* succeeding. Certainly such cynicism has been expressed outside of popular media, a point hinted to by Bridges:

> PlentyofFish.com (POF) operates a mostly free dating service that draws a diverse demographic and makes the argument that "pay" dating services have an interest in users continuing their search for partners over long periods of time while they make regular monthly payments; that, if anything, their real interest is in not finding their members a partner.[35]

Willard Foxton, in an article for the British newspaper *The Telegraph*, takes a more forceful stance on this same issue:

> One universal feature, regardless of business model to make money, is that the websites require you to keep visiting the site—so to make money, they need you to fail to find love right away. Equally, too much failure, and you'll leave the site. A dating website needs to strike a balance between sending you on good dates—but not the best dates. There's a massive tension between what works for the users, and what works for the shareholders.[36]

While Foxton's comments could be countered with DeMasi's arguments about the large and growing dating pool—and thus the reality that such companies will *always* have customers so don't need to actively sabotage—nonetheless, the simple premise is that there will always be far more people participating in online dating than those who actually successfully couple this way.[37] Part of this can be explained by the reasons why *any* couple fails, regardless of how they met. Other reasons, while not restricted in applicability to online dating, are amplified there. The first explored in this section centers on online dating not viewed exclusively as a way to meet a spouse, but rather as a recreational activity—a recreational *product*—of its own accord.

Dating as Recreation

In the "Dice" episode of the sitcom *New Girl* (2011–), Schmidt (Max Greenfield) and Jess (Zooey Deschanel) discussed Dice, a hook-up app that Schmidt had been using and which Jess tried for a day:

JESS: I just don't understand how what we did today is gonna help me find love.
SCHMIDT: Love? Why would you want to fall in love?
JESS: Why else would I go on dates?
SCHMIDT: The point of dating is just to keep on dating, and then never stop. It's like burning fossil fuels. Or seeing a therapist.
JESS: No. Schmidt, the whole point of going on dates is to fall in love and have a relationship. Like, don't you ever worry that you're missing out? I mean, you're plowing through all these girls, and some of 'em might be great, but you'll never know. Do you want to go through life that way?
SCHMIDT: Yeah.

Thinking about dating as recreation, as a pastime however, is by no means an Internet age phenomena: social theorists Ida Johnson and Robert Sigler, for example, identified that, "By the beginning of the twentieth century, dating as recreation was beginning to emerge as an activity not necessarily related to courtship."[38] Bill in *Must Love Dogs*, like Schmidt in *New Girl*, admitted to using the technology for this precise purpose: "I'm just out there passing the time, tap-dancing if you want the truth." A male online dater quoted by Slater was seemingly driven by similar motives: "Some of these women are sort of losers ... but they supplement my life while I pursue the long-term prospects."[39] One of the daters in Nick Paumgarten's *New Yorker* article, went so far as to describe online dating as a kind of sport, notably that it was akin to "target practice," and a way to "sharpen his skills."[40] Online dating, therefore—in all its unsuccessfulness at creating *lasting* relationships—may in fact have its greatest triumph in serving as a recreation product, a point made well by the sociologist Zygmunt Bauman:

> Shopping malls have done a lot to reclassify the labours of survival as entertainment and recreation. What used to be suffered and endured with a large admixture of resentment and repulsion under the intractable pressure of necessity has acquired the seductive powers of a promise of incalculable pleasures without incalculable risks attached. What shopping malls did for the chores of daily survival, internet dating has done for the negotiation of partnership.[41]

Whether online dating companies have caused, or simply exploited a culture where dating is now a pastime, the search for intimacy online has become an activity in its own right rather than exclusively a means to find a permanent partner. Equally, while some theorists have contended that online dating should be rebranded as online *introductions* given that the actual dating doesn't normally transpire "online,"[42] in fact, this isn't entirely accurate: for some people online browsing and meeting new people *is* actually the recreation; not all daters will seek in-person meetings. This point was discussed by sociologists Robert Brym and Rhonda Lenton who identified that one-quarter of those on dating sites (mostly women) never actually go on any dates, and that "online flirting is the most popular form of erotic activity."[43] A man quoted by sociologist Helene Lawson and Kira Leck personalized this idea:

> The Internet is a place where people can take risks without consequences. You can experiment with people you wouldn't normally meet or get involved with. You can grocery shop. There are more people to meet. You can play games for a long time. You can look at so many pictures; it's fun like a candy store.[44]

On screen this idea is well illustrated in Grace's (Jane Fonda) comments about her online dating forays to friend Frankie (Lily Tomlin) in "The Earthquake" episode of the comedy-drama *Grace and Frankie* (2015–):

FRANKIE: What is the point of doing all this if you never go out with anybody?
GRACE: Well, maybe that is the point. I enjoy the positive feedback of a tickle and I never have to leave the house.[45]

For some participants, the activity of searching—or *shopping*—for a partner actually serves as the endgame; perhaps also providing an explanation as to why there are many more screen displays of characters simply engaged in the activity of online dating rather than actually happily coupling this way and also potentially why there is so much more data on real-life Internet *dating* rather than online-aided *marriages*. The focus on the search makes complete sense: the pastime of shopping, after all, is not necessary about the *buying* so much as the browsing. The sociologist Eva Illouz discussed this very idea:

> This "shop-and-choose" outlook is the effect not only of a much wider pool of available partners but also of the pervasion of romantic practices by a consumerist mentality: the belief that one should commit oneself only after a long process of information gathering.[46]

Certainly on screen this "shop-and-choose" idea is readily identifiable. In the gay-themed drama *Breaking the Cycle* (2002), Jason (Carlos da Silva) was a regular user of sex chatrooms. Via voiceover he divulged: "What am I doing? Cruising the chatrooms again? I just had sex, but somehow I'm drawn to these chatrooms. Scared that if I'm not online I'll miss the perfect person." Jason's idea of the *perfect person* alludes to the consumerist fear of missing out—a sentiment regularly encouraged by, and also *exploited* by, retailers[47]—an impulse driven by the lure of (perhaps) something better being out there so one has to keep actively hunting for "perfection" else live in perpetual unhappiness.[48] This idea, in fact, was addressed by the economist Paul Oyer in his book *Everything I Needed to Know About Economics I Learned From Online Dating*:

> In the online dating world, this means I know that looking at one more profile creates some chance that this person will turn out to be the absolute love is my life and will make me happier than any woman ever could. When I think of it that way, I almost feel a *responsibility* to go look at another profile.[49]

The idea of *the search* being the recreation is underpinned by several key factors. First, as noted at the beginning of this section, online partner-browsing fits into a culture (a) that is already versed in eschewing formal courting rituals, (b) where premarital sex is common and (c) where marriage is being delayed. In the very same safety-in-numbers way that online dating gets normalized, participant numbers also *facilitate* daters becoming preoccupied with the search, something Bridges identified:

> One service provides five new matches daily for its members. If you don't like the ones it sends today, five more choices will arrive tomorrow, and then another five on the next day, and so on … To one of my respondents, this practice is "like promoting Dating ADD."[50]

Using a similar metaphor to the man in Lawson and Leck's study quoted earlier, Kaufmann claims that "[a] woman on the net is like a child who has been let loose in a sweetshop."[51] Certainly this was the experience for an online dater quoted by Slater:

> I'm an average-looking guy. I wasn't used to picking and choosing that way. All of a sudden I was going out with one or two very pretty, ambitious women a week. At first I just thought it was some kind of weird lucky streak.[52]

With all the apparent options, there is, seemingly, enough to keep some people—like Grace in *Grace and Frankie*—sufficiently entertained at their computer, let alone ever needing to go on any physical dates (an idea, potentially, contributing to the *loneliness* identified in research on Internet addiction; see Chapter 3). This spoiled-for-choice idea is nicely illustrated by the "Date with an Antelope" episode of the animated series *Johnny Bravo* (1997–2004), when the title character sits down at his computer and exults: "Millions of chicks at the push of a button!" In the "Digging the Dirt" episode of the supernatural series *The Gates* (2010), Devon (Chandra West) makes a similar comment, "I'm telling you, dating in the Internet era is a revelation.

I get 100 messages a day. Eliminate the losers, there's still dozens of handsome, successful men who'd kill to meet me." This online-specific idea of an enormous range of people actively *wanting* to be pursued allows a person—on screen or off—to make browsing their pastime, to make the searching and evaluating and flirting the source of entertainment. A side effect of so much choice however, is the reality that dating online can become a numbers game, both in terms of juggling options and in gaming to increase matches.

The Numbers Game

In the thriller *Untraceable* (2008), Jennifer (Diane Lane) and her colleague Griffin (Colin Hank) discussed the latter's online dating adventures:

JENNIFER: Alright, I'll see you Sunday.
GRIFFIN: Wait … Sunday?
JENNIFER: Annie's birthday.
GRIFFIN: Oh, shit, I forgot. Okay, can I bring a date?
JENNIFER: Are you kidding? You don't even know if you like this girl.
GRIFFIN: No, no, no no not Peggy. Melanie, she's a social worker. She likes
    sushi and rock-climbing and Dickens. It's a number game.

This *numbers game* idea of dating widely in the hope of perhaps striking gold is also detected in other examples whereby characters use the technology to bulk date. This idea is illustrated in the "Jenny & Christian" episode of the British drama series *Dates* (2013), in a conversation where Christian (Andrew Scott) asked his date Jenny (Sheridan Smith) how many online dates she had been on:

CHRISTIAN: Oh, you've been on a few of these, have you?
JENNY: You could say that.
CHRISTIAN: Cool, cool. How many's that?
JENNY: Seven, last week. Four this week, well three, you're the fourth.

In *In Search of a Midnight Kiss* this same *bulk date* idea is apparent when Vivian tells Wilson on their first date, "I mean, no offence, but I'm meeting three other guys before I meet you. I'm going to figure out which one I like best, okay?" In "The Lunar Excitation" episode of *The Big Bang Theory*, Howard (Simon Helberg) was also seemingly bulk dating: "I've had, like, eight dates in the last month. And twelve if you count the ones who showed up and left." Even in *Must Love Dogs*, Bill was similarly juggling multiple women, something evident in an exchange between him and his daughter Sarah on their accidental date:

SARAH: At least let me have the rose.
BILL: I can't. I'm seeing someone else at four o'clock.

In each of these examples, characters are seemingly spoiled for choice; thus, such scenes function to subtly subvert the idea of online dating being the method of the unfuckable. Instead, online dating is framed in these examples as a way for typically desirable—and in demand—people like Vivian to date, and alternatively, for less conventionally attractive people like nerdy Howard, or older men like Bill, to have a better chance than they would in the offline dating world, something attributable to high-level participation numbers.

An idea also at play in these examples—and something Vivian in *In Search of a Midnight Kiss* actually verbalized—is an ethos whereby the deluge of choice allows a person to be selective and thus also, potentially, *cavalier*, a topic returned to later in this chapter in the context of disposability.

Although the idea of a *numbers game* can reference juggling multiple options before perhaps settling on one,[53] another definition is about gaming to maximize opportunities for success—to put oneself in the position of getting to pick. The role of self-marketing is discussed in the next section, but here I am interested in gaming to produce a greater quantity of matches. In sexual health researchers Danielle Couch, Pranee Liamputtong and Marian Pitts' study on online dating, the authors discussed Cameron who "held two different online dating profiles on one website to intentionally attract different types of women, and that one of these profiles contained deceitful information."[54] Bridges identified something similar, noting, "many individuals maintain membership on several different websites, especially given that not all dating sites work the same way in presenting partners, and not all market the same end result."[55] *Must Love Dogs* provides a good screen illustration of this in a conversation between Sarah and Dolly (Stockard Channing), a woman Bill had met online:

DOLLY: You're on this, aren't you?

SARAH: PerfectMatch.com.

DOLLY: What? Just one site?

SARAH: Yeah.

DOLLY: Honey, you got to put more bets on the table. I'm on at least ten. You get to try out different personalities. Like here, I say, I'm into opera, antiques, poetry in the original Greek. In this one I like to skydive, ride motorcyles and enjoy rodeo … It's an ad. It's like those cars that say they get thirty miles to the gallon … You just want someone to take you out for a test drive.

SARAH: I'm just not comfortable advertising myself this way.

DOLLY: Honey, when you get to be my age and you're approaching your expiration date, it pays to advertise. This baby never sleeps, it's working for me twenty-four hours a day, God bless its little Pentium chip heart.

Dolly's *extra bets on the table* idea also plays out in the "Soulmates" episode of the sitcom *Parks and Recreation* (2009–15). Like Dolly, Tom

(Aziz Ansari) has multiple online dating profiles: "I made 26 profiles," he tells his colleague, Leslie (Amy Poehler), "each designed to attract a different type of girl. Tom A. Haverford, sporty and sexy. Tom B. Haverford, smooth and soulful." On one hand this behavior can be criticized as catfishing; a concept explained by Sherlock (Jonny Lee Miller) in the "On the Line" episode of the crime-drama *Elementary* (2012–): "Someone who uses social media to create false identities. Most typically for the purpose of pursuing online romance." For Dolly and Tom however, their methods were less about manipulation and more simply to get bites or, in Dolly's words, to be taken out for a test drive, a concept Oyer also discussed:

> [I]f I revealed my [favorite Internet] video and occasional smoke in my profile, that woman would never agree to meet me in the first place. So I make an executive decision. I, like many others, hide these minutiae. [56]

Certainly thinking about online dating as about casting lines in the hope of getting a nibble is widely apparent on screen: this very analogy, in fact, was used in *Da Kath and Kim Code* when Sharon, who had just started online dating, remarked, "I got a few bites tonight." [57]

Date Customization

One way for the economics of online dating to become more acceptable, more mainstream, is that rather than thinking of it as a product, instead, it becomes a *service*; that the *introduction* is purchased rather than the person. Such an idea is more palatable because we each like to think of ourselves as unique and not reduced to a set of preferences fed into a dating site. One area where uniqueness is seemingly catered to is the realm of customization whereby your "niche" desires can be serviced through tailored searches. In the "Red Lacquer Nail Polish" episode of *The Mentalist*, for example, Rigsby verbalized this idea: "You can customize the kind of woman you want to meet," he exulted, and in fact customized to the point where he was only matched with red-haired women who resembled Grace. In the drama *Men, Women & Children* (2014), customization transpired in the context of ordering an escort: Don (Adam Sandler) completed his online booking, customizing down to his preferred amount of pubic hair.

On one level, customization, in fact, is perfectly in line with the consumerism themes discussed throughout this chapter, and something that Slater explained well:

> We live in an age of customization. Homes, cars, vacations, college degrees, even children—they can all be specialized and designed to suit every need, fad, desire, and whim. Love and relationships have also become customizing things, defined in a boardroom, built to fit, and

pushed out by sites like eHarmony and Chemistry, or offered up by OkCupid and Match as one choice among many, as a box that can be checked along with other boxes, such as long-term dating, short-term dating, new friends, casual sex, activity partners.[58]

Customizing a potential partner positions the online search for intimacy ever closer to Kaufmann's analogy of obtaining yoghurt or Masciotra's purchase of a lawnmower, but can also be considered, simply, as just a way to expedite the process and filter out unsuitable prospects, as opposed to it necessarily being something shallow, dehumanizing or objectifying.[59] In *A Christmas Song*, for example, Jill (Ramona Milano) referenced this latter interpretation in her effort to convince her colleague Diana to date online: "Just look at it like a screening process." That said, being able to go online and specify—like Rigsby and Don did—for things as narrow as hair preferences, not only overtly links the search to online shopping, but reflects some of the unstated rules about the online dating game as related to the "products" that perform best in the market. In the pilot *A to Z*, for example, Andrew—who works for Wallflower—explained some market "truths" about online dating to Zelda:

ANDREW: There's a lot of things you don't know about the online dating world.
ZELDA: Oh my god, is that so? Please enlighten me.
ANDREW: Well for instance, when a guy chooses a girl on the site, guess how important it is that she have a college degree?
ZELDA: I'm going to go with of no importance.
ANDREW: Ding ding ding. You got it!

Andrew provides insights into the online dating landscape which, in fact, are applicable for dating *offline* too, whereby attributes like appearance are of greatest importance, particularly as related to the selection of women. The consequences of this, therefore, mean that while the young and attractive fair well, others get quickly dismissed based on appearance. This is akin to what transpires offline but is a dynamic exacerbated online because of factors such as scale[60] and, because rapid-fire judgments get made based on scant information and with participants not getting an opportunity to exhibit their other good qualities. In psychologists Rosanna Guadagno, Bradley Okdie and Sara Kruse's work on dating preferences, they identified that "short men and overweight women were the least likely to get emails through the dating site."[61] Diane Mapes hinted to something similar in her self-help book *How to Date in a Post-Dating World*:

According to Judy McGuire, who writes the syndicated column "Dategirl," it's simple. "Women worry that the guys they meet on the Internet are going to be serial killers. Men only worry that the women are going to be fat."[62]

On screen and the apparent nightmare of being matched with someone "unattractive" is a trope frequently used for laughs. The *short man* abhorrence for example, was apparent in the "Crossfire" episode of the crime-drama *Nash Bridges* (1996–2001). Inspector Michelle Chan (Kelly Hu) was undercover, going on online dates to catch a criminal. The following exchange transpired between her and one of her dates: a short, balding and bespectacled man named Kenneth (Bill Rafferty):

KENNETH: Are you disappointed? You look disappointed.
MICHELLE: Your profile said you were tall and muscular.
KENNETH: I took a little dramatic license.[63]

In "The Obstacle Course" episode of *Ally McBeal*, the same theme was at the heart of a court case about a woman's (Ann Cusack) feelings of deception after the man (Arturo Gil) she met online turned out to be a dwarf. *Fat abhorrence* has a similar screen presence. In a scene from *You've Got Mail*, when Kathleen hadn't yet realized that Joe was "NY152," Joe teasingly speculated about her online beau's likely appearance: "maybe he's fat, he's fat, he's a fatty." In *Perfect Romance*, Tess had told Jenny about Peter in the lead-up to their first meeting. He hadn't supplied a photo, something Jenny found egregious: "Mom! He could be fat, hideous, sporting a comb-over." Referencing the idea of the fat *woman* as the worst date imaginable, Vivian in her first phone conversation with Wilson in *In Search of a Midnight Kiss* jokingly described herself, "I'm three hundred pounds, I'm into bondage and I like Hello Kitty." Mickey's (Katt Williams) horror at the obese woman who opened her door to him on their first date in the comedy *Internet Dating* (2008) is another example of this. The lack of popular demand for certain aesthetic qualities highlights a theme discussed in Chapter 4 where characters like Kenneth in *Nash Bridges* are motivated to lie about their appearance to secure a date.

Fears of meeting someone unattractive are a concern both on screen and off, but consumerism allows a person to effortlessly extricate him- or herself from any unpleasantness—aesthetic or otherwise—and alternatively to leave any liaison that fails to satisfy all his or her needs[64]: in such a large market, unwanted products are effortlessly discarded and easily replaced.

Date Disposability

Even prior to Vivian's first in-person date with Wilson in *In Search for a Midnight Kiss*, over the phone she sidelined pleasantries and stated bluntly, "I'll give you a shot, but listen, I'm not wasting my New Year's Eve on somebody I don't like. So we'll meet and within five minutes I'll know if I like you or not. Where do you want to meet?" While this abruptness provided an insight into Vivian's personality—as well as her temporal desperation to find the "right" person to spend New Year's Eve with—it is also indicative of some of the consumerist themes discussed thus far, notably a consequence of choice: with so many options, the concept of *settling* seems ludicrous and unnecessary.[65]

Slater discussed choice as related to online dating, noting that it "influences mate seekers in at least two ways. First, there's the choice one confronts at the selection phase. Second, there's the mere existence of online dating as an easy, discreet mate-finding channel *after* selection has occurred."[66] This latter point is particularly important because the same abundance of options that facilitated a couple's initial online introduction *remains* after the dyad is established. In consumer culture, dissatisfaction is constantly encouraged[67]; after all, if we are content with what we have, we will have few incentives to return to the market. Thus, within a culture underpinned by the mentality of constant upgrade, it is no surprise that the same methods used to find intimacy are used to find *more intimacy*, an idea discussed in the context of infidelity in Chapter 6.

Something apparent in research on Internet communications is the notion of "weak ties," an idea explaining that without proximity and feelings of obligation, relationships formed online are often considered more disposable because lives are not enmeshed as they would be had a workplace, school or church meeting transpired, and thus exiting such relationships is easier.[68] Such disposability is evident in the experiences of online daters in social scientist Jo Barraket and Millsom Henry-Waring's research:

> I think the fact that you never have to see them again is wonderful. You know, if it's family or friends, or work or whatever, and it doesn't work out, then you've got all the awkwardness … that carries into your life and relationships.[69]

> I wonder whether it makes everything too easy, so it can lend itself to becoming even more impermanent, relationships even more fragile. It's just too easy to meet people, too easy to cycle through people, so it kind of accelerates the disintegration of long-term relationships, that sort of thing.[70]

The philosopher Dan Silber explored this same issue:

> Most of us are repelled when we consider the world of dating as a market because doing so seems to threaten all of its participants with objectification. Each individual, with his or her gifts and powers, is simply an exchangeable object that may be traded for another of equal value.[71]

A good illustration of these *weak ties* transpires in *Breaking the Cycle*. In one scene, Jason exchanged phone numbers with a man he met online. The two have phone sex but as soon as the other guy reached orgasm, he terminated the call. When Jason called him back the guy pretended to be a

Chinese restaurant, clearly feeling no obligation to provide Jason anything more than the brief amount of dirty talk. Weak ties manifesting in a cavalier attitude toward relationships and disposability is also illustrated in the thriller *Net Games* (2003). In one scene, Ray (Sam Ball) touted the benefits of a sex chat site to his friend Adam (C. Thomas Howell):

> You've got bored housewives, college co-eds, divorcees, widows ... You get to have cybersex with absolutely no commitment. You don't like one chick, you click on another one. You don't like that chick, click. You don't like her, click. Click, click. Whatever. You don't like 'em all, just one click, you log off, you never hear from any of them again.

Ray's comments appear less like he is talking about real people behind disembodied exchanges, and more so about consumer goods able to be browsed and rejected at will.

Another aspect of disposability worth considering is online relationships used for low-risk experimentation, for example, to try out an alternate sexual identity without actually committing to it.[72] The philosopher Aaron Ben-Ze'ev discussed this idea:

> In offline personal relationships, such as marriage, there is less room for mistakes: one or several significant mistakes may wound the spouse in a way that will terminate the relationship or severely harm its quality.[73]

Going online gives a person the opportunity to play with identity—to try out a new sexual personae, perhaps (Chapter 6)—without risking one's offline relationship or reputation in the process.

With the online dating landscape so crowded, burdens exist to make yourself—*your product*—stand out from the crowd. This alludes to another economics aspect of the online dating landscape; the need to self-promote, something discussed by Oyer:

> Sure, there are a lot of differences between someone selling a used bowling ball on eBay and someone signing up for Match.com, but the basic idea is the same. The bowler needs to think about how to present his bowling ball to get what he wants (money, presumably) just as the Match.com participant needs to present himself to get what he wants (a partner in most cases, casual sex in others).[74]

All methods employed to find a partner necessitate some level of self-marketing—for example, grooming—but such promotions are turned up a notch online because a pitch is the dominant way of making an impression and securing matches and how well you sell yourself has direct impact on success. As Bridges notes, "In online dating (OLD), the profile is initially the only way to "get one's foot in the door" and have a chance at a potential sale."[75]

Online Self-Promotion

In the aforementioned scene from *Must Love Dogs*, Dolly explicitly stated, "it pays to advertise." This active marketing approach is, in fact, widely identifiable. In the "Zero Dark Forties" episode of *The Exes*, Holly's (Kristen Johnston) friends decide to post an online dating profile for her and in turn verbalize the necessity for self-promotion:

HASKELL (WAYNE KNIGHT): Let me see what you wrote. "Holly: Tall, strong-minded, Forty-ish divorce lawyer." Why don't you just put "angry old giraffe wants to die alone"?
STUART (DAVID ALAN BASCHE): I-I don't understand. What's wrong with it?
PHIL (DONALD FAISON): We're competing with every other woman out there, man. You gotta sell the goods. Put 'em in the window, baby.

Stuart's first draft of Holly's profile resulted in her failing to get any hits. Haskell then rewrote it and suddenly she was inundated: "First, she's not tall, she's statuesque ... With legs built for danger ... She's 30-something ... Who cares if the "something" is 13 more years."

This scene illustrates numerous market tenets well. First, akin to Dolly's comments in *Must Love Dogs*, it emphasizes the importance of advertising, of actively selling oneself. Second, it alludes to competition, that your product is *competing* for attention in a market demanding ever newer (read: younger) offerings.[76] Third, and something evident in numerous screen examples, it shows that profiles are *embellished* as part of a sales pitch. While outright deceptive posts are discussed further in Chapter 4—for this section I am specifically interested in examples where profile exaggeration is rationalized as necessary to remain competitive. In the romantic-comedy *The Perfect Man* (2005), adolescent Holly (Hilary Duff) and her friend Amy (Vanessa Lengies) tried to arrange an online date for Holly's mom (Heather Locklear) which involved some strategic exaggerations; as Amy remarked, "Everyone lies in cyberspace." The same attitude is identifiable in *Breaking the Cycle*, when Sammy (Stephen Halliday) encouraged Chad (Ryan White) to try online dating and made some suggestions for his profile:

SAMMY: Age, nineteen.
CHAD: Oh, I'm not nineteen.
SAMMY: Honey, everybody lies about their age. Everyone makes themselves a little bit younger, okay?

Similar embellishment was normalized in the "The Online Date" episode of the comedy-drama series *Jane By Design* (2012). Jane's (Erica Dasher) mother, Kate (Teri Hatcher), created an online dating profile for Jane's boss, Grey (Andie MacDowell):

JANE: "Easygoing and affectionate, enjoys long walks on the beach"— Grey's none of these things!
KATE: Well, in the world of online dating illusion is everything. Trust me. She'll thank me later.

In the "May the Best Friend Win" episode of *Baby Daddy* normalized deception also transpired. After her son, Ben (Jean-Luc Bilodeau), and his friend, Riley (Chelsea Kane), found Bonnie's (Melissa Peterman) dating profile— and, notably, that she had lied about her age—Bonnie rationalized her deceit to Riley:

BONNIE: You listen up Little Miss You-Ain't-Going-to-Look-Like-That-Forever, yeah, you heard me—enjoy those while they're up high. This is how online dating works, okay. Everybody lies. It's like the weight on your driver's license. It's more of a suggestion.[77]

In each of these examples, deceit is engaged in not for the purposes of being predatory, but rather, to sell oneself in a marketplace that amplifies the biases and preferences of the offline dating world and whereby selection or rejection is happening constantly (something further exacerbated with the use of hook-up apps).[78] It is worth noting, that with lying so normalized and thus so readily assumed, it likely leads to *more* lying and normalized lying of the *everybody does it* kind mentioned on screen, something Oyer explained: "profile-inflaters ... have made it seem that because everyone is lying a little, to claim 'A Few Extra Pounds' would mean one is actually significantly overweight."[79]

Participants in Barraket and Henry-Waring's study appeared to have actually *internalized* the necessity to self-promote with one dater going so far as to explicitly see herself as a product for consumption with the burden of carving out a unique profile in a marketplace of similar packaged goods:

> I mean, you're a product on the shelf, literally on the shelf most of the time, and no-one's ever going to buy you if that's how you present yourself, both your picture and your profile. I mean they're so unimaginative that they talk about walks on the beach and romantic candlelit dinners, all of them.[80]

The final consumerism theme discussed in this chapter is efficiency. While Kaufmann and Masciotra's comments quoted earlier—likening online dating to shopping for consumer goods—hint to the lack of romance, the analogy also works in that a trip to the supermarket is the modern, efficient way to forage for food; going online to find a date can thus be construed similarly.

Drive-Thru Love[81]

In the "Two Bodies in the Lab" episode of *Bones*, Booth asked Temperance why she was dating online, to which she responded, "It's a practical way of objectively examining a potential partner without all the game-playing." This idea is bolstered by the name of the site that Temperance signed up with: SensiblePartners.com. Although practicality isn't really discussed in the episode, given the demanding nature of Temperance's employment as a forensic anthropologist, it stands to reason why efficiency may appeal; a theme, in fact, identifiable in several screen examples. During one of Daphne's interrogations of potential dates for her daughter in *Because I Said So*, she asked Jason (Tom Everett Scott), "Do you mind my asking why a man like you hasn't found a woman already?" Jason admitted to being a workaholic. Although Jason didn't explain himself further, it appeared that part of his rationale for online dating, like Temperance, was also expedience. Work hours were also a theme in *Birthday Girl*, apparent in John's explanation for pursuing an online mail-order bride service:

> Okay. When you think about it, England is just a small island. I mean, I know that gives you about 20 million girls to choose from, but if you live in a small town and you work long hours you're just not going to get the time to meet them all. I suppose I never really believed that stuff about falling in love with the girl next door … But where does it say you have to meet the love of your life in the local supermarket … Some people, on the face of it, might not understand what I'm doing. Might think it's a bit sad. I think it's quite a brave move. Quite a brave, reasonable thing to do.

Efficiency is also referenced in the "Crossfire" episode of the superhero series *Smallville* (2001–11), when one of the women Clark (Tom Welling) met online—a beautiful woman named Catherine (Emilie Ullerup), formerly a member of the Peace Corps and now writing a PhD—divulged her reasons for going online: "I'm kinda busy so I don't go on dates much." In the thriller *Murder Dot Com* (2008), the attorney Lauren (Robyn Lively) provided a similar rationale: "I work 18 hours a day, do you think it's easy to meet women in a courtroom? Give me a break." In the "Out in the Cold" episode of *Ally McBeal*, the attorney John (Peter MacNicol) similarly referenced efficiency in his explanation for going online to find intimacy: "I'm busy, I don't have time to trawl the single scenes. It just became easier for me to move the little mouse and click on escort services." Even outside of busyness, the simple idea of online dating being easier is referenced in several examples. In the gay-themed comedy *Eating Out 3: All You Can Eat* (2009), Harry (Leslie Jordan) identified how the Internet has changed the introductions game: "Your generation has it pretty easy when it comes to finding all the other fish in the sea." In the *Lip Service* episode discussed earlier, Frankie touted the benefits of online dating to Tess: "What you want, when you want it. Easy as ordering a pizza." In the "Naked and Afraid" episode of the sitcom *Hot in Cleveland* (2010–), Joy (Jane Leeves) made a similar comment, lauding the benefits of the "Sinder" hook-up app: "On Sinder, I can order my men the way I order my shoes."

Just as efficiency is detected on screen, it is also widely apparent in memoirs and academic research. Amy DeZellar in her memoir *Dating Amy*, for example, wrote, "Internet dating has a bloodless efficiency that is perfect for me. I was running a complex dating assembly line ... While I was getting ready to go out and meet one date, I was e-mailing new recruits and booking times with others."[82] De Masi similarly discussed these themes, noting, "Online dating effectively functions as a labor-saving device in the search for a partner,"[83] and notably spotlighted specific efficiencies in expanding the opportunities to couple, along with helping ethnic and sexual minorities.[84] James Houran, a psychologist for the TRUE.com dating website made a similar point:

> These busy singles are short on time and opportunities, so they are looking for an efficient and cost effective way to look for and cull qualified prospects. Online dating, therefore, is actually a savvy approach to the problem.[85]

Online quests for intimacy are often framed negatively, as discussed throughout this book. Efficiency however, is one way where the pursuit gets presented as a product of the zeitgeist rather than as something associated with the desperate or nefarious.

This chapter has begun the exploration of the Internet's role in overhauling the quest for intimacy as evidenced in screen fiction. As explored throughout this chapter, one of the biggest changes is how such quests have become guided—even *manipulated*—by the edicts of economics: that going to the market and using a service to search for a partner renders the search for intimacy akin to other online activities such as shopping. One element briefly referenced in this chapter—that the role of the market makes online dating *unromantic*—is expanded on in Chapter 2, where the notions of real romance, real love, real relationships and real sex are examined.

Notes

1. Interestingly, the notion of the park being a good and notably *normal* place to meet is actually alluded to in the romantic-comedy *Must Love Dogs* (2005). Sarah (Diane Lane) and Jake (John Cusack) exist as a rare screen example of a couple who meet online and stay together. Interestingly however, over the credits a variety of characters name good places to meet partners and Sarah and Jake name the park, in doing so they subtly edit out the role of the Internet in their introduction.
2. A "meet cute" is a device commonly deployed in romantic-comedies and describes how the romantic leads first meet. Although *meet cute* is the common

description, "cute meeting" also gets used in numerous discussions: Wheeler W. Dixon, *The Charm of Evil: The Life and Films of Terence Fisher* (Metuchen, NJ: Scarecrow Press, 1991), 147; Robert E. Kapsis, *Jonathan Demme: Interviews* (Jackson, MS: University Press of Mississippi, 2009), 30; Murray Pomerance, *City That Never Sleeps: New York and the Filmic Imagination* (Piscataway, NJ: Rutgers University Press, 2007), 41.

3. This references a scene from the romantic-comedy *The Perfect Man* (2005), when Jean (Heather Locklear) asked for her daughter, Holly's (Hilary Duff), help to set up a Match.com profile, to which Holly protested, "Can't you just wait this time and see if you meet a guy the normal way?"

4. Jean-Claude Kaufmann, *Love Online* (Malden, MA: Polity, 2012), 6.

5. David Masciotra, *Mellencamp: American Troubadour* (Lexington: University Press of Kentucky, 2015).

6. Michele Schreiber, *American Postfeminist Cinema: Women, Romance and Contemporary Culture* (Edinburgh: Edinburgh University Press, 2015), 76–77.

7. John C. Bridges, *The Illusion of Intimacy: Problems in the World of Online Dating* (Santa Barbara, CA: Praeger, 2012), 14.

8. Jean-Claude Kaufmann, *Love Online* (Malden, MA: Polity, 2012), 5.

9. John C. Bridges, *The Illusion of Intimacy: Problems in the World of Online Dating* (Santa Barbara, CA: Praeger, 2012), 43.

10. John T. Cacioppo, Stephanie Cacioppo, Gian C. Gonzaga, Elizabeth L. Ogburn, and Tyler J. VanderWeele, "Marital Satisfaction and Break-ups Differ Across On-line and Off-line Meeting Venues," *Psychological & Cognitive Sciences*, 110 (2013): 10135–40; Jeffrey A. Hall, "First Comes Social Networking, Then Comes Marriage? Characteristics of Americans Married 2005–2012 Who Met Through Social Networking Sites," *Cyberpsychology, Behavior and Social Networking*, 17, 5 (2014): 322–26.

11. Sidney L. Markowitz, *What You Should Know About Jewish Religion, History, Ethics and Culture* (New York: First Carol Publishing, 1992).

12. In the Italian film *L'amore in città* (*Love in the City*) (1953), a journalist goes undercover at a marriage agency. Marriage agencies are also themes in the American comedy *The Model and the Marriage Broker* (1951), the Romanian comedy *Occident* (2002), the romantic-comedies *The Matchmaker* (1958), *Crossing Delancey* (1988), *The Matchmaker* (1997), *Miss Match* (2003) and *Hitch* (2005), the thrillers *Birthday Girl* (2001) and *Fetish* (*Make Yourself at Home*) (2008), *The Girl with No Number* (2011) and the Korean romantic-drama *Pairan* (*Failan*) (2001). On television, in the "Marriage Broker" episode of the sitcom *The Real McCoys* (1957–63), the service of a marriage broker is sought to ward off deportation; in the "Domestic Trouble" episode of the sitcom *My Three Sons* (1960–72) a call is mistakenly made to a marriage agency instead of a maid agency. The Singaporean television series *Love at Risk* (2013) also featured a marriage agency. Matchmaking is even mentioned as part of Chang's (Lori Tan Chinn) backstory in the "Ching, Chong, Chang" episode of the comedy-drama series *Orange Is the New Black* (2013–). Psychologists Mette Kramer and Torben Gordal discussed the role of popular media in documenting the use of market-based matchmaking methods, "Since the mid-1960s the number and variety of dating and reality television shows with a matchmaking bent have been expanding worldwide, thereby supporting the long tradition of the theme of mate selection" (Mette Kramer and Torben Gordal, "Partner Selection and

Hollywood Films," in *The Psychology of Love*, volume 2, ed. Michele A. Paludi (Santa Barbara, CA: ABC-CLIO, 2012): 3–22, 3.

13. Dan Slater, *Love in the Time of Algorithms* (New York: Current, 2013). See also Harry Cocks, *Classified: The Secret History of the Personal Column* (London: Random House, 2009).

14. In the "The Great Dickdater" episode of the sitcom *3rd Rock from the Sun* (1996–2001), colleagues Dick (John Lithgow) and Mary (Jane Curtin) placed personal ads in the newspaper. They ended up matched with each other. Love sought through personals ads is also key in the plots of the American romantic-comedies *The Personals* (1982) and *Next Stop Wonderland* (1998), and the Taiwanese romantic comedy *Zheng hun qi shi* (*The Personals*) (1998).

15. See for example the American films *Shadow of a Doubt* (1943), *Lured* (1947), *Monsieur Verdoux* (1947), *The Honeymoon Killers* (1969), *Sea of Love* (1989) and *Lonely Hearts* (2006), the French films *Pièges* (*Personal Column*) (1939) and *Landru* (*Bluebeard*) (1963), the Mexican film *Profundo Carmesí* (*Deep Crimson*) (1996) and the Belgian film *Alleluia* (2014).

16. Ted Sutton, "Project Flame," *Slate*, March 4, 2014. Accessed June 25, 2015, from http://www.slate.com/articles/technology/technology/2014/03/before_okcupid_ and_match_com_there_was_project_flame_what_happened_when.html.

17. The comedy *Carry On Loving* (1970), centered on the "Wedded Bliss" computer dating agency. In a subplot of the comedy *Hi, Mom!* (1970), Jon (Robert De Niro) pretended to be his neighbor, Judy's (Jennifer Salt), computer-matched date. In the "Gloria, Hallelujah" episode of the sitcom *The Odd Couple* (1970–75), Oscar (Jack Klugman) tried computer-dating and was matched with his housemate, Felix's (Tony Randall) ex-wife. Similar themes were at the heart of the "Mate for Each Other" episode of the sitcom *Three's Company* (1977–84), when housemates Jack (John Ritter) and Janet (Joyce DeWitt) signed up for computer-matched dating and were matched with each other. This same theme transpired several decades later in the "Stop Will! In the Name of Love" episode of the sitcom *The Fresh Prince of Bel-Air* (1990–96) when Carlton (Alfonso Ribeiro) used a computer-matched dating service and was matched with his sister, Hilary (Karyn Parsons). Worth noting, this idea of characters matched with people already known to them—notably family members—is something I discuss in my book *Cyberbullies, Cyberactivists, Cyberpredators: Film, TV, and Internet Stereotypes* where I analyze this trope as widely apparent in online dating–themed plots (Lauren Rosewarne, *Cyberbullies, Cyberactivists, Cyberpredators: Film, TV, and Internet Stereotypes* [Santa Barbara, CA: Praeger, 2016]). A non-online computer-matched dating service even transpired in a distinctly World Wide Web–era example: in the "Matchmaker" episode of the sitcom *How I Met Your Mother* (2005–14), Ted (Josh Radnor) signed up with the "Love Solutions" agency.

18. Another example of video-dating on screen transpired in the "All You Need is Love" episode of the sitcom *Bosom Buddies* (1980–82). Video-dating also plays important roles in the comedy *You Can't Hurry Love* (1988), the thrillers *Deadly Messages* (1985) and *Dangerous Love* (1988), the drama *Singles* (1992), the romance *Meet Prince Charming* (2002), the musical-comedy *A Perfect Couple* (1979), the Australian comedy *The Sum of Us* (1994) and the Canadian vampire film *Karmina* (1996).

19. It is worth noting that many of the features of computer-dating and video-dating have been incorporated into modern online dating, thus blurring the distinction.

20. Al Cooper, "Sexuality and the Internet: Surfing into the New Millennium," *CyberPsychology & Behavior*, 1 (1998): 187–93.

21. Dan Slater, *Love in the Time of Algorithms* (New York: Current, 2013), 49.

22. Lauren Rosewarne, *Cyberbullies, Cyberactivists, Cyberpredators: Film, TV, and Internet Stereotypes* (Santa Barbara, CA: Praeger, 2016).

23. As Sam Yagan, co-founder of the dating site OKCupid, noted, "The only people online in the nineties were socially awkward geeks … So, by definition, they were the bulk of the people doing online dating" (in Dan Slater, *Love in the Time of Algorithms* [New York: Current, 2013], 42).

24. Sophia DeMasi, "Shopping for Love: Online Dating and the Making of a Cyber Culture of Romance," in *Handbook of the New Sexuality Studies*, eds. Steven Seidman, Nancy Fischer and Chet Meeks (New York: Routledge, 2006): 223–32.

25. Diana Senechal, *Republic of Noise: The Loss of Solitude in Schools and Culture* (Lanham, MD: Rowman and Littlefield, 2011), 162.

26. Rufus Griscom, for example, contended that "serendipity is culturally important— we have a collective investment in the idea that love is a chance event … But serendipity is the hallmark of inefficient markets" (Rufus Griscom, "Why Are Online Personals So Hot?" *Wired*, November 2002. Accessed July 16, 2015, from http://archive.wired.com/wired/archive/10.11/view.html?pg=2).

27. Sophia DeMasi, "Shopping for Love: Online Dating and the Making of a Cyber Culture of Romance," in *Handbook of the New Sexuality Studies*, eds. Steven Seidman, Nancy Fischer and Chet Meeks (New York: Routledge, 2006): 223–32, 225.

28. Hodgins's use of a safety-in-numbers plea can be likened to the one that Chloe (Chloe Wepper) ham-fistedly put forward in the "In the Mix, on the Books, and in the Freezer" episode of the sitcom *Manhattan Love Story* (2014): "Hey! Three out of five relationships start online. In a fact I just made up because I'm totally not defensive."

29. In the "Meet the New Boss" episode of the legal-drama *Suits* (2011–), the need to self-market in fact *sabotaged* Rachel's (Meghan Markle) online dating efforts: she sat down to write an online dating profile but didn't know how to begin and thus aborted the project.

30. Lauren Rosewarne, *Cyberbullies, Cyberactivists, Cyberpredators: Film, TV, and Internet Stereotypes* (Santa Barbara, CA: Praeger, 2016).

31. In Dan Slater, *Love in the Time of Algorithms* (New York: Current, 2013), 6.

32. This method can be likened to evidence-based policy making whereby proof that something works is used to legitimize an initiative.

33. Dan Slater, *Love in the Time of Algorithms* (New York: Current, 2013); Margo Strupeck, *Seven Deadly Clicks: Essential Lessons for Online Safety and Success* (San Francisco, CA: Zest Books, 2013); Michelle Martinez, "Dating Web Sites," in *The Social History of the American Family: An Encyclopedia*, eds. Marilyn J. Coleman and Lawrence H. Ganong (Thousand Oaks, CA: Sage Publications, 2014): 320–22.

34. As Jonathan Keats contends in his book *Control + Alt + Delete*, "Finding lasting love isn't equivalent to searching for home electronics on eBay, but for the planned obsolescence of most modern relationships, online dating services are

ideal" (Jonathon Keats, *Control + Alt + Delete: A Dictionary of Cyberslang* [Guilford, CT: Lyons Press, 2007], 54).

35. John C. Bridges, *The Illusion of Intimacy: Problems in the World of Online Dating* (Santa Barbara, CA: Praeger, 2012), 3.

36. Willard Foxton, "Online Dating: How Devious Companies Make Money Out of Heartache," *The Telegraph*, February 14, 2013. Accessed June 27, 2015, from http://blogs.telegraph.co.uk/technology/willardfoxton2/100008824/online-dating-how-devious-companies-make-money-out-of-heartache/.

37. The sociologist John Bridges made a similar point noting, "more people fail to fall in love than actually do discover it ... Even so, millions and millions of new users continue signing up for these services, membership fees are rising, and the websites appear to be thriving" (John C. Bridges, *The Illusion of Intimacy: Problems in the World of Online Dating* [Santa Barbara, CA: Praeger, 2012], 1–2).

38. Ida M. Johnson and Robert T Sigler, *Forced Sexual Intercourse in Intimate Relationships* (Brookfield, VT: Ashgate, 1997), 17.

39. In Dan Slater, *Love in the Time of Algorithms* (New York: Current, 2013), 124.

40. Nick Paumgarten, "Looking for Someone," *The New Yorker*, July 4, 2011. Accessed July 26, 2015, from http://www.newyorker.com/magazine/2011/07/04/looking-for-someone.

41. Zygmunt Bauman, *Liquid Love: On the Frailty of Human Bonds* (Malden, MA: Polity Press, 2003), 65–66.

42. Helen Fisher, an anthropologist employed by Match.com, commented, "It's a misnomer that they call these things 'dating services' ... They *should* be called 'introducing services.' They enable you to go out and go and meet the person yourself" (in Aziz Ansari and Eric Klinenberg, "How to Make Online Dating Work," *New York Times*, June 13, 2015. Accessed June 27, 2015, from http://www.nytimes.com/2015/06/14/opinion/sunday/how-to-make-online-dating-work.html).

43. Jean-Claude Kaufmann, *Love Online* (Malden, MA: Polity, 2012), 14.

44. In Helene M. Lawson and Kira Leck, "Dynamics of Internet Dating," *Social Science Computer Review*, 24, 2 (2006): 189–208, 195.

45. A "tickle" in this example is akin to kisses, or likes, used on other dating sites. In the "We Are Everyone" episode of the crime-drama *Elementary* (2012–), the TrueRomantix site used *winks*.

46. Eva Illouz, *Consuming the Romantic Utopia: Love and the Cultural Contradictions of Capitalism* (Berkeley: University of California Press, 1997), 173.

47. In marketing theorists Kit Yarrow and Jayne O'Donnell's work on retailing to young people, they recommend, "Create a sense of urgency and a fear of missing out. We think, 'If I don't buy it now it won't be there later.' For competitive-sport shoppers this is particularly irresistible" (Kit Yarrow and Jayne O'Donnell, *Gen BuY: How Tweens, Teens and Twenty-Somethings Are Revolutionizing Retail* [San Francisco, CA: Wiley, 2009], 55).

48. Lori Gottlieb discussed this issue in an article on marriage for the *Atlantic Monthly*, "it's not politically correct to get behind settling—it's downright un-American. Our culture tells us to keep our eyes on the prize ... and the theme of holding out for true love (whatever that is—look at the divorce rate) permeates our collective mentality" (in Nika C. Beamon, *I Didn't Work This Hard Just to Get Married: Successful Single Black Women Speak Out* [Chicago, IL: Lawrence Hill Books, 2009], 156). The abhorrence of settling was actually

presented as a joke as part of a skit in a 2015 episode of *Saturday Night Live* (1975–), where the "Settl" dating app was marketed through a fake commercial centered on several awkward couples who had "settled" for suboptimal partners so they could get married.

49. Paul Oyer, *Everything I Needed to Know about Economics I Learned from Online Dating* (Boston, MA: Harvard Business Review Press, 2014), 7–8.
50. John C. Bridges, *The Illusion of Intimacy: Problems in the World of Online Dating* (Santa Barbara, CA: Praeger, 2012), 69.
51. Jean-Claude Kaufmann, *Love Online* (Malden, MA: Polity, 2012), 7.
52. In Dan Slater, *Love in the Time of Algorithms* (New York: Current, 2013), 109.
53. It is also important to consider, as Dan Slater suggests, that online dating has a role in the erosion of monogamy (Dan Slater, "A Million First Dates: How Online Dating Is Threatening Monogamy," *The Atlantic*, 311, 1 (2013): 40–46). This topic is addressed further in Chapter 6.
54. Danielle Couch, Pranee Liamputtong and Marian Pitts, "What Are the Real and Perceived Risks and Dangers of Online Dating? Perspectives from Online Daters," *Health, Risk & Society*, 14, 7–8 (2012): 697–714, 705.
55. John C. Bridges, *The Illusion of Intimacy: Problems in the World of Online Dating* (Santa Barbara, CA: Praeger, 2012), 2.
56. Paul Oyer, *Everything I Needed to Know about Economics I Learned from Online Dating* (Boston, MA: Harvard Business Review Press, 2014), 27.
57. Online dating as a kind of fishing expedition is evident in the PlentyOfFish.com site title and is also a common metaphor applied to dating discussions, something indicated by the titles of a variety of dating self-help books: Steve Nakamoto, *Men Are Like Fish: What Every Woman Needs to Know about Catching a Man* (Hunting Beach, CA: Java Books, 2010); Nanci Williams, *Fishtails: Men Who Bite, Dates That Suck, and Other Cautionary Tales from a Mid-Life Fishing Expedition* (Cork: BookBaby, 2012); Samantha Brett, *The Catch: How to Be Found by the Man of Your Dreams* (Sydney: Allen and Unwin, 2012). It is also well illustrated in Harry's (Leslie Jordan) comment in *Eating Out 3: All You Can Eat* (2009): "Your generation has it pretty easy when it comes to finding all the other fish in the sea."
58. Dan Slater, *Love in the Time of Algorithms* (New York: Current, 2013), 115.
59. Customization for a partner was discussed in this section, and it is worth noting that customization for *victims* also occurs. In the "P911" episode of the crime-drama *Criminal Minds* (2005–), for example, customization is mentioned by FBI agent Aaron Hotchner (Thomas Gibson) in his explanation of the types of online pedophiles: "Situational and preferential. Situational offenders rarely seek out children but they'll take advantage of a situation if presented with it. Whereas preferential offenders actively target children by age group, hair color, they'll seek out jobs which give them as much access to children as possible."
60. One good illustration of this transpired in the romantic-comedy *You've Got Mail* (1998), when George (Steve Zahn) commented, "Well, as far as I'm concerned, the Internet is just another way of being rejected by women." Another example transpired in the "Follow Through" episode of the sitcom *Selfie* (2014) when Wren (Colleen Smith) remarked (in reference to a book club discussion of *Little Women*), "dying from scarlet fever sounds better than being ignored on Match.com every night."

61. Rosanna E. Guadagno, Bradley M. Okdie and Sara A. Kruse, "Dating Deception: Gender, Online Dating, and Exaggerated Self-Presentation," *Computers in Human Behavior*, 28 (2012): 642–47, 643.
62. Diane Mapes, *How to Date in a Post-Dating World* (Seattle, WA: Sasquatch Books, 2006), 106.
63. The same *dramatic license* idea is referenced in the romantic-comedy *Must Love Dogs* (2005), when Bill (Christopher Plummer) explained to his daughter (Diane Lane) why he lied about his age and pastimes in his profile: "Well think of it as poetry, darling. It's who I am in the bottom of my soul."
64. A good example of such extrication transpired in the comedy *Jack and Jill* (2011). Jill (Adam Sandler) was on her first date with a man she had met online, "Funbucket" (Norm MacDonald). At one point during the date—which Funbucket described as a "terrifying nightmare"—he went to the bathroom and never returned. While this kind of abandonment could, of course, happen regardless of *where* the relationship was initiated, the weakness of the ties between daters—based on how they came to be introduced—likely underpins a willingness to consider online-initiated dates as less serious than other kinds. The same idea is the basis of a joke in "The Lunar Excitation" episode of the sitcom *The Big Bang Theory* (2007–), when Howard (Simon Helberg) spoke of his "success" on an online dating website: "I've had, like, eight dates in the last month. And twelve if you count the ones who showed up and left."
65. The idea of choice enabling extrication from a suboptimal liaison is discussed by the psychologist Kimberly Young, "We're also driven by a fast-food mentality that demands immediate delivery of anything we want, coupled with the ability to instantly leave behind anything we find boring or tiresome" (Kimberly S. Young, *Caught in the Net: How to Recognize the Signs of Internet Addiction—And a Winning Strategy for Recovery* [New York: John Wiley & Sons, 1998], 29).
66. Dan Slater, *Love in the Time of Algorithms* (New York: Current, 2013), 119.
67. The criminologist Jeffrey Ross discussed this issue, noting that, "A unique feature of contemporary consumer culture is that insatiable desire—the constant demand for more—is now not only normalized but essential to the very survival of the current socioeconomic order" (Jeffrey Ian Ross, *Encyclopedia of Street Crime in America* [Thousand Oaks, CA: Sage Publications, 2013], 124). The theologian Mary Doyle Roche discussed this same idea in relation to the role of advertising: "the media keeps children (and adults) in a constant state of dissatisfaction while at the same time promising to relieve that dissatisfaction by introducing a new 'must have' product" (Mary M. Doyle Roche, *Children, Consumerism, and the Common Good* [Lanham, MD: Lexington Books, 2009], 35).
68. Robert Kraut, Michael Patterson, Vicki Lundmark, Sara Kiesler, Tridas Mukopadhyay and William Scherlis, "Internet Paradox: A Social Technology That Reduces Social Involvement and Psychological Well-Being?" *American Psychologist*, 53, 9 (1998): 1017–31; Monica T. Whitty and Adam N. Joinson, *Truth, Lies and Trust on the Internet* (New York: Routledge, 2009).
69. In Jo Barraket and Millsom S. Henry-Waring, "Getting It On(line) Sociological Perspectives on e-Dating," *Journal of Sociology*, 44 (2008): 149–165, 157.
70. In Jo Barraket and Millsom S. Henry-Waring, "Getting It On(line) Sociological Perspectives on e-Dating," *Journal of Sociology*, 44 (2008): 149–165, 161.

71. Dan Silber, "How to Be Yourself in an Online World," in *Dating—Philosophy for Everyone: Flirting with Big Ideas*, eds. Kristie Miller and Marlene Clark (Malden, MA: John Wiley & Sons, 2010): 180–94, 188.

72. Elsewhere I discuss this idea in the context of teen sexual experimentation (Lauren Rosewarne, *Cyberbullies, Cyberactivists, Cyberpredators: Film, TV, and Internet Stereotypes* [Santa Barbara, CA: Praeger, 2016]).

73. Aaron Ben-Ze'ev, *Love Online: Emotions on the Internet* (New York: Cambridge University Press, 2004), 34.

74. Paul Oyer, *Everything I Needed to Know about Economics I Learned from Online Dating* (Boston, MA: Harvard Business Review Press, 2014), 2.

75. John C. Bridges, *The Illusion of Intimacy: Problems in the World of Online Dating* (Santa Barbara, CA: Praeger, 2012), 66.

76. The same idea of competition is alluded to in the romantic-comedy *The Perfect Man* (2005): Jean (Heather Locklear) asked for her daughter's help to set up a Match.com profile: "Have you seen these lines? I'm in a race against time. Now get on in there and scan this thing. Every second counts. Tick tock, tick tock."

77. While in the examples discussed thus far self-promotion centered on crafting a profile, worth noting is the *continued* self-selling that occurs after a first date is secured. An unnamed episode of the British crime-drama *Scott & Bailey* (2011–) illustrated this idea well: Janet (Lesley Sharp) relayed her online dating experience to her colleague, Rachel (Suranne Jones), "Got out of the car, took one look at him and I thought I can't. I couldn't face trying to sell myself to some random stranger."

78. In the "Mano-a-Mansfield" episode of the sitcom *Ground Floor* (2013–15), Derrick (James Earl) was swiping with gay abandon on the Pynchr dating app: "You get a pynch. You get a pynch. Ooh, girl, you get a three-finger pynch!"

79. Paul Oyer, *Everything I Needed to Know about Economics I Learned from Online Dating* (Boston, MA: Harvard Business Review Press, 2014), 30.

80. In Jo Barraket and Millsom S. Henry-Waring, "Getting It On(line) Sociological Perspectives on e-Dating," *Journal of Sociology*, 44 (2008): 149–165, 162.

81. In the documentary *Hooked* (2003)—about the use of the Internet by gay men—one of the interviewees commented, "The Internet is the drive-thru for sex."

82. Amy DeZellar, *Dating Amy: 50 True Confessions of a Serial Dater* (New York: Hachette, 2006), ebook.

83. Sophia DeMasi, "Shopping for Love: Online Dating and the Making of a Cyber Culture of Romance," in *Handbook of the New Sexuality Studies*, eds. Steven Seidman, Nancy Fischer and Chet Meeks (New York: Routledge, 2006): 223–32, 229.

84. Sophia DeMasi, "Shopping for Love: Online Dating and the Making of a Cyber Culture of Romance," in *Handbook of the New Sexuality Studies*, eds. Steven Seidman, Nancy Fischer and Chet Meeks (New York: Routledge, 2006): 223–32.

85. In Monica T. Whitty and Adrian N. Carr, *Cyberspace Romance: The Psychology of Online Relationships* (New York: Palgrave Macmillan, 2006), 171.

2 The Authenticity of Online Intimacy

In the drama *Chloe* (2009), the title character (Amanda Seyfried) remarked, "I hate the Internet. Nothing is private. Nothing is real." A theme apparent in literature on online dating—but also one relevant to cybersex and other online quests for intimacy—is the notion of how "real" such intimacies are. *Real*—a term used to describe, most commonly, authenticity, along with qualities like longevity—is a concept problematized and examined herewith.

This chapter begins with an idea introduced in Chapter 1 about online dating being unromantic and thus, that the absence of chance—of *serendipity*—in a meeting renders intimate connections as less authentic. The authenticity of the meeting is then explored, followed by an examination of how notions of authenticity impact on communication, sex and even relationship dissolution. The chapter closes with the proposition that for some participants online relationships actually feel *more real* and more authentic than those experienced offline.

Unreal and Unromantic

In this section the idea of online dating—and online-exclusive relationships—as being *not real* lies in their supposed lack of romance; romance in this context being driven by the enduring Hollywood *meet cute* idea. Four underpinnings for this concept are proposed: the sullying influence of money, the unromantic nature of the meeting, the construction of the Internet as a place and last how computers—and technology more generally—are widely construed as soulless and, as in the words of feminist theorist Eileen Boris, "the antithesis of intimacy."[1]

The Unhappy Union of Love and Money

The Beatles' claim that *money can't buy me love*[2] underpins the notion that the involvement of the market—both the Internet as a consumer good as well, more specifically, as online dating as a product or service—frequently frames intimacies found online as less romantic and somehow less authentic.

In the drama *Temptation: Confessions of a Marriage Counselor* (2013), Harley (Robbie Jones) stated, "I prefer the old-fashioned way of meeting women." His affair partner, Judith (Jurnee Smollett-Bell)—who was employed as a psychologist for an online dating company—similarly commented, "I prefer the old-fashioned way of finding love." *Old-fashioned* alludes to two distinct ways of thinking about real love: (a) that it is incompatible with money (and with the economy more broadly) and thus can't be acquired through a market means like online dating, and (b) that it is somehow *organic*, that two people should simply—and, almost *literally*—bump into each other and be overcome by mutual attraction. The "naturalness" and inevitability of such a meeting means that seeking assistance—*paying* for assistance—is considered as tantamount to admitting to failing at what is supposed to come naturally[3] and injects money into an already fraught situation. Although, of course, online dating isn't about *buying a person*, nonetheless, the idea of buying an introduction works to link any relationship formed to the qualities associated with money and consumerism like power, class and, as discussed later in this chapter, *disposability*, and in turn distances the union from idealized imaginings of *real love*.

The ideas of offline relationships being *real* and real being separate from the market are, of course, severely flawed. The sociologist Eva Illouz discussed the "invisible, though powerful role"[4] of consumerism in love, albeit a role that is routinely denied: "When people recount moments they found romantic, they perceive them as entirely divorced from acts of consumption that made them possible."[5] Illouz spotlights the reality of people invariably editing out the financial aspects of the restaurant/evening out/holiday that they found so romantic and so real—they might in fact, actively *deny* that consumerism played any part at all—because the popular way of thinking about love is that the union is so strong that, even if *we ain't got money*,[6] we'd still be together.

Another problem with thinking about serendipitous love as real love lies simply in the popular deployment of the word *romance*. Romance is generally characterized as a *departure* from reality, as an exciting happening that exists *beyond* the ordinary; certainly the term *romanticize* is about something perceived as less real and more magical. Illouz in fact makes this point identifying how, "Romantic time feels like holiday time: it is perceived as different and special and is therefore experienced in the mode of celebration."[7] Although such definitions frame romantic love as something *less* real, they also allude to ways that online relationships can, albeit accidentally, be construed as *more real*. The properties of communicating in cyberspace—and the necessity to use imagination to substitute for a physical presence—potentially render online relationships as *more romantic* for some participants due to their existence outside of the banalities of real life[8]—a topic returned to at the end of this chapter.

As related to a discussion of money, it is worth briefly examining the idea of online dating being less romantic because the introduction was purchased, thus linking online quests for intimacy to other purchases made, perhaps, in the sex industry, where introductions—as well as access to people for intimacy purposes—are bought. In a scene from the horror film *Smiley* (2012), a young girl, Mary (Darrien Skylar), was using a chat roulette site. Her babysitter, Stacy (Nikki Limo), cautioned, "You shouldn't put yourself out there like that." The idea that communication online is about *putting one-self out there*—something that can be interpreted as *out there* into danger, or, as relevant to this discussion *out there* in a marketing sense—is a theme also apparent in narratives with online dating as a theme. The romantic-comedy *Because I Said So* (2007), for example, centers on Daphne's (Diane Keaton) attempts to find love online for her daughter, Milly (Mandy Moore). Daphne is suitably charmed by Jason (Tom Everett Scott) and sets him up with Milly. Jason's mother (Judi Barton) discussed her son's new relationship in a phone call to a friend: "[Milly] has the loveliest spirit about her but I still can't believe he found her on the *Internet*. Not like in our day. It somehow reminds me of writing a phone number on the back of a wall." More so than just being *not real* or *not romantic* because of the absence of serendipity, the online meet in this scene is framed as a low-brow way—if not a *whore-ish* way—for a woman to be met.[9] The same sentiment is verbalized in other examples. In an unnamed episode of the lesbian-themed Scottish series *Lip Service* (2010–12), Tess (Fiona Button) stated her opposition to online dating: "I'm not that desperate; it's for skanks and psychos." In the "Online Dating" episode of the sitcom *Hot Properties* (2005), Ava (Gail O'Grady) expressed her thoughts on online introductions: "the whole thing sounds so dirty. It's like saying you met someone under a pier." In the "Move Me" episode of the sitcom *Marry Me* (2014–15), Kay (Tymberlee Hill) described the "Boobr" hook-up app: "it's a dating app for lesbians, like Grindr is for gay men or Tinder is for straight men and whores." In each example, relationships instigated online are framed not merely as unromantic, but as tawdry because they transpire as part of a transaction. Women, notably, are the ones framed most disparagingly in these assessments.

The Lacklustre Meet

In Ellen Fein and Sherrie Schneider's 2002 book *The Rules for Online Dating: Capturing the Heart of Mr. Right in Cyberspace*, the duo answer a question they are apparently often asked in their date-coaching sessions:

Q: My boyfriend and I met through an online dating service. When people ask how we met, should I tell them? I'm kind of embarrassed about it.

A: Five years ago we might have told you to say you met "through friends," but not anymore. There's nothing to be embarrassed about now. Millions of men and women are meeting this way every day. It is no more contrived than a blind date or a singles dance.[10]

On one hand, over a decade on from the publication of *The Rules*, online dating has undergone a significant branding overhaul (Chapter 1). On the other hand, stigma remains, both in reality and most certainly on screen, working to undermine the possibility of online dating being viewed as romantic, despite the imagery rampant in advertising (Chapter 1). A central component of this lack of romance is the seemingly unserendipitous meeting.

At the end of the romantic-comedy *Must Love Dogs* (2005), a variety of characters offer tips on good places to find love. The protagonists, Sarah (Diane Lane) and Jake (John Cusack), suggest parks. Unlike what transpired at the end of the television thriller *The Husband She Met Online* (2013)—when, after a disastrous online dating experience, Rachel (Meredith Monroe) walked through a park and bumped into a nice man in a classic meet cute way—this isn't actually what happened in *Must Love Dogs*: instead, Sarah was on an online dating site, Jake's friend and lawyer, Charlie (Ben Shenkman), was on the same site; Charlie made a date with Sarah on Jake's behalf. A necessary question, therefore, is whether Sarah and Jake were *lying* in the film's final scene: did divulging how they really met embarrass them (in line with the embarrassment alluded to by Fein and Schneider), or in fact, did they not actually consider their first meeting as having happened until they met, in person, in the park? Certainly this is how the psychologist Gian Gonzaga in the eHarmony guide *Dating Second Time Around* suggests tackling such embarrassment:

Q: "But what will we tell people who ask how we met?"
A: You could, if you wish, choose the place where you had your first date, and say, for example, "We met in a coffee bar." But by the time you are telling your grandkids how you met, they will be astounded that anyone ever met in any other way besides the Internet.[11]

This latter point—indicative of a fervent belief that online dating is now perfectly normal—was alluded to in *Because I Said So*. When Milly discovered her mother's role in matching her and Jason, Milly was perturbed. Jason seemed confused by Milly's reaction and—unaware that Daphne had kept the details from her—assumed she was simply upset by the role of the Internet in their meeting: "What does it matter how we met?" he argued, "What matters is we did meet and how good this is between us."[12] For Jason, he considered the Internet as simply an efficient and unshameful way for the time-poor to connect.[13]

The embarrassment hinted at in *Must Love Dogs*, in the Fein and Schneider volume and by Gonzaga is identifiable in numerous published works. The sociologist John Bridges for example, discussed such embarrassment in his book *The Illusion of Intimacy*:

[D]uring the time the interviews were conducted for this book, several interviewees made reference to other couples whom they either knew or had heard about who had met online and married. Attempts to contact those couples or to persuade them to sit down for an interview were always rebuffed, however. Some couples seemed to want to deny that they met on the Internet, others had created a different cover story to use whenever the time came to explain how they first met their partner, and still others just refused to be interviewed.[14]

Natalye Childress in her memoir, *Aftermath of Forever*, referenced her own embarrassment: "I cringe a bit on the inside when I think of how we met—through a dating website."[15] In Michael Thomsen's memoir, he also discussed this issue, writing, "I've noticed that many of the women who date online prominently require their potential suitors to be willing to lie about how they met."[16] In her self-help book *Dating Confidential*, under the heading "Catchy Ad Headers for Personal Ads or Online Dating," Hedda Muskat suggested, "Willing to lie about how we met."[17] How-we-met embarrassment was again identified in Aziz Ansari and Eric Klinenberg's 2015 book *Modern Dating*:

> There can still be a social stigma with online dating sites, and people are sometimes afraid to admit that's how they met their partner. Their fear is that using an online site means they were somehow not attractive or desirable enough to meet people through traditional means ... Occasionally we interviewed people who felt embarrassed that they had met their mates online and crafted "decoy stories" for their friends and family.[18]

Concern about mode-of-meeting alludes to several key themes of this book. It confirms first, the popular perception that an online introduction is different than other kinds of meetings: people wouldn't hesitate, for example, to divulge a bar/workplace/school meeting, but one that transpires online apparently exists as proof at having failed at what is supposed to come naturally. A central underpinning to this, and one in line with themes already discussed in this chapter, is that the meeting is considered *less authentic* because it is seemingly *less romantic*. The philosopher Dan Silber explored this concept, where he identified the stranglehold that serendipity has on popular perceptions of real love:

> The serendipity of love is important, among other things, because it affords us the illusion of uniqueness. If our love relationships are serendipitous, then they are spontaneous and therefore (improbably) break free of the conditions that otherwise deterministically condition our lives. They are special and meaningful as islands of blissful freedom in a sea of mundane, mechanically ordered events.[19]

Film theorist Michele Schreiber made a similar point, observing how our culture "consistently celebrates the accidental and fortuitous as being *more authentic* ways of finding love ..."[20]

An online meeting thus exists in opposition to this; finding love online is finding it through a method that is not only commercial and "unoriginal" but that notably lacks that transformative power that an accidental meeting is assumed to have. Illouz notes that from the end of the nineteenth century, romantic love began to replace religion as the primary source of meaning and significance.[21] As relevant to this discussion, the unserendipitous online meeting, therefore, exists as less *divine*, less magical and ultimately less authentic inside a culture that bundles real love with qualities like spontaneity and chance.

Another aspect to online dating's *realness* is alluded to in Kayli Stollak's memoir *Granny Is My Wingman*. Stollak outlined some of the reasons that she, and her grandma, had previously rejected online dating: "And when it came down to it, we were both stuck on the serendipity of finding romance in real life."[22] Sally Brampton made the same point in her article for the British newspaper *The Telegraph*, identifying why she had stopped online dating, "It seemed to me too sterile, too fast, too lacking in the potential pleasure of love and serendipity."[23] The sociologist Ben Agger also used the S-word, contending that online dating "erases the role of serendipity, the sheer accident of romantic attraction, which may occur between seemingly unmatchable and different partners."[24] Even Match.com referenced this idea in a 2015 television commercial where a woman divulged her reasons for not having previously signed up with the site: "I'm holding out for that great story."

Thus far I have outlined the popular perception that love found online is less authentic because it lacks serendipity, but the countercase also needs examination. Dan Slater, for example, in his book *Love in the Time of Algorithms*, alluded to this: "I'd become conditioned to the message-in-a-bottle randomness of it all."[25] Ron Geraci, in his memoir *The Bachelor Chronicles* made a similar observation: "there's the draw of the serendipity of having a new, strange woman drop into your life via your e-mail inbox at any moment."[26] Although it is unlikely that these authors would construe the randomness of an online meeting as having the same romance as an offline one, it is nonetheless worth considering the possibility of rethinking online meetings as a kind of orchestrated quest for serendipity, as opposed simply to the lackluster, polar-opposite-of-a-meet-cute; an idea certainly applicable in a large dating landscape but also one where the algorithms used are routinely thought of, as Sheldon (Jim Parsons) described them in "The Lunar Excitation" episode of the sitcom *The Big Bang Theory* (2007–) as "hokum" or, as Elizabeth (Melissa Sagemiller) in the television holiday film *All I Want For Christmas* (2013) dubbed them, "absurd."[27]

The Internet as a Place

An interesting underpinning of the unromantic and less-real perception of love online centers on the technology and, more specifically, on the consumer good of the Internet. Most relevant for this discussion is the notion of thinking of the Internet as a place; an idea discussed by digital ethics researcher Annette Markham:

> Many users and researchers conceptualize the Internet as a place as well as a tool. From this perspective, the Internet describes not only the network that structures interactions but also the cultural spaces in which meaningful human interactions occur.[28]

More than being just *any* place, as I discuss in my book *Cyberbullies, Cyberactivists, Cyberpredators: Film, TV, and Internet Stereotypes*, the Internet is commonly portrayed as a somewhere that a person can be from.[29] In the romantic-comedy *Can't Hardly Wait* (1998), for example, an exchange between two teenage nerds, Geoff (Joel Michaely) and Murphy (Jay Paulson), illustrated this idea:

GEOFF: Isn't this the weekend that you're supposed to meet your girlfriend from the Internet?
MURPHY: Yeah, but she has some photo shoot in Fiji ... for a catalog or something.
GEOFF: Oh, man. That sucks.
MURPHY: Yeah. I guess that's just the price you pay for dating Christie Turlington.

This scene is one of many where the idea of a person being *from* the Internet is presented. In the "Hammerhead Sharks" episode of the legal-drama *The Practice* (1997–2004), the sibling (Dreya Weber) of a murder victim claimed of her sister, "Well, I can't believe she would go off and meet up with some stranger from the Internet." In the gay-themed comedy *Eating Out 3: All You Can Eat* (2009), when Zack (Chris Salvatore) introduced Ryan (Michael E.R. Walker) to his friends, he announced: "this is Ryan from the Internet." In the "Four to Tango" episode of the drama series *Dawson's Creek* (1998–2003), a teacher (Gloria Crist) quipped, "You know, I dated a guy from the Internet once. Hideous." Through this *from the Internet* claim, the Internet is framed not merely as a means to meet a person, but rather, as a place and, more specifically, a kind of badlands or Wild West. In turn, such ideas come to quietly influence our perceptions of relationships instigated online. The idea of thinking of the Internet as a place to date—to perhaps even live out entire relationships—rather than just a mode of introduction was, in fact, briefly alluded to in a 2015 *New York Times* article. Helen Fisher, an anthropologist employed by Match.com, for example, contended, "It's a misnomer that they call these things 'dating services' ... They *should* be called 'introducing services.' They enable you to go out and go and meet the person yourself."[30] This might seem like a semantic point, but it provides much insight into popular perceptions about online dating. Rather than Fisher's idea of online dating being merely a means of introduction, in fact, it is far more commonly viewed as a place where people are from, where people get met and, most curiously, where the dating and relationship happen.

An extension of the Internet as a place is the idea that people from there are *less* real: that they are more likely to be duplicitous about attributes, for example, like gender, age or appearance (Chapter 4).[31] The *stranger from the Internet* phrase used in the aforementioned episode of *The Practice* is a bogeyman idea widely apparent on screen whereby the people encountered online are routinely assumed to be psychos, weirdos and other miscreants. Part of this idea is predicated on the notion that people *from* the Internet—or at least met there—are less able to be fully known as compared with those met spontaneously offline, due to weak ties as well as the inextricable link that the Internet has with anonymity: as Mark Penn and Kinney Zalesne identified in their book *Microtrends*, an enduring perception of online dating was people "with something to hide."[32] A good screen verbalization of this idea transpired in the "Two Bodies in the Lab" episode of the crime-drama series *Bones* (2005–). The protagonist, Temperance (Emily Deschanel), had signed up with a dating site and after a lengthy email exchange arranged to meet her match, David (Coby Ryan McLaughlin), in person. Temperance's colleague, Booth (David Boreanaz), chided, "You don't even know who this guy is that you're meeting." The underpinning of Booth's comments, and a topic returned to at different junctures in this chapter, is that people met online are perceived as fundamentally *less real* than those met offline, *real* in this context being linked to the concept of authenticity and thus referencing the screen's frequent reference to the bogeyman (discussed further in Chapter 4).[33]

Computers as Soulless

In the opening of the sci-fi film *Surrogates* (2009), the narrator proclaims, "We're not meant to experience the world through a machine." This comment alludes to another underpinning of the perception that online dating is unromantic and less authentic: that by using a computer,[34] the experience is less about two souls coming together in a beautiful union and instead becomes about bits, bytes and algorithms and the unreality of cyberspace. Thinking of computers this way, of course, is nothing new. The history of *technophobia*,[35] and more recently *cyberphobia*, is laden with assumptions about the dangers that technology poses to humanity:

> "Cyberphobia" is in part based on the futuristic fear that impersonal and inhuman machines could eventually govern society, and that the differences between people and machines would eventually become hazy.[36]

> Cyberphobia is not a new disease. Humans have been afraid of machines in one way or another since time and humans began together. What many in this position fail to realize is that they're up against

their own definition of life; if it's limited and the machine exceeds their definition of themselves, then it's conceivable the machine could overpower them.[37]

The fear and the fascination, the technophobia and technophilia centre on the as yet, or ostensibly, ungoverned possibilities of cyberspace ... Cyberspace is immersive and unreal, 'the new final frontier' where we can boldly go but may get lost, go mad, do something terrible or forget our way home.[38]

A key component of both techno- and cyberphobia is the fear of computers dehumanizing us—that the distinction between the two will blur, that we will become *less real* if real is defined as human—a concept, needless to say, frequently at the heart of artificial intelligence–themed narratives.[39] Such dehumanization, in fact, is mentioned in a brief quip in the drama *Downloading Nancy* (2009), a film centered on the depressed title character's (Maria Bello) use of the Internet to find someone to kill her. In one scene, Billy (David Brown)—a friend of Nancy's husband, Albert (Rufus Sewell), and aware of Nancy's Internet addiction—asked Albert whether Nancy "has finally morphed into a digital entity." The undercurrent here is that there is a cost to so much time spent online—a cost to living our intimate lives *through a machine*—notably that it makes a person *less human*. For those relationships instigated online and lived out exclusively in cyberspace, the question of reality relates to whether the couple remains *real*—as in human, as in flesh and blood—or whether the online nature of the dyad renders a relationship something new, something *other*, if not something potentially *creepy*.[40]

In the "Newer Elements of Our Defense" episode of the Canadian sci-fi series *Orphan Black* (2013–), Felix (Jordan Gavaris) tried to convince Cosima (Tatiana Maslany) to use the "Sapphire" hook-up app. Cosima protested, "I'm not gonna let an app decide who I love." Although Cosima doesn't elaborate on her remark, it makes complete sense in a world where computers are invariably perceived as cold, calculating by their very nature and far removed from love and romance. To have, therefore, a computer involved in love can be construed as not merely unromantic, but rather, as infusing the relationship with the cold calculations of a machine; that the relationship is somehow less special, less *authentic*, not merely because it was acquired by entering the dating market (Chapter 1), but because it was instigated in cyberspace, a place more commonly deemed separate from reality rather than just another medium for it to play out.

In the next section, the idea of *real* as applied to online communication is explored.

The Real of Communication

From emails to chatroom and social media exchanges, in this section the authenticities of online interactions are examined.

Curated Communication

In the romantic comedy *You've Got Mail* (1998), Kathleen (Meg Ryan)—
who is easily tongue-tied and flustered in real life—is able to carefully craft
her messages to NY152/Joe (Tom Hanks), presenting herself as thoughtful and composed rather than scatterbrained. In the drama *In Search of
a Midnight Kiss* (2007), the protagonist, Wilson (Scoot McNairy), drafts
an email to his ex-girlfriend. His first attempt is depressing, divulging his
suicidal impulses. Wilson then deletes it all and types an upbeat version
which he sends. In the drama *Men, Women & Children* (2014), the teenager
Tim (Ansel Elgort) drafts a first Facebook message to send to his classmate Brandy (Kaitlyn Dever). Like Wilson, Tim starts off with an emotive,
confessionary message and then deletes it and just sends the line, "had a
good time talking today." In the romantic-comedy *Something's Gotta Give*
(2003), Erika (Diane Keaton) and her houseguest, Harry (Jack Nicholson),
take to communicating via instant message even though they are in the same
house. In one scene, Harry begins a message to Erika stating that he misses
her, but then abruptly deletes it.

The first point to be taken from these scenes is that online communication is frequently edited. In each example, characters had the opportunity
to consciously manipulate how they wanted to be perceived; the men in
In Search for a Midnight Kiss, Men, Women & Children and *Something's
Gotta Give*, each elected to suppress their initial inclinations to be emotional, confessionary and to show weakness and instead opted for more
detached, impersonal messages. Such editing in fact was explicitly discussed
in the "Empathy Is a Boner Killer" episode of the comedy-drama *Orange is
the New Black* (2013–). Sam Healy's (Michael Harney) mail-order bride,
Katya (Sanja Danilovic), claimed to have been "catfished" by him: "You're
not the man you say to me on the Internet. You catfish! ... [to Red (Kate
Mulgrew) who was translating] I thought he'd be funny. He seemed funny
online when he could edit himself."[41] Such editing thus raises the question
of which communication—which *self*—is real: Is it the initial inclination to
emote or the self that has time to reflect and revise? Is it the bumbling real-
world self or the articulate and funny version presented online? Does time
and the ability to redraft make an interaction—a *person*—any less authentic? Alternatively, could such exchanges, in fact, be construed as *more real*
given a character's ability to fully express him- or herself without the sabo-
teurs of nerves or social awkwardness? A good screen exchange about this
topic transpires in "The Waitress is Getting Married" episode of the sitcom
It's Always Sunny in Philadelphia (2005–). Dennis (Glenn Howerton) and
Mac (Rob McElhenney) were drafting a dating profile for their friend Charlie
(Charlie Day) who had recently been badly stung by hornets:

DENNIS: First thing we gotta do is we gotta take your picture for the profile.
MAC: [to Dennis] So do you have the make-up?

CHARLIE: Oh, no make-up. Come on.

DENNIS: Those hornet stings are pretty bad, buddy, so I think we're going to have—

CHARLIE: Yeah, but I am who I am.

DENNIS: Right, but let's do who you are minus the hornets.

MAC: Let's pretend like you're not who you are and attract a woman.[42]

While Charlie channelled Popeye's "I yam what I yam," as Dennis implied, editing online can simply be construed as eliminating trivial, nonessential qualities, i.e., Charlie is *not* his hornet stings, akin to how Kathleen in *You've Got Mail* is *not* her nerves or social awkwardness. While determining "real" is impossible—and equally would problematically presume that there is a singular and *genuine* self that exists to use as comparison, as opposed to multiple and often *compartmentalized* selves (Chapter 6)—such issues nonetheless allude to how the Internet—perhaps more so than any other medium—enables self and identity to be played with.[43]

The Orchestrated Self

In Chapter 1, I discussed narratives including *Must Love Dogs* and the "Soulmates" episode of the sitcom *Parks and Recreation* (2009–15), whereby characters admitted to having posted multiple dating profiles in the hope of increasing their chances for a match. In a world preoccupied with cybersecurity, it is logical to read such behavior as catfishing, but another interpretation— and equally one relevant to the message—editing that transpired in *You've Got Mail*, *In Search for a Midnight Kiss*, *Men, Women & Children*, *Something's Gotta Give* and *Orange is the New Black*—is that the Internet simply provides the opportunity to try out different personalities, to amplify, perhaps, traits normally downplayed. In philosopher Aaron Ben-Ze'ev's discussion on online dating, he noted, "Cyberspace is similar to fictional space in the sense that in both cases the flight into virtual reality is not so much a denial of reality as a form of exploring and playing with it."[44] The psychologists Monica Whitty and Adam Joinson posed a related question in their discussion of the appropriateness of dubbing such behavior as *deceit*: "Lies or a different presentation of self?"[45] While such analyses are one way to interpret the multiple dating profiles in *Must Love Dogs* and *Parks and Recreation*, it is also an idea spoken aloud in several narratives. In *Men, Women & Children*, for example, Brandy confessed to Tim, "I have a secret, a Tumblr account, and it's like the only place I can go to where I can just be myself." Brandy's online identity—a goth aesthetic—existed in sharp contrast to the self she presented *offline*. In the "Mikado" episode of the sci-fi series *Millennium* (1996–99), identity-play was verbalized in a conversation between protagonist Frank (Lance Henriksen), his colleague Peter (Terry O'Quinn) and the IT specialist Brian (Allan Zinyk) in the context of the online activity of a murder victim:

FRANK: Her pseudonym online was Queen Libido.
PETER: These [emails] are quite explicit. Doesn't sync with a librarian from the Sheboygan Conservatory of Music.
BRIAN: Some people feel liberated from their normal self when they adopt an Internet persona. In the anonymity of cyberspace people are free to experiment. Online I've changed my name, my appearance, sexual orientation. Even gender.
PETER: That's more personal information than I need, Brian.

The same point was made in the horror film *Strangeland* (1998), when Angela (Amy Smart) touted the wonders of the Internet: "I don't have to be me. I mean, sometimes I pretend I'm some goody two-shoes prom queen and then I can change my online name and become a hellraising b-girl."

In an early scene in *Must Love Dogs*, Sarah and her father Bill (Christopher Plummer)—both who had posted online profiles—were matched, in line with a common screen trope,[46] because Bill had lied in his profile:

SARAH: A young fifty, Dad? You're seventy one! And when was the last time you rode a bike? Meandering or any other way.
BILL: Well think of it as poetry, darling. It's who I am in the bottom of my soul.

A similar plea played out in the controversial documentary *Catfish* (2010),[47] centered on Yaniv "Nev" Schulman's experience being catfished by a woman, Angela, who posed as several characters online, including "Megan," a woman Nev ended up falling in love with. After she was exposed, Angela explained her actions: "A lot of the personalities that came out were just fragments of myself. Fragments of things I used to be, wanted to be, never could be." This idea of multiple online personalities, in fact, gets verbalized in *Downloading Nancy*, in a conversation between Nancy and Louis (Jason Patric), a man she first met online and then started seeing in real life:

NANCY: [Referring to a dress she had put on] You know, this isn't me.
LOUIS: What is you? We met online, is that you?
NANCY: There are a lot of mes online.

The same idea plays out in the British film *Chatroom* (2010), a film where online interactions get acted out for dramatic effect. In one scene, the meek Emily (Hannah Murray) takes her online model friend Eva (Imogen Poots) into her "room" (read: her social media profile); pictures of Condoleeza Rice and Angela Merkel adorn the walls:

EVA: This is your room?
EMILY: This is it.
EVA: This is your personality?
EMILY: This is an aspect of my personality.

The identity-play ideas transpiring in these scenes coincide well with psychologist Sherry Turkle's work on gamers who identify—and enjoy—the malleability of their own identities online:

> On MUDs [multi-user domain], Gordon has experimented with many characters, but they have something in common. Each has qualities that Gordon is trying to develop in himself. He describes one current character as "an avatar of me. He is like me, but more effusive, more apt to be flowery and romantic with a sort of tongue-in-cheek attitude toward the whole thing."[48]

A gamer in sociologist Dennis Waskul's work on online gaming made a similar point: "Each of my screen names is a different representation of my multi-faceted personality."[49]

The identity-play apparent in *Must Love Dogs*, *Catfish* and *Chatroom* can be construed as akin to the personality-experimentation in *Men, Women & Children*, *Millennium* and *Strangeland*, but another interpretation is that for Bill in *Must Love Dogs* and Angela in *Catfish*, their *ideal selves* were being presented, an idea Whitty and Adrian Carr discussed:

> The 'actual self' is the representation of how you or another actually believes you are; the 'ideal self' is the representation of how you or another would like to see yourself, including hopes and wishes for you; and the 'ought to self' represents the attributes that you believe you should possess.[50]

The lies told by Bill and Angela centered on qualities like age and attractiveness which are things online daters regularly exaggerate about (Chapter 4), not exclusively because they can, but rather, because they want to improve their chances of being selected in a crowded dating market (Chapter 1).

Another take on the different-selves idea is apparent in sociologist Jean-Claude Kaufmann's book *Love Online*. He suggested that rather than the focus being on multiple selves or *ideal* selves, rather, that the nature of the medium simply necessitates *different selves*:

> A lot of people fail to show up for the [online] dates they have arranged. The main reason why they do so is that, despite what everyone may think, a date is not just a follow up to their online conversations. A date brings together two people who really are different from who they were on the net. They are not more 'real' or more 'authentic', but they are different. In a sense, a date is a fresh start because the cards have been reshuffled. Which explains why the rituals have to be codified: the transition from net to real life has to be as normal and as neutral as possible.[51]

Waskul suggested something similar in his work on online gaming: "When people interact by mediums of communication, they must translate themselves through the conventions of the media, and in that process, selfhood is necessarily transformed."[52] The comedy *Geography Club* (2013) and the "Four to Tango" episode of *Dawson's Creek* provide two good screen illustrations of these ideas. *Geography Club*, for example, opened with teen Russell (Cameron Deane Stewart) in a gay chatroom scheduling an in-person meeting:

72FINS: I have these sick shades. Orange frames. I'll wear those.
RUS96: Cool. I'll be wearing a green shirt with a cartoon lizard on it. Don't be jealous.
72FINS: Ha. Okay.
RUS96: Look … it's really important you don't tell anyone.
72FINS: For sure. Same here.
RUS96: I mean, I'm not even sure I'm … you know.
72FINS: Totally get it. I don't like labels either.

While Russell went to the park as planned, 72FINS failed to show. Something similar transpired in *Dawson's Creek* when the gay teens Jack (Kerr Smith) and Ben (Tony Schnur)—who had been corresponding online—decided to meet offline. Like 72FINS, Jack didn't end up going through with the date, explaining his reasoning to his sister, Andie (Meredith Monroe):

> Andie, this is different. This is a whole new level of my life that I don't even know if I'm ready for. When I walk through that door and I say hello to this guy my entire life is going to be different. I'm not just going to be telling the world that I'm gay, I'm actually going to *be* gay.

While both 72FINS in *Geography Club* and Jack in *Dawson's Creek* considered themselves as gay—and were certainly both gay in their online presentations of self—owning their sexual identity in real life was a step too far. Not proceeding with the planned meeting didn't make either character any less gay, but as Kaufmann alludes, is indicative of the two selves being *different*, being separate.

The Real of the Relationship

In the television thriller *Every Mother's Worst Fear* (1998), adolescent Martha (Jordan Ladd) is abducted by a cyberpredator whom she met in a chatroom. In the aftermath, Martha's best friend, Sherry (Chiara Zanni), tried to assuage her own mother's fears about online communication, saying, "It's like dating without having to put up with the person." Although Sherry proposes a dating-as-recreation idea akin to those discussed in Chapter 1, her comments also hint to the idea that relationships carried out online are often different to those happening offline, most notably in that real-life dates don't ever have to transpire. A relationship existing wholly online, therefore, poses a multitude of questions related to the concept of authenticity.

In *Love in the Time of Algorithms,* Slater proposed that "online dating adds a new wrinkle: What *is* togetherness? Do e-mail and text messages count?"[53] On screen the idea of relationships being not-real due to the absence of a physical presence is spotlighted. Quoted earlier was the scene from *Can't Hardly Wait* where Murphy spoke of his "girlfriend" even though the two had never met. This idea of perceiving oneself in a relationship despite no offline meetings occurring is a theme apparent in a range of narratives. In the "Leave Me Alone" episode of the comedy-drama *Girls* (2012–), Hannah (Lena Dunham) referenced the death of her "Internet boyfriend" who seemingly died before they had ever met. In the Canadian comedy-drama *Control Alt Delete* (2008), the protagonist Lewis (Tyler Labine) told a story of having chatted with a woman online whom he had scheduled to meet but who stood him up: "I always consider her my first girlfriend, even though we never actually met." In the comedy, *Napoleon Dynamite* (2004), Kip (Aaron Ruell) was asked about his "new girlfriend" to which he explained: "Things are getting pretty serious right now. I mean, we chat online for like two hours every day so I guess you could say things are getting pretty serious." The two had never met. The same idea was also apparent in the "The One with Barry and Mindy's Wedding" episode of the sitcom *Friends* (1994–2004), in a conversation about Chandler's (Matthew Perry) "new girlfriend":

PHOEBE (LISA KUDROW): Ooh, someone's wearing the same clothes they had on last night. Someone get a little action?
CHANDLER: I may have.
MONICA (COURTENEY COX): Woo hoo, stud!
ROSS (DAVID SCHWIMMER): What's she look like?
CHANDLER: Well, we haven't actually met. We just stayed up all night talking on the Internet.
MONICA: Woo hoo, geek!

In the British biopic *One Chance* (2013), this same idea was referenced in an exchange between the protagonist Paul (James Corden) and his co-worker Braddon (Mackenzie Crook):

BRADDON: And how's your girlfriend?
PAUL: Oh, she's brilliant. She really is. She's absolutely fantastic.
BRADDON: And are you actually planning on meeting her at any point?
PAUL: She keeps asking me down there, but …
BRADDON: But what? You've been texting her for over a year now. What are you waiting for?

These scenes allude to a range of important topics relevant to analyzing the authenticity of relationships forged online, notably, that cyberpartners are the solution for losers. Something that unites each of the daters in *Can't*

Hardly Wait, *Girls*, *Control Alt Delete*, *Napoleon Dynamite*, *Friends* and *One Chance* is that these aren't characters with enormous social status or career success, rather, they each struggle in the offline dating world due to factors including nerdiness, social awkwardness, unattractiveness and naiveté. It is important, therefore, to consider that their online relationships can be construed as less commentary about the changing nature of relationships in the Internet age, and more so a means to demonize a character. This is certainly a point I made in *Cyberbullies, Cyberactivists, Cyberpredators*, where I identified that the existence of a cyberpartner is often used on screen to compound a character's geekiness: that such (generally male) characters are not *man* enough to get a flesh and blood partner so they turn to *machines* to fulfil their needs.[54]

The Lonesome Loser Solution[55]

While online daters being framed as "losers" is part of the screen's demonizing of the Internet—and of technology and its users more broadly—it is also worth exploring how the "lonesome" part fits into research about online relationships. On one hand, and a topic expanded on in chapter 3, is that for characters with social anxieties the Internet can be a highly useful tool to socialize. However, the rarity of this succeeding—happily ever after couplings in *Napoleon Dynamite* and *One Chance* exist as rare exceptions—hints to the idea that any social triumphs reaped are likely short-lived. Communications scholars James Katz and Ronald Rice suggest that rather than online dating being positive for lonely people, it can exacerbate dire social predicaments: "the postmodern view [is] that the Internet only temporarily shields but ultimately heightens the despair and emptiness of existence."[56] The authors summarize much of the "dystopian" literature on online relationships, identifying that such unions have been considered "antithetical to the nature of human life," socially isolating, psychologically depressing and lacking in the interdependence, commitment and permanence that characterize offline relationships.[57] The social scientist Norman Nie made similar points, alleging that the Internet causes "aloneness and anomie."[58] Conversely, for some participants these relationships—whatever their duration—are incredibly important. While they may not always end in marriage, for some the Internet facilitates socializing that wouldn't happen in real life; for others, such relationships prove an essential lifeline.[59]

Regardless of whether online relationships are perceived as good or bad, what is most relevant for this chapter is simply the recognition that they are *different* from offline ones, but not necessarily less authentic. The question of authenticity was addressed by Ben-Ze'ev:

> Cyberspace is part of reality; it is, therefore, incorrect to regard it as the direct opposite of real space. Cyberspace is part of real

space, and online relationships are real relationships ... It is a space where real people have actual interactions with other people, while being able to shape, or even create, their own and other people's personalities.[60]

Similar points are made by psychologists Katelyn McKenna and John Bargh:

[T]hese relationships are not of lesser quality than real-life relationships; instead, they become real-life relationships. People tend to bring their Internet friends and romantic interests into their real life by talking on the telephone, exchanging pictures and letters, eventually meeting many of them in person.[61]

While the depth of offline relationships—sometimes which in fact, *exceed* offline relationships—is examined later in this chapter, the simple idea of them often not actually existing exclusively in cyberspace but rather incorporating other media and potentially even physical meetings is an important consideration, and something with heightened relevance as technology advances into "intimate computing"[62] and physical separation becomes less of a barrier.[63] While such in-person meetings didn't transpire in *Can't Hardly Wait*, *Girls* or *Control Alt Delete*, conversely, in *Napoleon Dynamite*, *Friends* and *One Chance* the characters did actually meet their online partners, and in both *Napoleon Dynamic* and *One Chance* the narratives ended with successful dyads.

While relationships formed online, or even lived out exclusively online, are commonly perceived as *different* to those offline, an important aspect to this is the veracity of the depth of feelings attached, in turn sparking the question of how authentic the love experienced within them is.

The Real of the Love

In *Catfish*, Nev reflected on his online relationship with "Megan": "There were moments when I felt like genuine, like I really care about this girl." In the comedy *Ten Inch Hero* (2007), Jen (Clea DuVall) spoke to her colleagues about her online beau, "Fuzzy": "And I know it's crazy, but ... I feel really close to him." Both Nev and Jen appeared to acknowledge that their sentiments were unorthodox in a world where love online is construed as less real, but for both, their feelings were nonetheless genuine. Ben-Ze'ev addressed this idea in his book *Love Online*:

Despite the fact that the partner is physically remote and is to a certain extent anonymous, in one important aspect this relationship is similar to an offline romantic relationship—the emotion of love is experienced as fully and as intensely as in an offline relationship.[64]

Ben-Ze'ev's point coincides with findings in other studies. Whitty and Jeff Gavin, for example, noted that some online-exclusive relationships were, in fact, considered as real and as satisfying as many others.[65] The psychologists Martin Lea and Russell Spears made the same point, identifying that for some people online relationships can be as intimate as any other.[66] In film and television, however, the authenticity of online love is presented as more complicated. In this section, themes including love online being construed as a game and such love being less authentic due to the centrality of imagination are explored.

The Game of Love

The Korean romantic-comedy *Baram-pigi joheun nal* (*A Day for an Affair*) (2007) centered on two married women who go online in pursuit of an affair. In one scene, one of the women, Tweetie (Jin-seo Yoon), has an in-person conversation with her unnamed online lover (Jong-hyeok Lee):

HIM: You love me, don't you?
TWEETIE: Don't talk nonsense. Love? In the chatroom yes. Not in reality.

Something similar transpired in *Downloading Nancy* in an offline conversation between Nancy and Louis, the latter who had—during their online conversations—agreed to kill her:

NANCY: Do you want to kill me in this dress?
LOUIS: No. I don't want to kill you.
NANCY: You coward.
LOUIS: Just listen.
NANCY: No! You're a coward—
LOUIS: Listen! You came to me with this idea and it's not real for me anymore. It's not.
NANCY: You're an arsehole! You arsehole!
LOUIS: I won't do it.
NANCY: Yes you are!
LOUIS: No I'm not.
NANCY: You, you, you, you made me a promise. We made an agreement.
LOUIS: On the fucking computer? This is real!

In the television thriller *Web of Desire* (2009), a perceived separation between online intimacy and real life also transpired. An unhappily married couple, Beth (Dina Meyer) and Jake (Adrian Hough), had separately entered chatrooms in pursuit of distraction and both ended up meeting the same insane woman, Finn (Claudette Mink). Toward the end of the film, Finn tracked down Jack, in person, to confront him about why their online love hadn't moved offline:

FINN: Jake, you told me how much you wanted to touch me. Well I'm here now, Jake. Touch me.

JAKE: I also said that I'd never go through with it because despite everything I still love my wife. Finn, it's the Internet. How could you take that seriously? I didn't even know your real name. I stopped emailing you. I cancelled my account.

In the thriller *Net Games* (2003), a similar theme is evident: Adam (C. Thomas Howell) wasn't having sex with his wife so sought relief and distraction in a sex chatroom. The first woman he had cybersex with, Angel (Lala Sloatman), became obsessed, harassing him at home, wanting to move their online encounter offline.

Tweetie in *Baram-pigi joheun nal*, Jake in *Web of Desire* and Adam in *Net Games* illustrate something Ben-Ze'ev considers to be a central use for online romantic relationships: "as a means of escaping from forming offline relationships."[67] (Jake in *Web of Desire* actually explicitly verbalized this idea, telling Finn, "I needed an escape, alright?") In such narratives, love becomes a pastime, played with as a distraction from unhappy marriages and in some cases exists as a way to even avoid *physical* infidelity by servicing certain needs within the parameters of cyberspace (Chapter 6).

For Tweetie, Jack and Adam, their online relationships were about playing with love, romance and sex without actually having to make the investment of a real-life commitment. For Tweetie and Jack, notably, online love was more of a game—akin, perhaps, to Second Life role-play where different identities and alternate realities are experienced—and is a concept personalized in comments made by the sociologists Robert Brym and Rhonda Lenton, who noted that one-quarter of those on online dating sites (mostly women) never actually go on a single date, and that "online flirting is the most popular form of erotic activity."[68] Whitty and Carr made a similar point, noting, "cyberspace is a unique space. It is a place where one can be playful with presentations of self. It is also a space where one can '*play at love*'."[69] This concept, in fact, was part of the undercurrent of Carol's (Laura San Giacomo) accusation to her husband, Thomas (Garret Dillahunt), in the television biopic *Talhotblond* (2012), after she had stumbled on his cyberaffair: "you've been out here [on the computer] playing at love." In previous research I have examined how behaviors like cyberbullying and cyberstalking can transpire because people have difficulties separating the game-play they conducted on their computers and the real-life consequences that such behavior can have.[70] In the context of online dating, these ideas were briefly spotlighted in communication scholar Yann-Ling Chin's study where a female online dater described her experiences:

> Games are governed by rules, online romance also has its rules. The rule is never take it too seriously, if not, it would lose its mysterious and ideal perfect features, pain would also ensure subsequently.[71]

While for some participants online dating can be exclusively recreational and love can be just a lark dabbled in akin to any emotional highs experienced while online,[72] it should be noted that for others—like Finn in *Web of Desire* or Angel in *Net Games*—love can be perceived as something more serious, more *real* and more significant.

The Idea of Love

In the television thriller *Cyberstalker* (2012), Aiden (Mischa Barton) was cyberstalked. Her perpetrator emailed her ceaselessly and left messages on the family's answering machine. "She's never even met you!" Aiden's mother, Michelle (Chantal Quesnelle), yelled at the answering machine. Michelle's retort alludes to an interesting way to think about relationships formed online: that real—that even *obsessive*—feelings can be experienced in spite of two people never having physically met. While these ideas are hinted at in *Baram-pigi joheun nal*, *Web of Desire* and *Net Games*, at least in these examples some reciprocity of communication transpired. In examples like *Cyberstalker* however, the communication was exclusively one-sided. Similar, one-way interactions were apparent in the "Chinese Walls" episode of the British crime-drama *The Inspector Lynley Mysteries* (2001–7). Murder suspect Tanner (Wayne Foskett) was a frequent visitor to an erotic webcam site. He became obsessed with one of the cam girls, Emily (Isabella Calthorpe), who later is found murdered. While Tanner told police, "she's just an image on my computer," this isn't quite how he construed the situation; Tanner pursued Emily offline, so serious were his feelings. In one scene Tanner tried to justify his offline stalking to detectives: "I wanted to get closer. I wanted to know her as a person. And yeah, I know how sad and deluded that sounds." Something similar transpired in the drama *On_Line* (2002). John (Josh Hamilton) spent the majority of the film watching a webcam site operated by his ex-girlfriend, Angel (Liz Owens). Watching her webcam—akin to the many cyberstalking scenes apparent in popular media[73]—allowed John the opportunity to feel as though his romantic relationship was continuing even though the "communication" was one-sided. By the end of the film however, when Angel was shown via webcam to have recoupled, John decided to stop watching her, explaining, "It's much easier to love an image than a real person … As long as you were alone I could bounce that love off your image like a mirror and somehow feel it coming back to me. But now I can't even pretend anymore." Although this comment illustrates the capacity for feelings to be cultivated for a disembodied image, John's comment about *bouncing love* off Angel's image alludes to another element working to downplay the authenticity of online love on screen: objectification and projection.

Objectification and Projection

Discussed earlier was the documentary *Catfish*. The same team produced a follow-up short titled *Catfish: Meeting the Girl in the Pictures* (2010), centered on Nev tracking down the woman, Aimee Gonzales, whose photos had (unbeknownst to her) been used by Angela to pose as "Megan":

NEV: I know this sounds crazy, but I fell in love with you. You know what I mean?
AIMEE: With my picture, not with me as a person.

Projection and objectification is similarly alluded to in the Canadian drama *Adoration* (2008), during a video chat between teenage Simon (Devon Bostick) and his classmate Hannah (Katie Boland):

SIMON: You never know when or how something might affect you …
HANNAH: Well, Simon, I think I'm losing you right now. Because if you think that it's easier to project your feelings onto a thing rather than a person then I'm wondering your response to what you're looking at right now. Because right now I'm just a thing on whatever it is you are watching me on.

A slight variation on these themes played out in the "Kitty" episode of the crime-drama *CSI* (2000–2015). David Berman (David Phillips) was having an online affair, or at least he *thought* he was having an affair: it turned out the "woman" was actually only an avatar. Something similar transpired in the "Road Kill" episode of the crime-drama *NCIS* (2003–), where a fake website had been set up to lure adulterous men using the fabricated profile of "Jodie." An idea apparent in *On_Line, Catfish: Meeting the Girl in the Pictures, Adoration, CSI* and *NCIS*—and in fact, one also relevant to *Can't Hardly Wait, Girls, Control Alt Delete, Napoleon Dynamite, Friends* and *One Chance* discussed earlier—is that they each hint to an Internet-specific issue about the capacity for *real affections* to be cultivated without a body and with often only scant visual content to assist. (In some examples, like *Her* [2013] discussed later, relationships exist with *no* visual content whatsoever.) More so, they allude to the capacity for both objectification and transference to happen in the absence of shared physical intimacy.

While the objectification that the Internet is normally associated with centers on the *sexual* objectification of women by male users of netporn and webcam sites,[74] and equally the economics of online dating lends itself to such an analysis,[75] the examples discussed in this section highlight another kind whereby an online love interest becomes an object that the viewer can project fantasies and personality onto: as John in *On_Line* said in reference to Angelcam, "I could bounce that love off your image."[76] While this behavior can actually *exacerbate* the depth of feelings experienced in these kinds of relationships (explored later in this chapter), it can also fuel the interpretation that characters aren't experiencing *real* love, but rather, are engaging in what psychologists term *erotic transference*,[77] an idea explained in the context of online relationships by communications theorists Julie Albright and Eddie Simmens:

> Both anonymity and the lack of physical proximity of online communicators can enhance projection, both through the ability to create a carefully crafted and edited "persona" to attract an online lover, and by encouraging the fantasies and desires of the online Other to proceed unchecked, extending the projection process beyond the bounds possible in a face-to-face interaction. ... The projection process of mutual supplementation of an optimized self and an idealized other online has been termed the "virtual mirror" where the screen of the computer becomes a kind of mirror, where one projects a best self and sees in the reflection an "Other" shaped to one's own desires.[78]

A woman quoted in sociologists Helene Lawson and Kira Leck's study personalized these ideas, highlighting both the appeal of such relationships but also a shortcoming of their authenticity:

> There is no real environment. So, people make a fake environment. It's an artificial sense of intimacy. Talk relationships are the drama people are missing in their lives. You can be anything you want to be. It's exciting like a first kiss.[79]

These ideas are particularly applicable to understanding why so few online matches in film and television actually end in a happily ever after: that the real of online chemistry is often difficult to sustain *offline*. In *On_Line* for example, John and Jordan (Vanessa Ferlito) had excellent cybersex; upon meeting in person however, they had no chemistry: their cyberspace connection couldn't be sustained in person. In the "Sex, Lies and Monkeys" episode of *The Practice* something similar played out: Ellenor (Camryn Manheim) had developed a close relationship with George (Michael Monks) both online and over the phone, but upon their first in-person meeting, for Ellenor there was no spark. Although there are a variety of reasons why online relationships fail in real life—including a lack of physical attraction—the reality is that while much scope exists online to fill gaps in knowledge with desirable content,[80] these gaps get promptly filled with *reality* upon an offline meeting. (Such ideas also allude to why, for some participants, online relationships are considered *superior* and even *more real* because the anticlimax of reality has no capacity to intrude, discussed later in this chapter.)

A theme connected to the idea of objectification is that without the physical presence of a lover, the relationship is less personal, less specific and perhaps closer to netporn-aided masturbation than sex: *On_Line*, as well as the suburban drama *Little Children* (2006), illustrate this well. In one of their cybersex sessions in *On_Line*, John asked Jordan whether she had ever had a real orgasm on webcam. The *why* of John's question isn't explained, but it appeared that he was seeking out something that could make their disembodied exchange seem special, seem unique, seem as though real intimacy was transpiring rather than an impersonal disembodied interaction. Something similar transpired in *Little Children*. In one scene, the narrator (Will Lyman) discussed middle-aged Richard (Gregg Edelman) who was having difficulty successfully masturbating to a photo of the webcam performer (Sarah Buxton) whom he had become obsessed with: "Though, as close as Richard sometimes felt to SluttyKay, as much as he believed that he knew her, he could never get past the uncomfortable fact that she existed for him solely as a digital image." Akin to John wanting Jordan to have a *real* orgasm during their cybersex session, for Richard, merely masturbating to the image of SluttyKay was insufficient; he needed something tangible to make the experience *more real* (something accomplished by ordering a pair of her worn panties from her website).[81] It could be contended, therefore, that the yearning for more is testimony to such relationships not actually being properly satisfying, an idea expanded on in the context of sex in the next section.

The Real of the Sex

In his chapter on virtual infidelity, Jim Thomas acknowledged that, "Even in the tactile, corporeal world, what counts as sex varies."[82] Offline this idea is perfectly illustrated by the Bill Clinton sex scandal of the 1990s, whereby the veracity of Clinton's claim of not having had sexual relations with Monica Lewinsky is wholly dependent on our definition of sex. Similarly, as Christa Worthington contended in her article on virtual infidelity, while the sex happening online might be *different*, it would be incorrect to consider it *absent*: "The flesh is certainly involved. The glands do engage in cybersex, even if bodies never do."[83] On screen, however, the story is a bit more complicated. In this section the authenticity of sex in cyberspace is examined from the idea of it being merely glorified masturbation through to the real of the pleasure.

Romanticized Masturbation

Watching netporn and stimulating one's own genitals for pleasure exists as an obvious illustration of masturbation: it centers on one person using a visual aid to self-gratify. Beyond netporn, however, the Internet offers a range of other means to experience sexual pleasure, notably with someone else, something Ben-Ze'ev discussed:

> Compared with offline masturbation, cybersex (like phone sex) is a much more social interaction, as it is done while communicating with another person. While in offline masturbation, orgasm comes courtesy of the person's own hands and mind, in cybersex, orgasm comes courtesy of another person's mind. Cybersex narrows the gap between

masturbation and offline sex, as it involves the active contribution of another person.[84]

A good illustration of the high-level contribution of *someone else* to masturbation—in turn transforming cybersex beyond standard perceptions of self-stimulation—transpires in the speculative future film *Her*. Theodore (Joaquin Phoenix) had fallen in love with his operating system Samantha (voiced by Scarlett Johansson). In one scene the two consummate their union by engaging in a romantic kind of dirty talk; Theodore masturbates throughout and through her moans Samantha implied that she was doing the same. On one hand, in line with Ben-Ze'ev's ideas, this scene could simply be likened to phone sex. *Her*, however, is specifically about the growing and deepening of Theodore's relationship with his operating system—and, in fact, the growing and deepening of an entire population's relationships with their systems. Therefore, while technically Theodore was only masturbating, to dismiss this scene as just one of autoeroticism is inaccurate; Theodore feels both additionally connected to Samantha through the cybersex and heightened anomie without her physical presence in the aftermath, akin in fact, to the many screen examples of characters feeling miserable after masturbation that I discuss elsewhere whereby something—*somebody*—is missed.[85]

Something that problematizes the authenticity of the sex in *Her* is the very fact that Samantha can be construed as an extension of Theodore's conscience: she adapts throughout the narrative to meet all his needs; something I have addressed previously:

> In a number of scenes, Theodore wakes and the very first thing he experiences is the warmest of warm greetings from his operating system. Part of Samantha's appeal—part of the plausibility of him falling for her—is that she anticipates his every need. She (learns to) laugh at his jokes and put up with his ukulele playing and be present—and absent—all at a push of a button.[86]

The fact that Samantha evolves based on Theodore's needs and wants, in fact, renders her a projection of his fantasies, to—as Anna Shechtman contended in *Slate*—serve as a blank canvas:

> When confronted with Samantha's husky voice and a black screen, we, like Theodore, are left to our own psychosexual devices. We can project whatever image of female pleasure onto the film's flat surface—onto Samantha's flat surface—that we want … [O]ur collectively imagined Scarlett-body is not Scarlett Johansson. It is a vague sketch of sex appeal, easier to control—and to fetishize—than any actual woman-seen.[87]

The sex in *Her*, therefore, is open to interpretation as resembling the objectification that transpires in netporn masturbation, or in association with erotic webcams as in *On_Line* and *Little Children* discussed earlier, where the act is more akin to self-stimulation to a fantasy than sex with a real and *free-thinking* person.

Another interesting component of the "sex" scene in *Her* is Samantha and Theodore's articulation of wanting something more physical with each other: part of their dirty talk centers on both characters musing about how they would touch each other *if they could*. While Samantha's pining is a manifestation of Theodore's fantasies—*he* wants a woman who desperately wants more of him—their mutual articulation of wanting *more* is also a way that cybersex is presented as *less real* on screen, serving to demonstrate that cybersex can't ever be solely sufficient.[88] Ben-Ze'ev in fact, alluded to this idea when he noted, "The wish to transform an online romantic relationship into an actual one is an indication of its incompleteness."[89] This desire for *more* is illustrated in numerous screen examples each conveying the idea that the not-real of online sex lies in its inability to be fully satisfying. *Net Games*, along with the Belgian speculative future film *Thomas est amoureux (Thomas in Love)* (2000), offer alternative takes on this issue of authenticity. *Net Games*, for example, opened with Angel and Lawrence (Reggie Lee), masturbating while engaged in a steamy cyberchat:

ANGEL: I have to stop, Lawrence. Sorry.
LAWRENCE: Stop? Why?
ANGEL: This is making me crazy. You make me so hot Lawrence. It's all becoming too much of a tease. I need you for real.
LAWRENCE: I don't get it?
ANGEL: I'm talking for real. I want to meet you.

While the *Net Games* plot is convoluted—and the identity of Angel and her motives for cybersex are permanently unclear—the idea of wanting *more*, of Angel supposedly needing Lawrence *for real*, hints to the idea that cybersex is often not construed as solely satisfying; a theme also apparent in *Thomas est amoureux*. The agoraphobic Thomas (Benoît Verhaert) has cybersex with Melodie (Magali Pinglaut). Afterward Melodie outlined her problems with intimacy transpiring in this manner:

MELODIE: It was creepy actually. I thought it was creepy. I can't do it like that. You know, I have to see you.
THOMAS: But you do see me.
MELODIE: You know what I mean. I want you here with me. I want to touch you. Feel you.

While the desire for more makes sense in a world where "real" and "normal" relationships necessitate in-person physical intimacy, another component is the psychological aspects of physical presence, of touch, that enhances the sexual experience and is something absent in cybersex. In my book *Masturbation in Pop Culture: Screen, Society, Self,* I explored the idea that both in real life and also on screen, masturbation is often construed as an insufficient sexual experience[90]; an idea that often underpins perceptions of online sex as lackluster. Communications scholar Hannu Eerikäinen discussed this notion in his summary of the work of the French philosopher Paul Virilio who argued that real sex and cybersex are in fact fundamentally different:

> [Virilio] sees cybersex in a dystopian perspective of alienation and loneliness effected by new technologies. For him cybersex is not a medium for togetherness and communion, but quite on the contrary, a "sex machine for mediatic masturbation," "remote control masturbation practice" and a "cosmic brothel" ... Instead of creating contacts worldwide, cybersex for Virilio is a high-tech form of monadic isolation, a technology driving people apart, far away from each other.[91]

Virilio's arguments, in fact, are echoed in a range of screen narratives. In a humorous example from the "Y2dicK" episode of the sitcom *3rd Rock from the Sun* (1996–2001), Dick (John Lithgow) experienced a brief Internet addiction and reflected, "I made such a mistake. I thought all this technology would help me wrap my arms around human kind but I was wrong! All it gave me was a raging case of carpal tunnel syndrome. ... I wasn't connected to anything, I was separated." A more serious version of these sentiments transpired in the Argentinian drama *Medianeras* (*Sidewalls*) (2011), where the protagonist, Martín (Javier Drolas), described his life online:

> The Internet brings me closer to the world, but further from life. I do banking and read magazines on the Internet, download music and listen to the radio on the Internet, order food on the Internet, watch films on the Internet, chat on the Internet, study on the Internet, play on the Internet, have sex on the Internet ...

Martín's point was that the Internet, while aiding him in doing the vast majority of things that once necessitated human interaction, simultaneously *isolated him.* A similar observation was made by Max (Paul Bettany) in the sci-fi film *Transcendence* (2014) in the aftermath of a blackout that halted online communications: "The Internet was meant to make the world a smaller place, but it actually feels smaller without it." Even in the lighthearted holiday film *A Snow Globe Christmas* (2013), a similar statement is made about the Internet: in the perfect world within the snow globe, the Internet had not been invented.

Virilio's work, and the comments of Dick in *3rd Rock from the Sun*, Martín in *Medianeras* and Max in *Transcendence* are in line with some of the themes of cyberphobia, whereby exchanges online are construed not merely as *inauthentic* but more so as dehumanizing and leading us away from the real intimacies and personal experiences that apparently define us.

More than Masturbation

In a scene from *Net Games*, Adam tells his best friend, Ray (Sam Ball), that his cybersex exchange was "the closest thing I've had to sex in about eight months." While Adam didn't describe his cybersex *as sex*, nonetheless, it seems clear that he didn't think of it as merely masturbation either; an idea bolstered by the fact that he told Ray about it, something that presumably wouldn't have transpired had he just masturbated. Cybersex participants appear to echo Sam's distinction:

> With netsex, it is fantasies. My MUD lover doesn't want to meet me in RL [real life]. With *Playboy*, it was fantasies too, but in the MUD there is also the other person. So I don't think of what I do on the MUD as masturbation. Although you might say that I'm the only one who's touching me.[92]

> I felt like I had had the wildest sex of my life and it had seemed so intensely REAL. When I think back to it now, even if the details are hazy, I see not me sitting at my computer but me and Gersh on my desktop, clothes dishevelled and in the grip of wild passion—although strangely we look a lot like our avatars![93]

While for Adam in *Net Games* and Theodore in *Her* the sexual pleasure experienced appeared genuine—appeared *real*—we don't have the information to compare this to the pleasure they may have derived strictly from masturbating without a cybersex component, nor if they had physical sex. It seems, however, reasonable, to consider the pleasure felt during cybersex as real—as genuinely pleasurable—without committing to deeming the sex *itself* as real; that its authenticity lies in it serving as a kind of bridge between the real and virtual worlds, offering at least some of the physical sensations without wholly substituting.

While thus far I have discussed the concept of the real of love for those inside online relationships, worth also considering is the real of these unions for those outside, notably, for offline partners of online affair participants, a topic explored further in Chapter 5.

The Real of the Longevity

In 2015, Match.com ran television commercials claiming that their matching system leads to more second dates and marriages than any other site. Such a claim—while working to provide an evidence-base for their product (Chapter 1)—also subtly counters the presumption that online relationships are transitory and disposable.

Something often discussed in research about online dating is longevity, about whether unions *last*. While length of a union is, of course, only one determinant of the success of a relationship, certainly in the context of a discussion on *authenticity*, the length of a relationship is a significant way to compare it to those transpiring offline, particularly given the reputation of the Internet in serving up quantity rather than quality of matches.

The Real of the Hook-up

In numerous screen examples, the Internet is presented as doing its best work in helping people connect for sex rather than to meet their life partner. While, of course, this might be all that is desired by some participants—as I discussed in Chapter 1, for many users, the ability for the Internet to facilitate dating rather than coupling is a central appeal—for other users the difficulty of finding something enduring online is noted both on screen and off.

The gay-themed comedy-romance *Is It Just Me?* (2010) opens with Blaine (Nicholas Downs) penning his column for a newspaper:

> I am writing today's article about my seemingly neverending quest to find true love. Is it just me, or am I the only one who can't seem to find someone special? I beg the question, am I the only gay man looking for more than what's behind a zipper?

Later, to illustrate Blaine's predicament, he goes into a relationships chatroom and finds himself asked about how "big" he is. Something similar occurs in the gay-themed drama *Breaking the Cycle* (2002), where Jason (Carlos da Silva) reflected on his online dating experiences: "These guys I'm meeting on the Web just want to screw and leave. I want more. I want the perfect dude."

On one hand, these two examples tie in well with literature documenting how useful the Internet has been in facilitating hook-ups up for sexual minorities (Chapter 6). While the Internet might be experienced by many homosexuals as primarily being about hooking up and recreational intimacy—regardless of whether this is what is actually sought—heterosexuals, in fact, often face the same predicament, both on screen and off. In the "E Is for Ectoplasm" episode of the sitcom *A to Z* (2014–15), set around the Wallflower Internet dating company, the manager Lydia (Christina Kirk), asked her employees to nominate romantic success stories that they could use in an advertising campaign. Howard (Ben Falcone) explained that such stories are not so easily found:

> Speaking of choking [he stares at the old Wallflower's "Golden Couple" poster] that's exactly what he did to her last night on a cruise ship … According to reports, after days of relentless arguing, Donna Henry brained Jim Henry with a shuffle board puck. A double choking then ensued and they both went over the side of the Moonlight Deck.

Lydia then prompted Howard, as well as Dinesh (Parvesh Cheena) and Lora (Hong Chau), for other suggestions:

HOWARD: Well, we've been through all of them and of the four that are local, two are divorced and one started a polygamist cult. We're waiting for an update on the fourth.
DINESH: Well we found them.
LORA: On a county coroner's website. They murdered each other two years ago.

These comments work to further the ideas that online dating is danger-ous and that the Internet is a badlands populated by nefarious characters (Chapter 4). Another explanation more relevant to the themes of this chap-ter, however, is the not so subtle contention that offline relationships simply don't last. Gonzaga, an eHarmony psychologist, in fact alluded to this idea: "You could say online dating allows people to get into relationships, learn things, and ultimately make a better selection."[94] The economist Paul Oyer spotlights a similar issue in the context of the consumerist underpinnings of online dating: "even when you are in a long-term relationship, you will constantly be deciding whether the relationship you have is better than the alternative of breaking it off and trying for a better one."[95] Although most research examines the impact of online dating in the formation of relation-ships, scant work has been done on tracking entrance into—and endurance of—*marriages*, or even long-term partnerships, formed this way. The psy-chologist John Cacioppo et al. did do some work in this area, however, and found that of the couples who married between 2005 and 2012, 34.5% met online; more than any other single venue.[96] The communications theorist Jeffrey Hall, however, cautions, "online" in the Cacioppo study represents more than simply online dating and includes people meeting undeliberately via social networking sites.[97] Other commentators identify that in fact, the online dating model, in fact, is actually *designed* to fail. While, as discussed in Chapter 1, part of this lies in the supposed *planned obsolescence* inher-ent in the business model, another explanation centers on the algorithms. The economist John Jensen in his book *The Marriage MBA* suggested that "matching based on similarity increases early satisfaction in couples, but is not predictive of longevity in relationships."[98] While in academic literature the usefulness of the matching algorithms has been extensively critiqued,[99] the "Soulmates" "episode of *Parks and Recreation* provided an illustration of some of the shortcomings when Tom (Aziz Ansari) is matched with his colleague, Leslie (Amy Poehler), not because they are a perfect match but because Tom had gamed the system by establishing multiple profiles.[100]

Although the *Parks and Recreations* scene illustrates the perception of algorithms as—to use *The Big Bang Theory*'s Sheldon's word—"hokum," it is also one of several examples where characters feel inclined to in fact *trust* the system: Leslie, for example, despite being surprised at being matched with her colleague Tom, nevertheless felt she should at least give the union a try. A similar idea is referenced in *Thomas est amoureux* (*Thomas in Love*). Thomas meets a woman, Vanessa (Dominique Baeyens), via an online dating site and the following exchange transpired:

THOMAS: Why did you join a dating club?
VANESSA: Everybody does it.
THOMAS: Yes. But guys hit on you. Right?
VANESSA: Of course! But how do I know if he's the ideal person?
THOMAS: Because I'm the ideal person?
VANESSA: The computer selected you for me among thousands of candidates.

The idea is also a theme in the Canadian romance *Perfect Romance* (2004) when Peter (Henry Ian Cusick) kept trying to make the in-person relationship with Jenny (Lori Heuring) work—despite being more drawn to her mother (Kathleen Quinlan): he had faith in the matching system. The television holiday film *A Very Merry Mix-Up* (2013) also referenced this idea: despite Alice's (Alicia Witt) instant chemistry with Matt (Mark Wiebe) whom she met serendipitously at an airport, she was inclined to believe that her engagement to Will (Scott Gibson) whom she met on Mates.com—with a 75% compatibility rating—was the more authentic union. Equally, the startling success of Sheldon and Amy's (Mayim Bialik) match in "The Lunar Excitation" episode of *The Big Bang Theory* serves as further testimony to this idea: that two such strange characters were matched—and were such a perfect fit—serves as proof of the usefulness of algorithms.

The Real of the Success Stories

While the screen has a long history of demonizing intimacies found online, in a small number of cases, a counternarrative is offered whereby real is demonstrated through cases of success. In the aforementioned "Two Bodies in the Lab" episode of *Bones*, the success story idea is alluded to in a conversation between David and Booth:

BOOTH: So, this whole you know, online thing, how long does it last? Because if it's just a way to, you know, hook up, I gotta tell you it's pretty low.
DAVID: Yeah, one of my partners met his wife online.
BOOTH: You're kidding?
DAVID: No. They've been married five years.
BOOTH: Doesn't mean it's not creepy.

While in *Bones* the relationship is only spoken about, the screen offers several happily ever after narratives working to convey the idea that coupling permanently is actually possible. In narratives including *Napoleon Dynamite, One Chance, Must Love Dogs, You've Got Mail, Meet Prince Charming* (2002), *A Cinderella Story* (2004), *Christian Mingle* (2014), *Perfect Romance* and *The Big Bang Theory* couples meet online, have offline romances and actually stay together. While such examples are the exception and not the rule—more commonly online dating is a comic detour in the journey to finding real love *offline*—they nevertheless exist as screen fiction examples showcasing the possibility.

Just as it is worth examining the authenticity of love online, it is equally important to examine the real of the pain felt.

The Real of the Pain

In the Taiwanese drama-romance *Ci qing* (*Spider Lilies*) (2007), Jade (Rainie Yang), a webcam performer, was crying. Her grandmother (Hsiu Li), comforted her and questioned, "A computer can make you cry like this?" Grandma was astonished that a machine—that disembodied exchanges—could have such an emotional impact, in-sync with popular perceptions about computers being soulless and interactions online being shallow. The fact that Jade was crying, however, highlights that for some people the emotions experienced online are real and that this *real* encompasses feelings of love as well as pain. While such pain can be illustrated via online activity such as characters addicted to gaming,[101] in this section real pain is explored in the context of the demise of online romances.

In a scene from *Chloe*, Michael (Max Thieriot) was chatting via webcam with his girlfriend Anna (Nina Dobrev):

ANNA: Look, Michael, it's not like we're engaged. Okay? If there are other guys, it's got nothing to do with you.
MICHAEL: Alright. I need to see you, okay? This … This is weird.
ANNA: You are seeing me.
MICHAEL: I mean … I mean face-to-face. This is … This is fucked.
ANNA: I know, but look, we are face-to-face, okay?

Anna and Michael had an offline relationship but the fact that their break-up was happening online was something Michael appeared to think was problematic; the exchange was seemingly missing the face-to-face realness he thought was owed to such a serious situation. In other examples, the entirety of a relationship—from start to finish—plays out online, in turn, delivering its own kind of pain. In the aforementioned "Leave Me Alone" episode of *Girls*, Hannah told her tale of love online:

> I met Igor online, in a chatroom for fans of an obscure punk band my vegan friend Marina liked. Igor's screen name was Pyro000, which belied a level of articulation unusual for an Internet boyfriend. So he became my Internet boyfriend for six blissful months until his friend IM'd me to say that he had died. Died!

This scene is noteworthy for several reasons. First, we don't know whether Hannah actually spent time with Igor in person or whether her phrase

"Internet boyfriend" meant that they were an online-exclusive couple. Equally, we don't actually know whether Igor had actually died or, in fact, whether he—wanting out of the entanglement—just got a friend to message Hannah, or perhaps pretended to be a 'friend' himself,[102] we nonetheless do have the real of an ending. Something similar transpired in the television drama *The Bride He Bought Online* (2015). The narrative centered on John (Travis Hammer) who is catfished by a group of teenage girls. In one scene he goes to the airport to meet his supposed bride who, of course, never arrives. Later, after John seeks revenge on the girls, he tells one of them, Mandy (Lauren Gaw), "The pain I felt at the airport was real!" Certainly the real of the pain felt by Hannah and John is identified in research, something the psychiatrist Avodah Offit identified:

> I've seen people become quite depressed over what should have been ephemeral relationships with people they've never met, who suddenly dump them on e-mail. They have every bit as much emotion as if they'd met and had a torrid relationship.[103]

While "weak ties" is a concept often thought to haunt online relationships,[104] for some people—something undoubtedly heightened for a socially isolated character like John who had invested so heavily in his online relationship—its ending can be particularly traumatic.

In the final section of this chapter the idea of online relationships being perceived as *more real* is explored.

Heightened Authenticity

As discussed throughout this chapter, the popular way to think about online-instigated, or online-only relationships, is that the Internet makes them less real. It is, however, essential to outline the counter case where not only is the *less real* argument denied, but where such encounters are portrayed as *more real*. *More real* in this context centers on factors including the confessionary nature of the written word, the speed of rapport, the intensity of intimacy and last, the elimination of the deleterious intrusions of real life.

Confession

Discussed earlier were scenes from *In Search of a Midnight Kiss, Men, Women & Children* and *Something's Gotta Give* where male characters edited their communications to downplay their sensitivity. This, of course, doesn't always transpire, and in other examples, the anonymity and distance fostered by the Internet, in fact, leads to characters being *more* emotionally forthcoming. The gay-themed romantic-drama *Ciao* (2008) presents a very good illustration of this. The backstory is an online relationship between two men: Andrea (Alessandro Calza) from Italy and Mark (Chuck Blaum) from the United States. After Mark's sudden death, his friends Jeff (Adam Neal Smith) and Lauren (Ethel Lung) discussed the contents of Mark and Andrea's email exchange:

JEFF: They seemed to have similar interests and opinions. They talked about film, music, politics, current events, things like that. It was like when I was with him but it was different.

LAUREN: How?

JEFF: He was a lot more open with the way he expressed himself.

LAUREN: What do you mean?

JEFF: Well like, there was this one email where he described this experience he had with his mom at college. She was picking him up at the airport for Thanksgiving. He noticed that she had a hole in her stockings then he started to cry in the car because she had spent $300 on a plane ticket and neglected to buy herself a new pair of stockings. He never told me that story before. I just can't see Mark being that emotional about things.

LAUREN: People usually are when they write. You just share all these things that you wouldn't share with people around you.

Miles (Giovanni Ribisi) in the thriller *Perfect Stranger* (2007) made a similar point about the Internet, "Sometimes you'd tell a perfect stranger something you wouldn't even tell your best friend, especially if you're anonymous."

Lauren and Miles both touch upon what is often termed the *stranger-on-the-train* phenomenon, a concept pioneered by the sociologist Georg Simmel, and one with great relevance to understanding online interactions:

> With the objectivity of the stranger is connected the phenomenon chiefly (but not exclusively) true of the stranger who moves on. This is the fact that he often receives the most surprising openness—confidences which would be carefully withheld from a more closely related person.[105]

The stranger-on-the-train idea is discussed widely in research on online relationships. Ben-Ze'ev for example, contended, "It is easier to open up to a faceless stranger that you do not have to look at while revealing your secret or to see the next morning."[106] Whitty and Joinson similarly identified that, "people are more likely to disclose information about themselves on the Internet compared to equivalent face-to-face (FtF) encounters."[107]

While not all online exchanges are as time-bound as an encounter between two passengers on a train, the reality is that *they could be*, that if things get too intense or too difficult, that a person can simply log-off with scant consequence—can disappear completely like Igor in *Girls*—in turn illustrating uncharacteristic and medium-generated openness and also weak ties and the capacity for relationship disposability (Chapter 1).

Speed of Rapport

Bridges identified the hastening of courtship timelines online which bring two people together far quicker than would occur in person:

> Online dating is unique in creating this type of linkage in would-be partners. Individuals online are often drawn very quickly to a potential partner; that is, a *speedup* in the relationship occurs and connections, though recent, are also accelerated.[108]

> The resulting collapse of time and the acceleration of the dating timeline are unique to digital technology.[109]

The psychologists Al Cooper and Eric Griffin-Shelley made a similar point:

> Computers speed things up. With regard to sexuality, this shift in speed evokes intense emotional reactions. For instance, flirtation and innuendo, long the staples of leisurely seduction, can rapidly escalate into frank sexual discussions and proposals on the Internet.[110]

Online dating participants similarly identify this acceleration; a man quoted by Lawson and Leck for instance, spoke of his experiences online:

> Internet people are more desperate; things move fast in weird ways … You get too intense too soon. There's like a speed to get to know each other. All you have is conversation that becomes exaggerated and magnified.[111]

In such relationships, the openness and confessions indulged in often lead to feeling "known" quickly, and thus participants perceiving themselves in a relationship more rapidly than would happen offline. A good illustration of this transpires in one of Kathleen's emails to Joe/NY152 in *You've Got Mail*:

> I like to start my notes to you as if we're already in the middle of a conversation. I pretend that we're the oldest and dearest friends—as opposed to what we actually are, people who don't know each other's names and met in a chatroom where we both claimed we'd never been before.

Slater discussed some of the unique properties of online romance and made a simple point about the *why* of hastened intimacy: "if she's on a dating site there's a good chance she's eager to connect."[112] For Kathleen, quite clearly the capacity, as well as *desire*, for her to conceive of herself in an established relationship underpinned some of the appeal. Worth noting of course, is that while the Internet may have its own accelerated timeline, offline the timelines get reset, highlighting why oftentimes relationships that work in cyberspace struggle offline.

Intensity of Intimacy

Relationships experienced exclusively online, alternatively ones transpiring online prior to an in-person meeting, are largely sustained by the written word. As discussed earlier, the nature of this contact is often highly revelatory, whereby participants feel that rather than just generically getting to know someone, more so, that they are getting to know the other person's *soul*; that online a person has the time to be more thoughtful, and to articulate complicated ideas without interpretation, in turn, rendering many emails and chatroom exchanges akin to diary entries.[113] This is a worthwhile interpretation for why in *Ciao,* Mark's online relationship with Andrea was deeper than his real-life relationship with Jeff and likely also why Kathleen in *You've Got Mail* perceived her online relationship with Joe as deeper than her offline relationship with her spouse Frank (Greg Kinnear).

Researchers identify some interesting consequences of the level of intimacy forged online. The psychiatrist Esther Gwinnell discussed in her 1998 work, for example, the interesting phenomena of what happens to participants in relationships that don't have a physical form, but rather, unfold largely on a keyboard and notably inside the minds of participants:

> When Internet lovers leave the computer to go to other activities, they may feel as though the other person is "inside" them. As they go through their daily routine, they may be thinking of what to say to her or what she'll say later on.[114]

The film *Her* presents this idea in a near-literal display: Theodore has Samantha with him all of the time; the second he wakes, Samantha is there with him until he falls asleep. Illouz discussed similar issues in her book *Consuming the Romantic Utopia*:

> The Internet seems to sustain relationships precisely through the ways it creates a phantasmatic presence. A phantom limb is a limb that has been amputated but whose neurological presence is still felt by the subject. Similarly, the technology of the Internet creates phantom sentiments—sentiments that are lived as sentiments based in real-life stimuli, but whose actual object is absent or non-existence. This is made possible through technological devices that mimic presence.[115]

This level of intensity, in fact, is referenced in *Little Children* as related to Richard's preoccupation with SluttyKay: as the narrator explains, "Lately, SluttyKay had become a problem. He thought about her far too often and spent hours studying the thousands of photos available to him."

While the relationship might not be *the same* as an offline one with a shared physical component, the depth of sentiment that participants in the online relationship feel for their partner—feel *transformed* by the depth of that connection—is worth highlighting. Equally, such connection is something that modern technology like smartphones facilitates with an online lover able to be in your pocket all day akin to what transpired in *Her*; something which, incidentally, enables offline relationships to potentially survive periods of separation (Chapter 5).

Real Life Ruins Everything

In a scene from *A Cinderella Story*, Sam (Hilary Duff) tells her friend Carter (Dan Byrd) that she is worried about meeting her online beau Austin (Chad Michael Murray) offline because, "this guy's too good to be true ... What if I meet him and I'm not what he expects? Maybe this whole relationship's just better for cyberspace." Sam's concerns highlight a central component as to why some online relationships are considered to be as satisfying if not *more* satisfying because they are able to be contained, controlled and can exist in a bubble, separated from everyday life.[116]

In *Baram-pigi joheun nal* (*A Day for an Affair*), Tweetie was disappointed that in person her unnamed online lover was very reluctant to extensively converse with her or to tell her erotic stories as he had done online. Tweetie had been expecting an extension of their six-month-long, prose-driven romantic online courtship; in person, however, he just wanted intercourse. On one hand, such a dynamic relates to the idea of females being drawn to words and aroused by ideas more so than visual material,[117] this scene also highlights a distinct shortcoming of offline relationships whereby in-person precise verbal communication is often less important. The sexologists Sandra Leiblum and Nicola Döring illustrated this idea by quoting a woman who had extensive experience meeting men online: "The men often talk a good game, but are so socially unskilled that meeting them in person shatters all of my illusions!"[118] A woman in Ben-Ze'ev's work made a similar point:

> The only complaint I have is that I miss the relationship we used to have online. There was no routine, no garbage to take out and most of all, uninterrupted, deep conversations. I think there is no better way to meet someone and get to know them from the inside.[119]

As Ben-Ze'ev observes, "many people testify that their virtual cybersex is much more active and intense than their actual offline sex."[120]

Given that communication is a recurrent theme in real-life relationship breakdowns and given that for an online couple all they do is communicate, it seems reasonable that online relationships often seem *more* real and *more* intimate in comparison. An extension of this idea—and something that underpins other challenging unions like long-distance relationships, prison relationships, military relationships and infidelities—is a desperate longing to be together. Ben-Ze'ev, for example, spotlights how, "Numerous novels and movies deal with romantic relationships that are not complete, and this aspect helps to maintain the intense excitement of the affair."[121] Once an offline relationship forms, however, all of the longing dissipates and either the relationship survives or it withers when the shared struggle to be together is gone.[122]

This chapter examined the complicated notion of authenticity as it pertains to love and sex online. Chapter 3 moves the discussion toward the lovelorn, examining the screen stereotypes constituting the typical online dater.

Notes

1. Eileen Boris, *Intimate Labors: Cultures, Technologies, and the Politics of Care* (Stanford, CA: Stanford University Press, 2010), 13.
2. The Beatles, "Can't Buy Me Love" (1964).
3. As Sara Eckel reflects in her dating self-help book, "When I started Internet dating, it felt like defeat. I had failed to meet someone 'naturally'; my soul was a dud" (Sara Eckel, *It's Not You: 27 [Wrong] Reasons You're Single* [New York: Penguin, 2014], 79).
4. Eva Illouz, *Consuming the Romantic Utopia: Love and the Cultural Contradictions of Capitalism* (Berkeley: University of California Press, 1997), 124.
5. Eva Illouz, *Consuming the Romantic Utopia: Love and the Cultural Contradictions of Capitalism* (Berkeley: University of California Press, 1997), 147–48.
6. This is a reference to Kenny Loggins' "Danny's Song" (1971).
7. Eva Illouz, *Consuming the Romantic Utopia: Love and the Cultural Contradictions of Capitalism* (Berkeley: University of California Press, 1997), 115.
8. A good illustration of this played out in the Canadian comedy *Control Alt Delete* (2008). The protagonist, Lewis (Tyler Labine), told his colleague, Jane (Sonja Bennett), about the failed relationship he had with his first girlfriend. They had a relationship online, arranged to meet in person but she never showed up. As Jane consoled, "Maybe Gladreal was happy to keep your relationship in the abstract. ... That way she could imagine meeting you the way that she wanted to, right?"
9. This is an example of older people portrayed as being out of touch with new technology and, specifically, online dating, something evident in other examples. A good illustration of this transpired in "The Practice Around the Corner" episode of the British comedy-drama series *Doc Martin* (2004–) when Al (Joe Absolom) told his father, Bert (Ian McNeice), that he had started online dating and Bert remarked, "that's for losers." Bert is presented as out-of-touch in this scene, rather than it being an indictment on Al's behavior.
10. Ellen Fein and Sherrie Schneider, *The Rules for Online Dating: Capturing the Heart of Mr. Right in Cyberspace* (New York: Pocket Books, 2002), 205.
11. Gian Gonzaga, *eHarmony Guide to Dating the Second Time Around* (London: Hachette, 2011), ebook.
12. Jason in this scene accepts online dating as an efficiency service and appears disinterested in the vagaries of romance and the capacity to have a good story to tell others.
13. The same point was made in a 2015 Match.com advertisement: "If you're sitting at dinner with Mr. Right, does it matter where you met him?"
14. John C. Bridges, *The Illusion of Intimacy: Problems in the World of Online Dating* (Santa Barbara, CA: Praeger, 2012), 105.

15. Natalye Childress, *Aftermath of Forever: How I Loved, Lost, and Found Myself* (Portland, OR: Microcosm Publishing, 2014), 129.

16. Michael Thomsen, *Levitate the Primate: Handjobs, Internet Dating and Other Issues for Men* (Alresford, Hants: Zero Books, 2012), 3.

17. Hedda Muskat, *Dating Confidential: A Singles Guide to a Fun, Flirtatious and Possibly Meaningful Social Life* (Naperville, IL: Sourcebooks, 2004), 103.

18. Aziz Ansari and Eric Klinenberg, *Modern Dating* (New York: Penguin, 2015), ebook.

19. Dan Silber, "How to Be Yourself in an Online World," in *Dating—Philosophy for Everyone: Flirting with Big Ideas*, eds. Kristie Miller and Marlene Clark (Malden, MA: John Wiley & Sons, 2010), 180–194, 188.

20. Michele Schreiber, *American Postfeminist Cinema: Women, Romance and Contemporary Culture* (Edinburgh: Edinburgh University Press, 2015), 76. [My emphasis].

21. Eva Illouz, *Consuming the Romantic Utopia: Love and the Cultural Contradictions of Capitalism* (Berkeley: University of California Press, 1997).

22. Kayli Stollak, *Granny Is My Wingman* (New York: Houghton Mifflin Harcourt, 2013), 30.

23. In Brigid Delaney, *This Restless Life: Churning Through Love, Work and Travel* (Carlton: Melbourne University Press, 2009), 38.

24. Ben Agger, *Oversharing: Presentations of Self in the Internet Age* (New York: Routledge, 2012), 31.

25. Dan Slater, *Love in the Time of Algorithms* (New York: Current, 2013), 4.

26. Ron Geraci, *The Bachelor Chronicles* (New York: Kensington Books, 2006), 64.

27. Susan Sprecher, Amy Wenzel and John H. Harvey, *Handbook of Relationship Initiation* (New York: Psychology Press, 2008); Eli J. Finkel, Paul W. Eastwick, Benjamin R. Karney, Harry T. Reis and Susan Sprecher, "Online Dating: A Critical Analysis from the Perspective of Psychological Science," *Psychological Science in the Public Interest*, 13, 1 (2012): 3–66; Dan Slater, *Love in the Time of Algorithms* (New York: Current, 2013); Amy Webb, *Data, A Love Story: How I Cracked the Online Dating Code to Meet My Match* (London: Dutton, 2013).

28. Annette N. Markham, "Internet Communication as a Tool for Qualitative Research," in *Qualitative Research: Theory, Method and Practice*, ed. David Silverman (London: Sage Publications, 2011): 95–124, 99.

29. Lauren Rosewarne, *Cyberbullies, Cyberactivists, Cyberpredators: Film, TV, and Internet Stereotypes* (Santa Barbara, CA: Praeger, 2016).

30. In Aziz Ansari and Eric Klinenberg, "How to Make Online Dating Work," *New York Times*, June 13, 2015. Accessed June 27, 2015, from http://www.nytimes.com/2015/06/14/opinion/sunday/how-to-make-online-dating-work.html.

31. Lauren Rosewarne, *Cyberbullies, Cyberactivists, Cyberpredators: Film, TV, and Internet Stereotypes* (Santa Barbara, CA: Praeger, 2016).

32. Mark Penn and E. Kinney Zalesne, *Microtrends: The Small Forces Behind Tomorrow's Big Changes* (New York: Twelve, 2007), 22.

33. Lauren Rosewarne, *Cyberbullies, Cyberactivists, Cyberpredators: Film, TV, and Internet Stereotypes* (Santa Barbara, CA: Praeger, 2016).

34. While in this chapter—and book—I don't really discuss the physical hardware used to access the Internet, a good illustration of the perceived unsexiness of computers was articulated in the biopic *Jobs* (2013) when Johnny (Giles

Matthey), one of the designers at Apple, remarked: "There's no sex left in computers. No curves."

35. Daniel Dinello, *Technophobia! Science Fiction Visions of Posthuman Technology* (Austin: University of Texas Press, 2005).

36. Joel Mokyr, *The Gifts of Athena: Historical Origins of the Knowledge Economy* (Princeton, NJ: Princeton University Press, 2002), 247.

37. Brian R. Smith, *Soft Words for a Hard Technology: Humane Computerization* (Englewood Cliffs, NJ: Prentice Hall, 1984), 142.

38. Sarah Kember, "Feminist Figuration and the Question of Origin," in *Futurenatural: Nature, Science, Culture*, eds. Jon Bird, Barry Curtis, Melinda Mash, George Robertson, Tim Putnam and Lisa Tickner (New York: Routledge, 1996): 253–66, 254.

39. For example *Metropolis* (1927), *Bicentennial Man* (1999), *A.I. Artificial Intelligence* (2001), *Big Hero 7* (2014) and *Ex Machina* (2015).

40. In the "Two Bodies in the Lab" episode of *Bones* (2005–), Agent Booth (David Boreanaz) refers to online relationships as "creepy."

41. This is a good illustration of philosopher Aaron Ben-Ze-ev's findings: "women can be more sexually expressive than they are in offline relationships and men may be more emotionally sensitive" (Aaron Ben-Ze'ev, *Love Online: Emotions on the Internet* [New York: Cambridge University Press, 2004], 44).

42. Charles's "I am who I am" plea can be likened to the assertion that Lina (Ali Wong) makes in the "Sweet Little Lies" episode of the drama series *Black Box* (2014) when she first posts an online dating profile: "Any potential date or one-night stand has got to love the real me."

43. Lauren Rosewarne, "The Hacking of Ashley Madison and the Fantasy of Infidelity," *The Drum*, July 23, 2015. Accessed July 25, 2015, from http://www.abc.net.au/news/2015–07–23/rosewarne-ashley-madison-and-the-fantasy-of-infidelity/6641742.

44. Aaron Ben-Ze'ev, *Love Online: Emotions on the Internet* (New York: Cambridge University Press, 2004), 3.

45. Monica T. Whitty and Adam N. Joinson, *Truth, Lies and Trust on the Internet* (New York: Routledge, 2009), 80.

46. Lauren Rosewarne, *Cyberbullies, Cyberactivists, Cyberpredators: Film, TV, and Internet Stereotypes* (Santa Barbara, CA: Praeger, 2016).

47. Controversial as pertaining to its veracity. See Andrew O'Hehir, "Untangling the 'Catfish' Hoax Rumors," *Salon*, October 14, 2010. Accessed July 7, 2015, from http://www.salon.com/2010/10/14/catfish/; Ryan Gilbey, "Trust Me, I'm a Film-Maker: The Men Behind Catfish Come Clean," *The Guardian*, November 19, 2010. Accessed July 7, 2015, from http://www.theguardian.com/film/2010/nov/20/catfish-fact-or-fiction-film.

48. Sherry Turkle, *Life on the Screen: Identity in the Age of the Internet* (New York: Simon and Schuster, 1995), 190.

49. In Dennis D. Waskul, *Self-Games and Body-Play: Personhood in Online Chat and Cyberspace* (New York: Peter Lang, 2003), 60.

50. Monica T. Whitty and Adrian N. Carr, *Cyberspace Romance: The Psychology of Online Relationships* (New York: Palgrave Macmillan, 2006), 23.

51. Jean-Claude Kaufmann, *Love Online* (Malden, MA: Polity, 2012), 28.

52. Dennis D. Waskul, *Self-Games and Body-Play: Personhood in Online Chat and Cyberspace* (New York: Peter Lang, 2003), 25.

53. Dan Slater, *Love in the Time of Algorithms* (New York: Current, 2013), 177.

54. The fantasy film *Weird Science* (1985) for example, centered on two nerds who used a computer to build a perfect woman, is an extreme illustration of this. The same idea is referenced in a quip made by the title character (Michael Fassbender) in the biopic *Steve Jobs* (2015): "… the same way you get over your high school sweetheart: you build a new one."

55. "Lonesome loser" is a reference to the song of the same name by The Little River Band (1979).

56. James E. Katz and Ronald E. Rice, *Social Consequences of Internet Use: Access, Involvement and Interaction* (Cambridge, MA: MIT Press, 2002), 10.

57. James E. Katz and Ronald E. Rice, *Social Consequences of Internet Use: Access, Involvement and Interaction* (Cambridge, MA: MIT Press, 2002), 204.

58. In James E. Katz and Ronald E. Rice, *Social Consequences of Internet Use: Access, Involvement and Interaction* (Cambridge, MA: MIT Press, 2002), 10.

59. While this book focuses on romantic and sexual intimacies, the screen depicts a number of other intimacies aided by the Internet, particularly in the context of friendship and well-being. In the thriller *Copycat* (1995), for example, after a panic attack, Helen (Sigourney Weaver)—who had become agoraphobic following an attack by a serial killer—goes into a chatroom and types "Anybody awake? Need to talk." In the drama *Mojave Phone Booth* (2006), Glory (Joy Gohring) gets involved in an online support group for depression. This also transpires in the British film *Chatroom* (2010), as well as in the drama *On_Line* (2002). In *Disconnect* (2012), Cindy (Paula Patton), who had lost her son, spends time in a grief chatroom. In *Men, Women & Children* (2014), Allison (Elena Kampouris) seeks support and encouragement for her eating disorder in an online pro-ana group. In the Belgian speculative future film *Thomas est amoureux* (*Thomas in Love*) (2000), the agoraphobic Thomas (Benoît Verhaert) gets all of his needs met online, including seeing a psychologist. Internet-based counselling is also the subject of the sitcom *Web Therapy* (2011–).

60. Aaron Ben-Ze'ev, *Love Online: Emotions on the Internet* (New York: Cambridge University Press, 2004), 2.

61. Katelyn Y.A. McKenna and John A. Bargh, "Plan 9 from Cyberspace: The Implications of the Internet for Personality and Social Psychology," *Personality and Social Psychology Review*, 4, 1 (2000): 57–75, 68.

62. As explained by technology theorist Adrian Cheok, "The term 'intimate computing' refers to technologies that enhance or make possible forms of intimacy between remote people that would normally only be possible if they were proximate … Very little work has been done in this area." (Adrian David Cheok, *Art and Technology of Entertainment Computing and Communication* [New York: Springer, 2010], 132).

63. In "The Infestation Hypothesis" episode of the sitcom *The Big Bang Theory* (2007–), Howard (Simon Helberg) builds a machine that can facilitate kissing between two geographically separated characters using the Internet.

64. Aaron Ben-Ze'ev, *Love Online: Emotions on the Internet* (New York: Cambridge University Press, 2004), 4.

65. Monica Whitty and Jeff Gavin, "Age/Sex/Location: Uncovering Social Cues in the Development of Online Relationships," *CyberPsychology and Behavior*, 4 (2001): 623–30.

66. Martin Lea and Russell Spears, "Love at First Byte? Building Personal Relationships Over Computer Networks," in *Understudied Relationships: Off the*

Beaten Track, eds. Julia T Wood and Steve Duck (Thousand Oaks, CA: Sage Publications, 1995): 197–233.

67. Aaron Ben-Ze'ev, *Love Online: Emotions on the Internet* (New York: Cambridge University Press, 2004), 219.

68. Jean-Claude Kaufmann, *Love Online* (Malden, MA: Polity, 2012), 14.

69. Monica T. Whitty and Adrian N. Carr, *Cyberspace Romance: The Psychology of Online Relationships* (New York: Palgrave Macmillan, 2006), 1.

70. Lauren Rosewarne, *Cyberbullies, Cyberactivists, Cyberpredators: Film, TV, and Internet Stereotypes* (Santa Barbara, CA: Praeger, 2016).

71. Yann-Ling Chin, "'Platonic Relationships' in China's Online Social Milieu: A Lubricant for Banal Everyday Life?" *Chinese Journal of Communication*, 4, 4 (2011): 400–416, 411.

72. Lauren Rosewarne, "The Hacking of Ashley Madison and the Fantasy of Infidelity," *The Drum*, July 23, 2015. Accessed July 25, 2015, from http://www.abc.net.au/news/2015-07-23/rosewarne-ashley-madison-and-the-fantasy-of-infidelity/6641742.

73. Lauren Rosewarne, *Cyberbullies, Cyberactivists, Cyberpredators: Film, TV, and Internet Stereotypes* (Santa Barbara, CA: Praeger, 2016).

74. Lauren Rosewarne, *Cyberbullies, Cyberactivists, Cyberpredators: Film, TV, and Internet Stereotypes* (Santa Barbara, CA: Praeger, 2016).

75. The philosopher Michael Bruce for example, in a discussion on college students' use of dating sites, identified, "On the dating sites there is a culture of extreme objectification, and even *expert objectification*" (Michael Bruce, "The Virtual Bra Clasp: Navigating Technology in College Courtship," in *College Sex—Philosophy for Everyone*, eds. Michael Bruce and Robert M. Stewart [Malden, MA: John Wiley & Sons, 2010]: 40–50, 45). The philosopher Dan Silber also drew attention to this issue noting, "Most of us are repelled when we consider the world of dating as a market because doing so seems to threaten all of its participants with objectification" (Dan Silber, "How to Be Yourself in an Online World," in *Dating—Philosophy for Everyone: Flirting with Big Ideas*, eds. Kristie Miller and Marlene Clark (Malden, MA: John Wiley & Sons, 2010): 180–94, 188).

76. The same idea of objectification through use of technology transpires in the comedy *Paul Blart: Mall Cop* (2009), the Singaporean romantic-drama *Be with Me* (2005) and the Uruguayan drama *Gigante* (*Giant*) (2009) where male security guards develop strong feelings for women they didn't know but spy on using CCTV cameras.

77. Sherry Turkle, *Life on the Screen: Identity in the Age of the Internet* (New York: Simon and Schuster, 1995); Ann G. Smolen, "The Multiple Meanings of the Electrified Mind," in *The Electrified Mind: Development, Psychopathology, and Treatment in the Era of Cell Phones and the Internet*, ed. Salman Akhtar (Lanham, MD: Roman & Littlefield, 2011): 129–40.

78. Julie M. Albright and Eddie Simmens, "Flirting, Cheating, Dating and Mating in a Virtual World," in *The Oxford Handbook of Virtuality*, ed. Mark Grimshaw (New York: Oxford University Press, 2014): 284–303, 290.

79. In Helene M. Lawson and Kira Leck, "Dynamics of Internet Dating," *Social Science Computer Review*, 24, 2 (2006): 189–208, 198.

80. The psychologist Kimberly Young makes this point, noting "Even if we never actually meet this cyber-hero or heroine, we're still filling in the blanks of their identity and relating to the person we've created, rather than the actual person who may be sitting at the other computer" (Kimberly S. Young, *Caught in the*

Net: How to Recognize the Signs of Internet Addiction—And a Winning Strategy for Recovery [New York: John Wiley & Sons, 1998], 102).

81. Such scenes can be likened to those transpiring in the sci-fi film *I Origins* (2014), as well as the "Andare Pescare" episode of the drama series *Sons of Anarchy* (2008–14) where men use the perfumes worn by dead lovers as an accoutrement during masturbation.

82. Jim Thomas, "Cyberpoaching Behind the Keyboard: Uncoupling the Ethics of 'Virtual Infidelity'," in *Net.seXX: Readings on Sex, Pornography and the Internet*, ed. Dennis D. Waskul (New York: Peter Lang, 2004): 149–77, 156.

83. Christa Worthington, "Making Love in Cyberspace," *The Independent* (October 6, 1996). Accessed June 30, 2014, from http://www.independent.co.uk/arts-entertainment/making-love-in-cyberspace-1356977.html.

84. Aaron Ben-Ze'ev, *Love Online: Emotions on the Internet* (New York: Cambridge University Press, 2004), 6.

85. Lauren Rosewarne, *Masturbation in Pop Culture: Screen, Society, Self* (Lanham, MD: Lexington Books, 2014).

86. Lauren Rosewarne, "Her, Hungry Ghosts and Rethinking Intimacy," *The Conversation*, February 11, 2014. Accessed July 9, 2015, from http://theconversation.com/her-hungry-ghosts-and-rethinking-intimacy-22757.

87. Anna Shechtman, "What's Missing from Her," *Slate*, January 3, 2014. Accessed July 9, 2015, from http://www.slate.com/blogs/browbeat/2014/01/03/her_movie_by_spike_jonze_with_joaquin_phoenix_and_scarlett_johansson_lacks.html.

88. This can be likened to the bodiless cybersex scenes transpiring in films like the sci-fi mini-series *Wild Palms* (1993), and the sci-fi films *Demolition Man* (1993), *Strange Days* (1995), *Virtuosity* (1995) and *Surrogates* (2009), where "intercourse" is a cerebral rather than corporeal experience, a topic I discuss further elsewhere (Lauren Rosewarne, *Cyberbullies, Cyberactivists, Cyberpredators: Film, TV, and Internet Stereotypes* [Santa Barbara, CA: Praeger, 2016]).

89. Aaron Ben-Ze'ev, *Love Online: Emotions on the Internet* (New York: Cambridge University Press, 2004), 134.

90. Lauren Rosewarne, *Masturbation in Pop Culture: Screen, Society, Self* (Lanham, MD: Lexington Books, 2014).

91. Hannu Eerikäinen, "Cybersex: A Desire for Disembodiment. On the Meaning of the Human Being in Cyber Discourse," in *Mediapolis: Aspects of Texts, Hypertexts, and Multimedial Communication*, ed. Sam Inkinen (Berlin: Walter de Gruyter, 1998): 203–42, 228 n. 38.

92. In Sherry Turkle, *Life on the Screen: Identity in the Age of the Internet* (New York: Simon and Schuster, 1995), 21.

93. Carol Parker, *The Joy of Cyber Sex* (Kew, Victoria: Mandarin, 1997), 52–53.

94. In Dan Slater, "A Million First Dates: How Online Dating Is Threatening Monogamy," *The Atlantic*, 311, 1 (2013): 40–46, 42.

95. Paul Oyer, *Everything I Needed to Know about Economics I Learned from Online Dating* (Boston, MA: Harvard Business Review Press, 2014), 8.

96. John T. Cacioppo, Stephanie Cacioppo, Gian C. Gonzaga, Elizabeth L. Ogburn and Tyler J. VanderWeele, "Marital Satisfaction and Break-Ups Differ across On-line and Off-line Meeting Venues," *Psychological & Cognitive Sciences*, 110 (2013): 10135–40.

97. Jeffrey A. Hall, "First Comes Social Networking, Then Comes Marriage? Characteristics of Americans Married 2005–2012 Who Met Through Social Networking Sites," *Cyberpsychology, Behavior and Social Networking*, 17, 5 (2014): 322–26.

98. John B. Jensen, *The Marriage MBA: The 7 Things You Need to Know about Dating and Relationships* (Victoria, BC: Friesen Press, 2014), 4.

99. John B. Jensen, *The Marriage MBA: The 7 Things You Need to Know about Dating and Relationships* (Victoria, BC: Friesen Press, 2014); Paul Oyer, *Everything I Needed to Know about Economics I Learned from Online Dating* (Boston, MA: Harvard Business Review Press, 2014).

100. The television holiday film *A Christmas Song* (2012) presents a similar take on this: after nemeses Diana (Natasha Henstridge) and Ken (Gabriel Hogan) are matched online, they both construct profiles with polar-opposite information about themselves; they get matched a second time.

101. A good example of this in the context of gaming transpired in the "Bullseye" episode of the crime-drama *Law & Order: Special Victims Unit* (1999–) where Jeff (Daniel Stewart Sherman) and Amber (Melissa Rain Anderson) were so obsessed with their online game-playing that, after they were arrested for neglecting their real child, they expressed genuine concerns about their online avatar child.

102. Lena Dunham—the creator and star of *Girls* (2012–)—wrote in her memoir about an online relationship that she had when she was twelve years old with a boy named Igor who apparently died of a drug overdose before they got to meet in person (Lena Dunham, *Not That Kind of Girl: A Young Woman Tells You What She's Learned* [New York: Random House, 2014]).

103. In Christa Worthington, "Making Love in Cyberspace," *The Independent* (October 6, 1996). Retrieved June 30, 2014, from http://www.independent.co.uk/arts-entertainment/making-love-in-cyberspace-1356977.html.

104. Wenhong Chen, "Internet Use, Online Communication, and Ties in Americans' Networks," *Social Science Computer Review*, 31, 4 (2013): 404–23; Barbara Barbosa Neves, "Does the Internet Matter for Strong Ties? Bonding Social Capital, Internet Use, and Age-Based Inequality," *International Review of Sociology*, 24 July (2015): 1–19.

105. Georg Simmel and Kurt H. Wolff, *The Sociology of Georg Simmel* (Glencoe, IL: The Free Press, 1950), 216.

106. Aaron Ben-Ze'ev, *Love Online: Emotions on the Internet* (New York: Cambridge University Press, 2004), 36.

107. Monica T. Whitty and Adam N. Joinson, *Truth, Lies and Trust on the Internet* (New York: Routledge, 2009), 1.

108. John C. Bridges, *The Illusion of Intimacy: Problems in the World of Online Dating* (Santa Barbara, CA: Praeger, 2012), 27.

109. John C. Bridges, *The Illusion of Intimacy: Problems in the World of Online Dating* (Santa Barbara, CA: Praeger, 2012), 42.

110. Al Cooper and Eric Griffin-Shelley, "Introduction. The Internet: The Next Sexual Revolution," in *Sex and the Internet: A Guidebook for Clinicians*, eds. Al Cooper and Eric Griffin-Shelley (New York: Brunner-Routledge, 2002): 1–15, 5.

111. In Helene M. Lawson and Kira Leck, "Dynamics of Internet Dating," *Social Science Computer Review*, 24, 2 (2006): 189–208, 203.

112. Dan Slater, *Love in the Time of Algorithms* (New York: Current, 2013), 125.

113. In the novel *The Rosie Effect*, the protagonist Don commented, "One of the advantages of text is that the other person cannot interrupt." (Graeme Simsion, *The Rosie Effect: A Novel* (New York: Simon and Schuster, 2014), 109).

114. Esther Gwinnell, *Online Seductions: Falling in Love with Strangers on the Net* (New York: Kodansha International, 1998), xix.

115. Eva Illouz, *Why Love Hurts: A Sociological Explanation* (Malden, MA: Polity, 2012), 236.

116. Such ideas can be likened to work on infidelity whereby affairs are construed as a bonus round and experienced as separate from real life (Lauren Rosewarne, *Cheating on the Sisterhood: Infidelity and Feminism* (Santa Barbara, CA: Praeger, 2009). These ideas also relate to the appeal of relationships such as those with prisoners whereby the relationship is not subjected to the tribulations and boredoms of everyday normal life.

117. Lauren Rosewarne, *Masturbation in Pop Culture: Screen, Society, Self* (Lanham, MD: Lexington Books, 2014).

118. In Sandra Leiblum and Nicola Döring, "Internet Sexuality: Known Risks and Fresh Chances for Women," in *Sex and the Internet: A Guidebook for Clinicians* eds. Al Cooper and Eric Griffin-Shelley (New York: Brunner-Routledge, 2002): 19–45, 42.

119. In Aaron Ben-Ze'ev, *Love Online: Emotions on the Internet* (New York: Cambridge University Press, 2004), 147.

120. Aaron Ben-Ze'ev, *Love Online: Emotions on the Internet* (New York: Cambridge University Press, 2004), 12.

121. Aaron Ben-Ze'ev, *Love Online: Emotions on the Internet* (New York: Cambridge University Press, 2004), 138.

122. This idea is actually referenced in feminist scholars Sally Lloyd and Beth Emery's work where they note, "'You and me against the world' may have particular meaning for the couple as a metaphor for what is right within the relationship and what is wrong with everything else" (Sally A. Lloyd and Beth C. Emery, *The Dark Side of Courtship: Physical and Sexual Aggression* Thousand Oaks, CA: Sage Publications, 2000], 27).

3   The Dateless and the Desperate

In the "Joint Custody" episode of the animated series *American Dad!* (2005), Roger jibed, "If I can't make friends with Jeff face-to-face, I'll have to do it the way fat people do: over the Internet." This comment introduces numerous themes explored in this chapter. First, it hints to the ability for the Internet to thwart—or, at least, delay—the face-to-face judgments that often plague people in real life who exist outside of society's notions of "attractive," for example, as Roger alluded, *fat people*. Second, it references the idea of the Internet as particularly appealing for outliers, as a place for them to retreat to, as well as socialize. *Outliers* in this context refers to the *unfuckable*, encompassing the fat, the disabled, the socially awkward, the unattractive, and, generally, characters who encounter difficulties in succeeding in the offline dating landscape. (The *sexually* outlier are discussed in Chapter 6.)

This chapter uses terms like *unfuckable*, *undateable* and *undesirable* interchangeably to reference many of the screen's online dating participants. The first point to be made here is that quite obviously unattractiveness is completely subjective; in fact, despite the narrow beauty aesthetic suggested by Hollywood, attraction is substantially more nuanced.[1] Equally, as explored throughout this book, the Internet has proven itself quite a boon for connecting the supposedly unattractive as well as those whose tastes—aesthetic, sexual or otherwise—deviate from the mainstream, something that pre-Web would have been more difficult. This *boon*, however, has meant that those socially excluded whom the Internet has been distinctly advantageous for have come to dominate the *who* of online dating both in the popular imaginary and notably on screen. This chapter focuses on those Internet users who exist outside of Western notions of attractiveness who have come to dominate popular perceptions of the stigmatized *who* of online dating.

This chapter begins with a discussion of the loser stereotype and then explores themes including desperation and loneliness.

Online Losers

In Chapter 2 I discussed a range of narratives where online daters had successfully turned online relationships into something lasting *offline*: outcomes experienced by Kip (Aaron Ruell) in the comedy *Napoleon Dynamite*

(2004) and Paul (James Corden) in the British biopic *One Chance* (2013). Kip in *Napoleon Dynamite* is a tall, awkward, unemployed aspiring cage fighter; he is also a prototype loser: odd looking, and spending all of his time at his computer. In *One Chance*, Paul is an overweight phone-store worker and aspiring opera singer. Paul is also a loser: clumsy and having shyly delayed an in-person meeting with his online girlfriend for six months. Both characters illustrate perfectly the losers assumed to use the Internet to couple. Another example of this is evident in the multiseason relationship of Sheldon (Jim Parsons) and Amy (Mayim Bialik) who were matched online in "The Lunar Excitation" of the sitcom *The Big Bang Theory* (2007–): both are prototype nerds employed as scientists. While these examples make the simple point that long-term relationships are indeed possible for people who meet online, more problematically, they also illustrate that a *certain kind* of person couples online.[2] While in *Napoleon Dynamite*, *One Chance* and *The Big Bang Theory* the online dating loser is personified, in a variety of others, this idea is spoken.

In "The Practice Around the Corner" episode of the British comedy-drama series *Doc Martin* (2004–), Al (Joe Absolom) revealed to his father, Bert (Ian McNeice), that he had started online dating, to which Bert responded, "that's for losers." In the comedy-drama *Burn After Reading* (2008), Linda (Frances McDormand) showed her colleague, Chad (Brad Pitt), her BeWithMeDC. com matches: "Loser. Loser. Loser. They should call this MrLoser.com," she lamented. In "The Gang Wrestles" episode of the sitcom *It's Always Sunny in Philadelphia* (2005–), Dennis (Glenn Howerton) and Mac (Rob McElhenney) discovered that Dee (Kaitlin Olson) had been chatting online:

DENNIS: Who's "Soldier of Fortune"?
DEE: He's just this guy I've been chatting online with. Whatever.
DENNIS: So that would make you "Desert Rose"?
DEE: Yes it would.
DENNIS: [scoffs]
MAC: Wow! What a couple of losers!

In the comedy *Paul Blart: Mall Cop* (2009), the head hostage-taker (Keir O'Donnell) tormented the title character (Kevin James) about his online dating profile: "Wow. Our boy Stuart [Stephen Rannazzisi] just turned me on to your profile on lonelyloser.com. Likes morning rain, walks on the beach. Who are you, Olivia Newton John?" In the "Digging the Dirt" episode of the fantasy series *The Gates* (2010), Devon (Chandra West) described her online dating experiences: "I'm telling you," she gushed, "dating in the Internet era is a revelation. I get 100 messages a day. Eliminate the losers, there's still dozens of handsome, successful men who'd kill to meet me." The horror film *Pulse 2: The Afterlife* (2008) opened with Michelle (Georgina Rylance) reading from her diary: "September fourteenth. Forty-three days single. Terry signed me up for the dating service. All losers ..." In "The Cinderella in the Cardboard" episode of the crime-drama *Bones* (2005–), the murderer, Kurtis (Kevin Christy)—who had hunted victims using a hook-up app— claimed, "All these beautiful women on my service, but none of them will look at me. I'm better than half the losers that sign up." In the pilot of the sci-fi series *Mr. Robot* (2015–), Elliot (Rami Malek) identified that his psy- chologist, Krista (Gloria Reuben), had been "dating losers on eHarmony" since her divorce. In "The Fall" episode of the comedy-drama series *Grace and Frankie* (2015–), the loser idea had apparently been internalized when Grace (Jane Fonda) explained her reluctance to upload a profile: "If I press that button, everybody in the world who looks at this site is going to know I'm a desperate loser," to which her daughter, Brianna (June Diane Raphael) responded, "Yes. But Mom, they're all desperate losers, too."

Verbally linking online dating to the word "loser" works to reinforce that there is something wrong with people who date online; *wrong* in this context being that they lack the qualities that would make them conventionally fuckable offline. Such screen examples, however, can only function as "reinforcements" within a culture where this idea *already* has traction. In Chapter 1 I noted that online dating has undergone a reputational overhaul with it mainstreaming substantially since its inception in the early 1990s. Although this may be true, the loser-archetype still has a distinct screen presence, and equally so is an idea still clinging to relevance in broader culture. Newspaper reports, for exam- ple, still—well into the 2000s—use *loser* in article headlines, for example: "Single white female seeks anyone other than these losers,"[3] "Online dating: Is everyone a catfish, conman, liar, cheater, predator or loser?"[4] and "Online losers are easy to spot; Danger signs in Internet dating."[5] Even articles which attempt to take a modern stance and reflect contemporary mainstreaming still use the word, in turn helping to echo it in the mind of readers already familiar with the stereotype: "Online dating not for losers,"[6] "Online dating not just for lovable losers"[7] and "Online dating no longer loser central."[8] The *why* of this loser association stems from two central factors: (a) the stereotypes of the earliest users, and (b) the nature of the technology.

Sam Yagan, cofounder of the dating site OKCupid, discussed the brand- ing problem that online dating has long suffered: "The only people online in the nineties were socially awkward geeks … So, by definition, they were the bulk of the people doing online dating."[9] A similar point was made by John Dvorak, Chris Pirillo and Wendy Taylor in their book *Online!*:

> In the early 1990s, it was far more likely to meet someone with similar interests and goals online, because the only people online were fellow geeks. In fact, the first online dates resembled a game of Dungeons & Dragons, the entire date taking place in cyberspace with characters created by users.[10]

During the early 1990s, a time before widespread domestic Internet use, the technology was used predominantly by actual geeks and nerds: these were computer people who understood the technology and were communicating with like-minded—and like-*skilled*—peers. Decades on and the typical 1990s user is still easily detectable in screen fiction. As I have discussed elsewhere, nerds and geeks in popular culture are invariably depicted in disparaging ways, commonly viewed as machine-like, robotic, hermitted and asexual[11]; thus, these qualities have come to shape our collective understanding about the type of people who use the Internet to find intimacy. While well into the 2000s Internet use has become near universal and online dating has become mainstream, as apparent in the majority of examples discussed in this chapter, in film and television the stereotypes of nerds-as-losers and losers-as-online-daters are still widely portrayed. Equally, given that use of the Internet is now common and thus going online shouldn't really prove much of an insight into a character, the fact that a person is depicted having to use this technology—that love hasn't found them *serendipitously*—positions an online dater as having failed at something that should come naturally. The economist Paul Oyer addressed this perception in his book *Everything I Needed to Know about Economics I Learned from Online Dating*:

> People who are desirable can generally find mates using standard methods, such as meeting people at work, meeting people at school, or being fixed up by friends. But undesirable people can't use those methods because the people they interact with on a daily basis have recognized their nondesirability and will not enter into a relationship with them, nor enthusiastically recommend them to their friends.[12]

Jeff Bercovici, writing for *Forbes*, made a connected point, identifying, "If people think online dating is for losers, it's partly because the experience of it makes them feel like losers."[13] Sophia Dembling in her book *Introverts in Love* also discussed this idea in the context of her patient Taylor, who claimed:

> I don't like how pathetic it makes me feel, stalking around looking at girls' photos and trying to think of something absolutely fascinating to message her and get her attention.[14]

Bercovici and Dembling hint to the idea that rather than the *technology* being the problem, within our couple-centric world, people are encouraged to feel bad—to feel like losers—because they are single and because they have entered the market to seek remedy. While simply going online to search for a partner doesn't suddenly make a person less attractive or less fuckable, one's self-perception, based upon negative cultural messages, means that he or she is cajoled into feeling this way.

A trope often used to illustrate the unfuckable *who* of online dating is the parade of losers encountered on screen: a hyperbolic supposed *encapsulation* of the online dating landscape.

The Loser Parade

A device frequently used on screen to frame online dating as comic is a freaks and weirdos parade. This trope usually transpires when a character starts online dating and thus moves quickly through a procession of strange and often farcically unsavory characters, subtly demonstrating what is *out there* in terms of the dating landscape. Worth noting, the characters in these freaks and weirdos parades are invariably men. While this links to the pervert assumption discussed further in Chapter 4, it also ties in with the earliest perception about *who* is online: the Internet has long been dominated by the belief that cyberspace is populated by geeks and that these geeks are men.[15]

As early as 1998 the loser parade was used in the "Crossfire" episode of the police-drama *Nash Bridges* (1996–2001). Inspector Michelle Chan (Kelly Hu) was undercover, trying to track down a criminal by going on online dates. Her first date, Kenneth (Bill Raferty), had lied that he was tall and muscular; he was actually short and balding. Her second date was seemingly suicidal, telling her:

> It's not like I would commit suicide per se, because I have too much respect for human life, however, sometimes I'm hitchhiking, I think that if a car were to veer off the road and hit me, eviscerating me instantly, some part of me would be profoundly relieved.

Another of Michelle's dates was married, another arrived eating a piece of toast, and another was transsexual. The loser parade in *Nash Bridges* is a trope apparent in a range of online dating–themed scenes. The romance *Meet Prince Charming* (2002), for example, opened with consecutive clips from dating videos to give insight into who is out there: an awkward shy guy, a woman craving a large penis, a bisexual, a woman who can kill chickens with her bare hands, a biker-fetishist and a very desperate man who stated, "I used to have a lot of standards I was looking for, but I don't date much so I've been dropping those off. So now, just, someone who's female." In the "Zero Dark Forties" episode of the sitcom *The Exes* (2011–), Holly's (Kristen Johnston) friends Phil (Donald Faison), Haskell (Wayne Knight) and Stuart (David Alan Basche) secretly uploaded a profile for her on a dating site and were prescreening men before orchestrating a meet cute. One man they met with had claimed to be a former Olympic water polo player: a very old man turned up; he had competed in the *Helsinki* games. The next date was accompanied by his mother (who insisted he play the harmonica for them); one weird date nursed a box throughout the meeting: as Haskell pronounced at the end of the parade, "After seeing this creep show, I'm just gonna come out and say it: I'm a freakin' catch!" In the "Dice" episode of the sitcom *New Girl* (2011–), Schmidt (Max Greenfield) scheduled a series of dates for the protagonist, Jess (Zooey Deschanel), via the titular dating app Dice. Jess's loser parade involved a man who grew raisins and had been in prison, a comedy-magician, and a man who admitted to getting into a lot of fist fights. In the romantic-comedy *Because I Said So* (2007), Daphne (Diane Keaton) had gone online to find a partner for her daughter, Milly (Mandy Moore). Like Holly's friends in *The Exes*, Daphne was prescreening suitor possibilities for Milly. One date had bad teeth, another was hypoglycemic, one had poor English skills, another was allergy prone, one was a drag queen, another twitchy, and there was also a hippy, an alcoholic, a ventriloquist and a punk. In the romantic-comedy *Must Love Dogs* (2005), among Sarah's (Diane Lane) suitors met online was a man wanting to arm-wrestle her, one who greeted her by lamenting that he thought she would be younger, and another who was sobbing. In the comedy *Internet Dating* (2008), Mickey (Katt Williams) similarly encountered a parade of strange and unappealing characters: a fat and constantly eating woman, a boxer looking for a fight and a horny Asian lady. In the "Attack of the Killer Kung-Fu Wolf Bitch" episode of the animated series *The Boondocks* (2005–), among the online dates that grandpa had arranged, his loser parade included a transsexual, a frightfully ugly woman and a very old lady. The loser parade is also a trope detected in advertising.[16]

Most obviously in each of these examples, this loser parade is deployed for laughs. Equally, it functions as a modern example of the familiar bad-date montage used on screen whereby bad experiences are made funny through exaggeration; one bad experience might be sad, but six clustered together is hilarious; speed-dating scenes, for instance, frequently use this device.[17] While such scenes are partly funny because they are hyperbolic, the weird daters portrayed are nonetheless the very people who are assumed to populate cyberspace. These are the unfuckable characters who would have little hope in offline dating so have taken their chances online; such scenes are humorous because they exploit preconceptions, if not potentially also fuel them.

Such scenes are a way to mock the online dating landscape, but it is also worth considering that they also say something about the protagonist daters *within* the narrative: the parade of freaks and losers works, for example, as a sharp contrast to the apparent normalness and relative fuckability of characters like Michelle in *Nash Bridges* or Sarah in *Must Love Dogs*, in turn conveying the impression that such women shouldn't *really* be in such a dating pool—in fact, they are fish out of water, hence why the scenes are so funny. That these women find themselves in such a pool is simply because they have been unlucky-in-love; as Daphne says about Milly in *Because I Said So*, "She's at a crossroads in her life." Such a reading, therefore, exists as a somewhat modern, almost positive portrayal: yes, our worst suspicions get confirmed by the loser parade but such scenes also prove that normal people—like Michelle, like Sarah—date online, too. Bolstering this idea, the fact that Samantha (Tia Carrere) and Jack (David Charvet) met online in *Meet Prince Charming* and ended up together, ditto for Sarah and Jake (John Cusack) in *Must Love Dogs*, and that Holly met Alex (Grant Show)— and had sex with him—in *The Exes*, proves that encountering someone nice and normal online is possible.

The perception that online dating is for losers is at the heart of a variety of screen presentations. In the next sections, the loser-assumption is conveyed via characters having to be strongly encouraged to embark on this modern matchmaking method, often against their will.

The Coerced Profile

In the aforementioned film *Pulse 2: The Afterlife*, Michelle noted that a "Terry" had signed her up for a dating service.[18] Such coerced participation, in fact, plays out in a range of narratives whereby characters are either pushed to sign up, alternatively, are just signed up by well-meaning family and friends, each scene serving as subtle testimony to stigma.

In Chapter 1, I discussed scenes from the Scottish lesbian-themed series *Lip Service* (2010–12) and *How I Met Your Mother* (2005–14), where well-meaning people suggested to single friends that they should try online dating. In both examples, the single characters, while initially reluctant, did end up participating. In the drama *In Search of a Midnight Kiss* (2007), Wilson (Scoot McNairy) is similarly nagged into putting up an ad by his housemate; as he does, he grumbles throughout: "This is humiliating," he says, "Misanthrope seeks misanthrope. Honestly, if you respond to this ad, you're probably not the kind of woman I'd go out with. I guess I'm lonely and it's New Year's and I'm willing to embarrass the hell out of myself with this ad." In the "In the Mix, on the Books, and in the Freezer" episode of the sitcom *Manhattan Love Story* (2014), Amy (Jade Catta-Preta) downloaded Tinder onto Dana's (Analeigh Tipton) phone to force her to expand her intimacy options. A variation on this theme transpired in the "We Are Everyone" episode of the crime-drama *Elementary* (2012–): Emily (Susan Pourfar) gave her friend Joan (Lucy Liu) a 6-month membership to a dating website TrueRomantix, fearing that Joan was becoming too absorbed in her work. In these examples, characters are pushed to date online—a push, seemingly needed because of the stigma attached—but each demonstrate varying degrees of initiative themselves by actually sticking with it; Wilson, Amy and Lucy for example, proceeded to schedule their own dates. In other examples, the push is more forceful.

Must Love Dogs is an example of a narrative that on one hand challenged some perceptions about online dating—after all, the couple at the center of the narrative, Sarah and Jake, were attractive and successful divorcees who used the technology to lastingly couple—in other ways, however, the film reiterates some well-established negative stereotypes, for example, use of the loser parade. Another negative framing of online dating is evident in Sarah's initial reluctance to get involved. The narrative catalyst is Sarah's friend, Carol's (Elizabeth Perkins), "dating intervention"; as she tells Sarah: "Don't be mad at me for this, okay? … I went online, pretended I was you, and put your profile on PerfectMatch.com." While akin to what transpired in *In Search of a Midnight Kiss* and *Elementary*, Sarah eventually does submit herself to the online dating game; in other examples, the dater is in much less control. As noted, *Because I Said So* centered on Daphne's attempts to find love online for her daughter Milly. Daphne wrote the profile for Milly and even met up with possible dates before orchestrating an accidental meet cute; Milly was kept away from the entire process. The same idea was at the heart of the Canadian television drama *Perfect Romance* (2004): Tess (Kathleen Quinlan) had gone online to find a partner for her daughter, Jenny (Lori Heuring), and met Peter (Henry Ian Cusick), and invited him to the house for a meeting. In the "Zero Dark Forties" episode of *The Exes*, Holly's friends had, unbeknownst to her, posted her profile and, like Daphne in *Because I Said So*, interviewed the candidates before orchestrating a meet cute. In *Paul Blart: Mall Cop*, a dating profile was put up for the title character by his daughter Maya (Raini Rodriguez) and his mother (Shirley Knight). "The Online Date" episode of the comedy-drama series *Jane By Design* (2012) centered on the title character (Erica Dasher) mother, Kate (Teri Hatcher), creating an online dating profile for Jane's boss, Grey (Andie MacDowell), in the hope, seemingly, of distracting Grey from micromanaging her daughter. Similar ideas played out in the "The Barbarian Sublimation" episode of *The Big Bang Theory*: Penny (Kaley Cuoco) had become addicted to online gaming so Sheldon uploaded a dating profile for her in an attempt to distract her from the game. Distraction was also a motivation in "The Waitress is Getting Married" episode of *It's Always Sunny in Philadelphia* when Dennis and Mac posted a profile for their friend Charlie (Charlie Day) so that he would stop pining for The Waitress who, as suggested by the episode title, was getting married. In the "Erica & Callum" episode of the British drama series *Dates* (2013), Erica (Gemma Chan) had been going on dates with men because her brother had been arranging them to steer her away from lesbianism. In the pilot of the sitcom *A to Z* (2014–15), it turned out that Zelda (Cristin Milioti) only had a profile on the Wallflower dating site because her friend, Stephie (Lenora Crichlow), had signed her up. In "The Lunar Excitation" episode of *The Big Bang Theory*, the only reason Sheldon was on the dating site was because his friend Raj (Kunal Nayyar) had signed him up.

The fact that characters in these examples each had to be coerced to try online dating is indicative of internalized stigma about this matchmaking method; seemingly the single characters hadn't already signed themselves up because they were aware of the negativity. While a character's reluctance works to reference the idea that online dating is a *different* way of meeting, it also hints that apprehension—about the technology, about the people met and even about the ego ramifications—is warranted. Although there is not a deluge of information about real-life online dating coercion, the topic does get briefly addressed in Julie Subotky's self-help book, *Consider It Done: Accomplish 228 of Life's Trickiest Tasks*:

> For many, joining an online dating pool is admitting defeat; others fear they'll be relegated to the world of weirdos … But if your friend is still reluctant, it may just be your job to convince him or her. Why bother? Because it's nice to care about your friends.[19]

Although these scenes can be considered as helping to reinforce the problematic perception that online dating is for weirdos, it is worth considering other interpretations. The very fact that friends were *suggesting* online dating indicates that, as Subotky alluded, they cared enough to do so, that they believed that their friend was dateable and just needed some help, a push, and determined that going online was the most practical option. While this, of course, doesn't preclude a possible belief that their single friend is a bit of a loser, it does somewhat dilute the assumption that the Internet is exclusively populated by unlikeable or nefarious characters. Equally, while I have been operating under the presumption that a character's reluctance to sign up stems from the method's beleaguered reputation, in fact, this could be attributable to other things. Addressed later in this chapter, for example, are factors including shyness and social awkwardness that inhibit a character from embarking on the search for love. While in some of these cases the Internet serves to overcome these problems, it is worth considering that if a character is extremely shy or socially anxious, alternatively if they have recently suffered great heartbreak, they may not even consider exposing themselves to *more rejection*, something the Internet is also commonly associated with, as apparent in numerous examples. In the romantic-comedy *You've Got Mail* (1998), for example, George (Steve Zahn) made a comment encapsulating this idea, "Well, as far as I'm concerned, the Internet is just another way of being rejected by women." Wren (Colleen Smith), in the "Follow Through" episode of the sitcom *Selfie* (2014), made a similar remark, "dying from scarlet fever sounds better than being ignored on Match.com every night." In the drama *The Center of the World* (2001), the ability to temper rejection online is also addressed by the Internet mogul Richard (Peter Sarsgaard):

> You don't need to open your door. You don't need to leave. You create a frontier to put your mattress with the cables and the CPUs, and you claim that piece of space. The world breaks in waves at your fingertips. You make its choices. You decide. And it sings for you when you ask.

Coerced profiles is one way that online dating is presented as something associated with losers, if not explicitly, the unfuckable. In the next section, an extension of this idea is explored where a character's own internalized apprehensions about dating are made evident in their profile.

The I-Can't-Believe-I'm-Doing-This Profile

Dan Slater, in his book *Love in the Time of Algorithms*, quoted an online dater who remarked, "I hate when they write on their profile that they find online dating bizarre. Do they really expect me to be impressed that they're above this shit, when their method of telling was their fucking online-dating profile?"[20] In Sam Greenspan's dating self-help book, he alluded to a similar idea, advising that when writing an online dating profile, avoid clichés such as: "I can't believe I am doing this, but here I am."[21] This very idea, in fact, is referenced in the title of Evan Katz's self-help book *I Can't Believe I'm Buying this Book: A Commonsense Guide to Successful Internet Dating.*[22]

While a person might include an "I can't believe ..." line in a profile because they think they are "above" such behavior—certainly a reasonable assumption for Wilson in *In Search for a Midnight Kiss* who alleged that he wouldn't actually be interested in dating anyone who was drawn to his miserable profile—other possibilities exist. Another reading, for example, is *hedging*, a topic discussed by communications theorists Leanne Knoblock and Kelly McAninch:

> Individuals may hedge against embarrassment in uncertain situations by *framing messages*, using humor prospectively or backtracking retrospectively, *employing ambiguity* to hide the central thrust of the message, *utilizing disclaimers* to circumvent negative reactions, *using retroactive discounting* to soften a declaration, and *controlling the floor* by requiring the other person to do the talking. In sum, planning and hedging help people produce messages in the midst of uncertainty.[23]

The idea of not committing fully to online dating—hedging, for example, by exhibiting reluctance or disbelief—is a way both to distance oneself from the negative stereotypes about online dating and to temper possible rejection and/or judgment. In Wilson's profile, for example, he exhibited embarrassment, humiliation and predicted—if not also, seemingly, *guaranteed*—future rejection. Another example of this transpired in "The Friendly Skies" episode of the crime-drama *Without a Trace* (2002–9). The episode centered on a woman, Linda (Heather Donahue), who had been murdered. Linda had an online dating profile which read, "I think I'm funny and charming and sensitive, and I'm very romantic and I love to travel, and generous and warm ... Oh God, this is so embarrassing." These two examples are subtle but contribute to the notion that online dating is commonly perceived as different to other introduction methods and that being embarrassed or anxious about the process is justified because in participating one is outed as being alone and having failed at what is supposed to come naturally.

Thus far I have discussed the popular perception of online daters as losers. A key component of this is desperation, an idea common both in screen presentations of online dating and also in published discussions.

The Desperate and the Dateless

In her memoir, *Just Don't Call Me Ma'am*, Anna Mitchael posed the question, "Was online dating actually a tattoo of desperation?"[24] In the "We Are Everyone" episode of *Elementary*, the same idea was alluded to in an exchange between Sherlock (Johnny Lee Miller) and his colleague Joan:

SHERLOCK: What are you doing?
JOAN: I'm looking at profiles of guys who winked at me on TrueRomantix.
SHERLOCK: I weep for the whole desperate lot of you.

Mitchael's question and Sherlock's jibe highlight a theme identifiable widely both off screen and on: the persistent coupling of online dating with desperation. For a person to date online, apparently he or she has failed to do that one thing that is supposed to come naturally, organically, a point made by Mark Penn and Kinney Zalesne in their book *Microtrends*:

> [Online dating] smacked of geeky antisocialness—people who couldn't make it in the "real" dating world. People with something to hide. People so desperate for a date they would seek out strangers at odd hours, from their lonely, maybe even creepy dens.[25]

In the "In the Mix, on the Books, and in the Freezer" episode of *Manhattan Love Story*, Peter (Jake McDorman) described online dating as "kinda desperate." Desperation was also mentioned by Elizabeth (Melissa Sagemiller) in the television holiday film *All I Want For Christmas* (2013) when she first logged onto MatchMe.com: "Am I that desperate that I need a website to find the love of my life?" Such desperation is similarly referenced in dating advice books where daters are advised, for example, to "write your ad so it doesn't reek of desperation"[26] and warned that "men can read desperation a mile away (and it's not pretty)."[27] In academic research this topic is also explored; an online dater quoted by sociologist Helene Lawson and Kira Leck, for instance, spoke of his experiences with desperation:

> Internet people are more desperate; things move fast in weird ways ... You get too intense too soon. There's like a speed to get to know each other. All you have is conversation that becomes exaggerated and magnified.[28]

An online dater quoted by the sociologist John Bridges equally identified her own desperation as a motivation for her cybersex forays:

> It was a "high" ... it was drug-like ... guys would write and tell me they thought I was hot ... they wanted to date me ... I got sexual proposals ... they thought I was just what they wanted for a partner ... I know now I was kind of "desperate," but I was wounded and broken and it made me feel better.[29]

On one level, desperation references the ideas outlined by Penn and Zalesne—as well as those presented in Chapter 1—whereby an online dater is frequently framed as someone who has failed at doing the "natural" thing of finding love. Equally, it can be contended that the desperation is in fact part of the underpinning of (or consequence of) the hastened intimacy discussed in Chapter 2. Other ideas, however, compound this: for example, the active *search* for love serves as a public declaration of inadequacy, if not, also as explored later in this chapter, *loneliness*.

On screen desperation plays out in various ways. In this section I examine notions of diminished self-perception and the concept of an expiry date.

The Pathetic Self

As explored throughout this chapter, there is much published research, along with a range of popular media depictions, working to frame online dating as desperate and pathetic. In numerous screen examples, characters have *internalized* this idea. While there is not a great deal of academic research on the internalization of such perceptions, research does identify internalized ideas about partner preferences notably in regard to age,[30] socioeconomic status, physical appearance, and personality,[31] and also ideas about racism and self-hatred.[32] The latter provides a hint to the possibility that this could apply, more generally, to the internalization of negative perceptions about going online for intimacy. In the *In Search of a Midnight Kiss* and *Without a Trace* examples, such internalization was conveyed via characters using words like *humiliated* and *embarrassed* to describe their own participation: they seemingly *knew* to feel bad about seeking intimacy online. In *Grace and Frankie*, Grace spoke of being a loser, in *All I Want for Christmas*, Elizabeth had internalized the idea that she was desperate. Even prior to signing up to date online, the perception of the activity as "pathetic" was referenced in a conversation between Wilson and his housemate, Jacob (Brian McGuire), in *In Search of a Midnight Kiss*:

JACOB: All you gotta do, my friend, is put up on an ad on the Craigslist.

WILSON: No, I don't know, man. The whole online dating thing, I think is a little bit too, you know, pathetic for me.

JACOB: It's not pathetic. I mean, everybody does it.

Pathetic is also mentioned by Vivian (Sara Simmonds) on her first date with Stevie (Bruce Jay) in the same film: "Why are you posting ads on Craigs-List?" she asked. "I mean, don't you think that's a little pathetic?" In the "Mano-a-Mansfield" episode of the sitcom *Ground Floor* (2013–15), online dating also gets described as pathetic when it is presented as a social option to Harvard (Rory Scovel): "I don't know," he says, "online dating just seems so pathetic." The term is also used in the "Slow Night, So Long" episode of medical-drama *Grey's Anatomy* (2005–). After lasting less than an hour on her date, Teddy (Kim Raver) met up with her colleagues, including Derek (Patrick Dempsey), in a bar:

TEDDY: Okay, so get this. His very first question "so what's your favorite food?"

DEREK: This is why you don't meet people on the Internet.

TEDDY: You're married, you don't get to have an opinion on my pathetic forays into Internet dating.

In *Meet Prince Charming*, the same ideas are alluded to via the word *hopeless*. Samantha's screen name was "Hopeless," and her online profile simply stated, "I think I've finally hit rock bottom." Jack, who was using the screen name "Hopeless-1," read Samantha's profile and remarked aloud, "You and me both." Both characters had, seemingly, internalized the perception that online dating outed them as desperate and dateless; that it *makes* them desperate and dateless. Such examples allude to internalized negative self-perceptions underpinning (a) one's status as single, (b) public declarations of singleness and (c) efforts to rectify this by going online. These ideas are taken a few steps further in *Because I Said So*. During a counseling session, Stuart (Tony Hale) is asked by his therapist, Maggie (Lauren Graham), how his experience with online dating went: "It was a nightmare, Doctor Wilder-Decker, it made me want to kill myself. Even more than the last time." Although we don't know from where Stuart's self-perception derives, the fact that his therapy sessions focused on his lack of success with women is likely a key clue: Stuart had seemingly *internalized* the idea that he is inadequate without a partner, and such feelings create desperation which, in turn, scares off potential dates and thus perpetuates his angst. Tony's internalized dissatisfaction could, in fact, be used to interpret the distress of the crying man who appeared in Sarah's loser parade in *Must Love Dogs* as well as the man with the death wish in Michelle's parade in *Nash Bridges*—both equally perceiving *themselves* as desperate losers, both in turn *presenting* themselves as desperate losers.

Notions of online dating perceived as pathetic are also apparent in published works. The sociologist Ben Agger in his book *Oversharing: Presentations of Self in the Internet Age*, for example, tabled the question: "Is online dating pathetic or a definite improvement over meeting romantic partners in a crowded, smoky bar?"[33] This question offers a useful way to think about the modern depiction, and perception, of online dating: the well-established view of it being pathetic versus the modern idea that it is efficient and effective compared to other methods (Chapter 1).

The *pathetic* idea is also identifiable in memoir. Christine Stapleton, for example, divulged, "I am not going to go so far as to say I'm pathetic, but I am a 50-year-old woman who has spent more nights snuggled up to a dog than a man. So I went against my daughter's edict—that she would divorce me if I ever stooped to Internet dating—and I stooped to Internet dating."[34] In Rosy Edwards's book *Confessions of a Tinderella*, she referenced the same idea:

> A coffee shop is a natural choice of venue for this onerous task, as in my head, writing a dating profile somewhere social makes it marginally less pathetic than writing it alone in my flat, although I'm down £4.20 (soya chai latte and a biscotti for sustenance) and have a feeling I am as pathetic as ever.[35]

Like Harvard in *Ground Floor*, Teddy in *Grey's Anatomy*, Samantha and Jack in *Meet Prince Charming* and Stuart in *Because I Said So*, both Stapleton and Edwards have seemingly internalized an idea that dating online makes them a loser. Such presentations work to connect online dating with the word *pathetic* for audiences.

Akin to those aforementioned newspaper articles trying to convince readers that online dating *isn't* for losers, self-help literature tackles the "pathetic" issue in the same way by attempting to counter fears, strangely, by repeatedly using the word and thus underlining the link: "Get over the idea that internet daters are all geeks. Online dating is pro-active, not pathetic," argues Liz Wilde in *A Girl's Guide to Dating*.[36] Janice Lieberman and Bonnie Teller make the same point in *How to Shop for a Husband*: "In our opinion, for those last remaining few who still believe Internet dating is slightly pathetic and only for losers, it's time to get real."[37] The pathetic perception is mentioned in these books and while an attempt is made to counter it, they present an acknowledgement that this process is not yet complete and stigma remains relevant.

The Expiry Date

A significant underpinning of portrayals of desperation centers—in varying degrees of subtlety—on the notion of a shelf life. In a 2015 episode of *Saturday Night Live* (1975-), a sketch centered around a commercial for the faux-dating product "Settl": an app that advocates for participants to lower their expectations in regard to finding a partner online. At the end of the commercial the voiceover warns "tick-tock." In *Must Love Dogs*, a poignant conversation transpires between Sarah and Dolly (Stockard Channing) illustrating this same idea:

SARAH: I'm just not comfortable advertising myself this way.
DOLLY: Honey, when you get to be my age and you're approaching your
    expiration date, it pays to advertise. This baby never sleeps, it's working
    for me twenty-four hours a day, God bless its little Pentium chip heart.

In the romantic-comedy *The Perfect Man* (2005), the same themes are more subtly conveyed in an exchange between Jean (Heather Locklear) and her teen daughter Holly (Hilary Duff):

JEAN: Can you scan this into Match.com?
HOLLY: Mom, I'm busy.
JEAN: Doing what?
HOLLY: Do you have to do this right away? Can't you just wait this time and
    see if you meet a guy the normal way?
JEAN: Have you seen these lines? I'm in a race against time. Now get on in
    there and scan this thing. Every second counts. Tick tock, tick tock.

Even in *In Search of a Midnight Kiss*, the expiry date idea is hinted at when Wilson's friends Jacob (Brian McGuire) and Min (Kathleen Luong) identify that Wilson should start online dating promptly: "He should do it before it's too late."

These examples tap into the idea of people having a use-by or *expiry date*,[38] whereby their looks, health and fertility are constantly declining, thus making their quest to couple harder each day. This burden is even more pronounced for women, whereby youthful looks and fertility are factors impacting on their fuckability in ways more significant than for men.

The fact that the *Saturday Night Live* sketch as well as Jean in *The Perfect Man* both mention a *ticking clock* hint to the notion of a competition whereby participants are in a dating market alongside younger people, in turn having to find ways to successfully self-market (Chapter 1), and alternatively be motivated to deceive to remain *in the game*. A good explanation for these ideas was articulated in the romantic-comedy *Something's Gotta Give* (2003), when Zoe (Frances McDormand)—a women's studies professor—delivers a poignant diatribe about dating, directing her comments to her sister Erica (Diane Keaton) and to Harry (Jack Nicholson), the older man whom Erica's daughter, Marin (Amanda Peet), had just started dating:

> Let's take you and Erica [Diane Keaton] for example. Harry, you've been around the block a few times, am I right? What are you, around sixty? Sixty-three! Fantastic. Never married, which, as we know, if you were a woman would be a curse. You'd be an old maid, a spinster. Blah blah blah. So instead of pitying you, they write articles about you. Celebrate your never marrying. You're elusive and ungettable. A real catch. Then, there's my gorgeous sister here … Look at her! She is so accomplished, the most successful playwright since who? Lillian Hellman? She's over fifty, divorced, and she sits in night after night after night because the available guys her age want someone—forgive me for saying this, hon—but they want someone that looks like Marin. So, the whole over-fifty dating scene is geared towards men leaving older women out. And as a result, the women become more and more productive and therefore, more and more interesting. Which, in turn, makes them even less desirable because, as we all know, men—especially older men—are threatened and deathly afraid of productive and interesting women.

The landscape Zoe describes is the environment where women like Sarah and Dolly in *Must Love Dogs*, Jean in *The Perfect Man* and Erica in *Something's Gotta Give* are attempting to sell themselves and to compete for attention with other women and thus why they each find coupling difficult; it is a place where looks and youth are prized over the qualities that Zoe mentioned.[39] The importance of looks and youth over other factors is actually discussed in the pilot of *A to Z*, when Andrew (Ben Feldman)—an employee at the Wallflower online dating company—explained the dating landscape to his love interest, Zelda:

ANDREW: There's a lot of things you don't know about the online dating world.
ZELDA: Oh my god, is that so? Please enlighten me.
ANDREW: Well for instance, when a guy chooses a girl on the site, guess how important it is that she have a college degree?
ZELDA: I'm going to go with of no importance.
ANDREW: Ding ding ding. You got it!

This notion of an expiry date within a landscape that prioritizes female youth and attractiveness over qualities like *productivity*, *interesting* and *educated* means that for characters like Dolly in *Must Love Dogs* and Jean in *The Perfect Man*, they feel under pressure—they *feel desperate*—to couple quickly, something Penn and Zalesne alluded to:

> At a minimum, online dating brought to mind older, unsuccessful singles whose dating years were waning and whose biological clocks were ticking. Going online was your Hail Mary effort to find a mate before you got too old.[40]

This *Hail Mary* idea, in fact, was verbalized in the "Internet Dating" episode of the sitcom *The Millers* (2013–15), when Adam (Nelson Franklin) mentioned a dating site for older people titled FinalChanceForRomance. com. Carol (Margo Martindale), in the episode, in fact, embarked on her own *final chance* quest by signing up for online dating after her separation from her husband.

These presentations, of course, are in sync with research identifying that desperation *does* sometimes motivate a person to date online, something Bridges addressed: "Aging, declining attractiveness, and the fear of being, and dying alone also strengthen the desire to search harder in an effort to find someone as quickly as possible."[41] This points to an interesting, albeit contentious, reality: that the dating landscape that Zoe described in *Something's Gotta Give*—and one apparently internalized in *Must Love Dogs* and *The Perfect Man*—is actually also a reality.

In their study on online dating and age preferences, psychologists Michael Dunn, Stacey Brinton and Lara Clark identified that there exists a growing disparity between men's own age and the preferred age of their partner, whereas women show a preference for partners around their own age or older.[42] Sociologists Jan Skopek, Andreas Schmitz and Hans-Peter Blossfeld undertook a similar study and unearthed comparable findings: men increasingly preferred younger women as they aged, whereas women's age preferences remained diverse.[43] Another of their findings was that age preference correlated strongly with perceptions of an ideal mate. This is particularly interesting because on one hand, the authors explain how we each internalize perceptions of norms regarding partners while also highlighting something mirrored by, and perhaps even *shaped* by, popular media depictions:

> Age norms for partnerships are stabilized by social sanctions penalizing those who violate the norm. As a consequence, individuals learn to desire the "normal" and reproduce this conception through their own mating decisions. From this perspective, preferences regarding a partner's age are essentially expressions of internalized conventions of what is perceived as acceptable in society.[44]

Such norms dictate that a "normal" age difference between a man and a woman is that the man should be slightly, but not too much, older than the woman. However, the older the person gets, the less binding these norms are because there are less penalties to their violation, hence why older characters like Harry in *Something's Gotta Give* can socially afford to date someone as young as Marin.

While the screen has a role in normalizing these perceptions—after all, the older man/younger woman configuration is effortlessly detected—it is worth considering that such narratives simply reflect zeitgeist realities whereby fears harbored by women and preferences held by men play out.

When Dolly in *Must Love Dogs* refers to her encroaching expiration date, while the obvious interpretation is the ticking clock on her eligibility, another is the quite literal notion of *physical* expiry. While this has relevance for women as related to the cessation of fertility,[45] this idea—something Bridges alluded to above—highlights the *dying alone* underpinning to desperation on screen, and something relevant for both sexes.

Dying Alone

In the "Pilgrimage" episode of the comedy-drama series *Nurse Jackie* (2009–), in the lead up to Dr. Cooper's (Peter Facinelli) fortieth birthday, he was lamenting all that he has failed to achieve in his personal life. His ruminations led him to a dating site. Although only a subtle idea in the narrative, Cooper was thinking about his legacy, his mortality, and potentially—as focused on in this section—his fears of dying alone. While the general concept of loneliness is discussed later in this chapter, as relevant for this section, the idea simply centers on fears of *dying alone* and thus the failure to achieve that great life objective of romantic companionship. As in the *Nurse Jackie* scene, a subtle allusion to this theme is apparent in "The Practice Around the Corner" episode of *Doc Martin* in an exchange between Al and his father, Bert:

AL: She's agreed to meet me. Tonight.
BERT: Nosferatu?

AL: Nefertari.

BERT: It's a bad idea ...

AL: It's my night off. It's only over in Wainbridge.

BERT: Yeah, but searching for love on the Internet, I mean that's for losers.

AL: Yeah, it's been ages since I've been out with anyone. I don't want to end up sitting on my tod in front of the TV every night. No offence, Dad.

It is low key in this scene, but Al was contrasting his wants in life with his father's predicament. In other examples, the *dying alone* fear is presented more overtly. In the "Furt" episode of the comedy-drama series *Glee* (2009–15), after Sue (Jane Lynch) was told by a love rival, "Face it Sue, you're never gonna find someone and you're gonna die alone," she promptly signed up for online dating. In the "Digging the Dirt" episode of *The Gates*, after Devon mentioned her online dating success, she sarcastically remarked to her neighbor Karen (Andrea Powell), "Karen, darling. You should give it a whirl. No need to grow old sad and alone." In the "C Is for Curiouser & Curiouser" episode of *A to Z*, Stu (Henry Zebrowski) attempted to help Stephie rewrite her online dating profile. When Stephie protested that his advice—lowering her salary, replacing the photo of her with a diploma—were sexist, he retorted, "Do you want to die alone?" In the "Zero Dark Forties" episode of *The Exes*, Haskell examined Stuart's first attempt at a profile for Holly: "Let me see what you wrote. 'Holly: Tall, strong-minded, Forty-ish divorce lawyer.' Why don't you just put 'angry old giraffe wants to die alone'?" In each example, desperation is linked to online dating through the idea that it is a kind of *last resort* for people who are not merely unfuckable, but are facing the prospect of dying alone.

The *dying alone* fear that propels characters to "do something drastic" is not a screen narrative exclusively associated with the Internet: in the 1992 pre-Web "Black Widower" episode of the animated series *The Simpsons* (1989–), for example, Patty described her sister's desperate predicament to Lisa and Bart, identifying similar concerns: "You see, Aunt Selma has this crazy obsession about not dying alone. So in desperation, she joined this prison pen-pal program. Her new sweetie's a jailbird." Viewing the *dying alone* fear as comic makes sense—after all, in an environment where online dating still has a branding problem, it seems logical to view going online as a desperate move akin to getting a jailbird as a sweetie. This, however, is not the only interpretation. In Slater's discussion about perceptions of online dating—and, specifically, mail-order brides—he posed the question: "Do we mock what we don't understand? Or do we mock what we understand all too well: lonely/desperate/horny people trying to be less lonely/desperate/horny?"[46] This notion that loneliness is real and horrible means that while on one hand we can laugh at Sue's rapid-fire response to her predicament in *Glee*, there is also potentially some gallows humor at play, recognizing that this isn't a Sue-specific problem, but rather an insight into the human condition.[47]

Only the Lonely

The idea that someone who felt lonely would start online dating seems completely logical when considered in an economic sense: as discussed in Chapter 1, identifying a need and going to the market to satisfy it is perfectly rational. Admitting publicly, however, that one *lacks* in an area like love is done reluctantly for fear of coming across as desperate, as needy, as a failure. Loneliness, however, is a motivation for real-life online dating and also underpins its screen depiction.

Owning the Lonely

Loneliness is undoubtedly a factor motivating many online dating forays,[48] and in some screen examples the idea actually gets verbalized. In the aforementioned *In Search of a Midnight Kiss*, Wilson admitted in his profile, "I guess I'm lonely." In the Australian comedy *Da Kath and Kim Code* (2005), Sharon (Magda Szubanski) stated, "I'm Internet dating. I've made a vow, I'm not going to spend Christmas on my own again." In the "Generation of Vipers" episode of the British police-drama *Lewis* (2006–), the murder victim at the center of the narrative, Professor Miranda Thornton (Julia Cox), similarly spoke aloud—*spoke publicly*—her loneliness in her dating website video profile:

> I don't care what you do, what you look like or how much you earn. I just want someone to be with. To talk to, to make love to. I'm tired of wasting my life. I'm tired of lonely weekends. I feel like I've had my life on pause and now I want to press Play. So, if you feel like I do, then please take a risk. I have.

Loneliness was also verbalized in the "David & Ellie" episode of *Dates*, in an exchange between Ellie (Montanna Thompson) and her date David (Will Mellor):

ELLIE: Why did you start Internet dating?
DAVID: Because I was lonely.

Given the amount of stigma attached to having "failed" at life's great ambition of coupling, characters' admitting that such failure has an emotional cost, exist as interesting and also *outlier* presentations. While for Sharon in *Da Kath and Kim Code* her loneliness can, in fact, be construed as comic due to her being a dowdy, overweight character who is presented as permanently pitiful (and in turn, the *caricature* of desperation), the portrayals of Wilson, Miranda and David in fact, are each more sympathetic and thus can be construed as reflective of the real-life reasons that people go online to find love.

There is substantial research on lonely people using the Internet as a way to feel less so,[49] something that stands to reason given, as expanded on later in this chapter, the Internet offers a low-pressure way for people to socialize. Conversely, however, research has also contended that Internet use creates and even *exacerbates* loneliness, something documented in psychological literature,[50] and something I have discussed previously as playing out in screen narratives where characters become addicted to the Internet and physically isolate themselves.[51] In the pilot episode of the sci-fi series *Mr. Robot* (2015–), this idea is briefly alluded to when the hacker protagonist Elliot (Rami Malek) comments about, "social media faking as intimacy." As specifically related to online dating, it seems predictable that research links online dating to loneliness. Psychologists Jacqueline Olds and Richard Schwartz, for example, contend that "online dating has been a boon to some of our loneliest patients."[52] Diana Senechal, in her book *Republic of Noise*, similarly identifies that widespread loneliness created the need for online dating, but also actually keeps us in this state (undoubtedly linking to some of the *planned obsolescence* ideas discussed in Chapter 1): "Loneliness has given rise to numerous online dating and networking services, which seem to take away the need ever to be lonely again. Yet we remain doggedly lonely."[53] While loneliness is perceived as a negative and often an *indicting* trait—something driving desperation—it is also a portrayal that mirrors the very reason why online dating is such a lucrative industry in real life: loneliness might be stigmatized but it is also ubiquitous.

The remaining sections of this chapter examine why the online dating landscape is so suited to outlier characters like the shy, the socially awkward, the fat, the ugly and the gullible.

The Shy and Socially Awkward

In *A to Z*, the online dating company that Andrew works for is named Wallflower. *Wallflower*, of course, is a common stereotype of people who date online: shy and socially awkward people are drawn to the Internet because it is a place where they are buffered from stressful face-to-face interactions and can come out of their shells gradually.

Anonymity is often discussed as an appeal in online dating; thus, the ability to shield identity undoubtedly helps a person with social anxieties to feel more confident in a new social situation. These are ideas that are easily detected on screen. In discussing the appeals of online dating, Laura in the "Generation of Vipers" episode of *Lewis* noted, "Online you can reveal yourself relatively painlessly." The same idea is hinted at in a range of screen examples. At the beginning of *You've Got Mail*, for example, one of Joe's early emails to Kathleen contained the lines, "I would send you a bouquet of newly-sharpened pencils if I knew your name and address. On the other hand, this not knowing has its charms." Kathleen similarly requested "no specifics" in her correspondence with Joe, also seemingly finding appeal in the *not knowing*. In an early scene in the "Two Bodies in the Lab" episode of *Bones*, when Temperance's online match, David, suggested a meeting, she initially appeared reluctant: "I'm enjoying the anonymity." In "The Practice Around the Corner" episode of *Doc Martin*, Al discussed with his father, Bert, his online dating adventures and similarly noted, "It's anonymous so it keeps it interesting." Anonymity was also enjoyed in the gay-themed drama *Breaking the Cycle* (2002), when Jason (Carlos da Silva) was arranging a hook-up with a man in a chatroom and his date commented, "That's the fun part of it ... The thing that I like about this is that we don't know each other except on the Internet." While anonymity is a drawcard for lots of Internet users—particularly in an environment hyperconscious about cyber-security—for characters like the socially awkward Kathleen in *You've Got Mail*, she distinctly benefited from being able to pace her online interactions with Joe. Equally, for Temperance in *Bones*—a character suspected of having Asperger's[54]—online dating catered to her social deficits. A woman in psychologist Kimberly Young's research actually personalized these issues, noting, "I get tongue-tied in real life, but I don't get finger-tied on the Net."[55]

Much more socially anxious than Kathleen or Temperance, however, is Thomas (Benoît Verhaert), the agoraphobic protagonist in the Belgian speculative future film *Thomas est amoureux* (*Thomas in Love*) (2000). Thomas conducted *all* of his socializing online, including sex. Agoraphobia is also apparent in other Internet-themed narratives. In the "Kitty" episode of *CSI* (2000–2015), the online dating profile photo of a murder suspect showed overstuffed trash cans and food containers. The crime scene investigators Avery (Patricia Arquette) and Nick (George Eads) discussed the possible social anxieties that led to the suspect going online for romance:

NICK: Cans are stuffed. To-go cups, food containers, he orders in a lot.
AVERY: He's agoraphobic. He doesn't like to leave, even to eat.

In the "Sweet Little Lies" episode of the drama series *Black Box* (2014), the agoraphobic Lina (Ali Wong) posted an online dating profile (although didn't go on any dates). While the agoraphobic Helen (Sigourney Weaver) in the thriller *Copycat* (1995) wasn't *dating* online, she too conducted all her socializing in chatrooms.

The value of online dating for people with social anxieties—and online socializing more generally—has been discussed by numerous theorists. Psychologists Monica Whitty and Adam Joinson, for example, drew attention to this, noting:

> Some people arguably benefit more from the unique space that is cyberspace. Shy and socially anxious individuals have been found to prefer many spaces online to get to know others. In particular, it has been found that shy people enjoy meeting potential romantic partners in newsgroups and on online dating sites.[56]

Another component of this—and a factor relevant to anybody with attributes that make them feel socially vulnerable—is that the Internet serves as terrain where some users feel more in control of outcomes, a point Joinson alluded to: "As the risk of rejection increases, people are more likely to use email over FtF [face to face] options."[57] For characters who want to feel more buffered in their social interactions, the Internet creates this capacity.

Just as online dating appeals to the shy and social awkward, equally it functions similarly for characters rendered physically unattractive in the offline dating game.

The Fat, the Ugly, the Infirm

In the "Who is Max Mouse—Part 1" episode of the children's series *Ghostwriter* (1992–95), middle-school student Erica (Julia Stiles) lauded the benefits of cyberspace, "It's a world where you are judged by what you say and think, not by what you look like. A world where curiosity and imagination equals power." Jeff (Patrick Wilson) in the thriller *Hard Candy* (2005) made a similar remark: "I think it's better to meet people online first sometimes. You get to know what they're like inside." Bryant (Cameron Mathison) in the television drama *The Wife He Met Online* (2012) made the same point, "At least with online you get to know a little bit about the person before you talk to them."[58]

On one level, these comments are in sync with the ideas presented earlier about pacing social interactions online: that self-revelation only comes when a person is a ready. More so, while the Internet has progressively become more visual, it doesn't have to be and thus a person can elect to only show themselves physically when they feel truly comfortable.[59]

For characters who exist outside of conventional attractiveness, online dating may be a way to get a *foot in the door* by being judged according to attributes like personality and humor rather than appearance. This is particularly important for the overweight or the disabled, for example, who have battled preconceived appearance-centered prejudices in ways that conventionally good-looking and able-bodied people don't. Discussed earlier was Sharon in *Da Kath and Kim Code*: as an overweight, unattractive character, online dating was a perfect social vehicle for her to play to her strengths. The "2Shy" episode of the sci-fi series *The X-Files* (1993–2002) centered on shy, overweight women using the Internet to date. Overweight Eleanor (Camryn Manheim) in the crime-drama *The Practice* (1997–2004) chose to date online; ditto the overweight title character in *Paul Blart: Mall Cop* and the overweight Lloyd (Michael McShane) in the "Witchcraft" episode of the sitcom *Brotherly Love* (1995–97), each character having previously been unsuccessful in the offline dating market.

Erica's comments in *Ghostwriter* hint to some interesting themes apparent in research on the Internet. Media theorist John Campbell, for example, reflected on the "bodily transcendence in cyberspace" ideas apparent in sci-fi films such as *The Lawnmower Man* (1992), *Johnny Mnemonic* (1995) and *The Matrix* (1999) and examined how such concepts have been discussed in academic literature:

> In the final decade of the twentieth century, a number of Western intellectuals began postulating that a new subjectivity was evolving from online interaction. Perhaps prematurely, some argued that this emerging online subject would be like the Greek god Proteus, possessing the ability to transform the self at will … Freed from our burdensome material selves, they proclaim, we become fluid entities, overcoming those societal stigmas inscribed on the body—race, gender, age, size, beauty, what have you.[60]

For characters whose physical bodies have restricted them—they are too shy to leave the house, perhaps, or too fat to be considered fuckable—the Internet exists as an opportunity to transcend corporeal limitations. While in the context of online dating, for a relationship to exist offline, one's physical self will eventually need to be exposed. For some characters, however, online socializing constitutes the entire recreation and no physical intimacy is sought (Chapter 1). Gorge (Ramsey Moore) in the sci-fi film *Gamer* (2009), for example, is an overweight, wheelchair-bound man. He spends his time playing online sim-games where he gets to experience—among other things—sex via the use of avatars; something unavailable to him in his real life. Disability is similarly a theme in the television dramas *Intelligence* (2014) and *Flashpoint* (2008–12). In the "Cain and Gabriel" episode of *Intelligence*, despite the fact that Jonathan Cain (Alan Ruck) was a housebound quadriplegic, he was—through his use of the Internet—able to orchestrate elaborate acts of bioterrorism from his wheelchair. By going online Jonathan was able to feel connected, feel productive, without moving from his monitor. In the "Eyes In" episode of the Canadian crime-drama *Flashpoint*, this idea had specific relevance to a discussion on intimacy: Stuart (Kris Lemche) had been paralyzed by a stroke; with the help of his webcam he could display himself on camera in a way that disguised his limp and engage with women on a (seeming) *level playing field*.

This idea of the Internet serving as a leveler is also worth examining. In reference to online dating, Steve Paganuzzi, a New York matrimonial attorney, commented, "Everybody's in the privacy of their own home. Everyone's equalized and available."[61] For Paganuzzi, the concept of the Internet as a leveler centers on online daters each outing themselves online as lovelorn, a unique situation that doesn't usually transpire offline where one's availability is normally ambiguous. The philosopher Aaron Ben-Ze'ev discussed this same idea in more detail:

> [E]asily discernible features such as unattractive external appearance, stereotypic characteristics, visible shyness, or social anxiety—which

might be an obstacle to the establishment of any close relationship. These gates often prevent people from developing relationships to the stage at which disclosure of intimate information could begin. Such barriers are typically absent in cyberspace and hence do not obstruct the early stages of potentially rewarding relationships.[62]

While Ben-Ze'ev subtly spotlights how the idea of the Internet as a leveler has most applicability at the *early stages* of an online relationship (and becomes less relevant if a relationship progresses and one party wants to meet), certainly the technology serves as a leveler for initial access in a manner without an offline equivalent because aesthetic factors frequently inhibit people from making intimate connections.

The final archetype of the screen's online dater discussed in this chapter is the loser who is defined by gullibility.

The Gullible

In their book on truth and the Internet, Whitty and Joinson contended, "some people trust others a little too readily on the Internet."[63] This idea is illustrated well in screen examples where a character is framed as a loser through their apparent obliviousness to the dangers of cyberspace. In the "On the Line" episode of *Elementary*, for example, Sherlock provided a definition of catfishing: "Someone who uses social media to create false identities. Most typically for the purpose of pursuing online romance." While such catfishing scams get extensive news media attention—for example in the well-publicized real-life catfishing case of the American footballer Manti Te'o[64]—on screen the presence of such a storyline is more modest. In the British drama *Birthday Girl* (2001), John (Ben Chaplin) gets embroiled in an online mail order bride scam; his bride (Nicole Kidman) was part of a band of thieves. A similar scam played out in a subplot of the drama *You and I* (2011). In *Da Kath and Kim Code*, while it is not explored in any great detail, it appears Sharon fell victim to a similar dating scam: in one scene she goes to the airport to meet her new online partner who never arrived. This same narrative played out for John (Travis Hammer) in the television drama *The Bride He Bought Online* (2015): he had been catfished by three teenage girls playing a prank.

Discussed earlier was the episode of *Ground Floor* where Harvard begins online dating. During the narrative, he in fact gets involved in an online relationship: "She's beautiful," he tells his colleague, "we have a lot of common interests … She's a Nigerian princess. Right now her money is tied up in this kind of weird legal situation." In the "Oh Honey" episode of the sitcom *How I Met Your Mother*, Honey (Katy Perry) referenced the same scam, musing, "Maybe I should feel weird about giving a stranger my Social Security Number, but the guy's a Nigerian prince!"[65] The documentary *Catfish* (2010) centered on Nev being catfished by the overweight

Angela who was posing as a range of different characters including the young and attractive "Megan." The idea of a person playing out a variety of identities online, including a love interest, also transpired in the British biopic *UWantMe2KillHim?* (2013). The documentary *Talhotblond* (2009), and the 2012 television biopic of the same name, charted similar terrain, centering on the real-life story of a 47-year-old man, Thomas Montgomery, who posed online as an eighteen-year-old man "Tommy" in correspondence with the eighteen-year-old, "Jessi." While "Tommy" was a constructed identity, so too in fact was Jessi: she was actually Mary Shieler who was using her daughter's likeness online; they were catfishing *each other*. While Honey in *How I Met Your Mother* was beautiful (read: fuckable) but stupid, for Harvard in *Ground Floor*, Nev and Angela in *Catfish*, Thomas in *Talhotblond*, Sharon in *Da Kath and Kim Code* and John in *The Bride He Bought Online*, these were characters who were desperate for intimacy and rather than thinking critically about the too-good-to-be-true offer presented, they simply allowed themselves to be seduced by it.[66]

Even outside of dating scams, desperation exists as inextricably linked to a character's possible online exploitation. In Miranda's profile in the "Generation of Vipers" episode of *Lewis*, she claimed not to care what her suitor looked like or what he earned; she just wanted *someone*. Miranda was murdered shortly thereafter, and the question thus raised was whether her desperation placed her in jeopardy. While in *Lewis*, Miranda's murder turned out to have had nothing to do with her online dating—indicative of the Internet red herring often deployed on screen[67]—this same theme was apparent in the television thriller *Every Mother's Worst Fear* (1998). Moments after her boyfriend dumped her, Martha (Jordan Ladd) entered a chatroom and typed "I need a friend." Seconds later the predator, Scanman (Ted McGinley), was shown at his computer, typing and saying—in a sinister voice—"An opportunity has come up." Scanman then arranged for another man to groom and then kidnap Martha. Martha's desperation for (platonic) intimacy put her in jeopardy: as Scanman said to Martha: "I found you because I wanted you to be found." In fact, predators preying upon the vocally vulnerable transpires in other examples. In "The Kindness of Strangers" episode of the police-drama *The District* (2000–2004), part of Icarus's (John Sloan) online grooming of 12-year-old Amy (Destiny Edmond) involved comments such as, "I know what you're feeling, Amy, my parents got a divorce too. I want to hold you and kiss you and make it better. I want to make love to you." The grooming of adolescents more broadly—an age group that is notoriously impressionable, prone to melancholy and risk-taking—transpires in a range of narratives on screen (Chapter 4).

Such ideas exist as an interesting screen union of both the desperate and losers and their active want for a partner, whereby people who go online are, seemingly, willing to accept anything; that their lack of selectiveness in fact makes them losers and that losers fall victim to criminals,[68] a concept discussed further in Chapter 4.

This chapter has examined the idea of *who* is dating online on screen, and what these ideas reveal about anxieties around online socializing. Chapter 4 furthers the discussion of stereotypes of Internet users, examining the notion of cyberspace being a place filled with nefarious characters eager to prey on vulnerable intimacy seekers.

Notes

1. Lauren Rosewarne, "The Fat Ugly Truth about Dating," *The Conversation*, July 10, 2015. Accessed July 12, 2015, from https://theconversation.com/the-fat-ugly-truth-about-dating-44515.

2. The psychologist David Anderegg addressed this issue in his book *Nerds* in the context of the sitcom *The Big Bang Theory* (2007–): "What *The Big Bang Theory* teaches us is that sometimes geeky guys can get a girl, but usually the less geeky guys are the ones who succeed, and when the really geeky guys get a girl, it's often an equally geeky girl" (David Anderegg, *Nerds: How Dorks, Dweebs, Techies and Trekkies Can Save America* [New York: Penguin, 2011], 14).

3. Claudia Connell, "Single White Female Seeks Anyone Other Than These Losers," *Daily Mail (London)*, January 20, 2011, 56.

4. Kevin Darné, "Online Dating: Is Everyone a Catfish, Conman, Liar, Cheater, Predator or Loser?" *Chicago Examiner*, March 4, 2013. Accessed July 11, 2015, from http://www.examiner.com/article/online-dating-is-everyone-a-catfish-conman-liar-cheater-predator-or-loser.

5. Dawn Fallik, "Online Losers Are Easy to Spot; Danger Signs in Internet Dating," *The Philadelphia Inquirer*, November 19, 2006, F02.

6. Amy Busby, "Online Dating Not for Losers," *Pearland Journal*, March 26, 2009, A2.

7. Amy Harmon, "Online Dating Not Just for Lovable Losers," *Lexington Herald-Leader*, June 29, 2003. Accessed July 11, 2015, from LexisNexis.

8. "Online Dating No Longer Loser Central," *Corpus Christ Caller-Times*, June 29, 2003. Accessed July 11, 2015, from LexisNexis.

9. In Dan Slater, *Love in the Time of Algorithms* (New York: Current, 2013), 42.

10. John Dvorak, Chris Pirillo and Wendy Taylor, *Online! The Book* (Upper Saddle River, NJ: Pearson Education, 2004), 183.

11. Lauren Rosewarne, *Cyberbullies, Cyberactivists, Cyberpredators: Film, TV, and Internet Stereotypes* (Santa Barbara, CA: Praeger, 2016).

12. Paul Oyer, *Everything I Needed to Know about Economics I Learned from Online Dating* (Boston, MA: Harvard Business Review Press, 2014), 132.

13. Jeff Bercovici, "Love on the Run: The Next Revolution in Online Dating," *Forbes*, February 14, 2014. Accessed July 11, 2015, from http://www.forbes.com/sites/jeffbercovici/2014/02/14/love-on-the-run-the-next-revolution-in-online-dating/.

14. In Sophia Dembling, *Introverts in Love: The Quiet Way to Happily Ever After* (New York: Perigee Books, 2015), ebook.

15. Lauren Rosewarne, *Cyberbullies, Cyberactivists, Cyberpredators: Film, TV, and Internet Stereotypes* (Santa Barbara, CA: Praeger, 2016).

16. Interestingly, a 2015 eHarmony television commercial attempted to subvert this trope. In the commercial, a blonde woman confidently asserts that she doesn't need online dating because "I can get my own dates." eHarmony founder Dr. Neil Clark Warren then asks her, "how's that going for you," and the ad cuts to the

woman's own bad date montage: her on a date with a man and his mother, her on a date with a man dressed like a teenager and playing a computer game. Apparently these bad dates were the ones she sourced *without* the assistance of online dating. She then concedes to needing eHarmony's help.

17. See, for example, speed-dating loser parade scenes in *The 40-Year-Old Virgin* (2005), as well as in the "Don't Ask, Don't Tell" episode of *Sex and the City* (1998–2004), the "Private Lives" episode of *House* (2004–12), and the "Singled Out" episode of *NCIS* (2003–).

18. It is unclear in the narrative who Terry is (i.e., whether male or female or friend or family member).

19. Julie Subotky, *Consider It Done: Accomplish 228 of Life's Trickiest Tasks* (New York: Random House, 2011), 70.

20. In Dan Slater, *Love in the Time of Algorithms* (New York: Current, 2013), 105.

21. Sam Greenspan, *11 Points Guide to Hooking Up* (New York: Skyhorse, 2011), ebook.

22. Evan Marc Katz, *I Can't Believe I'm Buying This Book: A Commonsense Guide to Successful Internet Dating* (Berkeley, CA: Ten Speed Press, 2003).

23. Leanne K. Knoblock and Kelly G. McAninch, "Uncertainty Management," in *Interpersonal Communication*, ed. Charles R. Berger (Berlin: Walter de Gruyter, 2014): 297–320, 300.

24. Anna Mitchael, *Just Don't Call Me Ma'am: How I Ditched the South, Forgot My Manners, and Managed to Survive My Twenties with (Most of) My Dignity Still Intact* (Berkeley, CA: Seal Press, 2010), 207.

25. Mark Penn and E. Kinney Zalesne, *Microtrends: The Small Forces Behind Tomorrow's Big Changes* (New York: Twelve, 2007), 22.

26. Ellen Fein and Sherrie Schneider, *The Rules for Online Dating: Capturing the Heart of Mr. Right in Cyberspace* (New York: Pocket Books, 2002), 20.

27. Joel D. Block and Kimberly Dawn Neumann, *The Real Reasons Men Commit: Why He Will—or Won't—Love, Honor and Marry You* (Avon, MA: Adams Media, 2009), 206.

28. In Helene M. Lawson and Kira Leck, "Dynamics of Internet Dating," *Social Science Computer Review*, 24, 2 (2006): 189–208, 203.

29. John C. Bridges, *The Illusion of Intimacy: Problems in the World of Online Dating* (Santa Barbara, CA: Praeger, 2012), 84–85.

30. Jan Skopek, Andreas Schmitz and Hans-Peter Blossfeld, "The Gendered Dynamics of Age Preferences: Empirical Evidence from Online Dating," *Journal of Family Research*, 3 (2011): 267–90.

31. Andreas Schmitz, Jan Skopek, Florian Schulz, Doreen Klein and Hans-Peter Blossfeld, "Indicating Mate Preferences by Mixing Survey and Process-Generated Data: The Case of Attitudes and Behaviour in Online Mate Search," *Historical Social Research*, 34, 1 (2009): 77–93.

32. Glenn T. Tsunokai, Allison R. McGrath and Jillian K. Kavanagh, "Online Dating Preferences of Asian Americans," *Journal of Social and Personal Relationships*, 31, 6 (2014): 796–814.

33. Ben Agger, *Oversharing: Presentations of Self in the Internet Age* (New York: Routledge, 2012), 35.

34. Christine Stapleton, "Online Dating Preferences Not Subject to Debate," *Palm Beach Post* (Florida), July 12, 2009, 3D.

35. Rosy Edwards, *Confessions of a Tinderella* (New York: Cornerstone, 2015), ebook.

36. Liz Wilde, *A Girl's Guide to Dating* (New York: Ryland Peters & Small, 2005), 28.
37. Janice Lieberman and Bonnie Teller, *How to Shop for a Husband: A Consumer Guide to Getting a Great Buy on a Guy* (New York: St Martin's Press, 2009), 87.
38. This idea was referenced in Sunny Singh's essay on dating as an older, single woman: "Once I reached my marriage 'expiry' date at the ripe old age of thirty, no one bothered about my solo status anymore" (Sunny Singh, "Fear of Meeting Mr. Right," in *Single Woman of a Certain Age: Romantic Escapades, Shifting Shapes, and Serene Independence*, ed. Jane Ganahl [Maui, HI: Inner Ocean, 2005]: 113–20, 114).
39. It is interesting to note that in the comedy-drama *Burn After Reading* (2008)—which has online dating as a major theme—when middle-age Linda (Frances McDormand) was introduced she was in a consultation at a cosmetic surgery clinic getting advised on a wide variety of procedures. (Later she explained to her health insurer that she was trying to "reinvent" herself.).
40. Mark Penn and E. Kinney Zalesne, *Microtrends: The Small Forces Behind Tomorrow's Big Changes* (New York: Twelve, 2007), 22.
41. John C. Bridges, *The Illusion of Intimacy: Problems in the World of Online Dating* (Santa Barbara, CA: Praeger, 2012), 42.
42. Michael J. Dunn, Stacey Brinton and Lara Clark, "Universal Sex Differences in Online Advertisers Age Preferences: Comparing Data from 14 Cultures and 2 Religion Groups," *Evolution and Human Behavior*, 31, 6 (2010): 383–93.
43. Jan Skopek, Andreas Schmitz and Hans-Peter Blossfeld, "The Gendered Dynamics of Age Preferences: Empirical Evidence from Online Dating," *Journal of Family Research*, 3 (2011): 267–90.
44. Jan Skopek, Andreas Schmitz and Hans-Peter Blossfeld, "The Gendered Dynamics of Age Preferences: Empirical Evidence from Online Dating," *Journal of Family Research*, 3 (2011): 267–90, 270.
45. Lauren Rosewarne, *Periods in Pop Culture: Menstruation in Film and Television* (Lanham, MD: Lexington Books, 2012).
46. Dan Slater, *Love in the Time of Algorithms* (New York: Current, 2013), 167.
47. Worth noting, sociologists Helene Lawson and Kira Leck in their study of online dating noted, "Regardless of their marital status, respondents of all ages tended to report being lonely" (Helene M. Lawson and Kira Leck, "Dynamics of Internet Dating," *Social Science Computer Review*, 24, 2 [2006]: 189–208, 192).
48. The economist Paul Oyer wrote, "loneliness—that biggest fear that leads us to online dating ..." (Paul Oyer, *Everything I Needed to Know about Economics I Learned from Online Dating* [Boston, MA: Harvard Business Review Press, 2014], 18).
49. Janet Morahan-Martin and Phyllis Schumacher, "Loneliness and Social Uses of the Internet," *Computers in Human Behavior*, 19 (2003): 659–71; Yair Amichai-Hamburger and Elisheva Ben-Artzi, "Loneliness and Internet Use," *Computers in Human Behavior*, 19 (2003): 71–80.
50. Robert Kraut, Michael Patterson, Vicki Lundmark, Sara Kiesler, Tridas Mukopad-hyay and William Scherlis, "Internet Paradox: A Social Technology That Reduces Social Involvement and Psychological Well-Being?" *American Psychologist*, 53, 9 (1998): 1017–103; John T. Cacioppo, James H. Fowler and Nicholas A. Christakis, "Alone in the Crowd: The Structure and Spread of Loneliness in a Large Social Network," *Journal of Personality and Social Psychology*, 97, 7 (2009): 977–91; James E. Katz and Ronald E. Rice, *Social Consequences of Internet Use: Access, Involvement and Interaction* (Cambridge, MA: MIT Press, 2002).

51. Lauren Rosewarne, *Cyberbullies, Cyberactivists, Cyberpredators: Film, TV, and Internet Stereotypes* (Santa Barbara, CA: Praeger, 2016).
52. Jacqueline Olds and Richard S. Schwartz, *The Lonely American: Drifting Apart in the Twenty-First Century* (Boston, MA: Beacon Press, 2009), 110.
53. Diana Senechal, *Republic of Noise: The Loss of Solitude in Schools and Culture* (Lanham, MD: Rowman and Littlefield, 2011), 162.
54. Lauren Rosewarne, *Cyberbullies, Cyberactivists, Cyberpredators: Film, TV, and Internet Stereotypes* (Santa Barbara, CA: Praeger, 2016).
55. Kimberly S. Young, *Caught in the Net: How to Recognize the Signs of Internet Addiction—And a Winning Strategy for Recovery* (New York: John Wiley & Sons, 1998), 12.
56. Monica T. Whitty and Adam N. Joinson, *Truth, Lies and Trust on the Internet* (New York: Routledge, 2009), 2.
57. Adam N. Joinson, "Self-Esteem, Interpersonal Risk and Preference for E-mail to Face-to-Face Communication," *CyberPsychology*, 7 (2004): 472–78.
58. Interestingly, in both *Hard Candy* and *The Wife He Met Online*, despite the men's comments about the benefits of getting to know people online first, in both examples the men fell victim to women who, in fact, they *never* really knew.
59. In real life, nearly all online dating sites and hook-up apps make use of photos: while inclusion of one on a profile is not mandatory, it is certainly common. On screen, however, the premise of many narratives is that for some reason dates were arranged *without* photos. In *Must Love Dogs* (2005), for example, had photos been exchanged during the online courtship, father and daughter would never have met up; equally, the absence of photos underpins two colleagues being matched—twice!—in the television holiday film *A Christmas Song* (2012).
60. John Edward Campbell, *Getting It On Online: Cyberspace, Gay Male Sexuality and Embodied Identity* (New York: Harrington Park Press, 2004), 5.
61. In Christa Worthington, "Making Love in Cyberspace," *The Independent* (October 6, 1996). Accessed June 30, 2014, from http://www.independent.co.uk/arts-entertainment/making-love-in-cyberspace-1356977.html.
62. Aaron Ben-Ze'ev, *Love Online: Emotions on the Internet* (New York: Cambridge University Press, 2004), 37–38.
63. Monica T. Whitty and Adam N. Joinson, *Truth, Lies and Trust on the Internet* (New York: Routledge, 2009), 6.
64. Ned Zeman, "The Boy Who Cried Dead Girlfriend," *Vanity Fair*, June 2013. Accessed August 20, 2015, from http://www.vanityfair.com/culture/2013/06/manti-teo-girlfriend-nfl-draft; Ben Zimmer, "Catfish: How Manti Te'o's Imaginary Romance Got Its Name," *The Boston Globe*, January 27, 2013. Accessed August 20, 2015, from https://www.bostonglobe.com/ideas/2013/01/27/catfish-how-manti-imaginary-romance-got-its-name/inqu9zV8RQ7j19BRGQkH7H/story.html; Ilana Gershon, "The Samoan Roots of the Manti Te'o Hoax," *The Atlantic*, January 24, 2013. Accessed August 20, 2015, from http://www.theatlantic.com/entertainment/archive/2013/01/the-samoan-roots-of-the-manti-teo-hoax/272486/.
65. While in these examples the Nigerian money scam was mentioned in the context of dating scams, worth noting, the same scam is mentioned in other contexts. In a scene from the Argentinian film *Medianeras (Sidewalls)* (2011), for example, Martín (Javier Drolas) mentioned that a friend had written to him from Oman: "He happens to be visiting Yemen and needs my help withdrawing 9.5 million dollars from a local bank. He hasn't written for a while. It's an imprudent, one-sided friendship." A similar idea was mentioned in the "Michael's Birthday"

episode of the sitcom *The Office* (2005–13), when Michael (Steve Carell) remarked, "When the son of the deposed King of Nigeria emails you directly asking for help, you help." The scam is also referenced in the "Crappy Birthday to You" episode of the Canadian comedy series *jPod* (2008) when Carol (Sherry Miller) tried to avoid a meeting by claiming, "a man in Nigeria emailed me, he needs help with a banking task."

66. A variant on the gullible romance-seeker is the gullible *friendship* seeker. In the British comedy *The Inbetweeners 2* (2014), adolescent Neil (Blake Harrison) naively commented, "I've got this amazing app called Grindr, made loads of new mates through it." Neil, of course, is referring to the homosexual hook-up app; his quest for friends, in fact, had put him in contact with men who wanted to have sex with him. Such a joke can be likened to the "Cartman Joins NAMBLA" episode of the animated series *South Park* (1997–), when Cartman joined the North American Man/Boy Love Association to make adult male friends (friends whose interests in boys weren't as platonic as Cartman's).

67. Lauren Rosewarne, *Cyberbullies, Cyberactivists, Cyberpredators: Film, TV, and Internet Stereotypes* (Santa Barbara, CA: Praeger, 2016).

68. Lauren Rosewarne, "Love Is a (Regulatory) Battlefield: The ACCC Takes on Dating Website Scammers," *The Conversation*, February 20, 2012. Accessed July 26, 2015, from https://theconversation.com/love-is-a-regulatory-battlefield-the-accc-takes-on-dating-website-scammers-5377.

4 Online Deception, Offline Disaster

In "The Friendly Skies" episode of the crime-drama *Without a Trace* (2002–9), Detective Fitzgerald (Eric Close) remarked, "I tell you, a scary world this Internet dating." Detective Monk (Richard Belzer) made a similar comment in the "Chat Room" episode of *Law & Order: Special Victims Unit* (1999–): "I love the information superhighway. You can meet creepazoids from all over the world without leaving the comfort of your own home."

Of the many stereotypes associated with Internet use, one of the most common is the villain who goes online to prey upon unsuspecting Web users. The idea that daters—and that intimacy seekers more broadly—have something to fear by going online is underpinned by the archetype of the cyberpredator. This nefarious figure takes advantage of the hope, the naiveté and the gullibility of intimacy seekers, and exploits their yen for connection. At the tamest end of the spectrum is deception centered on appearance; white lies told to secure intimate interest. In more extreme presentations, untruths are told about age, meetings are orchestrated with violent intent and the lovelorn get raped, kidnapped and murdered.

I begin this discussion with the premise of the Internet as dangerous, a belief widely held and one loudly echoed in screen fiction. I then discuss the two key concepts underpinning the supposed danger: (a) the Internet as a badlands, and (b) the notion of the cyberbogeyman. The remainder of this chapter focuses on the wide range of deceptions transpiring on screen. From assumed duplicity to actual acts of it, as well as those many lies told to win dates or entrap victims, each cast light on our techno- and cyberphobias, partner preferences and gender relations both on screen and off.

The Internet as Dangerous

When Detective Fitzgerald in *Without a Trace* spoke of the "scary world" of Internet dating, he contributed to a perception of the World Wide Web that has been consistent since its inception and one that is a contemporary incarnation of the technophobia of past eras whereby things that·are new are construed as scary and capable of jeopardizing not merely safety but *humanity*. This idea was perfectly encapsulated in a scene from the thriller *NetForce* (1999), when the cybercop Steve Day (Kris Kristofferson), lamented that "sometimes I think the growth of technology has outstripped our sense of morality." A similar remark was made in the romantic-comedy *You've Got Mail* (1998) when the newspaper columnist, Frank Navasky (Greg Kinnear), declared of the Internet: "It's the end of Western civilization as we know it … You think this machine's your friend, but it's not."

Discussed already in this volume are the triple-A factors of the Internet—affordability, accessibility and anonymity[1]—that have driven the mainstreaming of the Internet and more specifically problematic online behaviors including addiction. Such factors also provide the underpinning for why the Internet has dangers that are construed as disproportionate. With going online being so easy and with access being ubiquitous, a person with ill-intent—who can effortlessly hide their identity and can access the technology cheaply and portably—can use the Internet to commit bad acts. Some of these bad acts can be accomplished exclusively online—accessing child porn for example or hacking—but for others, a villain can meet and groom a person in a chatroom or via social media and then arrange an offline meeting to commit a physical bad act.

As discussed in the introduction to this book, activity conducted online is very rarely completely new in either motive or execution. This idea applies to intimacy quests generally, but also to the harm that may come to those using the technology for such pursuits. Cyberpredators, therefore, who prey upon the lovelorn, both on screen and off—can be viewed as an extension of the lonely hearts criminals who found victims via personals columns in previous eras.[2]

A theme underpinning the supposed dangers of the Internet is thinking of it less as a tool or a type of technology and more so as a place.

The Badlands of the Internet

In a scene from the horror film *Smiley* (2012), a preteen girl, Mary (Darrien Skylar), was using a chat roulette site. Her babysitter, Stacy (Nikki Limo), cautioned, "You shouldn't put yourself out there like that." *Out there* is open to interpretation, but in this scene it hints to the idea that the Internet has the capacity to be construed as a *somewhere*—a somewhere that you can go to communicate, a somewhere where bad things can happen and also a somewhere that can be traversed in order to inflict real-life harm.

In Chapter 2, I introduced the idea of thinking about the Internet as a place, a concept evident in a range of screen examples where characters speak of friends or lovers being *from the Internet*. While *from the Internet* conjures thoughts of strangers and cyborgs, most relevant for this chapter is that *from the Internet* is often tantamount to *from the badlands*. Thinking about cyberspace as a kind of dystopia is, of course, nothing new: in 1990, John Perry Barlow described cyberspace in ways that have shaped thinking in the decades since: "the actual natives are solitary and independent, sometimes to the point of sociopathy. It is of course a perfect breeding ground for outlaws and new ideas about liberty."[3] Barlow's notion of *outlaws* notably ushered in a metaphor that has become common in discussions of the Internet in the years since: the "Wild West." In 1997, social theorists John Arquilla and David Ronfeldt identified a range of parallels between the Internet and the Wild West, in turn spotlighting the endurance of this metaphor, one that is easily detected in news media commentary[4]:

- In the Wild West almost anything could occur. There was no one to enforce overall law and order, only isolated packets of local law. The same is true in cyberspace.
- There were both "good guys" and "outlaws" in the Wild West, often very difficult to tell apart. "Friends" were the only ones a person could trust, even though he or she would frequently have to deal with "strangers." This is also true in cyberspace.
- Outside of the occasional local enclaves of law and order, everyone in the Wild West was primarily dependent for security on their own resources and those of their trusted friends. This is also true in cyberspace.[5]

Like the Wild West, the notion of the Internet as *ungovernable* has long shaped thinking, and is a theme at the heart of narratives like *NetForce*, with the narrative centered on a team of cybercops attempting to track criminals in an elusive "place" that cannot be seen or touched. More recently the crime-drama *CSI: Cyber* (2015–) has attempted to explore similar material. In early screen examples like *NetForce*, the Internet was portrayed as both generically lawless and as providing endless opportunities to exploit vulnerability. The thriller *Copycat* (1995) provides another good early illustration of how such dangers were fictionalized on screen. The narrative centered on Helen (Sigourney Weaver) who had been living a reclusive lifestyle since nearly falling victim to a serial killer. In one scene she received by email a photo of one of the killer's new victims. In response, Helen frantically unplugged her computer: "It's an open window. He can crawl in anytime he likes," she said, panic-stricken. The aforementioned "Chat Room" episode of *Law & Order: Special Victims Unit* from 2000 presented a similar verbalization of fears when Detective Stabler (Christopher Meloni) lamented the difficulty of policing cyberspace to his wife, Kathy (Isabel Gillies):

KATHY: It scares me.
ELLIOT: Honey, it scares me too. But I can't just walk into a room a restrain the guy.
KATHY: Why not?
ELLIOT: I mean, these predators. You tell me where they are. I can't hear them, I can't see them.

Later in the same episode, Stabler commented to his daughter, "You know how I lock up all the doors and windows? Now they're coming in through there," he said, gesturing to the computer. A decade on and this point is still identifiable. In *The Craigslist Killer* (2011), Detective Bennett (William Baldwin) described a similar, lawless terrain: "Used to be able to see who the bad guys were, right? Now it's all text and emails and websites. Creeps are hiding in our houses and we don't even know who they are."

More recent narratives like *CSI: Cyber* have moved the discussion away from the generic idea of ungovernable technology or an ungovernable place—in line, likely, with cybersecurity now already being on the agenda for most governments—and focuses more specifically on the dangers of the *deep Web*, a concept explained by Russell Kay in an article for *ComputerWorld*:

> The deep Web, also called the invisible Web, refers to the mass of information that can be accessed via the World Wide Web but can't be indexed by traditional search engines—often because it's locked up in databases and served up as dynamic pages in response to specific queries or searches.[6]

A similar definition was offered by the journalist, Greer (Jonathan Marballi), in the "Chapter 15" episode of the political-drama *House of Cards* (2013–):

> Ninety-six percent of the Internet isn't accessible through standard search engines. Most of it's useless. But it's where you go to find anything and everything: child porn, bitcoin laundering, mail-order narcotics, hackers for hire.

The deep Web is referenced in a variety of narratives: as a place, for example, where terrorists hide as in the "Cry Havoc" episode of the legal drama *State of Affairs* (2014–); as a way misogynistic videos get uploaded as in the "Intimidation Game" episode of *Law & Order: Special Victims Unit*; as a place to buy drugs as in "The Deep Web" episode of the legal-drama *The Good Wife* (2009–) and "The Bogeyman" episode of the police-drama *Blue Bloods* (2010–), for human trafficking as in the television drama *The Bride He Bought Online* (2015), and as a hideout for pedophiles as in the "P911" episode of the crime-drama *Criminal Minds* (2005–), the "Kidnapping 2.0" episode of *CSI: Cyber,* and the "Chat Room" episode of *Law & Order: Special Victims Unit*.

The notion of the Internet being either lawless—or at least with pockets of lawlessness—creates an influential impression of cyberspace harboring bad people who both live *in* the Internet and use this technology to access innocents.

The "Who" of the Cyberbogeyman

In the "Juliet Takes a Luvvah" episode of the comedy-crime series *Psych* (2006–14), Shawn (James Roday) walked in on his colleague Gus (Dulé Hill) taking selfies:

SHAWN: Uh, what are you doing?

GUS: Look, it's not what it looks like. I'm just taking additional photos for my soulmateconnect.com online dating profile.

SHAWN: Phew. I thought there was something truly embarrassing going on in here.

GUS: Look, I need to be in love, Shawn. Everyone I've gone after over the last year has either been a killer or dating a killer.

SHAWN: Oh, well, by all means, let's scour the Internet, the place where everyone knows it's just decent, normal, sane people looking for true love.

Shawn's sarcasm serves as an illustration of the *out there* fears harbored about cyberspace, something widely identifiable in narratives, whereby characters in online dating–themed narratives express concern about who might be *out there*. Akin to *Psych*, something similar is evident in the "Do You Wanna Dance?" episode of the legal-drama *Ally McBeal* (1997–2002). The title character (Calista Flockhart) had begun online dating and her roommate, Renee (Lisa Nicole Carson), cautioned, "You realize this guy's probably got two heads and a criminal record?" The *Psych* and *Ally McBeal* scenes hint to a popular way that the bogeyman fear is executed on screen: that those encountered are presumed to be criminals.

The Murderous Bogeyman

In the opening of the comedy *EuroTrip* (2004), Scotty (Scott Mechlowicz) was emailing his German penpal, "Mike." Watching him, Scotty's friend, Cooper (Jacob Pitts), outlined the potentially murderous perils of meeting people online:

> You meet a [quote] cool guy [quote] on the [quote] Internet [quote], okay. This is how these sexual predators work. Next thing you know he's going to want to [quote] arrange a meeting [quote] where he will gas you and stuff you in the back of his van and make a wind chime out of your genitals.

Fears of murderous bogeymen, in fact, appear in a wide range of screen examples. In the British biopic *One Chance* (2013), Paul (James Corden) and Julz (Alexandra Roach) were on their first in-person meeting when Julz received a telephone call: "Oh, it's just my mum," she said, "making sure that I'm still alive and you haven't murdered me." In the romance *Meet Prince Charming* (2002), during a chatroom exchange with her online admirer, Jack (David Charvet), Samantha (Tia Carrere) expressed her apprehensions: "What if you're a psycho killer?" In *You've Got Mail* the same fears were evident in a scene when Kathleen (Meg Ryan) speculated with her employees Christina (Heather Burns) and George (Steve Zahn) about why her online date hadn't shown up to the café as planned. Kathleen and

Christina pondered an elaborate accident scenario when George held up a newspaper emblazoned with the headline "Cops Nab Rooftop Killer":

KATHLEEN: What are you saying?
GEORGE: It could be. He was arrested two blocks from the café.
CHRISTINA: Is there a picture? [They leaf through the newspaper] So that explains it.
GEORGE: He was in jail.
CHRISTINA: And there was a phone—
GEORGE: But he got only one call and he had to use it to call his lawyer.
CHRISTINA: You are so lucky.
GEORGE: You could be dead.[7]

In the comedy *Ten Inch Hero* (2007), worried about her colleague Jen's (Clea DuVall) burgeoning online relationship, Piper (Elisabeth Harnois) cautioned, "So basically he could be Charles Manson with a laptop?" In the "A League of their Own" episode of the sitcom *Ugly Betty* (2006–10), in the aftermath of Betty's (America Ferrera) breakup, her friend Christina (Ashley Jensen) suggested online dating: "There are freaks online," protested Betty, "Why don't you just chop me into pieces yourself, and we can cut out the middleman?" In the television thriller *The Girl He Met Online* (2014), while scanning through profile photos, Gillian (Yvonne Zima) gave a running commentary, "Momma's boy, no thank you, uggh, you're like a hundred years old, redneck trailer trash, too young … serial killer." In "The Fall" episode of the comedy-drama series *Grace and Frankie* (2015–), Grace (Jane Fonda) stated her objection to online dating: "I choose not to be murdered by a stranger that I met online." In the "In the Mix, on the Books, and in the Freezer" episode of the sitcom *Manhattan Love Story* (2014), the audience heard Dana's (Analeigh Tipton) internal monologue about her fears of her upcoming Tinder date: "Hoping he's not a seral killer."

This worst-case scenario fear of a dangerous person—a *dangerous man*—encountered online is explained by a range of factors. First, as discussed earlier, there exists in the cultural imaginary a well-established fear of people met through anonymous channels; something discussed by true-crime author William Webb in the context of real-life lonely hearts killers:

> Killers that connect with victims via the want ads are nothing new. The notorious lonely hearts killers of the 1940s, Raymond Fernandez and Martha Beck, met each other and found victims through a "lonely hearts" magazine. Harvey Louis Caringnan, a Minnesota serial killer, is known as the "want ad killer" because he used newspaper ads to lure women to their deaths. An even more infamous lonely hearts killer was Henri Desire Landru, who met at least 11 women through want ads in French magazines during World War 1 and murdered them.[8]

In recent years, the news media have granted extensive attention to real-life Internet-era villains who have met their victims in similar ways. In 2004, Lisa Montgomery met her victim—a pregnant woman whose baby Lisa planned to steal—in a rat terrier fanciers chatroom called "Ratter Chatter."[9] In 2007, Michael John Anderson became the first person to be dubbed "The Craigslist Killer" after he met his victim, Katherine Olsen, on the site. Later, the same moniker was applied to Philip Markoff who, in 2009, murdered one woman, and assaulted others he had met on the site.[10] In 2014, husband and wife killers, Miranda Barbour and Elytte Barbour, were charged and convicted of murdering a man they met through Craigslist.[11] While in these examples *Craigslist* was the focus, in others, purpose-built online dating sites have been implicated in offline crime. In 2012, Elaine O'Hara in Ireland was stabbed, raped and eventually gagged and murdered by Graham Dwyer, a man she had met on the Alt.com "erotic dating" site.[12] In 2013, Sharon Siermans in Australia was beaten to death with a cricket bat by a man she met on the dating site PlentyOfFish.com.[13] Also in Australia in 2014, Tinder was implicated in the death of Warriena Wright.[14] Such cases, while small in number and certainly no more common than those transpiring following introductions made elsewhere—as Nick Paumgarten reminds us in his *New Yorker* article about online dating, "Bars don't do background checks, either"[15]—comply neatly with the techno- and cyberphobias well established in our culture and thus get additional news media attention because they prove deep-seated fears. Verbalized fears of murderous bogeymen in film and television both narrate offline fears and contribute to the idea of cyberspace as scary. The sociologist George Gerbner used the term *mean world syndrome* to describe the widespread belief that the world is a bad place full of people who can't be trusted; a belief Gerber suggested was fueled by a high diet of popular media.[16] With frequent and salacious news media reports on crimes linked to the Internet[17]—not to mention popular media's repeated fictionalization of this theme—a cycle is created where the screen mirrors our fears as well as fuels them.

Samantha in *Meet Prince Charming* feared encountering a *psycho*, and the title character in *Ugly Betty* worried about *freaks*. Both remarks hint to another common online dating fear: encountering somebody mentally unstable.

The Crazy Bogeyman

In an unnamed episode of the lesbian-themed Scottish series *Lip Service* (2010–12), Tess (Fiona Button) outlined her opposition to online dating: "No, absolutely not, I'm not that desperate; it's for skanks and psychos." In the "Two Bodies in the Lab" episode of the crime-drama series *Bones* (2005–), Temperance (Emily Deschanel) had just arranged her first in-person date with a man she met online. Temperance's colleague, Agent Booth (David Boreanaz), speculated, "So what if your computer date's psycho?" In the television drama

The Wife He Met Online (2012), an online dater commented, "So I almost didn't try this online dating thing. 'Cos I heard stories about getting matched up with these psychos." In the drama *On_Line* (2002), Moira (Isabel Gillies) told her friend, Ed (Eric Millegan), about her upcoming online date; Ed, concernedly, asked, "What if he turns out to be a complete psycho or something?" *Weirdo* is another way the same fears get verbalized. In the "Three Men and a Boubier" episode of the sitcom *Super Fun Night* (2013–14), Helen-Alice (Liza Lapira) responded doubtfully to her roommate's (Rebel Wilson) suggestion that they date online: "I don't know, Kimmie. There are too many weirdos online." In the *Catfish* (2010) documentary, a waitress provided Nev, the protagonist, her thoughts on online dating: "I know my friend, she actually just met a guy the other day off the Internet and he was a total weirdo." In the "I'm Moving On" episode of the drama *Hart of Dixie* (2011–15), Zoe (Rachel Bilson) started online dating and her friend, Wade (Wilson Bethel), cautioned, "Gotta be careful. Lots of freaks and weirdos online." In the "I Robot … You, Jane" episode of the supernatural series *Buffy the Vampire Slayer* (1997–2003), Buffy (Sarah Michelle Gellar) and Xander (Nicholas Brendon) discussed Willow's (Alyson Hannigan) new online relationship with "Malcolm":

XANDER: No, it's just this Malcolm guy. What's his deal? I mean, tell me you're not slightly wigged.
BUFFY: Okay, slightly. I mean, just not knowing what he's really like.
XANDER: Or who he really is. I mean, sure he says he's a high school student, but I can say I'm a high school student.
BUFFY: You are.
XANDER: Okay, but I could also say that I'm an elderly Dutch woman. Get me? I mean, who's to say I'm not if I'm in the elderly Dutch chatroom.
BUFFY: I get your point. I get your point. Oh, this guy could be anybody. He could be weird, or crazy, or old, or he could be a circus freak. He's probably a circus freak.
XANDER: Yeah, I mean, we read about it all the time. You know, people meet on the net, they talk, they get together, have dinner, a show, horrible ax murder.

In the Australian comedy *Da Kath and Kim Code* (2005), lovelorn Sharon (Magda Szubanski) began online dating and her friend, Kath (Jane Turner), commented, "Gee, Internet dating. I hope Sharon's careful. There's a lot of loonies out there."

These examples, of course, exist in the same culture that is fearful of encountering a murderer online; certainly as related to the real-life murders discussed above, *weirdo* and *psycho* seem like apt descriptions. Equally, in light of newspaper headlines like, "Is there a psychopath in your inbox?",[18] "Psychos Lurk Online,"[19] and "Weirdos are online and out of control,"[20] cultural chatter about online dating helps to normalize the idea that crazy people populate cyberspace. Of course, more than simply the interplay between news media and fictional depictions of the mentally unstable is the more general presentation that people online—those *from* the Internet or *lurking* on the Internet—are actually a different breed; that their use of the Internet for intimacy is only the tip of the iceberg of their strangeness. Portrayals of the Web commonly involve themes of duplicity, fake identities, *fluid* identities, that help shape our perceptions of the typical Internet user. In my book *Cyberbullies, Cyberactivists, Cyberpredators: Film, TV, and Internet Stereotypes*, for example, I discussed media stereotypes such as netgeeks and neckbeards who are invariably presented on screen as pasty and often sinister men typing on keyboards in darkened basements.[21] Such men look different and live differently, and these presentations hint to a *breed difference* idea, whereby the Internet is construed as its own place that produces its own nefarious population. While in reality, today we are *all* "Internet people" given our high-level use[22] on screen, and the Internet— particularly high-level use of it—continues to be a way a character is framed as different, if not notably strange or psycho.

Among the stereotypes I discussed in *Cyberbullies, Cyberactivists, Cyberpredators* was the cyberpervert. On screen this figure is another kind of online dating bogeyman, a sexually rapacious, if not dangerous figure assumed to lurk on dating sites.

The Perverted Bogeyman

In the romantic-comedy *Because I Said So* (2007), Daphne (Diane Keaton) went online to search for a partner for her daughter, Milly (Mandy Moore). Daphne's profile attempted to exclude those she assumed populated cyberspace: "Let me preference this ad by saying if you're a nut job, pervert, or fruit cake, move on …" In the "Online Dating" episode of the sitcom *Hot Properties* (2005), Ava (Gail O'Grady) explicitly described online dating as a "wonderfully efficient way for perverts around the world to check you out." In the "Dice" episode of the sitcom *New Girl* (2011–), Schmidt (Max Greenfield) coached the protagonist, Jess (Zooey Deschanel), on how to use the titular hook-up app; via role-play he tried to warn her about the kind of men that he predicted she would encounter:

SCHMIDT: Okay, first test. Now, I'm gonna say something, and you tell me what's really being said. "Oh, you know, I'm just staying in a hotel right now."
JESS: I like to travel.
SCHMIDT: Homeless. Pervert. "Oh, my God, my mom is just the most amazing woman."
JESS: Oh. I love my mother.
SCHMIDT: Virgin. And somehow also a pervert. "I kind of prefer public transportation." Jess: Oh. Earth-conscious.
SCHMIDT: Multiple DUIs. Pervert.

In the comedy *Celebrity Sex Tape* (2012), at the end of the film, after Ross (Jack Cullison) refused to lose his virginity on screen, he addressed the camera: "I'll have you know, there's only one girl I want to lose my virginity to. My ex-girlfriend Kim [Julie Barzman]. And she wouldn't be watching this because she's not that kind of girl like all you little perverts. She's pure. And I love that about her." In *Smiley*, as part of her advice to Mary about not using "Hide and Go Chat," Stacy cautioned that the site was "for people who do gross things to other people." A variation on this theme played out in the Canadian drama *Adoration* (2008) when Tom (Scott Speedman) was looking at his nephew Simon's (Devon Bostick) webcam chat interaction with an older man:

TOM: Who's he?
SIMON: Some guy.
TOM: Was he trying to pick you up? [laughter]

These examples comply with well-established negative perceptions about *Internet people*: given the long history of the marginalization of people with sexual interests deviating from the norm,[23] it is of course, no surprise that the concept of "pervert" would be used in the same manner that "murderer" might be. It is, however, reasonable to assume that in a world where people are seeking intimacy that bumping into a pervert—someone else seeking connection, albeit of an unorthodox kind—during such a search is a more likely occurrence than encountering a murderer.

While contact from perverts might actively be desired for intimacy seekers who subscribe to sites like Alt.com or FetLife, for people on putatively vanilla dating sites, spontaneously encountering a "pervert" is a potentially distressing situation documented repeatedly in academic research. In literature scholar Christyne Berzsenyi's work on online dating, she quoted "Juliet" who described her experiences: "I find that women of my age, including myself, get a number of responses from much younger men, twenties and thirties, who are perhaps either perverted with mother-obsessions or want to be supported financially by mother-substitutes."[24] Certainly a disproportionate number of responses from much younger men was 50-year-old Janet's (Lesley Sharp) online dating experience in the British crime-drama *Scott & Bailey* (2011–), and has relevance in several scenes discussed later in this chapter where adult women are courted online by teenage boys. A good screen illustration of an unexpectedly perverted encounter occurred in the "C Is for Curiouser & Curiouser" episode of the sitcom *A to Z* (2014–15) when Stephie (Lenora Crichlow) was reviewing her online matches: "wanker, wanker, oh, *actual* wanker." Something similar transpired in the "Mano-a-Mansfield" episode of the sitcom *Ground Floor* (2013–15) when Jennifer (Briga Heelan) spoke of her experiences using a hook-up app: "I was on Pynchr for, like, maybe a day. It's basically a delivery system for dick pics." The sociologist Adam Kotsko addressed this online pervert phenomenon in his book *Creepiness*:

Much has been said of the effect of internet anonymity in releasing people's primal id, and this seems to be above all the case when it comes to creepy behavior. Men routinely send pictures of their erect penises to women who venture into online dating services, and they post other repulsive sexually explicit material with no apparent self-awareness. In a particularly vivid example, one woman reported reading an online dating profile in which a man praises the virtues of the "cum socks" that he used to clean up after masturbating.[25]

Of particular interest is Kotsko's point about why such behavior plays out so frequently online: "What is creepy about them is not their sexual desire as such, but their insistence on *brandishing* it. Exhibitionism is the distinguishing trait of the pervert."[26] While exhibitionism is discussed further in Chapter 6, it is worth noting that another possibility for the presence of it in Internet-themed narratives centers on the medium being—both in reality and also in the popular imaginary—a site for sexually renegade behavior: that without having to expose identity or look into the eyes of one's victim,[27] the capacity to engage in such antisocial behavior, to release a person's *primal id*, is facilitated.

In this section I have alluded to some of the specific online bogeyman presentations that are depicted on screen; in the next section, the focus is on investigating the general presence of a cyberbogeyman; a focal point for fears about the Internet.

The "Why" of the Cyberbogeyman

In his discussion of the horror genre, the communications scholar Kendall Phillips identified the ever-presence of the bogeyman in popular culture:

> In a way, every tale of horror is a tale of the bogeyman. Folklorists trace the origin of this mythical figure of fear as far back as human history is recorded. ... While the form of the bogeyman varies across cultures and historical periods, the essential quality of the bogeyman is his (or, at times, her) relationship to cultural boundaries. The bogeyman exists at the boundary point between cultural notions of right and wrong, and his position at the boundary entails a number of important cultural implications. ... These kinds of monstrous figures have long served as warrants for the systems of morality—if you cross the boundaries of morality, these figures await you.[28]

Phillips' ideas are particularly useful in thinking about the role of the cyberbogeyman on screen—that it exists as an Internet-age embodiment—or, more aptly an Internet-age *disembodiment*—of fears well established in our culture. While, as discussed above, the cyberbogeyman exists in a variety of incarnations—as vague fears, for example, of murderers or perverts lurking on online dating sites—worth noting is a specific bogeyman that has received extensive real-life attention: Slenderman, a tall, faceless, ghost-like figure that began life as a meme in 2009. Tea Krulos, in his book *Monster Hunters*, discussed Slenderman describing him as "just a new version of an old, powerful archetype: the Bogeyman, that faceless, frightening creeper who has lived on in children's imaginations and nightmares for generations."[29] Dubbed the "Internet's best and scariest legend,"[30] Slenderman is a haunting presence online, one which was even thought to have "inspired" a real-life stabbing in Wisconsin in 2014.[31] The cultural impact of Slenderman is reflective of a desire to give bogeyman fears a *physical form*, to have an image to pin more generalized cyberspace fears to. While in popular media Slenderman has only a minimal presence—for example in the "#Thinman" episode of the sci-fi series *Supernatural* (2005–) and in Web series like *Marble Hornets* (2009–14) and *Jacob: The Series* (2015)—the enormous online presence of the character helps highlight, and explain, the popularity of the more generic cyberbogeymen common in Internet-themed narratives. In this section, some of these reasons, as specifically located within an intimacy quest, are explored.

A Consequence of Mainstreaming

The first explanation for the online bogeyman has its roots in the enormity of the modern dating landscape. In Chapter 1 I discussed how online dating is substantially more mainstream today than decades ago when the first such sites were established. Unlike personal ads and blind-dating of course, online dating is an enormous industry and has become the default method of purposeful partner procurement—so much so, in fact, that as the sociologist John Bridges noted, this method has replaced many others and is often conceived of as "the only game in town."[32] With increased participation, a greater number of people are feeling apprehensive about meeting a psycho, in turn normalizing this fear. Similarly, as Kristina Grish alluded in her self-help book *The Joy of Text: Mating, Dating, and Techno-Relating*, there is simply a greater likelihood of more psychos in a larger dating pool.[33]

The Beleaguered Reputation of the Online Dater

In the "How I Met Everyone Else" episode of the sitcom *How I Met Your Mother* (2005–14), Barney (Neil Patrick Harris) cautioned his friend Ted (Josh Radnor) about the perils of online dating, commenting: "the only hot girls that troll the Internet for dudes are crazy, hookers or dudes." In the comedy-drama *Burn After Reading* (2008), Linda (Frances McDormand) discussed her online dating experiences with her colleague Ted (Richard Jenkins). Two of Ted's cautionary remarks included, "Linda, what do you really know about this guy?" and—in line with the psycho and pervert fears discussed earlier—"You know, he could be one of these guys who cruises the Internet." A similar comment was made in the "Pilgrimage" episode of the comedy-drama series *Nurse Jackie* (2009–): Dr. Cooper (Peter Facinelli) had started online dating and his colleague, Dr. Roman (Betty Gilpin), cautioned, "Do you have any idea what kind of women troll those sites?" These scenes illustrate the point made by psychologists Monica Whitty and Adrian Carr: "the media would have us believe that cyberspace is full of an assortment of freaks and geeks."[34] While film and television unquestionably has a role in mainstreaming ideas about online daters being creeps and weirdos (Chapter 3), worth noting, this idea is not only detected on screen, but has extensive traction in published work where online dating is still perceived as unsafe. A survey, for example, conducted by the Pew Research Center, found that 66% of Internet users thought that online dating was dangerous and of those who had actually tried it, 43% believed it was risky.[35] In sexual health researchers Danielle Couch, Pranee Liamputtong and Marian Pitts' study on online dating, the authors quoted a number of participants who articulated their own cyberbogeymen fears: "Estelle," for example, noted, "i think your also hopeing that the person isn't like some serial killer" [sic], while "Tommy" claimed, "you never know if you're going to meet an axe murderer." "Clarissa" in the same study said, "I think dating sites are extremely dangerous. They are Psychopaths playgrounds."[36] Bridges, in his book *The Illusion of Intimacy*, quoted "Joyce" who had once been a former Match.com user and described her experiences: "they just feed on women and men who are hurting and all they do is provide a tool for perverts."[37] In *Cyberbullies, Cyberactivists and Cyberpredators* I similarly explored a range of self-help books that normalize the need to be extra careful when online dating compared to finding intimacy using other methods. Together such ideas help to explain the bogeyman presumption both on screen and in real life.

While the cyberbogeyman has much screen and social traction, in both contexts fears center simply on the idea of what *might* happen online. Something, however, that gives this idea gravitas is that, as alluded to earlier, bad things do happen online and such bad things are reported on extensively, potentially even disproportionately.[38] In the following sections fictionalized portrayals of those bad things happening are explored. This discussion begins with online deception; a theme that can be as innocuous as white lies told about attractiveness through to the concealment of malicious intent.

Dater Deception

As with bogeyman fears of online daters being murderers, psychos and perverts, the idea of such daters being duplicitous is a common screen presentation. In this section, speculation about identity deception as well as acts of it are explored.

Discussed earlier were scenes where bogeyman assumptions were articulated about the kinds of people assumed to be lurking on dating sites. Similar assumptions are made about the specific kinds of deceptions encountered on such sites, notably in relation to gender, age and identity. While such deception is frequently speculated on, equally so does it actually transpire.

Gender Deception

Xander's comments in *Buffy the Vampire Slayer* about his capacity to pose online as an "elderly Dutch woman," along with Barney's speculation in *How I Met Your Mother* about "the only hot girls that troll the Internet for dudes are crazy, hookers or dudes," are illustrative of the simple speculation that gender deception is likely online; a fear echoed in a range of scenes. In "The One with Barry and Mindy's Wedding" episode of the sitcom *Friends* (1994–2004), for example, Chandler (Matthew Perry) discussed his new online romance with his friend Phoebe (Lisa Kudrow):

PHOEBE: You know, I think it's so great that you are totally into this person and yet, for all you know, she could be ninety years old or have two heads or … It could be a guy.
CHANDLER: It's not a guy, alright? I *know* her.
PHOEBE: It could be a big giant guy.

In the "Girls, Girls, Girls" episode of *Supernatural*, Sam (Jared Padalecki) warned his brother, Dean (Jensen Ackles), about his match on the "Crush-Book" dating app: "It could be some Canadian trucker named Bruce." In the comedy-drama *Me and You and Everyone We Know* (2005), two young boys were in a chatroom and the older one, Peter (Miles Thompson), speculated about the woman they were chatting with: "Everyone just makes stuff up on these things. It's probably a man pretending to be a woman." The same assumption was made in the comedy *Sex Drive* (2008), when Ian (Josh Zuckerman) and his brother Rex (James Marsden) were driving and Ian divulged his new Internet romance:

IAN: There is a girl I've been, kind of—
REX: Alright, I'm listening. Where'd you meet her?
IAN: On the … online.
REX: [abruptly stops car] For fuck's sake, Ian! Don't you watch *Dateline*? [1992–] She's probably a guy. Some fat old dude who wants to ram you in the tail pipe.

In the drama *Disconnect* (2012), gender deception fears emerged when the journalist Nina (Andrea Riseborough) arranged to meet Kyle (Max Thieriot), an 18-year-old source for her story on cybercrime:

NINA: Listen Kyle, there's something I didn't tell you about myself.
KYLE: What are you, a dude?

These themes were also apparent in the documentary *Lil Bub & Friendz* (2013): one of the interviewees, Grant Mayland—termed "Minneapolis's #1 cat video fan"—reflected on his late-1990s experiences in chatrooms:

> It was 1998 when my mom got me AOL. I started going into cha-trooms and things just kind of grew from there. I went into a lot of the really dirty lesbian chatrooms ... I mean everyone was you know, probably either a 15 or 45 year old guy. I think at the time I was secretly aware but I fantasized that I wasn't ...[39]

While in these examples, gender being lied about is simply assumed; in others, such deception actually plays out.

In the "Surprise" episode of the sitcom *Mike & Molly* (2010–), Samuel (Nyambi Nyambi) mentioned the woman he had been exchanging emails with his friends Mike (Billy Gardell) and Carl (Reno Wilson), the latter who had experienced his own online gender deception:

SAMUEL: This is the woman I've been telling you about. She is also from Africa.

MIKE: That picture ain't Africa, that's Lincoln Park. I recognize the hot dog vendor. Gary. Or Jerry.

CARL: She is a beautiful woman if that is indeed her real picture.

SAMUEL: What are you talking about?

CARL: People lie all the time on these dating sites. I once tried hooking up with this hot Filipino chick. Ended up being a short Guatemalan man named Roberto.

In the "Girl Trouble" episode of the police-drama series *Nash Bridges* (1996–2001), Joe (Cheech Marin) assumed he was having an online romance with a woman; the "woman" turned out to be Pepe (Patrick Fischler) his office manager. In the "Mikado" episode of the sci-fi series *Millennium* (1996–99), the IT specialist Brian (Allan Zinyk) admitted, "Online I've changed my name, my appearance, sexual orientation. Even gender." In the "Serpent's Tooth" episode of the British sitcom *My Family* (2000–2011), Nick's (Kris Marshall) experience with gender deception was noted in a conversation with his mother Susan (Zoë Wanamaker) and father Ben (Robert Lindsay):

SUSAN: You're not chatting up girls on the Internet again?

BEN: What do you mean "again"? What, you've done this kind of thing before?

NICK: Yeah, and it worked really well. Tahlia, her name was. This 19-year-old cellist from Prague. We had a really deep and rewarding e-relationship going.

SUSAN: Until Tahlia turned out to be a 48-year-old gasfitter called Stuart from Sunderland.

NICK: Alright, so it was a man. It meant a lot to me while it lasted.

Later in the same episode, in order to secure a date with a lesbian model, Nick pretended to be a woman online. Something similar occurred in the "Past Tense" episode of the sitcom *Suddenly Susan* (1996–2000), when Todd (David Strickland) posed as a lesbian in a chatroom. Todd arranged to meet a woman offline; his "lesbian" turned out to be another man (Shawn Hoffman): both men had lied about their gender. In the "Joey and the Holding Hands" episode of the sitcom *Joey* (2004–6), the episode opened with a standard bogeyman-themed conversation between the title character (Matt LeBlanc) and his nephew Michael (Paulo Costanzo):

MICHAEL: Check it out. I just met the hottest girl on the Internet.

JOEY: Oh yeah, how do you know she's hot?

MICHAEL: 'Cos she described herself to me.

JOEY: Michael, it's the Internet. People lie. As I found when I got this authentic Stormtrooper helmet for five grand.

MICHAEL: You can be as cynical as you want, Joey, this is how my generation meets people, okay? She says she's a lovely young woman, I happen to believe her.

JOEY: Sorry. I'm sure you'll be very happy with [peers at the user name] SexySteve87.

MICHAEL: So what, Stevie Nicks is a woman. Steve can be a girl's name.

Upon arrival at the house, Michael's online date appeared to be a beautiful blonde woman: Joey's suspicions seemed unfounded. Michael then left with Steve only to return home soon after, alone, to concede to his uncle, "Yeah, it's a dude." In the drama *Closer* (2004), an experience of gender deception was exposed in a conversation between Anna (Julia Roberts) and Larry (Clive Owen):

LARRY: Where were you between the hours of six-forty-five and seven-PM?

ANNA: That's really none of your business. Where were *you*?

LARRY: On the net talking to you.

ANNA: [shakes her head]

LARRY: Well I was talking to someone.

ANNA: Someone pretending to be me. I think you were talking to Daniel Wolf [Jude Law].

LARRY: Who?

ANNA: This guy I know. It's him.

LARRY: No. I was talking to a woman.

ANNA: How do you know?

LARRY: Believe me. She was a woman. I got a huge ... She was a wo- ... She wasn't, was she? What a bastard.

In the "Erica & Callum" episode of the British drama series *Dates* (2013), Callum (Greg McHugh) divulged to his date Erica (Gemma Chan), "I've been on a lot of dates with a lot of girls ... Well, two including this one and the other 'so-called girl' turned out to be a ... that doesn't matter." In the teen-comedy *Geography Club* (2013), adolescent Ike (Alex Newell) met a "boy" online only to discover it was a girl once he had his hand down her pants.

While the Internet's role in facilitating attributes like gender being lied about are discussed later in this chapter, it is worthwhile briefly examining why gender is such a common focus of deceit. The most obvious explanation is that it reflects real-life anxieties. In communications scholar Jeffrey Hancock's work on digital deception, he identified that "gender deception is perhaps the most commonly discussed example of category deception online."[40] One likely reason for this is the very long history of such deception playing out online even prior to the Web. The writer Lindsy Van Gelder, for example, documented the case of "Joan," an online identity created by Alex, a male psychiatrist, who chatted on CompuServe, an hourly rate Internet service in the very early 1990s.[41] The psychologist Patricia Wallace discussed the fall-out from the case; tapping into themes that were referenced in the *My Family*, *Suddenly Susan* and *Lil Bub & Friendz* examples discussed earlier:

> Some were angry at any gender deception, while others, less concerned about online gender-swapping, were outraged by the thought that Alex was using the online "Joan" persona to front for him so he could hear intimate self-disclosure from women and also, experience lesbianism vicariously. Most, but not all, agreed that Alex violated some trust or other.[42]

More recent research documents that gender deception remains a popular real-life online pastime. In their survey of Internet-deception studies, psychologists Stefan Stieger, Tina Eichinger and Britta Honeder identified that, "The most prominent form of online deception is gender switching."[43] The authors discussed one study that showed that 18% of male and 11% of female chatroom users lied about their sex.[44] While mirroring reality is one explanation for screen speculation about gender deception, so too is gender deception's long history as a theme in entertainment products: the historian Elizabeth Reis, for example, traced cultural anxieties about such deception back to the 1500s[45]; Shakespeare's play *The Twelfth Night* from 1602 is one famous example. With gender deception being deemed amusing for hundreds of years, the involvement of the Internet is a way to give contemporary salience to this well-established storyline.

Another explanation for gender deception narratives is their mirroring of some specific real-life anxieties about gender and sexuality. In the vast majority of examples discussed in this section, the fears—as well as the eventuality—of online gender deception center on *men* being tricked into thinking that they are corresponding with women. Such a theme works as funny—and also potentially horrifying—because it taps into the notion of homosexual panic. In his work on homophobia, the sociologist Michael Kimmel identified men's serious fears of humiliation in relation to sexual matters.[46] Men's egos related to speculation about homosexuality, in fact, have been widely discussed.[47] Undoubtedly the idea that an online love interest could be a man and that that man might, as suggested in *Sex Drive*, want to "ram you in the tail pipe," helps exploit fears of humiliation, notably ones centered on unwanted homosexual advances. Larry's embarrassment in *Closer* exists as another good example of this: he was seemingly quite perturbed that the "huge erection" he got as a result of a steamy online chat was prompted by contact with another man and not Anna as he was led to believe. In line with stereotypes about homosexuality, to be assumed as gay is to be assumed as less masculine.

Another notable form of deception transpiring on screen relates to appearance—people will exploit opportunities to lie about their appearance simply because they can.

Appearance Deception

In the gay-themed drama *Breaking the Cycle* (2002), in one scene Jason (Carlos da Silva) wears a T-shirt reading "You looked better on the Internet!" This T-shirt illustrates some of the themes in the *Breaking the Cycle* narrative but also comically references the idea of the Internet as a place where appearances can be played with; a place where different, older or entirely fraudulent photos can stand in for your own.[48] On screen such deception is relatively common. In the aforementioned *Mike & Molly* episode, Carl speculated, "She is a beautiful woman if that is indeed her real picture." In this scene, much like characters simply assuming gender deception, Carl suspects that a person would lie about appearance because the technology enables it. One way that assumed deception transpires is characters exhibiting shock that their date actually looks like his or her photo (a popular trope discussed later in this chapter); in others, it involves appearance deception speculation and fears that a date might not be attractive. In *Meet Prince Charming*, for example, at one point Samantha messages Jack online, "What if you're yucky?" In *You've Got Mail*, prior to Joe (Tom Hanks) first seeing Kathleen in person, his colleague, Kevin (Dave Chapelle), warned him, "She could be a real dog." Later in the film—when Kathleen hadn't yet realized that Joe was NY152—Joe teasingly speculated to her about his likely appearance: "maybe he's fat, he's fat, he's a fatty." In the aforementioned "Juliet Takes a Luvvah" episode of *Psych*, Shawn warned Gus about his new online girlfriend, "Of course she looks all pretty online. When you show up at the restaurant, guess who's waiting for you at the bar? The New Delhi version of Colonel Sanders, with a wig." In the Canadian television romance *Perfect Romance* (2004), Tess (Kathleen Quinlan) went online to find her daughter, Jenny (Lori Heuring), a partner. The man Tess had chosen had not supplied a photo; something that Jenny found egregious: "Mom! He could be fat, hideous, sporting a comb-over."

Akin to gender deception, appearance deception is routinely speculated on and also regularly transpires on screen. In the "Crossfire" episode of *Nash Bridges*, for example, Inspector Michelle Chan (Kelly Hu) was undercover, going on dates to snare a predator. The following exchange transpired between she and one of her dates; a short, balding and bespectacled man named Kenneth (Bill Rafferty):

KENNETH: Are you disappointed? You look disappointed.
MICHELLE: Your profile said you were tall and muscular.
KENNETH: I took a little dramatic license.

In an unnamed episode of *Scott & Bailey*, Janet goes on her first online date, and described the man to her colleague, Rachel (Suranne Jones), "Shorter? He was definitely shorter." In the "Witchcraft" episode of the sitcom *Brotherly Love* (1995–97), the fat, bearded and middle-aged Lloyd (Michael McShane) had met a woman, Lotus (Megan Cavanaugh), online, and discussed his new romance with his young and hunky colleague Joe (Joey Lawrence), in turn divulging his own appearance-deception:

LLOYD: She wants to meet me.
JOE: You haven't met?
LLOYD: No, she just emailed me that she's coming into town for the comic book convention and she's rather insistent on dropping by.
JOE: So what's wrong with that?
LLOYD: Well, ah, I might not be exactly what she expects.
JOE: What do you mean?
LLOYD: Well, she might be expecting someone a bit younger. With a compact build and a leather motorcycle jacket.
JOE: Why would she expect that, Lloyd?
LLOYD: Oh because I sent her your picture.

The same situation transpired in a sketch from the "Cyber Girl" episode of the Canadian comedy series *The Red Green Show* (1991–2006), when nerdy Harold (Patrick McKenna) used a photo of his uncle, Red (Steve Smith), to woo a woman online. In "The Obstacle Course" episode of *Ally McBeal*, a court case centered on Rebecca's (Ann Cusack) feelings of deception after a man (Arturo Gil) she met online turned out to be a dwarf. The *Ally McBeal* creator, David E. Kelley, used the same storyline five years later in the "New Kids on the Block" episode of the legal-drama *Boston Legal* (2004–8) when Denny (William Shatner) was matched online with Bethany (Meredith Eaton), a midget. This narrative also played out in the "Eeny Teeny Maya Moe" episode of the animated series *The Simpsons* (1989–); Moe was matched with Maya and on their first meeting he discovered that she was a midget. The comedy *Bringing Down The House* (2003) opened with a legal-themed cha-troom exchange between Peter (Steve Martin) and Charlene (Queen Latifah). Charlene described herself as "31, with long, flowing locks and an athletic body" and Peter described himself as "a little older, 6'2", my hair is light, boyishly light." Charlene was actually a large black woman and Peter a grey-haired older man. The "Attack of the Killer Kung-Fu Wolf Bitch" episode of the animated series *The Boondocks* (2005–) opened with Riley narrating, "For most of my grandad's romantic life, the Internet hadn't been invented yet. So he was still discovering the dangers of online dating." Grandad was then shown opening his front door to numerous dates: each woman was shown next to the photo used online and the difference was marked: a transsexual, an ugly woman and an old woman each turned up, each in sharp contrast to the glamorous woman in the photo. A similar idea played out in the "The Barbarian Sublimation" episode of the sitcom *The Big Bang Theory* (2007–). Penny (Kaley Cuoco) became addicted to online gaming so to distract her from the game, Sheldon (Jim Parsons) posted an online dating profile for her. Penny's first date, Tom (Mark Hames), arrived to find her in the middle of a gaming binge and looking thoroughly disheveled. "I'm sorry dude," Tom says to Sheldon, "she doesn't look anything like her picture," to which Sheldon's roommate, Leonard (Johnny Galecki), commiserates, "they never do." In the comedy *Internet Dating* (2008), the first woman that Mickey (Katt Williams) arranged to hook up with turned out to be a fat woman (Lauren Christine Miller), who opened the door eating a tub of ice cream. In the "Gone Girl" episode of the Australian crime-drama *Winter* (2015–), Mel (Rachel Gordon) lamented to her sister about her failed online date: "Date from hell. This guy is nothing like his photo. I mean there should be some kind of law: your photo has to at least vaguely resemble who you are now not ten years ago."

Appearance deception on screen, of course, correlates strongly with the kind of deception that occurs in real life: as the economist Paul Oyer wryly observed in his book *Everything I Ever Needed to Know about Economics I Learned from Online Dating*: "if I had a nickel for every overweight per-son who describes him - or herself as "Athletic and Toned," … I would have a lot of nickels."[49] Psychologists Jessica Donn and Richard Sherman similarly documented widespread apprehensions among online daters about honesty regarding appearance.[50] Communications scholars Jennifer Gibbs, Nicole Ellison and Rebecca Heino found that most online daters *assume* that extensive misrepresentation about appearance transpires.[51] Couch, Liamputtong and Pitts also identified that most participants in their study were actively concerned about deceit: "These concerns tended to focus on inaccurate photos or the provision of incorrect details about relationship status."[52] While these studies reflect assumptions about deceit—something screen representations likely help fuel—research also spotlights the reality of such dishonesty. In communication scholars Hancock, Catalina Toma and Nicole Ellison's work, they found that both genders did actually lie about their weight and most men exaggerated their height.[53]

Many scenes of appearance deception can simply be explained akin to any online deception, as par for the course for the Internet (discussed later in this chapter). There are, however, some specific reasons why a person would exaggerate attractiveness, notably to improve one's chances in the dating market. In the romantic-comedy *Must Love Dogs* (2005), Dolly (Stockard Channing) explained why she embellished her dating profiles: "You just want someone to take you out for a test drive." Dolly's comment alludes to a simple self-marketing idea introduced in Chapter 1 whereby characters lie to remain competitive in a dating landscape that prioritizes attractiveness. Stieger, Eichinger and Honeder, in fact, linked such deception to biology:

> Sexual selection theory maintains that evolution is driven by strategies that provide mating advantages, such as outrivaling intrasexual competitors and, thus, increasing one's chance of being selected as a mate by a member of the opposite sex.[54]

Unsurprisingly, a dating market that rewards good looks is not just speculation; as Oyer explained:

> Looks are the single best predictor of how often someone on a dating site will be contacted by interested fellow daters. People in the most attractive 10 percent receive about twice as many e-mails as people who are average looking.[55]

An obvious explanation for appearance deception on screen is that it mirrors (as well as potentially *normalizes*) the perception that by dating online a person is simply likely to be duped. The assumption is that duplicity encourages more duplicity in order for participants to remain competitive. Widespread speculation about, and actual acts of deception online, help to mainstream the idea that being lied to is a valid fear and one substantiated in research.

Along with gender deception and appearance deception, another attribute commonly lied about on screen is age. In narratives where pedophilia is a theme, such deceit raises specific concerns; however, in most examples such deception centers on self-marketing.

Age Deception

In the "Zero Dark Forties" episode of the sitcom *The Exes* (2011–), Holly's (Kristen Johnston) friends secretly posted an online dating profile for her. Taking Phil's (Donald Faison) advice that, "You gotta sell the goods. Put 'em in the window, baby," Haskell rewrote the first draft amending Holly's age to "30-something ... Who cares if the 'something' is 13 more years," Haskell rationalized. This is an example of age deception whereby the motive centers primarily on being taken out for a test drive; an incentive motivating deception in a range of narratives. In the same episode of *The Exes*, one of Holly's matches selected by Phil, Haskell and Stuart (David Alan Basche) was a former Olympic water polo player. A very old man turned up to their prescreening; he had competed in the *Helsinki* games and had clearly misrepresented his age. Something similar transpired in the comedy *I Love You, Man* (2009). Peter (Paul Rudd) had used a website, FriendFinder.com, to make platonic male friends. He was matched with a man named Mel whose photo made him appear similar in age to Peter. When they met, Mel (Murray Gershenz) was elderly: "The picture is from a couple of years back," he explained. In an unnamed series 2 episode of the British series *Starlings* (2012–13), Grandpa (Alan Williams) tried online dating. While Grandpa was elderly himself, the woman he was matched with was in a vegetative state. In the aforementioned *Breaking the Cycle*, Jason mentioned meeting a man who had used the screen name "Young Jock Boy" but clearly was neither young nor a jock. In *Must Love Dogs*, the reason why Sarah's (Diane Lane) first online match, and date, was with her father, Bill (Christopher Plummer), was because the latter had lied about his age:

SARAH: A young fifty, Dad? You're seventy one! And when was the last time you rode a bike? Meandering or any other way.

BILL: Well think of it as poetry, darling. It's who I am in the bottom of my soul.

In the "May the Best Friend Win" episode of the sitcom *Baby Daddy* (2012–), Bonnie (Melissa Peterman) put up a dating profile and explained why she had lied about her age: "Everybody lies. It's like the weight on your driver's license. It's more of a suggestion." In the "Furt" episode of the comedy-drama series *Glee* (2009–15), middle-aged Sue Sylvester (Jane Lynch) stated in her profile that her age as 27.

While in these examples, age was downplayed so that characters could compete in a dating market that favors youth and attractiveness, the same thing transpires at the other end of the age spectrum when younger characters *overstate* their age for similar reasons. In *Me and You and Everyone We Know*, Peter and his younger brother Robby (Brandy Ratcliff) together pretended to be an adult male in a chatroom; Robby, too young to even read or write properly, actually set up an in-person date with a woman (Tracy Wright) they had chatted to. In the "Do You Wanna Dance?" episode of *Ally McBeal*, Ally's online beau, Chris (Jonathan Taylor Thomas), turned out to be a fifteen-year-old. The same thing transpired in "The Fifth Wheel" episode of the sitcom *The Nanny* (1993–99): CC (Lauren Lane) had become infatuated with a "man" she met online; her beau turned out to be her business partner's fifteen-year-old son Brighton (Benjamin Salisbury). This narrative also played out in *Must Love Dogs*: one of Dolly's online suitors, Jeremy (Will Rothhaar), ended up being a fifteen-year-old. In the "No Ordinary Mobster" episode of the superhero series *No Ordinary Family*

(2010–11), teen JJ (Jimmy Bennett) posted a profile pretending to be older so that he could communicate with his adult tutor, Katie (Autumn Reeser). In the "David & Ellie" episode of *Dates*, Ellie (Montanna Thompson)—in her efforts to find a better-quality suitor—had claimed to be twenty-five when, in reality, she was only nineteen.

In each of these examples, akin to the appearance-deception discussed earlier, the motivation for lying was simply to secure a first date; or in the case of JJ in *No Ordinary Family*,[56] to at least get closer. Just as such deception is experienced on screen, equally so does it play out in real life. Social researcher Dore Hollander, for example, reported that two-thirds of young adults surveyed found that people they had met online had lied about their age.[57] In Hancock, Toma and Ellison's study, they identified that one-fifth of people lied about their age.[58] Sociologist Benjamin Cornwell and David Lundgren similarly identified that almost one-quarter misrepresented their age online.[59]

An example that bridges the gap between lying to self-promote and lying to exploit transpired in the documentary *Talhotblond* (2009) and in the 2012 television biopic of the same name, both centered on the real-life story of a 47-year-old man, Thomas Montgomery, who posed online as an eighteen-year-old man, "Tommy," in correspondence with the eighteen-year-old, "Jessi." While "Tommy" was a constructed identity, as it turned out so too was Jessi: she was actually Mary Shieler who used her daughter's likeness to woo Thomas. While deception quite clearly was occurring, neither "Tommy" nor "Jessi" appeared intent on doing harm, rather their behavior was illustrative of *mutual catfishing*, in line with the definition offered by Sherlock (Jonny Lee Miller) in the "On the Line" episode of *Elementary* (2012–): "Someone who uses social media to create false identities. Most typically for the purpose of pursuing online romance." Unsurprisingly, the same thing played out in the aforementioned documentary *Catfish* centered on Nev who developed an online friendship with young "Abby" and an online romance with Abby's sister "Megan." It turned out that the Megan and Abby identities were fabricated by Angela, a middle-aged, overweight housewife. Again, Angela didn't wish to do anything physically harmful to Nev; her motivation was simply recreational cyberromance. In other examples, however, age deception transpires with harm as the central objective; the standard narrative being teenagers in chatrooms looking for fun and encountering a predator who poses as a peer.

In the "Cartman Joins NAMBLA" episode of the animated series *South Park* (1997–), the use of the Internet to groom young men was part of a joke; more commonly, however, such an idea is presented as part of a serious, if not *educative*, storyline. In the "Mother and Child Reunion: Part 1" episode of the Canadian drama series *Degrassi: The Next Generation* (2001–), adolescent Emma (Miriam McDonald) met "Jordan," a supposed fellow high school student, in a chatroom. Emma's friend, JT (Ryan Cooley), warned her, "I bet he lives in Scarborough and works at a video store … I bet he's forty and drools." JT's bogeyman suspicions were confirmed when Emma met "Jordan" in person in the "Mother and Child Reunion: Part 2" episode: he was a man (Jeff Gruich) in his forties. Something similarly transpired in "The Kindness of Strangers" episode of the police-drama series *The District* (2000–2004) when twelve-year-old Amy (Destiny Edmond) thought she was meeting "Icarus," a fifteen-year-old boy she had met online. Icarus turned out to be a predatory adult (John Sloan). While both Emma and Amy could have faced serious dangers, both girls left their encounters physically unscathed; an outcome of the kind that doesn't always play out on screen.

The television drama *Every Mother's Worst Fear* (1998) provided an early screen example of malicious age deception. Adolescent Martha (Jordan Ladd), who had just been dumped by her boyfriend, entered a children-of-divorce chatroom and typed, "I need a friend." Her quest for platonic intimacy led her to an online relationship with "Drew" (Vincent Gale). While initially Drew implied that he was similar in age to Martha, over the course of their correspondence, Drew admitted to being 34 and Martha inflated her age to 21. Drew was grooming Martha on behalf of a cyberpredator and trafficker, Scanman (Ted McGinley); Martha was then kidnapped. A cyber-instigated kidnapping similarly transpired in the Christian-drama *Finding Faith* (2013): a cyberpredator had posed as a peer and befriended the teenager Faith (Stephanie Bettcher) via a social networking site. Later Faith was kidnapped. This storyline also transpired in "The Hunt" episode of *Criminal Minds* where the intent was to eventually sell the kidnapped girls. In *The Bride He Bought Online*, John (Travis Hammer) turned the tables on the three teenage girls who had catfished him, by kidnapping them and attempting to traffick them via the deep Web. In the thriller *Trust* (2010), adolescent Annie (Liana Liberato) had been chatting online to "Charlie," an apparent fellow teen. When the two finally met in person, "Charlie" was, in fact, a middle-age man named Graham (Chris Henry Coffey) who then raped Annie. The horror film *Strangeland* (1998) opened with two fifteen-year-old girls, Genevieve (Linda Cardelllini) and Tiana (Amal Rhoe), using a teen chat site. They were corresponding with a supposed peer, "Capt Howdy" (Dee Snider), who invited them to a party. Tiana was found murdered; her body discovered with her lips sewn together, she had been tortured and died from a heart attack. The horror film *Megan Is Missing* (2011) followed a similar storyline: thirteen-year-old Megan (Rachel Quinn) met a boy, "Josh" (Dean Waite), online. Josh claimed to be a student at a nearby school. Josh kidnapped Megan before torturing and murdering her. Megan's best friend Amy (Amber Perkins) attempted to find her friend, and in the process also became one of Josh's victims. In the "Age of Innocence" episode of the police-drama series *Blue Bloods*, teenager Betsy (Stevie Steel) was found dead outside a hotel. Betsy had met a boy online via the "SocialGizmo" social media site; that boy turned out to be Howard (Austin Lysy), a middle-aged man. The British drama *Chatroom* (2010) provided another spin on this idea: across the course of the narrative, online interactions are acted out for dramatic effect; in one scene a middle-aged man, Tony (Gerald Home), entered the "Chelsea Teens" chatroom where adolescent William (Aaron Taylor-Johnson) was waiting:

TONY: Is this for teenage girls?
WILLIAM: Well, are you a teenage girl?
TONY: Yeah, I'm Tina.
WILLIAM: Tina the teenage girl.
TONY: Yeah. Are you a teenage girl?
WILLIAM: Yeah. And at the moment I'm touching myself.
TONY: Really? Are you good at it?
WILLIAM: Usually I'm a lot better when I'm not hacking into Tony Layton's home computer and putting his name on a sex offender's register. Pedo!

In this scene, William baited a would-be cyberpredator, something that transpires in numerous examples where age deception is part of a to-catch-a-predator storyline. In the "P911" episode of *Criminal Minds*, the FBI created a fake profile of twelve-year-old "Suzie" to trap a cyberpredator. The same thing occurs in *Finding Faith*, *Strangeland* and in the "Web" episode of *Law & Order: Special Victims Unit*. Similarly, in the "Killer Chat" episode of the crime-drama *Numb3rs* (2005–10), the father of a girl who had committed suicide following abuse by an online predator was part of the Parents Stop Predators group who snared pedophiles in chatrooms.

Each of these examples provides a worst-case scenario of what can happen online. The idea of the Internet aiding pedophiles getting access to children has been well documented in research on sex crimes and the Internet[60] and has received extensive media attention: the examples discussed in this section give voice to widespread child-safety fears dominant in the zeitgeist. Earlier I quoted Rex in *Sex Drive* who mentioned the investigative news program *Dateline*. *Dateline*, in fact, is a good example of a television show that has had a significant role in putting the spotlight on cyberpredators who target children, notably Chris Hansen's "To Catch a Predator" segment, which centered on baiting pedophiles in chatrooms and then ambushing the adult men who organized offline meetings. Worth noting, the cliché of Hansen's entrapments has been referenced in other examples, such as in the fourth season of the sitcom *Arrested Development* (2003–14) and the comedy *Trainwreck* (2015) where the snare was part of a joke.

In the examples discussed in this section, age deception transpired. In fact, beyond age, the predators in these examples also lied about their identity as criminals. In the following sections identity-lies such as name and marital status are explored.

Identity Deception

In *Must Love Dogs*, Sarah's first online date was with her father. In the aforementioned "I'm Moving On" episode of *Hart of Dixie*, Zoe's first date turned out to be one of her patients. In *You've Got Mail*, Shopgirl and NY152 were actually already known to each other as Kathleen and Joe, business rivals. In these examples, screen names disguised a person already known offline to a dater—a common screen trope. In the "C Is for Curiouser & Curiouser" episode of *A to Z*, Stephie's online date turned out to be her ex, Stu (Henry Zebrowski). In the "Emo-tion Caption" episode of the Canadian comedy series *jPod* (2008), Cowboy's (Benjamin Ayres) online hook-up turned out to be his sister, Jennifer (Dena Ashbaugh). In the "The One With Barry and Mindy's Wedding" episode of *Friends*, Chandler's online romance was with his offline ex-girlfriend, Janice (Maggie Wheeler). In the "Sexual Perversity in Cleveland" episode of the sitcom *The Drew Carey Show* (1995–2004), the protagonist (Drew Carey) had cybersex with a woman who turned out to be his colleague and nemesis, Mimi (Kathy Kinney). In the "California Girls" episode of the family-drama *Make It or Break It* (2009–12), Chloe's (Susan Ward) first in-person date was with the father of one of her daughter's gymnastics colleagues. In the "Girl Trouble" episode of *Nash Bridges*, Joe was unaware that the "woman" he was romancing online was Pepe, his office manager. In the television holiday film *A Christmas Song* (2012), teaching colleagues Diana (Natasha Henstridge) and Ken (Gabriel Hogan) only realized that they were matched online—twice—when they meet up for in-person dates. In "The Practice Around the Corner" episode of the British comedy-drama *Doc Martin* (2004–), the first online match that Al (Joe Absolom) met in person was his housemate Morwenna (Jessica Ransom). In fact, the only reason that the two were matched was because they had both lied about their identities:

MORWENNA: You said you were an entrepreneur.
AL: You said you were a doctor.
MORWENA: I said I was a medical professional.

While in these examples identity deception was largely accidental—with screen names concealing both daters' identities—a range of other kinds of identity deceptions transpire on screen.

Couch, Liamputtong and Pitts flagged that "incorrect details about relationship status" was a common form of online dating deceit.[61] Marketing theorists Günter Hitsch, Ali Hortaçsu and Dan Ariely made the same point noting that marital status was the most common thing lied about by men online,[62] and the Pew research cited earlier identified that 20% of men lied about their marital status online. Such deception certainly plays out on screen. In the pilot of the sci-fi series *Mr. Robot* (2015–), it was discovered that Krista's (Gloria Reuben) online beau was married. In *Burn After Reading*, the first man that Linda met online (and then had sex with) was married. The Swedish drama *Miss Kicki* (2009) opened with the title character (Pernilla August) speaking on a webcam to Mr. Chang (Eric Tsang) in Taiwan. Miss Kicki secretly traveled to Taiwan only to discover that Mr. Chang was married. In the "Jenny & Christian" episode of *Dates*, after Jenny (Sheridan Smith) and Christian (Andrew Scott) had sex, Christian's partner, Helen (Amanda Hale), walked in on them. In the gay-themed thriller *Truth* (2013), two men—Caleb (Sean Paul Lockhart) and Jeremy (Rob Moretti)—met via a hook-up app. Caleb neglected to divulge that he had a mental disorder; Jeremy similarly failed to disclose that he was married. Caleb, in fact, turned out to be a psycho and torturer. While infidelity was Caleb's justification for attacking Jeremy, Caleb also illustrates another form of identity deception: undisclosed mental illness. This was a central theme in *The Girl He Met Online*, whereby Gillian neglected to divulge to her online suitors that she was bipolar. In the television thriller *Web of Desire* (2009), Finn (Claudette Mink) had recently been released from a mental institution and wasn't the paramedic she claimed to be to the married couple she seduced online. In the thriller *Net Games* (2003), Adam (C. Thomas Howell) had cybersex with Angel (Lala Sloatman); when he missed their first scheduled phone conversation she became hysterical. When Adam attempted to sever ties, Angela's harassment amplified and he ended up conceding that she was a "fucking psycho." In *The Wife He Met Online*, Georgia (Sydney Penny) and Bryant (Cameron Mathison) meet online; Georgia neglected to divulge her homicidal schizophrenic tendencies. In the "Attack of the Killer Kung-Fu Wolf Bitch" episode of *The Boondocks*, Grandpa got involved with a woman named Luna: she turned out to be a mentally unstable kung-fu master who attacked him and one of his grandsons.

Outside of marital status and mental illness, the screen offers some other—sometimes more madcap—forms of identity deception to exaggerate, if not mock, the deception fears existing off screen. In the Christian-drama *Christian Mingle* (2014), lapsed Christian Gwyneth (Lacey Charbert) pretended to be devout in order to date on the titular website. In the comedy *Can't Hardly Wait* (1998), the nerdy Murphy (Jay Paulson) was under the (erroneous) impression that he was dating the model Christie Turlington online: while unspoken, obviously he had been catfished.[63] In the comedy *A Very Harold & Kumar 3D Christmas* (2011), Kumar's neighbor Adrian (Amir Blumenfeld) had lined up a date with a woman, Mary (Jordan Hinson), whom he had met online by claiming to be Robert Pattinson's acting coach. In the "Date with an Antelope" episode of the animated series *Johnny Bravo* (1997–2004), the title character met "Carol"; Carol turned out to be an antelope. In the "I, Robot ... You, Jane" episode of *Buffy the Vampire Slayer*, Willow's online "boyfriend" Malcolm turned out to be a cyber-demon. In the "Digging the Dirt" episode of the supernatural series *The Gates* (2010), Devon (Chandra West) neglected to divulge to her online suitor that she was actually a witch; she stole his eyes for a spell on their first date. In the "Valentine's Day in Quahog" episode of the animated series *Family Guy* (1999–), Meg's online beau, Toby, stole her kidney. Something similar transpired in the "Girls, Girls, Girls" episode of *Supernatural* where the woman Dean met through the dating app attempted to steal his soul. In the "2Shy" episode of the sci-fi series *The X-Files* (1993–2002), shy, overweight online daters were seduced by Virgil Incanto (Timothy Carhart), a fat-sucking vampire. In the British biopic *UWantMe2KillHim?* (2013), John (Toby Regbo) posed as several characters online including "Rachel" whom he used to seduce his friend Mark (Jamie Blackley), and "Janet" a supposed M15 agent. In the British mini-series *Killer Net* (1998), Scott met "Charlie" (Kathy Brolly) in a chatroom; Charlie turned out to be a liar and a thief and embroiled Scott in a murder. Theft was also a theme in the "Jenny & Nick" episode of *Dates*: Nick's online date, Jenny, was a kleptomaniac who stole his wallet. In the "Jenny & Christian" episode, Jenny stole Christian's wedding ring. Theft was also briefly referenced in the "A Muddy Road" episode of the crime-drama *Fargo* (2014–) when Patty's (Anna Sundberg) online date stole all her panties. In the Canadian drama *The Boy She Met Online* (2010), teen-age Cami (Tracy Spiridakos) met a boy, Jake (Jon Cor), online; Jake, unbe-knownst to her, was a prisoner; "she thinks I go to Penn State not the State Penn," he laughed. As in *Killer Net*, Cami's relationship with Jake culminated in theft, murder and also drugs. In the comedy *The Virginity Hit* (2010), Becca (Savannah Welch) had offered to help with Matt's (Matt Bennett) online virginity-loss quest; Becca was a grad student who was secretly doing a proj-ect on how men are like animals and illicitly filmed Matt doing things such as performing oral sex on a rubber doll. In the drama *Red State* (2011), Jarod (Kyle Gallner) and his friends found a woman through a website—"It's like Craigslist for people who want to get fucked"—and arranged a foursome. When Jarod woke, he found himself caged in the back of a Westboro-esque church, Five Points Trinity: the boys had been drugged, kidnapped and were to be punished for their sins. In the Taiwanese drama *Girl$* (2010), chatrooms were used to organize "paid dates": one of the men who arranged a paid date was a serial killer. This same theme was at the heart of *The Craigslist Killer*.

Akin to gender deception, some of these examples fit with the well-established entertainment motif of mistaken identity: *You've Got Mail*, for example, was a remake of the romantic-comedy *The Shop Around the Corner* (1940), a film based on the play *Illatszertár* (*Parfumerie*) written by Miklós László in 1937. In each narrative, love blossoms between two people already known to each other albeit in a different context. As transpired in *You've Got Mail*, the Internet exists as the perfect device for the mistaken identity narrative to play out: it makes complete sense that with physical separation and the use of screen names, such identity concealments are eas-ily accomplished. Equally, some of these narratives illustrate less accidental and more overt secret identities; themes long-standing in film and television.

The Why of the Lie

In the romantic-comedy *A Cinderella Story* (2004), during one of Sam (Hilary Duff) and Austin's (Chad Michael Murray) first in-person meetings, they had the following exchange:

AUSTIN: You do actually go to North Valley high school, right?
SAM: Of course.
AUSTIN: Well, I'm just checking, you never know with the Internet.

The same *you never know with the Internet* idea was alluded to in the "Body of Evidence" episode of the British crime-drama *New Tricks* (2003–), when the police department's IT expert, Xander (Andy Rush), explained how difficult it is to gauge identity online: "This is the Internet. The cloak of anonymity. Nobody knows who anybody is." A visual representation of the fears alluded to in these scenes was presented in *Chatroom*. Eva (Imogen Poots) had agreed to meet William (Aaron Taylor-Johnson) offline and was shown walking down a long corridor with many rooms leading off it; the corridor is used throughout the film as a metaphor for the many chatroom possibilities whereby scary, often leering characters lurk, akin to a seedy hotel. Eva's fears and vulnerability were a way to visually illustrate the idea that you don't ever really know the people encountered online. In this final section of this chapter, I examine some of the principles underpinning the recurrent theme of deceit in intimacy quests, notably that the medium itself facilitates deception and that the population drawn to using the Internet is by nature deceitful.

A Deceitful Medium

While online anonymity has its charms—Al in *Doc Martin* commented, "It's anonymous so it keeps it interesting," and Temperance in *Bones* noted "I'm enjoying the anonymity"—it also means that concealing things is made effortless: one's name, address, profession, age, appearance, marital status, etc., can all be easily suppressed or outright lied about online.

Anonymity has underpinned discussions of the Internet since the earliest writings about it. While people have indeed been able to be anonymous in personal ads and correspondence in past eras, the Internet makes doing so— frequently and with a vast number of different people—effortless. In fact, some sites use anonymity as a selling point; the infidelity website AshleyMadison. com is one such example, actively promoting "discrete encounters." In their book on truth and the Internet, Whitty and Adam Joinson spotlighted that, "both openness and deceit are encouraged online."[64] While openness leads to hastened intimacy as discussed in earlier chapters, the idea of deceit not merely being facilitated but *encouraged* is important. Earlier I quoted Brian's comments in the "Mikado" episode of *Millennium*, where he noted that he had changed his name, his gender and even his sexual orientation online: doing so was, seemingly, a game for him. More than just being a game, how-ever, it can, in fact, become an addictive pastime. In his book *Love Online*, the philosopher Aaron Ben-Ze'ev noted, "Anonymity is cyberspace can be compared to wearing a mask: in both cases, the sense of anonymity is pow-erful and makes you feel different."[65] Such an idea undoubtedly provides part of the appeal for some of the recreational deceptions that transpired in narratives like *Catfish*, where the motive was less about hurting others and more so about amusing oneself, playing with love and seeing how far a ruse could be taken. Such behavior can also be likened to that of trolls, neckbeards and hackers; screen archetypes I have discussed elsewhere who trade on being able to conceal their identity and to effortlessly create new ones, often purely to entertain themselves.[66]

Deception as a pastime was referenced by the sociologist Dennis Waskul who noted, "As almost everyone knows, the Internet provides a context for extreme fluidity; anyone can be anyone on the Internet."[67] *Fluidity* can refer to gender and sexual orientation, and it also highlights another complexity of deception online: that rather than it simply being a case of "stranger danger," the Internet facilitates a kind of multiple personality dilemma whereby the person encountered online seems real, seems genuine, but in real life is different. Therefore, the concern is not so much about picking real from false, but rather managing the idea of *multiple* realities (Chapter 2).

Another means by which the Internet is plagued by issues of authenticity is the unique nature of cyberspace liaisons; something psychologist Jo Lamble and Sue Morris discussed in their book *Online and Personal*: "As long as the relationship takes place solely online, doubt will always exist as to the truth of the written word."[68] For the reasons explored in Chapter 2, online relationships are often considered *inauthentic*: an aspect of this is that if these dyads play out exclusively on the Internet, then the exchanges are disembodied and will be permanently plagued by the suspicion that deception may be transpiring.

The medium itself of course, can't *make* people be liars, and thus, in line with the idea that people *from the Internet* are somehow different, in this section the idea of those online as more predisposed to lying is explored.

A Deceitful Population

In a 1996 article about online dating from the British newspaper *The Independent*, Christa Worthington discussed "Kerry":

> IRL (in real life), Kerry (not her real name) roller-blades into the Bowery Bar, a cool downtown restaurant in New York, to tell me her story. She is not fat. She is not ugly. She is attractive—a stage performer who moves in arty circles. She left her husband of five years for Jim, whom she met online.[69]

The fact that Worthington felt it necessary to identify that Kerry was not fat or ugly appears to be a reference to widespread presumptions about the typical online dater: that going online to meet people is a last resort for the unfuckable; that Kerry is an outlier, at least according to popular perceptions. As discussed throughout Chapter 3, the popular off and on screen perception is that people who date online are unfuckable losers. A component of this idea, therefore, is that such people have a reason to lie about themselves: that if Internet people are less attractive then they will have an incentive to present themselves otherwise. In Mark Penn and Kinney Zalesne's book *Microtrends*, the authors noted that the stereotype for online daters has long been "people with something to hide."[70] While Penn and Zalesne were speaking in the past tense, as discussed throughout this chapter, the notion of online daters as duplicitous remains a popular real-life trend—some academic research, in fact, identifies that 81% of online daters had actually told at least one lie in their profile, most involving small exaggerations[71]—as well as an enduring presence on screen.

I began this chapter with a discussion of the Internet as a kind of badlands; that bad people are bred there and that bad people use this technology to access and harm others. With this in mind, another consideration for online duplicity on screen is simply because it fits into the techno- and cyberphobias harbored about people who date online. That not only are they less attractive, but that their very nature means they have secrets and ill-intents that get concealed online.

Overblown Deceit

While I have discussed a range of examples where deceit is a key theme in a narrative, it is also important to explore the countercase. A good way this is illustrated on screen is when characters actually exhibit surprise that their date actually looks like their photo, thus countering widely held perceptions about people *from the Internet*. While such scenes are open to interpretation as being about bogeyman assumptions about online daters, equally they can be interpreted as a demonstration that (a) attractive people do actually date online (Chapter 1) and that (b) assumptions of deceit are often unfounded. In the "Two Bodies in the Lab" episode of *Bones*, for example, when Temperance first met David (Coby Ryan McLaughlin) in person he commented, "Your picture doesn't do you justice by the way," to which she responded, "Thank you. Yours either." In the "Jenny & Nick" episode of *Dates*, Nick (Neil Maskell) made a similar comment to Jenny: "your picture doesn't do you justice ... Different in the flesh. Prettier." In *The Wife He Met Online*, Bryant said to Georgia on their first date, "You are even more beautiful in person." In *The Girl He Met Online*, when Gillian first met Andy (Shawn Roberts) offline, Andy commented, "You're even more beautiful in person," to which Gillian replied, "Thank you. I guess you never know with someone you meet online." In *Must Love Dogs*, Jake (John Cusack) similarly was, predictably, very surprised when he met Sarah in person:

JAKE: Why did you write voluptuous? No ... I did not mean to be rude at all. It's just that voluptuous, you know, that tends to go the other way ... It's just one of those words they use in personal ads like rubenesque or weight proportionate to height. Right? ... If a girl says athletic she usually means flat-chested.

In the "Valentine's Day in Quahog" episode of *Family Guy*, when Meg first met her online beau, Toby, in person she remarked, "Wow, you look just like your picture," and Toby similarly responded, "You're much prettier in person." In *A Very Harold & Kumar 3D Christmas* (2011), when Adrian finally met Mary, she exclaimed, "Wow, you look just like your profile pic," to which he responds, "You look better." In *The Virginity Hit*, when Matt first met Becca, he commented, "You look even prettier than the pictures that you sent. You look prettier in real-life." In a scene from the thriller *Untraceable* (2008), Jennifer (Diane Lane) and her colleague Griffin (Colin Hanks) had a conversation about his online dating adventures and the same appearance incredulity was expressed:

GRIFFIN: I'm almost positive that my first date last night is eligible for the hall of fame. She was amazing, she looked exactly like her photo.
JENNIFER: You'll never see her again.
GRIFFIN: How do you know?
JENNIFER: Because you look nothing like yours.

In the horror film *Maniac* (2012), on her first date with Frank (Elijah Wood), Lucie (Megan Duffy) admitted that he was not what she had expected; her imaginings had involved "long black hair and greasy skin full of acne." In *Perfect Romance*, Peter (Henry Ian Cusick) complimented his date Jenny (Lori Heuring), "You're even more beautiful than your photograph."

In each of these examples, assumptions about being lied to proved to be unfounded; in line with research that indicates that while deception might be common online, it rarely involves deceits as large scale as those that often play out on screen. Sociologist Jean-Claude Kaufman addressed this issue, identifying:

> Anyone who is looking for a proper date is caught up in a logic of self-expression, and that encourages a minimal degree of honesty. They do tinker with the facts, but only to a limited extent. They know that if they cheat too much, they will pay for it sooner or later. The "misleading advertising" argument is therefore grossly over-stated. It is often a way of masking the fact that we are the source of the problem.[72]

Oyer made a similar point, noting that very few people tell bold lies: most center on things such as a few more inches, a few less pounds or years.[73]

It is also worth considering that sometimes people actually *want* to be deceived.[74] In Chapter 2, I explored the potential for online-only relationships to be construed as *more real* because reality wasn't impinging on a liaison. It is thus reasonable to presume that—particularly for relationships where an offline meeting will never transpire—some people *want* to imagine their partner as young and attractive; that with the relationship playing out predominantly in the participants' heads, that they would in fact *rather* the input be positive rather than necessarily truthful.

This chapter has examined the concept of deception transpiring in online quests for intimacy. Chapter 5 moves the discussion toward intimacy quests centered primarily on sex.

Notes

1. Al Cooper, "Sexuality and the Internet: Surfing into the New Millennium," *CyberPsychology & Behavior*, 1 (1998): 187–93.
2. Such themes have an extensive screen history, for example in the US films *Shadow of a Doubt* (1943), *Lured* (1947), *Monsieur Verdoux* (1947), *The Honeymoon Killers* (1969), *Sea of Love* (1989) and *Lonely Hearts* (2006), in the French films *Pièges (Personal Column)* (1939) and *Landru (Bluebeard)* (1963), in the Mexican film *Profundo Carmesí (Deep Crimson)* (1996) and in the Belgian film *Alleluia* (2014).
3. John Perry Barlow, "Crime and Puzzlement," *Whole Earth Review*, Fall (1990): 44–47, 45.
4. The Internet is linked to the Wild West in a range of reports, including recent ones: "Internet Is Rife with Fraud and as Lawless as Wild West, Warn Peers," *The Times* (London), August 10, 2007, 5; Jana Kasperkevic, "Cord Cutters on Net Neutrality," *The Guardian*, February 22, 2015. Accessed July 25, 2015, from http://www.theguardian.com/technology/2015/feb/22/cord-cutters-net-neutrality-end-wild-wild-west-nternet; Nicole Perlroth and David E. Sanger, "Obama Calls for New Cooperation to Wrangle the 'Wild West' Internet," *The New York Times*, February 13, 2015. Accessed July 25, 2015, from http://www.nytimes.com/2015/02/14/business/obama-urges-tech-companies-to-cooperate-on-internet-security.html?_r=0; Eric T. Schneiderman, "Taming the Digital Wild West," *Westchester County Business Journal*, May 5, 2015. Accessed July 25, 2015, from LexisNexis. Worth noting, this Wild West idea is also apparent in a range of books and journal articles: David Allweiss, "Copyright Infringement on the Internet: Can the Wild, Wild West Be Tamed," *Touro Law Review*, 15, 3 (1999): 1005–52; Robert W. Pearce and Cherie W. Blackburn, "'Wild, Wild West' of the Internet Collides with Trademark Law," *South Carolina Business Journal*, 19, 3 (2000): 7–10; Mark Franek, "Foiling Cyberbullies in the New Wild West," *Educational Leadership*, 63, 4 (2005): 39–43; Michael Fertik and David Thompson, *Wild West 2.0.: How to Protect and Restore Your Online Reputation on the Untamed Social Frontier* (New York: American Management Association, 2010).
5. John Arquilla and David Ronfeldt, *In Athena's Camp: Preparing for Conflict in the Information Age* (Santa Monica, CA: RAND, 1997), 242.
6. Russell Kay, "DeepWeb", *Computerworld*, December 19, 2005: 28.
7. Later in the film, the same criminal bogeyman fears were articulated when Joe (Tom Hanks)—Kathleen's Internet beau, although unbeknownst to her at that time—speculated that her online correspondent was probably "Mr 152 felony indictments."
8. William Webb, *The HTTP Murders: 15 Cyber Killers You Never Want to Meet Online* (Anaheim, CA: Absolute Crime Books, 2013), 31.

9. "Baby Found Alive; Woman Arrested," *CNN*, December 18, 2004. Accessed July 15, 2015, from http://www.cnn.com/2004/US/12/18/fetus.found.alive/index.html?eref=sitesearch.

10. Maureen Orth, "Killer@Craigslist," *Vanity Fair*, October 2009. Accessed July 15, 2015, from http://www.vanityfair.com/culture/2009/10/craigslist-murder200910.

11. Tracie Egan Morrissey, "Satan, Rape and Murder: The Life of Miranda Barbour, Craigslist Killer," *Jezebel*, February 21, 2014. Accessed July 15, 2015, from http://jezebel.com/satan-rape-and-murder-the-life-of-miranda-barbour-cr-1526169756.

12. Fiona Gartland, "Graham Dwyer and Elaine O'Hara: The Master-Slave Relationship," *The Irish Times*, March 30, 2015. Accessed July 15, 2015, from http://www.irishtimes.com/news/crime-and-law/graham-dwyer-and-elaine-o-hara-the-master-slave-relationship-1.2156173.

13. Mark Russell, "Rapist Jason John Dinsley on Parole When He Beat Sharon Siermans to Death with Cricket Bat," *The Age*, December 20, 2013. Accessed July 15, 2015, from http://www.theage.com.au/victoria/rapist-jason-john-dinsley-on-parole-when-he-beat-sharon-siermans-to-death-with-cricket-bat-20131219-2zoqq.html.

14. Kristian Silva, "Gable Tostee Granted Bail but Banned from Tinder," *Brisbane Times*, November 19, 2014. Accessed July 27, 2015, from http://www.brisbanetimes.com.au/queensland/gable-tostee-granted-bail-but-banned-from-tinder-20141119-11po6s.html.

15. Nick Paumgarten, "Looking for Someone," *The New Yorker*, July 4, 2011. Accessed July 26, 2015, from http://www.newyorker.com/magazine/2011/07/04/looking-for-someone.

16. George Gerbner, "Toward 'Cultural Indicators': The Analysis of Mass Mediated Message Systems," in *The Analysis of Communication Content: Developments in Scientific Theories and Computer Techniques*, eds. George Gerbner, Ole R. Holsti, Klaus Krippendorf, William J. Paisley and Philip J. Stone (New York: John Wiley, 1969); George Gerbner and Larry Gross, "Living with Television: The Violence Profile," *Journal of Communication*, 26, 2 (1976): 173–99.

17. Lauren Rosewarne, "Don't Blame Stephanie Scott's Murder on the Internet," *ABC The Drum*, April 15, 2015. Accessed April 30, 2015, from http://www.abc.net.au/news/2015-04-15/rosewarne-dont-blame-stephanie-scotts-murder-on-the-internet/6394560.

18. Kerry Daynes, "Is There a Psychopath in Your Inbox?", *The Telegraph*, February 2, 2012. Accessed July 15, 2015, from http://www.telegraph.co.uk/lifestyle/9064008/Is-there-a-psychopath-in-your-inbox.html.

19. Kaffie Sledge, "Psychos Lurk Online," *Columbus Ledger-Enquirer*, March 13, 2003. Accessed July 15, 2015, from LexisNexis.

20. Bruce Wilson, "Weirdos Are Online and Out of Control," *The Daily Telegraph*, January 20, 2001. Accessed July 15, 2015, from LexisNexis.

21. Lauren Rosewarne, *Cyberbullies, Cyberactivists, Cyberpredators: Film, TV, and Internet Stereotypes* (Santa Barbara, CA: Praeger, 2016).

22. The character Mercer makes a comment about this in the novel *The Circle*: "the world has dorkified itself" (Dave Eggers, *The Circle* [New York: Vintage Books, 2013], 133).

23. Lauren Rosewarne, *Part-Time Perverts: Sex, Pop Culture and Kink Management* (Santa Barbara, CA: Praeger, 2011).

24. In Christyne Berzsenyi, "Writing to Meet Your Match: Rhetoric and Self-Presentation for Four Online Daters," *Innovative Methods and Technologies for Electronic Discourse Analysis*, ed. Hewee Ling Lim (Hershey, PA: Information Science Reference, 2014): 210–34, 228.

25. Adam Kotsko, *Creepiness* (Alresford, Hants: Zero Books, 2015), 26.

26. Adam Kotsko, *Creepiness* (Alresford, Hants: Zero Books, 2015), 26.

27. Research on cyberbullying explores these ideas in greater depth. Psychologists Robin Kowalski, Sue Limber and Patricia Agatston, for example, discussed how not being able to see a victim makes disengaging morally and unguiltily from a situation easier: bullying "occurs via technology, as opposed to via face-to-face interactions, perpetrators cannot see the emotional reactions of their victims" (Robin M. Kowalski, Sue Limber and Patricia W. Agatston, *Cyberbullying: Bullying in the Digital Age* [Malden, MA: Wiley-Blackwell, 2012], 87).

28. Kendall R. Phillips, *Projected Fears: Horror Films and American Culture* (Westport, CT: Praeger, 2005), 132–33.

29. Tea Krulos, *Monster Hunters: On the Trail with Ghost Hunters, Bigfooters, Ufologists, and Other Paranormal Investigators* (Chicago, IL: Chicago Review Press, 2015), 268.

30. Caitlin Dewey, "The Complete, Terrifying History of 'Slender Man,' the Internet Meme That Compelled Two 12-Year-Olds to Stab Their Friend," *The Washington Post*, June 3, 2014. Accessed July 15, 2015, from https://www.washingtonpost.com/news/the-intersect/wp/2014/06/03/the-complete-terrifying-history-of-slender-man-the-internet-meme-that-compelled-two-12-year-olds-to-stab-their-friend/.

31. Caitlin Dewey, "The Complete, Terrifying History of 'Slender Man,' the Internet Meme That Compelled Two 12-Year-Olds to Stab Their Friend," *The Washington Post*, June 3, 2014. Accessed July 15, 2015, from https://www.washingtonpost.com/news/the-intersect/wp/2014/06/03/the-complete-terrifying-history-of-slender-man-the-internet-meme-that-compelled-two-12-year-olds-to-stab-their-friend/.

32. John C. Bridges, *The Illusion of Intimacy: Problems in the World of Online Dating* (Santa Barbara, CA: Praeger, 2012), 43. This "only game in town" idea was verbalized in an unnamed episode of the lesbian-themed Scottish series *Lip Service* (2010–12): Frankie (Ruta Gedmintas) suggested online dating to Tess (Fiona Button), Tess declined, and Frankie remarked, "What's the alternative?" Her comment implies that nowadays online dating is the default way to find companionship.

33. Kristina Grish, *The Joy of Text: Mating, Dating, and Techno-Relating* (New York: Simon Spotlight Entertainment, 2006), 123.

34. Monica T. Whitty and Adrian N. Carr, *Cyberspace Romance: The Psychology of Online Relationships* (New York: Palgrave Macmillan, 2006), 1.

35. Mary Madden and Amanda Lenhart, "Online Dating" (Washington: Pew Internet, 2006). Accessed January 18, 2015, from http://www.pewinternet.org/2006/03/05/online-dating/.

36. In Danielle Couch, Pranee Liamputtong and Marian Pitts, "What Are the Real and Perceived Risks and Dangers of Online Dating? Perspectives from Online Daters," *Health, Risk & Society*, 14, 7–8 (2012): 697–714, 708.

37. John C. Bridges, *The Illusion of Intimacy: Problems in the World of Online Dating* (Santa Barbara, CA: Praeger, 2012), 40.

38. Lauren Rosewarne, *Cyberbullies, Cyberactivists, Cyberpredators: Film, TV, and Internet Stereotypes* (Santa Barbara, CA: Praeger, 2016).
39. This same idea was referenced in an unnamed episode of the lesbian-themed Scottish series *Lip Service* (2010–12) when Tess (Fiona Button)—who had just started online dating—remarked, "You should look at some of these girls. Most of them are just desperate hets after a free lezzie floorshow." One date that Tess goes on actually does involve her inadvertently performing in a "free lezzie floorshow" when it turned out that her date had a husband who wanted to watch.
40. Jeffrey T. Hancock, "Digital Deception: Why, When and How People Lie Online," in *Oxford Handbook of Internet Psychology*, eds. Adam Joinson, Katelyn McKenna, Tom Postmes and Ulf-Dietrich Reips (New York: Oxford University Press, 2009): 289–302, 291.
41. Lindsy Van Gelder, "The Strange Case of the Electronic Lover," in *Computerization and Controversy: Value Conflicts and Social Choices*, eds. Charles Dunlop and Rob Kling (New York: Academic Press, 1991): 533–46.
42. Patricia Wallace, *The Psychology of the Internet* (New York: Cambridge University Press, 1999), 47.
43. Stefan Stieger, Tina Eichinger and Britta Honeder, "Can Mate Choice Strategies Explain Sex Differences? The Deceived Persons' Feelings in Reaction to Revealed Online Deception of Sex, Age, and Appearance," *Social Psychology*, 40, 1 (2009): 16–25, 16.
44. Monica T. Whitty, "Liar, Liar! An Examination of How Open, Supportive, and Honest People Are in Chat Rooms," *Computers in Human Behavior*, 18 (2002): 343–52.
45. Elizabeth Reis, "Impossible Hermaphrodites: Intersex in America, 1620–1960," *Journal of American History*, 92, 2 (2005): 411–41.
46. Michael S. Kimmel, "Masculinity as Homophobia: Fear, Shame and Silence in the Construction of Gender Identity," in *Gender Relations in Global Perspective: Essential Readings*, ed. Nancy Cook (Toronto: Canadian Scholars' Press, 2007): 73–82.
47. Willard Gaylin, *The Male Ego* (New York: Viking, 1992); Francis Mark Mondimore, *A Natural History of Homosexuality* (Baltimore, MD: The John Hopkins University Press, 1996).
48. Another example of this is Peter Steiner's 1993 cartoon published in *The New Yorker* where a dog is seated at a computer, captioned by the text "On the Internet, nobody knows you're a dog."
49. Paul Oyer, *Everything I Needed to Know about Economics I Learned from Online Dating* (Boston, MA: Harvard Business Review Press, 2014), 26.
50. Jessica E. Donn and Richard C. Sherman, "Attitudes and Practices Regarding the Formation of Romantic Relationships on the Internet," *CyberPsychology & Behavior*, 5, 2 (2002): 107–23.
51. Jennifer L. Gibbs, Nicole B. Ellison and Rebecca D. Heino, "Self-Presentation in Online Personals: The Role of Anticipated Future Interaction, Self-Disclosure, and Perceived Success in Internet Dating," *Communication Research*, 33, 2 (2006): 152–77.
52. Danielle Couch, Pranee Liamputtong and Marian Pitts, "What Are the Real and Perceived Risks and Dangers of Online Dating? Perspectives from Online Daters," *Health, Risk & Society*, 14, 7–8 (2012): 697–714, 702.

53. Jeffrey T. Hancock, Catalina Toma and Nicole Ellison, "The Truth about Lying in Online Dating Profiles," *CHI 2007 Proceedings* (2007): 449–52. Accessed July 25, 2015, from https://msu.edu/~nellison/hancock_et_al_2007.pdf.

54. Stefan Stieger, Tina Eichinger and Britta Honeder, "Can Mate Choice Strategies Explain Sex Differences? The Deceived Persons' Feelings in Reaction to Revealed Online Deception of Sex, Age, and Appearance," *Social Psychology*, 40, 1 (2009): 16–25, 17.

55. Paul Oyer, *Everything I Needed to Know about Economics I Learned from Online Dating* (Boston, MA: Harvard Business Review Press, 2014), 170.

56. The thriller *Perfect Stranger* (2007) provided a similar example of this whereby Miles (Giovanni Ribisi) pretended online to be Rowena's (Halle Berry) boss, Harrison (Bruce Willis), in order to get closer to her.

57. Dore Hollander, "Among Young Adults, Use of the Internet to Find Sexual Partners Is Rising," *Perspectives on Sexual and Reproductive Health*, 34, 6 (2002), 134–46.

58. Jeffrey T. Hancock, Catalina Toma and Nicole Ellison, "The Truth about Lying in Online Dating Profiles," *CHI 2007 Proceedings* (2007): 449–52. Accessed July 25, 2015, from https://msu.edu/~nellison/hancock_et_al_2007.pdf.

59. Benjamin Cornwell and David C. Lundgren, "Love on the Internet: Involvement and Misrepresentation in Romantic Relationships in Cyberspace vs. Realspace," *Computers in Human Behavior*, 17 (2001): 197–211.

60. Ethel Quayle and Max Taylor, *Child Pornography: An Internet Crime* (New York: Routledge, 2003); Dennis Howitt and Kerry Sheldon, *Sex Offenders and the Internet* (Hoboken, NJ: John Wiley & Sons, 2007); Richard Wortley and Stephen Smallbone, *Internet Child Pornography: Causes, Investigation, and Prevention* (Santa Barbara, CA: Praeger, 2012); Michael C. Seto, *Internet Sex Offenders* (Washington DC: American Psychological Association, 2013).

61. Danielle Couch, Pranee Liamputtong and Marian Pitts, "What Are the Real and Perceived Risks and Dangers of Online Dating? Perspectives from Online Daters," *Health, Risk & Society*, 14, 7–8 (2012): 697–714, 702.

62. Günter J. Hitsch, Ali Hortaçsu and Dan Ariely, "What Makes You Click: Mate Preferences in Online Dating," *Quantitative Marketing and Economics*, 8, 4 (2010): 393–427.

63. I discuss cyberpredator impersonation elsewhere (Lauren Rosewarne, *Cyberbullies, Cyberactivists, Cyberpredators: Film, TV, and Internet Stereotypes* [Santa Barbara, CA: Praeger, 2016]).

64. Monica T. Whitty and Adam N. Joinson, *Truth, Lies and Trust on the Internet* (New York: Routledge, 2009), 1.

65. Aaron Ben-Ze'ev, *Love Online: Emotions on the Internet* (New York: Cambridge University Press, 2004), 37.

66. Lauren Rosewarne, *Cyberbullies, Cyberactivists, Cyberpredators: Film, TV, and Internet Stereotypes* (Santa Barbara, CA: Praeger, 2016).

67. Dennis D. Waskul, *Self-Games and Body-Play: Personhood in Online Chat and Cyberspace* (New York: Peter Lang, 2003), 26.

68. Jo Lamble and Sue Morris, *Online and Personal: The Reality of Internet Relationships* (Sydney: Finch, 2001), 8.

69. Christa Worthington, "Making Love in Cyberspace," *The Independent* (October 6, 1996). Accessed June 30, 2014, from http://www.independent.co.uk/arts-entertainment/making-love-in-cyberspace-1356977.html.

70. Mark Penn and E. Kinney Zalesne, *Microtrends: The Small Forces Behind Tomorrow's Big Changes* (New York: Twelve, 2007), 22.
71. Jeffrey T. Hancock, Catalina Toma and Nicole Ellison, "Separating Fact from Fiction: An Examination of Deceptive Self-Presentation in Online Dating Profiles," *Personality and Social Psychology Bulletin*, 34, 8 (2008): 1023–36.
72. Jean-Claude Kaufmann, *Love Online* (Malden, MA: Polity, 2012), 34.
73. Paul Oyer, *Everything I Needed to Know about Economics I Learned from Online Dating* (Boston, MA: Harvard Business Review Press, 2014).
74. Lauren Rosewarne, "Happily, Willingly Manipulated," *The Conversation*, April 23, 2015. Accessed July 29, 2015, from https://theconversation.com/happily-willingly-manipulated-40710.

5   Seeking Stimulation Online

This chapter focuses on the Internet's role in the arrangement, participation in and maintenance of physical intimacy. While intercourse is obviously a key component of this—with characters turning to online dating and hook-up apps to arrange offline liaisons—in fact, the Internet assists with physical intimacy in a range of ways, notably catering to sexual needs exclusively within the parameters of cyberspace.

This chapter begins with a discussion of perhaps the most obvious of online sexual offerings: netporn. I present the case that self-stimulation is a kind of intimacy, albeit with the self, and that masturbation can constitute its own kind of sexuality. I then examine the role of the Internet in facilitating intercourse substitutions: while netporn-aided masturbation is one example, so too is cybersex. Finally, this chapter explores the Internet as an accoutrement in existing relationships, aiding, for example, couples who are geographically separated to maintain physical connection.

The Internet Is for Porn[1]

In the "Body of Evidence" episode of the British crime-drama *New Tricks* (2003–), one of the investigators, Gerry (Dennis Waterman), remarked, "In our day, we had to brave the top shelf and disapproving newsagents. But now, you can get an eyeful of anything and you don't have to leave the house. And it's free." Here, Gerry spotlights a changed landscape where, because of the Internet, porn has become more popular, more accessible and more acceptable and gets delivered to your house, your office, *your phone*, completely free of charge. In popular media the inextricable link between the Internet and porn is made repeatedly, whereby the technology is often framed as primarily being about transmitting explicit content; something encapsulated in an exchange between Jay (Jason Mewes) and Holden (Ben Affleck) in the comedy *Jay and Silent Bob Strike Back* (2001):

JAY: What the fuck is the Internet?
HOLDEN: The Internet is a communications tool used the world over. Where people can come together to bitch about movies and share pornography.

In this scene—and in a range of others discussed in this section—the Internet is framed as being inextricably linked to porn; both as a place awash with it, as well as today's default distribution method. In the 2002 "I Am Furious Yellow" episode of the animated series *The Simpsons* (1989–), for instance, Bart established a website featuring a mocking cartoon of his father, Homer. The site went viral—something Homer discussed with his colleagues:

CARL: [to Homer] You're the Internet's number one non-porno site!
LENNY: Which makes you ten-trillionth overall.

In the "The Great Wife Hope" episode of the same series, the same porn-everywhere idea is referenced in an exchange between Luanne and Marge at a bowling alley:

LUANNE: How did you ever come up with an idea like "crazy bowling"?
MARGE: I Googled "girls having fun," and after wading through 97,000 pages of porn, I found "crazy bowling."

In the "My Brother, Where Art Thou?" episode of the sitcom *Scrubs* (2001–10), this idea is again apparent in Dr. Cox's (John C. McGinley) quip, "I'm fairly sure if they took porn off the Internet, there'd only be one website left, and it'd be called 'Bring Back the Porn!'" In the "Babies & Bathwater" episode of the medical-drama *House* (2004–12), the title character (Hugh Laurie) explained why he wasn't in his office: "Because there is a computer in my office. If I log on, romance will ensue. My wrist might fall off." In the "Exam Time" episode of the British series *The Inbetweeners* (2008–10), the teenager Neil (Blake Harrison) observed: "I don't think I've ever been on the Internet and not ended up having a wank." In the "A Big Piece of Garbage" episode of the animated series *Futurama* (1999–2013), Fry—a present-day character transported to the future—reflected, "In my day the Internet was only used to download pornography," an observation apparently also accurate well into the future; as Professor Farnsworth countered, "Actually that's *still* true." In an exchange in the comedy *The Virginity Hit* (2010), teenager Matt (Matt Bennett)—who was on an online-advertised quest to lose his virginity—discussed some of the offers of "help" he had received with his friend Zack (Zack Pearlman):

MATT: Strangers kill other strangers.
ZACK: Strangers also blow other strangers. You're not making sense … This is exactly why God invented the Internet.
MATT: He invented the Internet for porn.

Each of these examples helps to reiterate—if not normalize—the idea that the Internet's biggest contribution to culture is sexually explicit content.

The majority of the scenes discussed thus far help to illustrate a point that I make in my book *Masturbation in Pop Culture: Screen, Society, Self,* whereby film and television persistently contend that the Internet is full of porn—that such material is consumed heartily—but simultaneously keeps largely silent about how the material gets used. While in the examples discussed thus far, porn-without-masturbation is spoken about rather than shown, the "Chapter 23" episode of the political-drama *House of Cards* (2013–) presented this idea visually. Francis (Kevin Spacey) was watching netporn on his laptop and while he eventually got caught—a standard trope in porn and masturbation-themed scenes[2]—he actually wasn't masturbating; he was just consuming the material like any other media. While there are a variety of reasons for this masturbation-avoidance portrayal— for example, (a) that porn has become a metonym for autoeroticism and thus, for reasons including taste and classification, it doesn't always need to be shown for the reference to be noted; and (b) continued cultural discomfort with speaking frankly about sexual matters[3]—worth noting is that with porn now so prevalent, and with *pornification* exemplified by sexual imagery widely apparent throughout the mainstream (Chapter 6), it is worth acknowledging that not every encounter with porn will lead to masturbation anyway. Arguably, as the *House of Cards* episode illustrated, in some contexts porn can just be consumed like any other kind of media.[4]

The aforementioned *House* and *The Inbetweeners* episodes, however, both provide a deviation from the masturbation-avoidance idea, demonstrating that sometimes porn and masturbation do actually get verbally coupled on screen and that sometimes the sexual arousal objective of such material is in fact revealed, in the process linking the Internet to porn, and in turn, the Internet to masturbation.

Before I explore the netporn-masturbation screen coupling, it is important to examine the interplay between masturbation and intimacy. In most literature, these two ideas are not merely viewed as separate, but in fact, masturbation is often considered to *thwart* authentic intimacy, to sabotage established romantic relationships and to inhibit the formation of new ones. Equally, masturbation is frequently framed on screen—and in society more broadly—as a lackluster substitute for intercourse. This isn't, however, the only interpretation. In *Masturbation in Pop Culture* I proposed the capacity for masturbation to be considered "not about a *lack* of something or a substitute for someone, nor is it about acting in opposition to heterosexuality, homosexuality or necessarily even about disrupting social norms, but that it is simply *another kind* of sexuality."[5] In line with this proposition, I would consider that masturbation is able to be interpreted as intimacy *with oneself*; as a kind of self-love making.[6] In that book I explored a range of screen presentations where masturbation is presented as a relaxation aid, a sedative and a mood enhancer and where time spent self-stimulating is framed as having positive physical and psychological benefits, in turn, sharing many qualities with physical intimacy had with another person. While the psychologists Steven Solomon and Lorie Teagno coined the term *self-intimacy* in reference to self-awareness and self-care and don't actually discuss masturbation,[7] I suggest that the term has relevance in the context of getting to know one's own body and in self-generating pleasure, hence the relevance for including masturbation in a discussion about intimacy. While this is not an area that has received extensive academic attention, the reality of it has nonetheless been referenced. In a case discussed by sex researchers Sandra Leiblum and Nicola Döring, for example, a woman used cybersex to overcome her embarrassment about her genitals: "I let myself be the sexual being I am and let myself enjoy the pleasure my body was capable of without embarrassment or shame. What freedom! What power! I slew a dragon!"[8] For this woman, the Internet—and, notably, the associated masturbation—seemingly enabled her to experience her sexuality in ways that she had been too ashamed to do previously; the Internet facilitated her *self-intimacy*.

In *Masturbation in Pop Culture* I conceded that on screen the depiction of masturbation as *another kind of sexuality* is relatively uncommon. When the act is depicted it is invariably used to reveal something disparaging about the character and most often—particularly when netporn is alluded to—injects themes of desperation, loneliness, addiction or depravity into a narrative. Rarely is autoeroticism a display of personal sexual liberation. Those rare times when masturbation is depicted as self-intimacy—most commonly, for example, in narratives where women self-stimulate—masturbation is presented as something "natural," as something woman-centered, if not *feminist*, and thus distinctly separate from netporn. This idea alludes to a broader gender difference between male and female masturbation portrayals: commonly women do it in the shower or bathtub, their only fuel being their romantic fantasies; men, conversely, frequently use an accoutrement like netporn. Such a display subtly presents men as more visually stimulated, if not also as more perverted and depraved. Exceptions to the perverted male masturbator stereotype do exist, however: a common one involves young male characters self-stimulating, for example, Alo (Will Merrick) in the "Alo" episode of the British drama *Skins* (2007–13), or Adam (Gabriel Basso) in the "Blue-Eyed Iris" episode of the comedy-drama *The Big C* (2010–13). In these examples, netporn-aided masturbation is less a way to convey perversion and instead is part of a *coming-of-age* story—this boy has now become a man.[9]

While arguably any character going online for material to masturbate to is engaged in a (self-)intimacy quest, for teenage characters waiting for an opportunity for intercourse, masturbation explicitly functions to help *tide them over*, an idea verbalized in dialogue between adolescents Kurt (Chris Colfer) and Blaine (Darren Criss) in the "Because Of The Layers" episode of the comedy-drama series *Glee* (2009–15). The duo had just started dating but had not yet had sex:

KURT: I'm just wondering have you ever had the urge to just rip off each other's clothes and get dirty?

BLAINE: Ah, yeah. But that's why they invented masturbation.

In *Masturbation in Pop Culture* I identified characters in a range of narratives—for example, in the aforementioned episodes of *Skins* and the *Big C*, as well as in *South Park* (1997–), *Family Guy* (1999–), *Two and a Half Men* (2003–), *Queer as Folk* (2000–2005), *Californication* (2007–14), *Being Erica* (2009–11) and *The League* (2009–) and in films including *Little Children* (2006), *2:37* (2006), *Afterschool* (2008), *Control Alt Delete* (2008), *Girl$* (2010), *Shame* (2011), *American Reunion* (2012), *Don Jon* (2013), *Thanks for Sharing* (2012), *Men, Women & Children* (2014) and *Wish I Was Here* (2014)—where characters masturbated while looking at netporn. As discussed, a common way to think about masturbation is it serving as a substitute: that self-sex is engaged in when the preferred kind of intimacy—*intercourse*—is unavailable. While unavailable sex is generally framed as acceptable for teenagers who are just beginning their sex lives, for adult characters an inability to access sex has connotations of desperation; that they are unfuckable and thus have had to *resort* to autoeroticism due to their paucity of other options. This concept quite obviously has a strong connection to the way online daters are portrayed (Chapter 3). In both cases, characters using a *computer* to cater to their intimate lives are framed as having failed to do what is expected to come naturally.

Just as the screen has a propensity to demonize the online dater—framing him or her, commonly, as either a loser (Chapter 3) or as dangerous (Chapter 4)—the netporn-masturbator gets similarly demonized; something that transpires on screen in a range of ways. Mentioned in the context of Francis in *House of Cards* was the notion of characters being walked in on during masturbation; while Francis wasn't actually "caught in the act," this does happen in other examples, in turn frequently (albeit subtly) demonizing both porn and masturbation by framing exposure as humiliating and shameful. In the drama *Don Jon*, the title character (Joseph Gordon-Levitt) is caught watching netporn by his girlfriend, Barbara (Scarlett Johansson), who brands the material as "sick" and Jon's consumption of it as "fucking disgusting." The verbalization of netporn consumption as disgusting transpires in a variety of screen examples. In the television drama *Cyber Seduction: His Secret Life* (2005), teen characters watch netporn. It is only, however, when the protagonist, Justin (Jeremy Supter), begins to consume progressively kinkier material that his friends began to articulate their disgust; "That stuff's way too twisted. Dude, you're getting scuzzy." Justin's friends accuse him of liking the real "freaky stuff" and eventually dub him "kinky the clown." In the drama *Disconnect* (2012), when Cindy (Paula Patton) and her husband Derek (Alexander Skarsgård) have their identities stolen, they initiate a private investigation into the man they deemed responsible, Stephen (Michael Nyqvist). As part of their inquiry, they combed through Stephen's bank statements to identify patterns of purchasing behavior:

DEREK: Look at this, look at this. Pay for view charge. Adult entertainment. $59.
CINDY: In one month?
DEREK: Yeah in one month. I knew he was a creep.

In *Disconnect*, consumption of netporn not only positions Stephen as a "creep" but apparently makes it more believable that he would also be a criminal; a theme identifiable in other examples. In the British mini-series *The Escape Artist* (2013), a central reason that Liam Foyle (Toby Kebbell) was suspected of committing a vicious murder was his enjoyment of violent porn. In the "Aftermath: Part 1" episode of the British police-drama *DCI Banks* (2010–), this link exists beyond mere conjecture: a man who had imprisoned women in his home was also revealed to be in possession of "extreme" netporn. This theme is also part of the plot of the drama *Afterschool*: the film opened with the teenager Robert (Ezra Miller) masturbating to porn involving strangulation; by the end of the narrative Robert had committed murder.

Don *Jon* and *Cyber Seduction: His Secret Life*, along with the drama *Shame*, each allude to another way that the netporn-masturbator gets demonized: through addiction. While addiction haunted the earliest writings about radio and then television and thus it is no surprise that it has plagued the Internet since the beginning,[10] a subcategory is *netporn addiction*. In a variety of narratives, netporn enters a narrative on the basis of its role in an addiction storyline; that it can't just casually be consumed as Francis did in *House of Cards*, but rather is used compulsively and becomes an instigator for a range of social problems and serves as a screen union between the techno- and cyberphobia literature and the radical feminist porn-harm rhetoric.[11]

In the "All Better Now" episode of the drama series *Queer as Folk* (2000–2005), Ted's (Scott Lowell) interest in netporn and self-intimacy was so fervent that he gets fired for watching it (and masturbating) at work. The same thing happens to Charlie (Evan Handler) in "The Great Ashby" episode of the drama series *Californication* (2007–14). While Ted's porn penchant gets channelled into establishing his own porn site, Charlie's addiction is more complicated. In the "Boys and Girls" episode of the series, for example, the character divulged, "I have been watching so much porn on the Internet lately that I've been seeking so much sexual gratification that it's like I don't even know how to relate to real women anymore." Charlie's inability to *relate to real women* is a theme apparent in other examples, whereby netporn and masturbation are framed as *thwarting* interpersonal intimacy and, more so, turning men into sex machines,[12] if not monsters. In *Cyber Seduction: His Secret Life*, as a result of Justin's increased netporn consumption, he begins to compulsively sexualize his female class-mates, something he didn't do prior to using porn. In the drama *Thanks for Sharing*, the film opens with Adam (Mark Ruffalo) walking through Manhattan. The character is constantly distracted by the female models in outdoor advertisements and the women walking on the street, casting them in sexual scenarios. His sexualizing is later revealed as linked to his porn-fueled sex addiction. In the Christian-drama *Uphill Battle* (2013), Erica's (Shelby Smith) ex-husband was addicted to pornography which led him, apparently, into infidelity, domestic abuse and then divorce. In *Don Jon*, Jon leaves Barbara in bed alone to watch netporn; in doing so Jon verbalizes a preference for it, identifying, "Real pussy's all good. But I'm sorry, it's not as good as porn." Jon's relationship with Barbara ends as a result of his disinclination to stop watching. In the Christian-drama *The Saber* (2007), Cameron's (Zac Klammer) netporn addiction leads to his expulsion from the military academy and the cessation of his relationship with his fiancé. The same subject matter was at the heart of the Christian-drama *Fireproof* (2008), where netporn addiction pushed Caleb (Kirk Cameron) and his wife Catherine (Erin Bethea) to the brink of divorce. In *Cyber Seduction: His Secret Life*, Beth (Briony Glassco), a friend of Justin's mom, Diane (Kelly Lynch), also attributed netporn to the split with her husband:

BETH: We stopped having sex. You know, I thought it was getting routine, so I tried to spice it up and he went into the den. The computer is in the den. Four in the morning I go in there and he's surfing porn and ... [cringes].
DIANE: What did you do?
BETH: I couldn't say anything, was too embarrassed. I was so hurt. I just turned around and went back to bed. I wanted us to do some therapy but he said there wasn't a problem ... He would stay up all night and watch that stuff but he couldn't bear to touch me. A real thing lying in the next room ...

Compulsive netporn was also named as a reason for a marriage breakdown in the drama series *Tell Me You Love Me* (2007).

In *Shame*, the sex addict protagonist, Brandon (Michael Fassbender), was so preoccupied with netporn and sex with prostitutes that when it came to having sex with a female colleague whom he had developed feelings for, he was unable to get erect. This kind of physical consequence is used in numer-ous examples to demonize explicit material and also, seemingly, to demon-strate awareness of the porn-harm arguments repeated in contemporary literature.[13] In the Canadian romantic-comedy *Love, Sex and Eating the Bones* (2003), Michael (Hill Harper) was addicted to netporn and when he and his girlfriend Jasmine (Marlyne Barrett) were about to have sex for the first time, like Brandon, he could not get hard. In *Men, Women & Children*, the netporn-addicted teenager, Chris (Travis Tope), was about to have sex for the first time and similarly he could not perform. These characters—these *men*[14]—are presented as being physically and psychologically damaged by netporn. They are presented as tragic figures of the Internet age where netporn has sabotaged their chance for real interpersonal intimacy, in line with the arguments apparent throughout porn-harm literature.[15]

Although these narratives work to demonize netporn—as well as the Internet as a delivery system—they are also indicative of the screen's presentation of netporn-aided self-intimacy as problematic and, in turn, frame intimacy with another person as the ideal, as natural, and the framing of those who fail at this are outlier, if not deviant.

While its addictive properties were identified in the earliest psychological research about the Internet,[16] more recently the addictive properties of netporn have been analyzed explicitly, and most research on sex addiction now addresses netporn-aided masturbation and cybersex as an outlet.[17] Some research in fact, identifies porn-addiction to be largely an *Internet-age* phenomenon, an idea presented by psychologists David Greenfield and Maressa Orzack who discuss two distinct types of sex addict, the first being someone would have consumed explicit material offline in previous eras and the second type being a product of the age:

> The secondary type of patient often has no prior history of compulsive sexual behavior, but the development of the compulsive pattern seems to occur almost concurrently with the introduction of the Internet … It is almost as if an arousal/compulsion cycle spontaneously ignites.[18]

While there is not universal agreement on sex and masturbation actually being addictive,[19] Internet theorists nonetheless identify attributes of the technology that, at the very least, facilitate excessive consumption, ideas which incidentally, also have relevance to other Internet-aided intimacy quests, notably infidelity (Chapter 6). One attribute discussed repeatedly in academic literature is time and the ability for perceptions of it to alter while online. The psychologist Kimberly Young—who undertook some of the earliest work on Internet addiction—examined this idea as early as 1998:

> Time seems to stand still on the Internet because no one's measuring time or keeping track of it. That's what separates the Internet from other time-consuming mediums. If you get mesmerized by TV over the course of an evening, the start of each new program reminds you that another hour has passed, and Jay Leno's monologue lets you know it's almost midnight.[20]

In recent years a number of other theorists have analyzed time in the context of cyberspace. The philosopher Aaron Ben-Ze'ev, for example, identified that "cyberspace enables people to lose track of time and space and to be drawn into an alternative, imaginary environment where the speed of time and the spatial location are more malleable."[21] The social scientist Norman

Nie also wrote about this, noting: "Many of us are familiar with that unique Internet characteristic of surfing that leads Internet junkies to sit down to do a single task and end up, hours later, with a loss of a sense of time, place, and original purpose."[22] While the idea of time being more *malleable* online has relevance to masturbation—and thus the specific capacity for a person to get stuck in a "porn cycle"[23]—it can also be an explanation for time lost shopping for a partner (Chapter 1) and, as discussed in Chapter 6, as facilitating infidelity transpiring within this blurry bonus round of cyberspace.

Alluded to earlier in the context of the teen masturbation in *Skins* and *The Big C* is the idea of netporn-aided masturbation as a kind of self-intimacy substituting for a more typical form—intercourse. In fact, netporn-aided masturbation as well as other sex-based Internet offerings are regularly understood as intercourse substitutes, thus tabling ideas, in varying degrees of subtlety, the intimacy-offerings of the Internet, notably in regard to how *real* such experiences are (Chapter 2).

The Online Substitution

In my book *Part-Time Perverts: Sex, Pop Culture and Kink Management* I discussed the notion of *substitution*, whereby kinky sex that is desired but inaccessible leads to arousal being channeled into other pursuits.[24] While similar to Sigmund Freud's work on *sublimation*, whereas Freud wrote about impulses being channeled into other, *nonsexual* pursuits,[25] I argue that sex remains the outlet, albeit taking different forms than originally fantasized.

Whereas masturbation is commonly framed as an intercourse substitute on screen,[26] some narratives explicitly spotlight a specific role for the Internet in substitution. In the comedy *Clerks II* (2006), for example, one of the protagonists, Randal (Jeff Anderson), remarked, "What's the point in having an Internet connection if you're not using it to look up weird, fucked-up pictures of dirty sex you'll never have yourself?" Here, Randal mentions using netporn as an intercourse substitute, as well as such material specifically providing a means to access sex *vicariously*. In the "Twanging Your Magic Clanger" of the sitcom *Two and a Half Men* (2003–), this same idea is alluded to: the second time Alan (John Cryer), is caught masturbating to netporn by his brother, Charlie (Charlie Sheen), Charlie commented, "Hey, I get it, you're bored, you're lonely, you can't afford a hooker." Alan didn't protest this assertion: he *was* masturbating because he didn't have access to a woman. While in these examples, netporn-aided masturbation substituted for intercourse in the generic sense, in other scenes it is more explicitly a response to intercourse that is withheld. In *Fireproof*, for instance, this idea was alluded to in an argument between Caleb and his wife Catherine:

CATHERINE: What do you do around here other than watch TV and waste time on the Internet? You know what, if looking at that trash is how you get fulfilled that's fine, but I will not compete with it.

CALEB: Well I sure don't get it from you.
CATHERINE: And you won't! Because you care more about saving for your
  stupid boat and pleasing yourself than you ever did about me.

A direct link is made in this scene between their lack of intercourse (and intimacy more broadly) and Caleb's use of netporn. While in *Fireproof* the intimacy substitute is netporn, other kinds are depicted on screen. In the thriller
Net Games (2003), friends Adam (C. Thomas Howell) and Ray (Sam Ball)
have a conversation about Adam's relationship with Jennifer (Monique
Demers), who, as part of her backstory, had been raped:

RAY: So let me ask you this. Are you guys, um—
ADAM: What?
RAY: You know -
ADAM: Sex? Not yet.
RAY: Good God! Are you serious?
ADAM: Yes.
RAY: You're going to like this <hands Ray a business card>. This is for you
  until you and Jen get back to normal.
ADAM: Cyber chat?

While initially Adam is reluctant, he visits the site immediately after his next
failed attempt to initiate sex with Jennifer. In the aftermath, Adam's cybersex
experience was explicitly understood as a substitute for intercourse—rather
than just masturbation—as apparent in the comments he made to Ray: "This
morning was the closest thing I've had to sex in about eight months." Adam
went online in pursuit of intimacy because it was denied to him by his partner.
Something similar transpired in the television thriller *Web of Desire* (2009):
Beth (Dina Meyer) attempted to talk to her husband, Jake (Adrian Hough),
about her stressful workday; Jake appeared uninterested so Beth entered a
chatroom and, resultantly, embarked on a relationship with Finn (Claudette
Mink). As it turned out, *Jake* had also been seeking solace in chatrooms and, in
a convenient coincidence, had also been involved in a relationship with Finn.
In the thriller *Downloading Nancy* (2009), the title character (Maria Bello)
lamented her miserable marriage to her therapist (Amy Brenneman), "Maybe
if I'd given birth to a set of golf clubs, I would have captured [husband] Albert's
[Rufus Sewell] interest." Although a little more complicated than Adam's
response in *Net Games* or Beth and Jake's in *Web of Desire*, Nancy's solution
to marital dissatisfaction was to go online to search for someone to kill her in
order to free her from her "fucked up life." This search led her into an online,
sadomasochist-themed affair with Louis (Jason Patric). When Albert confronts
Louis offline, the idea of substitution was explicitly discussed:

ALBERT: What the fuck have you been doing to my fucking wife?
LOUIS: What you haven't been doing to her, Albert.

In the gay-themed romance *eCupid* (2011), Marshall (Houston Rhines) and Gabe's (Noah Schuffman) relationship had become stale. One evening Marshall was watching late-night TV when he saw the "eCupid" app advertised. He completed the online questionnaire agreeing that his relationship did lack sex and that he was frustrated, feeling trapped and unsatisfied. In agreeing to the terms and conditions Marshall allowed the app to take control of his life, delivering him the kind of romantic and erotic thrills that his relationship with Gabe had been missing. Something similar transpired in *Men, Women & Children*. Don (Adam Sandler) and Helen (Rosemarie DeWitt)—a married couple in a sexless marriage—were lying in bed, using their iPads, the television on in the background. While the physical technology in this scene was subtly portrayed as a barrier to their intimacy, Internet connectivity serves an even more disruptive function: a television commercial for the AshleyMadison.com infidelity website came on, subtly planting the seeds of intimacy substitution. Shortly after, Helen posted a profile on the site and Don went online and procured the services of an escort.[27]

While infidelity is a theme in each of these examples—a topic explored in greater detail in Chapter 6—more simply, these scenes are illustrations of intimacy substitutes sought by people who would normally be expected to get their intimacy from within their committed relationship, in turn not only framing intimacy within couples as the norm, but presenting monogamy as the standard, albeit one that gets frequently challenged by the Internet.

For both Helen and Don in *Men, Women & Children*, their online search for an intimacy substitute led them to websites that facilitate the organization of offline liaisons. Be it for those within relationships seeking an intimacy substitute, or single characters simply seeking physical contact, the Internet makes arranging such liaisons effortless. This latter idea was illustrated well in the "She Said OK" episode of the comedy-drama series *Girls* (2012–). Hannah's (Lena Dunham) editor, David (John Cameron Mitchell), had arrived unexpectedly at her birthday party—after he had been stood up by a date. David's most pressing concern was borrowing Hannah's phone to download the Grindr hook-up app; he was keen to quickly arrange a substitute. This *Girls* scene provides a useful segue between the general idea of the Internet as a substitute for intimacy and the more specific use of hook-up apps to acquire new intimacies.

The Hook-Up

In this section this idea of the Internet used to orchestrate hook-ups is examined. While location-based apps like Tinder have been used for several years as part of the cross-platform marketing of films and television shows,[28] such apps are only just beginning to have a notable presence within narratives. I am using the term *hook-up apps* in this section because such technology is often popularly understood—and certainly presented as such on screen—as centered on recreational intimacy and as being different in motivation to online dating. It should, however, be noted that many online dating websites now have accompanying apps thus blurring the distinction between the two. Equally, online dating has, in practice, been also used for recreation (Chapter 1) and apps have been used to form relationships, thus highlighting that the distinction between the two is no longer clear; a complexity further fueled by hook-up apps occasionally being demurely referred to as *dating apps* within narratives.

The sitcom *Betas* (2014) centered on the development of a new, location-based hook-up app. The sitcom *A to Z* (2014–15) centered on the Wallflower online dating company; in the pilot the company launched a hook-up app to increase repeat custom; as manager Lydia (Christina Kirk) enthused, "They swipe, they click, they hook up. They swipe, they click, they hook up. They swipe, they click, they hook up." While in these examples the existence of the software is tabled rather than the practical application depicted, numerous other screen examples do have plots centered on app use. In the "In the Mix, on the Books, and in the Freezer" episode of the sitcom *Manhattan Love Story* (2014), for example, Amy (Jade Catta-Preta) downloaded Tinder onto her friend Dana's (Analeigh Tipton) phone, illustrative of themes discussed in Chapter 2 where one character's online dating reluctance gets usurped by a well-meaning friend. In the "The Cinderella in the Cardboard" episode of the crime-drama *Bones* (2005–), a hook-up app is at the center of an investigation when a photo of the analyst, Hodgins (T.J. Thyne), is found on the phone of a murder victim: they had both been using the location based hook-up app "Date or Hate?" In the "Dice" episode of the sitcom *New Girl* (2011–), the three women who Schmidt (Max Greenfield) had had sex with that week had each been met through "Dice," "it's kinda like Tinder," he explained to the protagonist Jess (Zooey Deschanel). In the "Naked and Afraid" episode of the sitcom *Hot in Cleveland* (2010–), Joy's (Jane Leeves) phone kept pinging thus forcing her to reveal to her roommates that she had just started using "Sinder." In the "Girls, Girls, Girls" episode of the fantasy series *Supernatural* (2005–), Dean (Jensen Ackles) used the "CrushBook" app. In several 2015 episodes of the Australian soap opera *Neighbours* (1985–), the "Ziva" app is used by characters including Paul (Stefan Dennis) and Naomi (Morgana O'Reilly). In the "Mano-a-Mansfield" episode of the sitcom *Ground Floor* (2013–15), Derrick (James Earl) enthusiastically used "Pynchr"; he then helped his colleague Harvard (Rory Scovel) set up a profile. In "The Gang Group Dates" episode of the sitcom *It's Always Sunny in Philadelphia* (2005–), the "Bunchers" app is mentioned; an app facilitating group dates. While in each of these examples heterosexual characters use these apps, in line with the standard portrayal of gay characters being defined by their sexuality—and more specifically using the Internet to arrange casual sex (Chapter 6)—hook-up apps also have widespread use among homosexual characters. David in *Girls* mentioned earlier is one such example of a character using Grindr. In the "Minimum Viable Product" of the comedy series *Silicon*

Valley (2014–), Grindr is also mentioned in the context of a tech-themed investment portfolio. The same app received a passing mention in the "And the Disappointing Unit" episode of the sitcom *2 Broke Girls* (2011–) when John (Patrick Cox) enthused about the "great business" his Grindr profile had received since he changed his username to "Suction Junction." In the "Looking for Home" episode of the gay-drama *Looking* (2014–15), a group of men were at a party matching Grindr profiles to attendees; in the process Patrick (Jonathan Groff) discovered that his boyfriend, Kevin (Russell Tovey), had an active profile. In the "Milk" episode of the Australian sitcom *Please Like Me* (2013–), Patrick (Charles Cottier) used Grindr to arrange a hook-up. In the "Present Tense" episode of the drama series *Faking It* (2014–), the gay hook-up app "Stubble" was mentioned; an app seemingly used by at least two of the gay male high schoolers in the episode. In "The City That Never Sleeps" episode of the police-drama *Blue Bloods* (2010–), closeted actor Russell (Marc Blucas) used "Tryster." In the "We're Not Friends" episode of the crime-drama *How to Get Away With Murder* (2014–), Connor (Jack Falahee) perused the offerings on "Humpr." In the thriller *Truth* (2013), Caleb (Sean Paul Lockhart) and Jeremy (Rob Moretti) met through "GuySpy." In the "Newer Elements of Our Defense" episode of the Canadian sci-fi series *Orphan Black* (2013–), the lesbian dating app, "Sapphire," is used by Cosima (Tatiana Maslany). "Boobr," is similarly used by Kay (Tymberlee Hill) in the "Move Me" episode of the sitcom *Marry Me* (2014–15): "Boobr: it's a dating app for lesbians, like Grindr is for gay men or Tinder is for straight men and whores," she explained.

While the examples discussed in this section center on hook-up apps, the idea of short-term, recreational intimacies being organized through the Internet actually transpires in a range of other examples. Mentioned earlier was Don in *Men, Women & Children* using the Internet to organize a sex worker and Helen using it to have an affair. In the drama *Red State* (2011), three teenagers used a classifieds website—"It's like Craigslist for people who want to get fucked"—to arrange a foursome. In the television biopic *The Craigslist Killer* (2011), the titular website was used by several characters for sexual liaisons; the classifieds site "Clicker" was similarly mentioned as used for hook-ups in an unnamed episode of the British crime-drama *Scott & Bailey* (2011–). Hook-up websites were also referenced in the thriller *Murder Dot Com* (2008) and the "Phobia" episode of the crime-drama *Stalker* (2014–15).

These screen examples showcase several aspects of the fusion of technology with recreational intimacy. First, of all the hook-up app scenes discussed thus far, characters only actually secured physical hook-ups in *New Girl*, *Marry Me*, *Orphan Black*, *Truth* and *Please Like Me*. A cursory explanation for this is sample size: hook-up apps do not yet have an enormous screen presence and thus when they are presented it is perhaps to be expected that characters are as apprehensive about the new technology as audiences. This explanation is in line with the techno- and cyberphobias rampant on screen, whereby worst-case scenarios of new technology frequently get fictionalized. Other explanations, however, are also at play. Of the examples where characters actually hooked up, in four of these narratives—*Marry Me, Orphan Black, Truth*, and *Please Like Me*—the app-users were homosexual. While the use of the Internet to organize nonvanilla intimacy is explored in greater detail in Chapter 6, it is worth speculating that there is perhaps greater audience acceptance for seeing homosexuals using such apps because doing so fits with popular assumptions about homosexual promiscuity[29] and more broadly, the well-established screen pattern of gay characters using the Internet to arrange sex. While such recreational intimacy might be expected, if not *tolerated* for gay characters, this is likely a more contentious issue for heterosexuals, particularly women; in *Marry Me* quoted earlier, Kay refers to Tinder as a place for "whores," indicative of a broader, enduring stereotype about women who use the Internet for intimacy as being somehow cheap or slutty (Chapter 2).[30] Equally, while sex outside of a relationship is, in fact, incredibly common on screen,[31] it might, however, be perceived as a step too far to have characters—particularly *attractive* characters who should be successful in *any* dating market—having to resort to using technology to arrange such liaisons. While use of such apps is, at least somewhat less stigmatized than online dating,[32] the use of this technology is still far from a serendipitous way of meeting a partner, and equally if a character was genuinely attractive and successful, presumably such technology wouldn't be needed. It is also worth spotlighting that when desirable characters do use hook-up apps, they are often resultantly punished; in turn serving as a subtle demonization, reprimand and also teachable moment. In the "Cinderella in the Cardboard" episode of *Bones*, for example, use of the "Date or Hate" app led to a murder. In "The City That Never Sleeps" episode of *Blue Bloods*, Russell is beaten up by his hook-up. In *Truth*, the psychotic Caleb imprisons and tortures Jeremy. In the "Dice" episode of *New Girl*, Jess's use of the app leads to a loser parade (Chapter 3) and for Schmidt, to a crisis of conscience. In the "Girls, Girls, Girls" episode of *Supernatural*, the hook-up that Dean arranged was with a woman working for a demon who was intent on stealing his soul. In the "Mano-a-Mansfield" episode of *Ground Floor*, a Nigerian money scam ensues. Equally, as apparent in the other online hook-ups—for example, the classifieds sites used to arrange recreational intimacies in *Red State, The Craigslist Killer*, Scott *&* Bailey, *Murder Dot Com* and *Stalker*—kidnapping, murder and stalking transpired, respectively. While it makes sense that such scenes are dramatic in the context of an entertainment product, it is also worth noting that such themes work as subtle condemnations—or, at the very least, *cautionary warnings*—about the technology.

The presence of hook-up apps on screen highlights a number of ideas relevant to a discussion of Internet-aided intimacy, notably in regard to motive. In Chapter 1 I introduced *efficiency* as a key reason that characters date online; Temperance (Emily Deschanel) in the "Two Bodies in the Lab" episode of *Bones* spoke of this exact thing in her rationale for signing up with SensiblePartners: "It's a practical way of objectively examining a potential partner without all the game playing." Hook-up apps take practicality to a new level, whereby in using the app, people out themselves as explicitly seeking recreational intimacy; after all, if they wanted a relationship they would have used a purpose-built online *dating* site.[33] In the *New Girl* episode, Schmidt spent a day coaching Jess through using "Dice"; by the end of the day, for a committed romantic like Jess it wasn't a good fit, Schmidt however, still saw great appeal:

JESS: I just don't understand how what we did today is gonna help me find love.
SCHMIDT: Love? Why would you want to fall in love?
JESS: Why else would I go on dates?
SCHMIDT: The point of dating is just to keep on dating, and then never stop. It's like burning fossil fuels. Or seeing a therapist.
JESS: No. Schmidt, the whole point of going on dates is to fall in love and have a relationship. Like, don't you ever worry that you're missing out? I mean, you're plowing through all these girls, and some of 'em might be great, but you'll never know. Do you want to go through life that way?
SCHMIDT: Yeah.

Schmidt, like the recreational daters discussed in Chapter 1, viewed the app as being about recreational intimacy as opposed to a means to find love or a relationship. This same casual sex-driver is mentioned briefly in *Murder Dot Com*, when Ben (Matthew Mahaney) explained the appeal of liaisons made through a hook-up site: "I mostly like it uncomplicated. Like the website." It is indeed feasible for hook-up apps to be conceived as ushering in and formalizing a market for casual sex outside of commitment. The sociologist Eva Illouz summarized the work of the philosopher Herbert Marcuse who argued, "that erotic desires could and should be liberated from the psychic demands of the capitalist system of production."[34] Arguably the use of apps may play a part in this. Of course, as evident in these examples, hook-up-app–aided casual sex actually transpires fairly *infrequently* on screen, and on those occasions when it does it is often connected to crime, thus working to frame the Internet, again, as a place where villains hunt prey (Chapter 4), as well as a kind of badlands that only the truly desperate would visit.

Desperation hints to another theme underpinning the use of hook-up apps on screen: that people go online when they fail in the "normal" offline dating landscape. This very idea was alluded to in the aforementioned *Hot in Cleveland* episode when Joy explained her reasons for using "Sinder":

I am done holding out for romance and happily ever after. That just leads to heartbreak. On Sinder, I can order my men the way I order my shoes.

While it is, of course, feasible that Joy simply liked sex and was thus just pursuing an avenue that created a ready supply—accurate, too, given that she had casual sex with a neighbor's contractor the same morning that she signed up with Sinder—there is also resignation on her part that she had failed to find intimacy in a romantic, serendipitous way and had to settle for intimacy supplied by technology.[35]

Just as the Internet can help characters without intimacy acquire it—as well as aid people with intimacy acquire more of it—it also has a role in deepening and strengthening the intimacy within an established dyad.

The Relationship Accoutrement

This section examines the Internet's role as a relationship aid in several key ways: as a tool for research, as a way to maintain intimacy in the face of geographic separation, and, more problematically, as a way to fuel romantic obsessions and, also, to make letting go more difficult.

Intimate Research

Dating self-help books invariably mention the importance of conducting an online background search on any potential date,[36] and in cultural anthropologist Illana Gershon's work doing so was identified as standard among college students:

> They also searched for information on new lovers, or possible lovers, occasionally going to great length to gather information. These searches could take hours in people's days, as they searched through posted photos and people's profiles that were linked to the person they were most interested in.[37]

It is, therefore, no surprise, that a key role for the Internet in intimacy quests on screen mirrors the real-life role of the Internet in prerelationship research. In the pilot of *Hot in Cleveland*, Joy jibed, "This is why the Internet was invented; for men to find pictures of naked celebrities and women to cyberstalk the men they trust." While in *Hot in Cleveland* this idea is presented as a joke, in other examples the use of the Internet for such purposes is less funny and more simply a standard step in modern courtship. In the pilot of *A to Z*, for example, the future couple at the center of the narrative, Andrew (Ben Feldman) and Zelda (Cristin Milioti), initially got to know each other by perusing each other's social media postings. In the "C Is For Curiouser & Curiouser" episode of the same series, Stephie (Lenora Crichlow) mentioned her use of "Lulu," an ex-boyfriend review site; as she justified, "Who meets without getting someone's information first?" A similar site, "Rater," was mentioned in "The Gang Group Dates" episode of *It's Always Sunny in Philadelphia*. In the "Feed the Need" episode of the Canadian comedy series *jPod* (2008), Ethan (David Kopp) and John (Torrance Coombs) conduct a "Google enhanced full cavity search" on their colleague, Kaitlin's (Emilie Ullerup), ex-boyfriend (Kyle Cassie). In the television holiday film *Annie Claus is Coming to Town* (2011), Ted (Sam Page) performed an online search of his love rival, Dean (Ryan Bittle). In another holiday film, *Christmas Bounty* (2013), Tory's (Francia Raisa) mom (April Telek) confessed to having Googled Tory's new boyfriend, James (Will Greenberg): "I gotta know what my little girl is up to." In the pilot of the sci-fi series *Mr. Robot* (2015–), the protagonist Elliot (Rami Malek) performs a background check on his therapist's boyfriend. In the gay-themed romantic-comedy *Eating Out: All You Can Eat* (2009), Tiffani (Rebekah Kochan) took these ideas further, suggesting to Casey (Daniel Skelton), "Don't you know anything about the Internet? You're supposed to make a fake profile … Pretend to be a total random stranger so you can find out all his personal details."

In the sci-fi film *I Origins* (2014), Ian (Michael Pitt), used the Internet to scour social media to locate a woman he had sex with at a party. In the romantic-comedy *A Case of You* (2013), Sam (Justin Long) similarly used Facebook to find a barista, Birdie (Evan Rachel Wood), whom he had a crush on. In *A Case of You*, the use of social media in romance was actually taken further when Sam's roommate, Eliot (Keir O'Donnell), advised, "That's the beauty of getting to see her Facebook profile. So much information on there. I mean, you could become the man of her dreams if you wanted," a suggestion Sam took heed of when he used the information on Birdie's Facebook page to become her perfect man. A similar narrative was deployed over a decade earlier in the pre-social-media "Civil War" episode of *Ally McBeal* (1997–2002) when, during a court case, Paula (Maria Pitillo) complained how she felt she had been manipulated into sex by a man who had used the Internet to obtain data on her:

> Everything we connected on he learned from my chatroom online. I'm in a circle group, women. And he, evidently, was in it, pretending to *be* a woman. So all the stuff about souls connecting first, I'd said that in the chatroom. He used it.[38]

On one hand, in a world where everything gets Googled and millions of people are on Facebook and LinkedIn and, in turn, everyone's connection to everyone else is information in the public domain, the notion of doing background research on a love interest seems fairly normal. Worth noting, however, are the amplified reasons that someone met online might *necessitate* such a "cavity search." Discussed in Chapter 4 was the idea that people *from the Internet* are viewed with more suspicion than the rest of the population. With this in mind, the use of an online background search has heightened relevance: *of course* a person met in the Internet badlands should be thoroughly investigated; it is only due diligence.

Another rationale for these cavity searches centers on the social circles that get expanded by online dating, something the sociologist John Bridges explains in his book *The Illusion of Intimacy*: "The technology, for example, does provide people who would otherwise never meet with the possibility of finding each other and arranging a meeting."[39] Here, Bridges' spotlights that not only does the Internet aid with connection, but notably it puts users in contact with people they wouldn't normally cross paths with, which is an idea working to further fuel the idea that people online are always ultimately just strangers.[40] As discussed throughout this volume, such strangers are assumed as more duplicitous than those met through a serendipitous meet cute. While this idea plays out in a range of narratives, the British mini-series *Killer Net* (1998), the comedy *Bringing Down the House* (2003), the Canadian drama *The Boy She Met Online* (2010) and the television drama *The Wife He Met Online* (2012) each illustrate this idea bluntly with law abiding, middle-class characters coming into contact with felons because of the Internet.

Maintaining Connectedness

Just as in previous eras where geography separated a couple (wartime, prison, etc.) and where letters and telephone calls functioned to bridge the intimacy gap, the Internet provides another means to do this—a more efficient way, for example, to "send" a letter or a photograph to a loved one. In more recent years the Internet has facilitated a much more intimate experience with couples able to make video calls and to engage in sexual intimacy that combines text as well as the visual and aural. Family therapist Katherine Hertlein discussed this idea in her work on intimacy and new technology noting, "Couples have the opportunity to stay connected in a way they never have had before."[41] While, as discussed already in this chapter, a number of films present cybersex as a theme, as relevant for this section are examples where it is used to bridge physical intimacy gaps for couples residing in separate locations. In *I Origins*, Ian and Karen (Brit Marling) stayed connected via video chat while in different countries. In the "Kitty" episode of the crime-drama series *CSI* (2000–2015), Susan (Torrey DeVitto) explained her use of the Web for such purposes: "My husband is stationed in Afghanistan. It's the only way we get to see each other ... I send Bradley photos and videos of the girls. I post whatever I can to bring our life to him." The "Connection Lost" episode of the sitcom *Modern Family* (2009–) centered on Phil's (Ty Burrell) use of the Internet to keep connected to his family while on a business trip. Certainly such uses reflect those documented in academic research. Psychologists Al Cooper, Coralie Scherer and David Marcus discussed this idea in one of their case studies:

> When Gordon was assigned a tour of duty in Istanbul, he and Ramona exchanged daily e-mails. They enjoyed combing the electronic card

Web sites for playful and erotic musical and animated e-greeting cards. When Gordon received a miniature digital camera in the mail, they set up simple videoconference calls, some of which become quite long and at other times had sexual interludes, which they felt kept them connected.[42]

While cybersex is not part of the video chats in *I Origins*, *Modern Family* or *CSI*, sex certainly constitutes part of Internet-aided connectivity in other examples. In the "Take Me with You" episode of the sitcom *The Mindy Project* (2012–), the title character (Mindy Kaling) and her boyfriend Casey (Anders Holm) practiced cybersex in preparation for an upcoming geographic separation. In the "The Infestation Hypothesis" episode of the sitcom *The Big Bang Theory* (2007–), Leonard (Johnny Galecki) and Priya (Aarti Mann) were already residing in different countries when they attempted cybersex. While both of these examples were deliberately comic—and thus their attempts were amusingly marred by technology failings and discomfort—these narratives do highlight the kind of real-life intimacy capabilities of the technology. A slightly sexier version transpired in the comedy *Good Luck Chuck* (2007). The film centered on Chuck (Dane Cook), who is bestowed with a mystical power enabling any woman who he has sex with to find love with another man immediately afterward. In light of his powers and his burgeoning love interest in Cam (Jessica Alba), Chuck insists that they communicate only via webcam instead of being in each other's physical presence and risking intercourse; the characters thus experienced sexual intimacy, albeit without being in the same room. The speculative future film *Her* (2013) provided a cybersex display more akin to sex scenes where the primary objective is eroticism not humor. The film centered on Theodore (Joaquin Phoenix) who is part of a generation who has taken connectivity to the nth degree; characters are in permanent contact with their operating systems, which constantly adapt to meet their needs. Like several other characters in *Her*, Theodore falls in love with his operating system, Samantha (voiced by Scarlett Johansson). Because Samantha doesn't have a body—because no capacity exists for Theodore to have physical contact with what is ostensibly only software—intimacy is restricted to talking: in one scene, the two engage in intimate dialogue while Theodore masturbates and Samantha makes noises to convey that she is doing the same. On one hand, this scene can be likened to any phone sex scene where "sex" is really just masturbation spurred on by disembodied voices,[43] on the other hand, the intimacy that Theodore had forged with Samantha—the fact that Samantha is with him constantly and permanently collating data to best meet his needs—in fact, positions the scene as *unimaginable* without the Internet.

With online technology facilitating loved ones keeping in contact, an interesting consequence is that when contact is absent—when a text message isn't replied to or a video call not taken—it can have negative impacts on self-esteem; something technology writer Brian Chen spotlighted in his book *Always On*: "So many of us like to text a lot because once we stop getting messages, we start to hurt, and then we become scared and unsure of ourselves."[44] The idea of esteem being attached to online communications is indeed identifiable on screen. Martín (Javier Drolas) in the Argentinian drama *Medianeras* (*Sidewalls*) (2011), for example, referenced this in his observation, "Is there anything more discouraging in the 21st century as an empty inbox?" While the comment was typical for the introspective Martín, it also provides insight into the modern-day blight of constant message-checking and social media updating as a way to say—and feel—*I was here*. In the holiday made-for-television film *All About Christmas Eve* (2012), the title character (Haylie Duff) is fired from her job and catches her boyfriend cheating on her; her dire predicament is made that bit worse the following morning when she looks at her phone and it reads "Calls: 0/ Messages: 0." A variant on this theme was apparent in the "The Importance of Not Being Too Earnest" episode of the drama series *Dawson's Creek* (1998–2003), when teen Audrey (Busy Philipps) mused on some of the pitfalls of email:

> E-mail expression is the scourge of the modern age. The Internet has made it way too easy to express oneself. Okay, you have some fleeting thought. You send it. It lands with a thud in some unsuspecting person's mailbox. Said person then reads it, gets irked because you've recapped a conversation that you presumably already had. They fail to respond. You feel slighted.

These examples are illustrative of some of the downsides of technology: the expectation of permanent connectivity, but also the minefield of problems that online communications create in accurately conveying information in the absence of face-to-face cues, and also the sense of loss in its absence.

As an Erotic Adjunct

While cybersex can help a geographically separated couple to remain sexually connected, the technology can also help add interest to relationships that aren't negatively impacted on by geography but are nonetheless seeking spice. The narrative catalyst for the television drama *Sexting in Suburbia* (2012), for example, was an erotic selfie that teenager Dina (Jenn Proske) sent to her boyfriend. Sure, Dina could have simply *shown* her scantily clad body to Mark (Ryan Kelley), but the eroticism here comes from daring to immortalize the image; to objectify oneself. Sexting, in fact, transpires in numerous examples. As in *Sexting in Suburbia*, in the "Shoot to Thrill" episode of the Canadian drama series *Degrassi: The Next Generation* (2001–), Alli (Melinda Shankar) took some sexy selfies and sent them to her boyfriend. In the "Hairography" episode of *Glee*, it is revealed that high school students Puck (Mark Salling) and Santana (Naya Rivera) had sexted. Teens similarly participated in sexting in the "Crush" episode of the crime-drama *Law & Order: Special Victims Unit* (1999–) and in the "Tin Man is Down" episode of the drama series *Homeland* (2011–). Akin to the demonized portrayal of hook-up apps on screen, it is necessary to spotlight that sexting in the majority of these examples is in fact *problematized* in narratives where youthful indiscretions, electronic footprints and slut-shaming frames the activity: in *Sexting in Suburbia*—in the predictable vein of made-for-television scaremongering—Dina's sexting is linked to her death. Interestingly, in examples where men sext on screen, while they aren't shamed as sluts, such scenes nonetheless also serve as lessons, as well as ripped-from-the-headlines fictionalizations of real-life scandals. In "The Rebuttal" episode of the sitcom *Alpha House* (2013–), for example, political aide James (Ben Rameaka) took a photo of his penis to send to his girlfriend Lola (Willa Fitzgerald); he accidentally Tweeted the photo using his boss's account. While a comic example, this scene references real-life sex scandals involving politicians; a storyline also apparent in other narratives. In the "October Surprise" episode of *Law & Order: Special Victims Unit*, Alex Muñoz (Vincent Laresca) is a political candidate who used social media to send erotic photos to women. The same thing occurred in the "Say Hello to My Little Friend" episode of the drama series *Scandal* (2012–) centered on Senator Richard Meyers (Patrick Fabian) who was sprung emailing photos of himself in his underwear. In the "Coon 2: Hindsight" episode of *South Park* this idea was again referenced when the character Captain Hindsight— alluding to a real-life scandal—commented, "Brett Favre should never have sent actual pictures of his schlong." Interestingly, while the sexting in each of these examples was conducted for the purposes of intimacy—either self-intimacy or as part of intimacy with a partner—again, the examples have negative consequences: humiliation, exposure and threatened political careers. Rather than sexting being framed as a way to bring two people closer together, in fact, it is invariably portrayed as a cautionary warning, and yet another problem caused by new technology.

The Fueling of Obsessions

In *Little Children*, middle-aged Richard (Gregg Edelman) had an obsession with the webcam performer SluttyKay. The idea of the Internet giving characters a way to become obsessed is, in fact, identifiable in a range of examples whereby regular "contact"—albeit often only one-way—conveys a semblance of intimacy that may be nonexistent offline but nevertheless functions to fuel obsessions. Similar to what transpired in *Little Children*, in the "Chinese Walls" episode of the British crime-drama *The Inspector Lynley Mysteries* (2001–7), Tanner (Wayne Foskett) became obsessed with the webcam performer Emily (Isabella Calthorpe); as he explained to investigators, "I wanted to get closer. I wanted to know her as a person. And yeah, I know how sad and deluded that sounds." While in these examples, webcams facilitated a sense of connection, in other scenes social media fulfils this role. In the "Lost and Found" episode of *Stalker*, Ian (Sterling Beaumon) maintained his crush on Jenny (Cole Bernstein) by accessing a Tumblr page that he had created full of photos of her, functioning as a kind of modern-day shrine. Something similar transpired in the British drama *Cyberbully* (2015), where an anonymous person whom teen Casey (Maisie Williams) had been exchanging emails with revealed that he had been collating all her social media activity and considered himself "a fan." In the first season of the crime-drama series *The Fall* (2013–), as married Paul's (Jamie Dornan) interest in his teen babysitter Katie (Aisling Franciosi) increased, so too did him watching her online singing videos: the videos were a way for him to have the kind of access to her that would have been problematic in real life. A variation on these ideas transpired in the Japanese drama *Riri Shushu no subete* (*All About Lily Chou-Chou*) (2001), where fans of the pop-singer Lily Chou-Chou bonded online over their shared interest. Similar bonding over music—specifically over an "obscure punk band"—was also referenced in the "Leave Me Alone" episode of *Girls*.

In these examples, akin to the cyberstalking scenes I discuss elsewhere,[45] the Internet acts to both convey a kind of faux intimacy between people and provide regular (albeit disembodied) contact where identity can be projected onto a set of images and a relationship can be conjured in one's imagination (Chapter 2).

While cyberstalking has a real, and sinister connotation that I explore elsewhere,[46] in popular parlance *stalking* has come to describe behavior that can include the aforementioned background searches but also, more commonly, serve as a way to surreptitiously keep tabs on someone. As "Amelie," a college student interviewed by Gershon, noted:

> I feel like people use "stalking" lightly now. So when I say I am Facebook stalking somebody, it doesn't mean that I am obsessed with them in the way that real-life stalking is. It just means that I might have checked their profile a few times but I've never met them.[47]

Here, Facebook stalking can be likened to the partner research discussed earlier, but can also provide a means to surreptitiously "connect" with a love interest.[48] Such behavior, of course, can also play a role in situations where a relationship may have ended but the Internet facilitates continued access—*continued contact*—even if it is one-way and unreciprocated.

Not Quite Letting Go

In Belinda Luscombe's *Time* article on Facebook and divorce, she noted, "For those who want to connect or reconnect with others, social-networking sites are a huge, glorious honeypot. But for those who are disconnecting, they can make things quite sticky."[49] These comments provide an interesting insight into the challenges that the Internet creates for terminated relationships that somehow "continue" because of the Internet.

Just as the Internet facilitates connection for people within relationships, the same technology exists after a breakup. In the "Un-Tag My Heart" episode of *Selfie*, for example, Eliza spoke about the role of social media in this regard: "Once the option of stalking your exes is presented, you can't not do it. It's like crack ..." Similar ideas were alluded to in the pilot episode of *Stalker*, when Lieutenant Beth Davis (Maggie Q) spoke about the impact that the Internet has had on human connectedness and, as specifically relevant for this discussion, access to exes:

> Stalking can be the result of a relationship gone wrong or delusional fixations that are pushed to extremes. Anyone can be a stalker. Ex-boyfriend, spouse, stranger. Anyone can be a victim, and it's on the rise. Facebook, Twitter, Instagram, Snapchat, Tinder, whatever app is hot today. We have too much access to one another. Social media is the number one reason stalking cases have tripled in the last decade. That's where I come in.

In the aforementioned *Selfie* episode, Eliza introduced her colleague, Henry (John Cho), to Facebook and in turn introduced him to the ability to stalk his ex-partners which, for the course of the episode, he became obsessed with doing. In the "Weirdos Need Girlfriends Too" episode of *Girls*, in the aftermath of Marnie's (Allison Williams) break up with Charlie (Christopher Abbott), she used Facebook to peruse photos of him in a manner that might have once manifested in a flicking-through-the-photo-album scene except that online that album keeps getting updated. In the drama *On_Line* (2002), John (Josh Hamilton) was a regular visitor to the Angelcam website. Angelcam in fact, was the webcam site of his ex-girlfriend, Angel (Liz Owens): by visiting the site, John was able to imagine he was still in a relationship with Angel, getting intimate access to her (in one scene he describes watching her get undressed), while also monitoring her behavior; it is, for example, through accessing her site that John discovers that she recoupled. Certainly this behavior fits in with Gershon's findings where she identified, that participants in her study "looked at their ex-lovers' profiles to see what was happening in the person's life."[50] Such behavior, of course, feeds into nostalgia (something discussed further in Chapter 6), as well as depression, and can delay closure and also result in unpleasant comparisons.[51] The "She Said OK" episode of *Girls*, provided a slightly different take on this idea. In the aftermath of Marnie's breakup with Charlie, she threw Hannah a birthday party and justified her kindness: "I'll have a bunch of, like, party pictures that I can post to Instagram, 'cos I know he [Charlie] checks it." For Marnie, her awareness that exes can, and do, continue looking at the social media updates of their former partners was a motivator for her to perform -and document- a happy/I've-moved-on/I-still-look-good life as a taunt to her boyfriend.[52]

Outside of social media, technology is shown to aid the "stalking" of loved ones in a range of other screen examples. In the comedy *Paul Blart: Mall Cop* (2009), Pahud (Adhir Kalyan) used GPS technology to track his ex-girlfriend's movements via her phone. In the "Sex, Lies and Politics" episode of *Ally McBeal*, a man kept tabs on his partner by tracking the movements of her wheelchair by using Lojack technology. In *Christmas Bounty*, James tried to convince Tory to use a GPS app so that they could always keep track of the other's movements. Parents also tracked children using GPS phone apps in *Men, Women & Children* and in the "Mia & David" episode of the British drama series *Dates* (2013).

While thus far I have discussed the capacity for the Internet to aid intimacy, it is worth noting the ability for technology to actually *thwart* it.

The Thwarting of Intimacy

Discussed earlier was the scene from *Men, Women & Children* where Don and Helen were lying in bed playing with their iPads; the technology clearly contributing to the distance between them. The Christian-drama *Online* (2013) provided another example of this: not only does reconnecting with an ex-girlfriend via social media erect a barrier between John (Morgan Ayres) and his wife Mary (Kelsey Sanders), but during the couple's estrangement, scenes dwell on John staying late in the office typing on his computer while Mary is at home, browsing on hers. A similar observation about technology's disruptive functions is made in the "Follow Through" episode of *Selfie* when Eliza realized that during most of the time she spent with her past boyfriends they had both been on their smartphones; that perhaps her relationships weren't as intimate as she had thought. This realization was bolstered in a scene where she walked into a restaurant and saw that this was, in fact, the case for most couples; each couple in the restaurant were using their phones while seated opposite each other. Outside of romantic intimacy, *Disconnect*, for example, showed a father, Rich (Jason Bateman), seated at the dinner table using his cell phone—the technology facilitated his emotional disconnection from his family members; something that transpires in the context of online gaming where characters like Jacob (Clark Duke) in the comedy *Hot Tub Time Machine* (2010), Tim (Ansel Elgort) in *Men, Women & Children* and Amber (Melissa Rain Anderson) and Jeff (Daniel Stewart Sherman) in the "Bullseye" episode of *Law & Order: Special Victims Unit* were each disengaged from their family members because of their online gaming. While, as discussed earlier, there is a range of research documenting the negatives that technology poses to relationships, there is also academic speculation about technology existing as a barrier to interpersonal connectedness: both as damaging to existing relationships and to the formation of new ones. The anthropologist Allen Batteau discussed this idea, observing, "As we become more connected with colleagues in China, we become less connected with our neighbors down the street."[53] The same idea has been explored by theorists such as psychologist Sherry Turkle in her book *Alone Together*,[54] and the political scientist Robert Putnam in *Bowling Alone*,[55] who both attempted to grapple with how notions of connectivity have changed because of the Internet, both in the creation of new options for connection and also in potentially weakening ties, too. Certainly films like *Men, Women & Children* and *Disconnect*—as well as *Selfie* and *A to Z*—attempted to tackle these issues within screen narratives.

As noted, while technology can be disruptive to existing relationships, the screen also contends that it can thwart their initiation in the first place. In one of the earliest World Wide Web–themed films, *The Net* (1995), the protagonist Angela (Sandra Bullock) conducted all her socializing inside a chatroom. In one scene, one of her chat companions "IceMan," wrote, "No one leaves the house anymore. No one has sex. The Net is ultimate condom." Here, IceMan touched upon a theme essential to technophobia—an underpinning, in fact, for each of the scenes discussed in this section—about the Internet making us less human, an idea with heightened relevance in the context of technology failing to deliver the promised whole new world of connectedness.[56] Another early screen example of this played out for Dick (John Lithgow) in the "Y2Dick" episode of the sitcom *3rd Rock from the Sun* (1996–2001) when, after he emerged from his Internet addiction, he commented, "I thought all this technology would help me wrap my arms around human kind but I was wrong … I wasn't connected to anything, I was separated." Martín in *Medianeras* (*Sidewalls*) had a similar realization: "The Internet brings me closer to the world, but further from life." Such failings were also articulated in the Japanese Internet-themed horror film *Kairo* (*Pulse*) (2001), in a conversation between Kawashima (Haruhiko Katô) and Karasawa (Koyuki):

KARASAWA: What got you started on the Internet?
KAWASHIMA: Nothing in particular.
KARASAWA: You don't like computers, right?
KAWASHIMA: No.
KARASAWA: Wanted to connect with other people?
KAWASHIMA: Maybe … I don't know. Everyone else is into it.
KARASAWA: People don't really connect, you know.
KAWASHIMA: What?
KARASAWA: Like those dots simulating humans. We all live totally separately. That's how it seems to me.

While evaluating the authenticity of online relationships is explored in Chapter 2, for this section it is worthwhile considering the capacity for such scenes to be both indicative of the failings of technology to truly connect us, but also as illustrative of how the Internet has actually kept people so distracted that making connections is thwarted; that the connectedness offered is superficial at best; as Elliot in the pilot of *Mr. Robot* observed, "our social media [is] faking as intimacy."

This chapter focused on the Internet's use in finding, having and keeping physically intimate relationships. Chapter 6 expands on these ideas, examining the role of film and television in portraying the Internet's involvement in nonmainstream sexual expressions such as infidelity and homosexuality.

Notes

1. This is a reference to the song of the same name from the musical *Avenue Q* (2003).
2. Lauren Rosewarne, *Masturbation in Pop Culture: Screen, Society, Self* (Lanham, MD: Lexington Books, 2014).
3. Lauren Rosewarne, "The Euphemisms Chapter," *American Taboo: The Forbidden Words, Unspoken Rules, and Secret Morality of Popular Culture* (Santa Barbara, CA: Praeger, 2013).
4. This situation, in fact, can be interpreted as a consequence of pornification, whereby material that was once considered salacious or titillating no longer is; something I have discussed elsewhere in reference, for example, to the once-arousing pin-up images of the 1940s and 1950s that are now innocuous enough to appear in cosmetics packaging (Lauren Rosewarne, *Sex in Public: Women, Outdoor Advertising and Public Policy* [Newcastle: Cambridge Scholars Publishing, 2007]).
5. Lauren Rosewarne, *Masturbation in Pop Culture: Screen, Society, Self* (Lanham, MD: Lexington Books, 2014), 267.
6. In a 1981 episode of the comedy series *Saturday Night Live* (1975–), musical theatre performer Bernadette Peters sang a song called "Making Love Alone" that equally illustrated these themes: "When one can't make love with another/ one can still make love alone."
7. Steven D. Solomon and Lorie J. Teagno, *Intimacy After Infidelity: How to Rebuild and Affair-Proof Your Marriage* (Oakland, CA: New Harbinger Publications, 2006).
8. In Sandra Leiblum and Nicola Döring, "Internet Sexuality: Known Risks and Fresh Chances for Women," in *Sex and the Internet: A Guidebook for Clinicians*, ed. Al Cooper (New York: Brunner-Routledge, 2002): 19–45, 42.
9. This *rite of passage* idea was apparent in an exchange in the television drama *Cyber Seduction: His Secret Life* (2005), when Diane (Kelly Lynch) spoke to her husband, Richard (John Robinson), about their son's apparent netporn addiction and Richard dismissed her concerns: "It's what teenage boys do. They look at pictures of girls with big boobs."
10. Nicola F. Johnson, *The Multiplicities of Internet Addiction: The Misrecognition of Leisure and Learning* (Burlington, VT: Ashgate, 2009); Mary Manjikian, *Threat Talk: The Comparative Politics of Internet Addiction* (Burlington, VT: Ashgate, 2012); Kimberly S. Young and Cristiano Nabuco de Abreu, *Internet Addiction: A Handbook and Guide to Evaluation and Treatment* (Hoboken, NJ: John Wiley & Sons, 2011).

11. Gail Dines, Robert J. Jensen and Ann Russo, *Pornography: The Production and Consumption of Inequality* (New York: Routledge, 1998).

12. The idea of men turned into sex machines via their use of the Internet is another illustration of techno- and cyberphobias where use of technology is thought to lead to dehumanization.

13. Pamela Paul, *Pornified: How Pornography Is Transforming Our Lives, Our Relationships, and Our Families* (New York: Times Books, 2005).

14. While female sex addicts do exist on screen—for example, Valérie (Belén Fabra) in *Diario de una ninfómana* (*Diary of a Nymphomaniac*) (2008) and Dede (Alecia Moore) in the drama *Thanks for Sharing* (2012)—the portrayal is most commonly male, and porn is more frequently an outlet for male addicts, whereas intercourse is the outlet for women.

15. Gail Dines, Robert J. Jensen and Ann Russo, *Pornography: The Production and Consumption of Inequality* (New York: Routledge, 1998); Pamela Paul, *Pornified: How Pornography Is Transforming Our Lives, Our Relationships, and Our Families* (New York: Times Books, 2005).

16. Kimberly S. Young, "Internet Addiction: The Emergence of a New Clinical Disorder," *104th Annual Meeting of the American Psychological Association*, August 16 (1996); Kimberly S. Young, *Caught in the Net: How to Recognize the Signs of Internet Addiction—And a Winning Strategy for Recovery* (New York: John Wiley & Sons, 1998).

17. Patrick Carnes, *Out of the Shadows: Understanding Sexual Addiction* (Center City, MN: Hazelden, 2001); Claudia Black, *Deceived: Facing Sexual Betrayal Lies and Secrets* (Center City, MN: Hazelden, 2009); Paula Hall, *Understanding and Treating Sex Addiction* (New York: Routledge, 2013).

18. David Greenfield and Maressa Orzack, "The Electronic Bedroom: Clinical Assessment of Online Problems and Internet-Enabled Sexual Behavior," in *Sex and the Internet: A Guidebook for Clinicians*, ed. Al Cooper (New York: Brunner-Routledge, 2002): 129–45, 135.

19. David J. Ley, *The Myth of Sex Addiction* (Lanham, MD: Rowman and Littlefield, 2012).

20. Kimberly S. Young, *Caught in the Net: How to Recognize the Signs of Internet Addiction—And a Winning Strategy for Recovery* (New York: John Wiley & Sons, 1998), 40.

21. Aaron Ben-Ze'ev, *Love Online: Emotions on the Internet* (New York: Cambridge University Press, 2004), 28.

22. Norman H. Nie, "Sociability, Interpersonal Relations, and the Internet: Reconciling Conflicting Findings," *American Behavioral Scientist*, 45, 3 (2001): 420–35, 431.

23. The term "porn cycle" comes from the "Parralox" episode of the British comedy series *Absolutely Fabulous* (1992–2012) when Gran (June Whitfield) remarked, "Once you're stuck in a porn cycle, you can be there for days."

24. Lauren Rosewarne, *Part-Time Perverts: Sex, Pop Culture and Kink Management* (Santa Barbara, CA: Praeger, 2011).

25. Patrick Gay Volney, *Freud on Sublimation: Reconsiderations* (Albany, NY: State University of New York Press, 1992).

26. Lauren Rosewarne, *Masturbation in Pop Culture: Screen, Society, Self* (Lanham, MD: Lexington Books, 2014).

27. This scene provides a very gendered response to the sexlessness in their marriage: whereas Don opts to pay for sex, Helen wants to be romanced within an affair.

28. Todd Spangler, "USA's 'Suits' Gets Down and Flirty with Tinder App," *Variety*, July 12, 2013. Accessed August 1, 2015, from http://variety.com/2013/digital/news/usas-suits-gets-down-and-flirty-with-tinder-app-1200562019/; Audra Schroeder, "Mindy Kaling Wants Tinder Users to Hook Up with Her TV Show," *Daily Dot*, January 2, 2014. Accessed August 1, 2015, from http://www.dailydot.com/entertainment/mindy-project-characters-fake-tinder-profiles/; Itay Hod, "Why Hollywood Is Hooking Up with Tinder, Grindr for Movie, TV and Music Projects," *The Wrap*, June 3, 2015. Accessed August 1, 2015, from http://www.thewrap.com/hollywood-swipes-right-for-tinder-grindr-to-market-movies-tv-and-music/.

29. Christian Klesse, *The Spectre of Promiscuity: Gay Male and Bisexual Non-monogamies and Polyamories* (Burlington, VT: Ashgate Publishing Company, 2007).

30. Kelsea Stahler, "Is Tinder Sexist? Why I Deleted Tinder on Principle, Even Though I Used to Love It," *Bustle*, July 10, 2014. Accessed August 22, 2015, from http://www.bustle.com/articles/30917-is-tinder-sexist-why-i-deleted-tinder-on-principle-even-though-i-used-to-love-it.

31. Robert Payne, *The Promiscuity of Network Culture: Queer Theory and Digital Media* (New York: Routledge, 2015).

32. Gabriela Barkho, "Have Hookup Apps Killed Digital Dating Stigma?" *The Daily Dot*, September 17, 2014. Accessed August 23, 2015, from http://www.dailydot.com/lifestyle/online-dating-stigma/; Amanda Hess, "Online Dating Will Soon Be Obsolete," *Slate*, October 21, 2013. Accessed August 21, 2015, from http://www.slate.com/blogs/xx_factor/2013/10/21/pew_study_on_internet_romance_online_dating_is_more_normal_than_ever_but.html.

33. Jill Stark and Laura Banks, "Love Me Tinder: Is the Hook-up Culture about Liberation or Exploitation?" *Sydney Morning Herald*, December 15, 2013. Accessed August 4, 2015, from http://www.smh.com.au/lifestyle/life/love-me-tinder-is-the-hookup-culture-about-liberation-or-exploitation-20131214–2ze9k.html.

34. Eva Illouz, *Consuming the Romantic Utopia: Love and the Cultural Contradictions of Capitalism* (Berkeley, CA: University of California Press, 1997), 7.

35. Such ideas have links to the way masturbation with sex toys is often framed on screen: "In doing so in these screen examples, the sex toy can be distanced from its status as an *object* and instead becomes imbued with qualities that make it more akin to a human sex partner. Thinking of vibrators this way can, of course, also signify a kind of sexual desperation: Helen [Dianne Wiest] in [the comedy] *Parenthood* [1989] for example, rhetorically asked her daughter, "Do you know why I'm having sex with machinery?" ... Helen presented sex-with-machinery as the *ultimate* desperation, debasement and notably *dehumanization*." (Lauren Rosewarne, *Masturbation in Pop Culture: Screen, Society, Self* [Lanham, MD: Lexington Books, 2014], 78).

36. Judith Silverstein and Michael Lasky, *Online Dating for Dummies* (Hoboken, NJ: Wiley Publishing, 2004); Bonnie Jacobson, *The Shy Single: A Bold Guide to Dating for the Less-Than-Bold Dater* (Emmaus, PA: Rodale, 2004); Laurie Davis, *Love at First Click: The Ultimate Guide to Online Dating* (New York: Simon and Schuster, 2013).

37. Ilana Gershon, *The Breakup 2.0: Disconnecting Over New Media* (Ithaca, NY: Cornell University Press, 2010), 147.

38. This scene connects to the deception discussed in Chapter 4, notably of the male characters posing as lesbians to get vicarious access to women.

39. John C. Bridges, *The Illusion of Intimacy: Problems in the World of Online Dating* (Santa Barbara, CA: Praeger, 2012), 6.

40. In numerous scenes, characters specifically refer to "people from the Internet" as strangers. In the drama *On_Line* (2002), Al (John Fleck) discussed with Jordan (Vanessa Ferlito) his burgeoning relationship with online Ed (Eric Millegan) and the possibility of moving things offline: "I-I don't have strangers over to my apartment." In the horror film *Smiley* (2012), Ashley (Caitlin Gerard) mused about online communications, "Why would you chat with strangers? Isn't that dumb?" In the "Generation of Vipers" episode of the British crime-drama *Lewis* (2007–), the title character Lewis (Kevin Whately) expressed wariness about online dating, "Exposing yourself to millions of strangers. I don't know."

41. Katherine M. Hertlein, "The Integration of Technology into Sex Therapy," *Journal of Family Psychotherapy*, 21 (2010): 117–31, 121.

42. Al Cooper, Coralie Scherer and I. David Marcus, "Harnessing the Power of the Internet to Improve Sexual Relationships," in *Sex and the Internet: A Guidebook for Clinicians*, ed. Al Cooper (New York: Brunner-Routledge, 2002): 209–30, 219.

43. See, for example, phone sex scenes in the crime-drama *Get Carter* (1971), the drama *Somewhere Tonight* (2011), the comedy-drama *Girl 6* (1996), the romantic-comedies *The Truth About Cats and Dogs* (1996), *Easier With Practice* (2000) and *Going the Distance* (2012) and the British drama *Burn It* (2003).

44. Brian X. Chen, *Always On* (Philadelphia, PA: Da Capo Press, 2012), 162.

45. Lauren Rosewarne, *Cyberbullies, Cyberactivists, Cyberpredators: Film, TV, and Internet Stereotypes* (Santa Barbara, CA: Praeger, 2016).

46. Lauren Rosewarne, *Cyberbullies, Cyberactivists, Cyberpredators: Film, TV, and Internet Stereotypes* (Santa Barbara, CA: Praeger, 2016).

47. In Ilana Gershon, *The Breakup 2.0: Disconnecting Over New Media* (Ithaca, NY: Cornell University Press, 2010), 146.

48. Ilana Gershon, *The Breakup 2.0: Disconnecting Over New Media* (Ithaca, NY: Cornell University Press, 2010).

49. Belinda Luscombe, "Facebook and Divorce: Airing the Dirty Laundry," *Time*, June 22, 2009. Accessed August 3, 2015, from http://content.time.com/time/magazine/article/0,9171,1904147,00.html.

50. Ilana Gershon, *The Breakup 2.0: Disconnecting Over New Media* (Ithaca, NY: Cornell University Press, 2010), 147.

51. Mai-Ly N. Steers, Robert E. Wickham and Linda K. Acitelli, "Seeing Everyone Else's Highlight Reels: How Facebook Usage Is Linked to Depressive Symptoms," *Journal of Social and Clinical Psychology*, 33, 8 (2014): 701–31.

52. In real life, the complexity of uncoupling on social media was acknowledged by Facebook in their 2015 efforts to help people reduce users' exposure to updates from ex-partners (Molly McHugh, "Facebook Breakups Just Got a Little Less Depressing," *Wired*, November 19, 2015. Accessed December 15, 2015, from http://www.wired.com/2015/11/facebook-breakup-tools/).

53. Allen W. Batteau, *Technology and Culture* (Long Grove, IL: Waveland Press, 2010), 114.

54. Sherry Turkle, *Alone Together: Why We Expect More from Technology and Less from Each Other* (New York: Basic Books, 2011).
55. Robert D. Putnam, *Bowling Alone: The Collapse and Revival of American Community* (New York: Simon and Schuster, 2000).
56. Daniel Dinello discussed this idea in his book *Technophobia!*: "Humans adapting to a machine environment get *less human* and more machine-like in the process. Technology creates its own requirements and forces humans to conform or die" (Daniel Dinello, *Technophobia! Science Fiction Visions of Posthuman Technology* [Austin, TX: University of Texas Press, 2005], 98).

6   The Quest for Kink

In the "Tongue-Tied" episode of the comedy-drama *Orange is the New Black* (2013–), Piper (Taylor Schilling) and Stella (Ruby Rose) were discussing the spectrum of fetishists, including bronies and furries, when fellow inmate Cindy (Adrienne C. Moore) interjected:

> See, that's the thing with the Internet. Nobody's a freak no more. See, it used to be all these weirdos sitting alone in their houses, jerking it to bugs or falling in love with their toasters, feeling all creepy and sad. Now, all they got to do is log on and find the same-minded toaster-loving peeps and, like, bam, suddenly shit be perfectly normal! Shawty, you could be into cannibalism or like being tickled. It don't matter. Somebody out there gonna like what you like.

Since the earliest days of the Internet—and something that has only exacerbated since—the technology has been used to link people with similar fringe interests. While initially those interests centered on computing, the technology very quickly became used to connect people with *sexual* interests—be it bug fetishes, or cannibalism as mentioned, or more commonly homosexuality and sadomasochism—that deviate from the norm.[1] In his work on online dating, cultural theorist Yow-Juin Wang contended that "cyberspace creates new possibilities for exploring one's sexuality,"[2] and certainly on screen the Internet is shown to serve as an important tool in helping people to explore their sexual selves and, more specifically, participate in their kinks.

This chapter focuses on nonvanilla activities. I use *nonvanilla* in this chapter to refer to sexual activity that is considered in some way renegade or, as described by queer theorist Gayle Rubin, *bad*:

> Bad sex may be homosexual, unmarried, promiscuous, non-procreative, or commercial. It may be masturbatory or take place at orgies, may be casual, may cross generational lines, and may take place in "public" or at least in the bushes or the baths. It may involve the use of pornography, fetish objects, sex toys or unusual roles.[3]

From acts of infidelity through to homosexuality, exhibitionism and voyeurism, this chapter focuses on the Internet's role in bad sex participation.

This chapter begins with a discussion of the Internet's involvement in the mainstreaming of nonvanilla activity and then examines specific sexual interests that get catered to by the technology. The role of the Internet in infidelity is then examined, with an exploration of how netporn, chatrooms and cybersex have each forced a rethink on what constitutes betrayal in the Internet age. Homosexuality as the most common sexual deviation on screen is then analyzed as an example of how fringe sexual practices have been revolutionized by the Web.

Mainstreaming the Perverse

It is impossible to have a conversation about nonvanilla sexualities and *not* mention the Internet. Pornification—something defined as the movement or, more critically, the *creep*[4] of the sex industry, specifically pornography, into other mainstream media including advertising, film and television—is routinely bundled with the Internet in academic discussions[5]: the Web has made access to pornography effortless, has made doing so anonymous and inexpensive and has helped to legitimize the consumption of this once taboo product.

Screen fiction has certainly had a role in contributing to Internet-aided mainstreaming: as discussed in Chapter 5, a range of narratives show characters masturbating while watching netporn and participating in cybersex (Chapter 5), helping to simultaneously normalize (as well as frequently demonize) the access of explicit material for self-stimulation. The mainstreaming of nonvanilla sexual practices in real life has also been credited to netporn: there is not merely a greater availability of sexually explicit material online, but more specifically, an availability of kinky content that, arguably, has stirred in us previously unrecognized sexual desires. Heterosexual anal sex, for example, which long existed as a taboo is now participated in at higher rates than ever before; a social change thought attributable—at least in part—to the high presence of the act in netporn.[6]

While certain nonvanilla sexualities discussed in this chapter have more taboo attached than others—child pornography being one example—this chapter isn't about the ethics or morality of accessing such material, rather, simply focuses on screen fiction mirroring and narrating a key role for the Internet.

Internet Temptations

In their discussion of the Polaroid camera, sociologists Charles Edgley and Kenneth Kiser wrote: "Every technological innovation creates deviant as well as respectable possibilities ... the machine itself does not dictate the moral choice; human beings do that."[7] The authors do, however, note that, "it would be foolish to believe that the availability of certain technologies did not make possible certain moral choices that were previously difficult or impossible to arrange."[8] This latter point certainly has traction on screen where the Internet is presented as creating a moral quandary for users as well as alerting them to sexual possibilities that may not have been properly considered previously. In the drama *Men, Women & Children* (2014), for example, fifteen-year-old Chris (Travis Tope) has specific sexual interests centered on dominance and submission. At one point in the narrative, the narrator (Emma Thompson) identified the Internet as having *dictated* Chris's perversions:

> Chris Truby began surfing pornography at the age of ten with a simple search of the word "boobs." This somewhat innocent query led to a series of clicks and within an hour of his first search Chris was watching a short video entitled "Titty Fucking Cum Queen." He might have thought this video to be unusual had it not already been viewed by three million others. By age fifteen, Chris found it difficult to achieve an erection without viewing a level of deviance that fell well outside societal norms.

The British drama *Chatroom* (2010)—where live-action displays dramatized chatroom exchanges—similarly hinted to a causal link between the Internet and deviance. In one scene, teenager Mo (Daniel Kaluuya) watched a young girl, Keisha (Rebecca McLintock), doing gymnastics (presumably a way to depict him watching an online video). Later, while in a chatroom, Mo asked William (Aaron Taylor-Johnson) whether seventeen is old enough to be called a pedophile:

WILLIAM: Have you tried anything?
MO: No! I'm ashamed of myself.

Chris in *Men, Women & Children* was presented as a young man who, at the "innocent" age of ten, had his entire sexuality corrupted by the Internet. This simplistic causal-link portrayal is undoubtedly what commentators had in mind when they criticized the film as a "trite fresco,"[9] "[a] clumsy, clammy critique of modern web culture"[10] and an "anti-Internet screed."[11] Mo in *Chatroom* is similarly presented as an impressionable teenager who has, apparently, been coached by the Internet to sexualize young women. While less heavy-handed than *Men, Women & Children*, *Chatroom* nonetheless presents the Internet as having the capacity to create desires and also provide an outlet for them. In both examples, neither of these male teens are presented as *naturally* deviant, but rather, both were apparently made deviant by the Internet.

The sociologist John Bridges discussed the role of the Internet in encouraging out-of-character sexual behavior:

> It can also evolve into a new type of impulsive "acting out"—a type of technological sex addiction that involves changes in behavior that are facilitated by the online technologies.[12]

Psychologist Robert Freeman-Longo took these ideas further, identifying cases of young people who, after viewing neporn, proceeded to sexually abuse siblings.[13] While Freeman-Longo presents a rather extreme—and controversial—view of the capacities of the media to affect, nonetheless, such ideas play out in *Men, Women & Children* and *Chatroom*: both Chris and Mo were tempted to act in sexual ways that offline seemingly had never previously occurred to them—the Internet *implanted* the temptation. These ideas align with research examining the Internet's role in arenas such as pedophilia where it exists as a constant source of temptation for pedophiles; something that the psychiatrist Fred Berlin discussed in the context of one of his patients:

> This is a wonderfully successful man, he teaches and has various other professional involvements, yet he's been struggling with not downloading images of child pornography from the Internet. He has never abused a child sexually, but if he gets caught doing this [viewing child porn] he will be a registered sex offender and he will go to jail for a long time. It's been a poignant struggle. He has been on the verge of suicide.[14]

While the Internet is, as discussed in the remainder of this chapter, more commonly presented as an *outlet* for pedophilia as opposed to (controversially) creating the initial desire for it, other screen examples frame the Internet as more explicitly responsible for temptation, notably in narratives where pornography and infidelity are themes; while both constitute *bad* sex, they are nevertheless substantially more socially acceptable than pedophilia or sadomasochism.

In the Christian-drama *The Saber* (2007), temptation is given physical form when a black-clad holographic woman appears by Cameron's (Zac Klammer) side while he sits at the computer: she exists as a figure to tempt him into the world of netporn. In the Christian-drama *Fireproof* (2008), Caleb (Kirk Cameron) is at his computer browsing the Internet when a pop-up ad for a porn site distracts him. These examples—both, unsurprisingly, situated within media content with a distinct morality agenda—portray the Internet as a constant source of temptation for sexual transgressions of the legal but perhaps not *moral* kind. Such themes, however, are also detected outside of Christian-drama. In the sex addiction–themed drama *Thanks for Sharing* (2012), sex-addicted characters have to physically remove temptations from their vicinity—for example, television sets and, notably, Wi-Fi–enabled laptops—for fear of succumbing to the great temptation of the Internet.

In *Men, Women & Children*, it is a television commercial for the website AshleyMadison.com that plants the seed of temptation for both Helen (Rosemarie DeWitt) and Don (Adam Sandler). While the sexless and unhappy nature of their dyad was evident from the beginning of the film—and while Don's use of netporn was established early into the narrative—it was only when the couple saw the television commercial with the "life is short, have an affair" tagline, that the idea of an affair appeared to seduce both. Similarly, it was a television commercial for an app that tempted Marshall (Houston Rhines) in the gay-themed romantic-comedy *eCupid* (2011), to betray his long-term partner.[15] These narratives, while not eliminating the capacity for "free will," frame the Internet as a quite literal temptation, as an explanation for transgression and also as something that constantly needs to be battled with, in line with techno- and cyberphobia presentations that frame new technology as fueling a constant struggle between man and machine.

In the next section this idea of infidelity is explored in greater detail with an examination of Internet-aided infidelity on screen. I explore how such scenes make defining cheating more complicated and assess the role of the Internet as a cause.

The Affair

In the "Looking for Home" episode of the gay-drama *Looking* (2014–15), Patrick (Jonathan Groff) discovered that his boyfriend, Kevin (Russell Tovey), had an active profile on the gay male hook-up app Grindr. Patrick construed the behavior as cheating even though Kevin seemingly hadn't actually hooked-up with anyone while he had been with Patrick; the fact that Kevin was still recreationally browsing created for Patrick *the capacity* for him to act. While the definitions of infidelity as pertaining to online conduct are contentious—something addressed later in this section—for the purpose of this section, I include all sex-themed acts of intimacy outside of a relationship as infidelity: Don and Helen's extramarital intercourse in *Men, Women & Children* is an obvious example, but equally so is the cybersex participated in by Adam (C. Thomas Howell) in the thriller *Net Games* (2003), along with the emotional affairs of Jake (Adrian Hough) and Beth (Dina Meyer) in the television thriller *Web of Desire* (2009). Even Patrick's browsing in *Looking* is an act of recreational intimacy and, in turn, constitutes infidelity for the purposes of this discussion, whereby Kevin is courting the *possibility* of future intimacy options. While I am using the term *infidelity*, this is not a moral condemnation of behavior but rather, simply a shorthand way to cluster Internet-aided sexual behaviors happening outside of a committed dyad.

Akin to what transpired in *Men, Women & Children*, the Korean romantic-comedy *Baram-pigi joheun nal* (*A Day for an Affair*) (2007), portrayed Internet-aided infidelity in line with a traditional, straight-forward extramarital-sex definition: two married women, Tweetie (Jin-seo Yoon)

and Dewdrop (Hye-su Kim), used the Internet to orchestrate online affairs
that eventually moved offline. Something similar transpired in the thriller
Downloading Nancy (2008), whereby unhappily married Nancy's (Maria
Bello) relationship with Louis (Jason Patric) began online and then became
physical offline. Most examples, however, frame Internet-aided infidelity as
more ambiguous, thus reflecting debates in the zeitgeist and academic literature about how betrayal needs to be rethought in a world of screen names
and cybersex. A humorous example of definitional contestation transpired
in the "Virtual Reality" episode of the sitcom *Mad About You* (1992–99),
when Paul (Paul Reiser) used a virtual reality headset and sensory gloves to
experience intimacy; something his wife, Jamie (Helen Hunt), construed as
betrayal:

PAUL: You can ski on the Alps. You're riding a raft through the Colorado
    River. You're in the space shuttle. You're flying all over the Earth. You
    can sing on Broadway. You're on-stage, singing. And everything you do,
    it's like you're doing it. You're right there.
JAMIE: Could we do these things together?
PAUL: Of course, yeah.
JAMIE: What did you do?
PAUL: I gave Christie Brinkley a massage. She had an itch. Listen, I gotta
    tell you, it's phenomenal. You really, you can't believe what this is. It's
    like, I'm like, it's Christie Brinkley. I'm looking at Christie Brinkley. I'm
    talking to Christie Brinkley. Christie Brinkley is talking to me. We're
    talking. Christie Brinkley and I were talk—You could see her. I could
    feel Christie Brinkley. You know? It's so funny. They had, like, lotion,
    this oil, so she asked me to put on some. I'm putting this lotion, and
    I'm rubbing oil right on her. And I'm telling you, you've never felt skin
    like this.
JAMIE: You're a little, little man.
PAUL: What?
JAMIE: You could choose anything and that's what you chose? To be with
    another woman?
PAUL: I was waiting for a bus. She started it. No, she did.
JAMIE: Have you no shame?
PAUL: Listen, it's not like I was really with her.
JAMIE: Yes, it was. You just got finished telling me how incredibly real it was.

Just as the simulated reality experience had felt real to Paul, it also felt real
to Jamie, a situation that Paul didn't understand until Jamie used the technology herself and he promptly feared that she would use it for sex with
another man.[16] The definition of cheating in the Internet age is also debated
in other screen examples. In the "Lifeline" episode of the lesbian-themed drama
series *The L Word* (2004–9), Tina (Laurel Holloman) used chatrooms to play
out her attraction to men. When her partner, Bette (Jennifer Beals) found

out, she considered this as betrayal even if Tina rationalized it as just play (Chapter 2). This can be likened to Patrick's (Teddy Sears) sadomasochistic chatroom participation in the "Rubber Man" episode of the horror series *American Horror Story* (2011–): Patrick construed his participation as just a masturbatory way to experience his interest in sadomasochism; his partner, Chad (Zachary Quinto), however, interpreted it as betrayal. In the drama *Chloe* (2009), Catherine (Julianne Moore) suspected her husband David (Liam Neeson) of infidelity: her suspicion was fueled when she saw him typing on his computer and laughing; Catherine appeared to assume that such a display was about intimacies shared outside of their marriage. These ideas were taken further in the suburban-drama *Little Children* (2006): Richard (Gregg Edelman) was obsessed with the SluttyKay [Sarah Buxton] webcam site and masturbated to it regularly, eventually getting caught by his wife, Sarah (Kate Winslet). So real was Sarah's sense of betrayal that the two began to sleep separately thereafter.

The examples discussed in this section highlight a range of topics worth unpacking, from definitional issues through to some of the unique properties of the Internet in the facilitation of sexual transgressions.

Defining Betrayal

While I deliberately used a very broad definition of infidelity earlier, the notion of what constitutes infidelity in the Internet age, in fact, is highly contentious. In their book *Sexual Arrangements*, psychologists Janet Reibstein and Martin Richards present a traditional definition of an affair: "a sexual relationship between people who are not married to each other and when at least one of the partners in this relationship is married to someone else."[17] Certainly this definition describes what transpired in *Men, Women & Children*, *Baram-pigi joheun nal* (*A Day for an Affair*) and *Downloading Nancy*. While *sexual relationship* might imply intercourse, it may not in fact be essential. Sociologists Arthur Neal and Sara Collas, for example, acknowledge that a physical component may not be needed for infidelity to transpire: "Secrecy, emotional intensity, and sexual chemistry (even if they don't touch) are the basic ingredients of an extramarital affair."[18] Certainly in narratives where the relationship is played out entirely online, the idea of what constitutes "sexual" gets problematized and emotional intimacy comes to have enhanced prominence. In the biopic *Talhotblond* (2012), for example—centered on a real-life catfishing case—Amanda (Courteney Cox) remarked, "It is the digital age. You don't have to leave your house to have an affair." In sync with Amanda's comment, Neal and Collas' definition provides a useful way to analyze Internet-aided relationships where the "cheating" may involve something other than extramarital intercourse. In *Little Children*, for example, it was clear that despite no physical touch with another person transpiring, Richard had become obsessed with SluttyKay and his (albeit one-sided) liaison had proven destructive for his marriage. In *Net Games*, while Adam had no offline sexual contact with Angel (Lala Sloatman), like Richard in *Little Children*, Adam's interactions with Angel were nonetheless experienced as erotic: genital stimulation still transpired; Angel in fact, surreptitiously photographed Adam masturbating at his computer as part of a blackmail strategy. The importance of genital stimulation, in fact, was addressed by Christa Worthington in her article about cyberinfidelity for the British newspaper *The Independent*: "The flesh is certainly involved. The glands do engage in cybersex, even if bodies never do."[19] In *Web of Desire*, while we don't know whether Beth or Jake masturbated during their chatroom encounters with Finn, we certainly know that intimate messages were exchanged and that Finn certainly believed that intimacy was transpiring; something evident in an offline altercation between Jake and Finn at the end of the film:

FINN: Jake, you told me how much you wanted to touch me. Well I'm here now, Jake. Touch me.
JAKE: I also said that I'd never go through with it because despite everything I still love my wife. Finn, it's the Internet. How could you take that seriously? I didn't even know your real name. I stopped emailing you. I cancelled my account.

Like Angel in *Net Games*, Finn construed the cybersex as real, as authentic, whereas Jake, akin to Adam, viewed the behavior online as recreational (and thus, *less real*).[20] In Chapter 2 I examined the concept of the authenticity of online-instigated relationships; the scenes discussed in this section provide interesting illustrations of this idea, whereby the liaisons may have felt real to the people betrayed even if for the participants it was construed only as play. A good illustration of this perception-disparity transpired in the drama *Disconnect* (2012). Cindy (Paula Patton) had lost her son and spent extensive time in a grief chatroom communicating with a man, Stephen (Michael Nyqvist), who is later suspected of stealing Cindy and Derek's (Alexander Skarsgård) banking information. Interestingly, despite the very platonic nature of Cindy's relationship with Stephen—"He talked to me when you wouldn't," Cindy explained to her husband—Derek still construed Cindy's online relationship as a betrayal. Derek, in fact, actually went after Stephen with a gun even *after* finding out that he hadn't been the identity thief; seemingly Stephen's true crime was his emotional intimacy with Cindy.[21]

Certainly in published literature on this topic, the complexity of infidelity in the Internet age—and the divide between those who think it is only fantasy-fueled masturbation versus others who contend that emotions and arousal make it cheating—are easily detected. The philosopher Aaron Ben-Ze'ev, for example, discussed a study whereby 75% of participants claimed to find it acceptable for their partner to visit a porn site, whereas 77% said it would be *unacceptable* for their partner to participate in an adult one-on-one video conversation: as Ben-Ze'ev surmised, "Due to the interactive nature of cyberspace, virtual activities on the Net are accorded moral significance."[22] A man quoted by Ben-Ze-ev certainly adhered to this distinction:

> Cybersex is closer to having a hooker than plain pornography because there is a real and active person involved on the other end. People are touching each others' minds in a mutual and cooperate way that silent fantasy does not permit.[23]

While it is not clear whether Sarah in *Little Children* quite knew the nature of Richard's relationship with SluttyKay, nonetheless, it was clear that she felt "something" was going on and that that something constituted a betrayal. Equally, Sarah may have interpreted that her husband was problematically spending his sexual resources on SluttyKay rather than inside their marriage; certainly these were the sentiments felt by Catherine in *Chloe* who was seemingly jealous of the pleasure her husband was reaping from his online communications, along with Derek's sentiments in *Disconnect* when his wife sought intimate counsel outside of their marriage. In *Don Jon* discussed earlier, Barbara clearly felt that Jon's continued use of pornography was a betrayal; while Barbara's views on this topic—beyond considering the material as "fucking disgusting"—were not discussed in the film, it appeared that she felt that she should be enough for him.

While in the examples discussed thus far online intimacies are construed as betrayal, in fact, some screen examples present an alternate take on this topic and depict partners with a substantially more liberal attitude; in turn, potentially serving as modern, Internet-age narratives whereby the opportunities presented by the technology are embraced rather than construed as threatening. In the "Chapter 23" episode of the political-drama *House of Cards* (2013–) for example, after Francis (Kevin Spacey) was caught watching netporn by one of his security personnel, he relayed the story to his wife, Claire (Robin Wright), who in fact found it hilarious. The scene served as an insight into the couple's unconventional relationship, and in fact, Francis being sprung became a catalyst for a later threesome. Similarly, in *Net Games*, despite Jennifer being a fragile character, she didn't, in fact, appear to find Adam's cybersex as a significant betrayal, rather she quickly banded with him to fight against the shared enemy of Angel; a response, noteworthily akin to narratives where betrayed wives choose to focus their blame on the *other woman* rather than their cheating husband (akin to Derek in *Disconnect* blaming Stephen instead of his wife).[24] Certainly this comparatively liberal attitude is a theme identifiable in published literature. A married female cybersex participant in Ben-Ze'ev's research, for example, clearly distinguished her behavior from infidelity: "it's a good way to act out fantasies of being with someone new, being with a stranger, etc. without actually doing it."[25] A married woman in Cathy Winks and Anne Semans' work similarly described, "My spouse is aware and approves and does the same himself. We consider it a healthy pressure valve for monogamy and we are brutally honest with our online partners about our unavailability in real life."[26] Sex researchers Sandra Leiblum and Nicola Döring discussed a husband whose affair had devastated his wife. He committed to never doing it again and decided to get involved with MUDs [Multi-User Dungeons], whereby he could play out little romances without "real" betrayal:

> Martin decided to tell Beth about his MUD sex life, and after reflection, she told him she did not mind. Beth made a conscious decision to consider Martin's sexual relationships on MUDs as more like his reading an erotic novel than his having a rendezvous in a motel room.[27]

Rather than the Internet immediately being exclusively construed as a threat, in fact, it is framed by Martin and Beth as potentially boasting safer, zeitgeist-abreast outlets for people in a world where temptation is ever-present, if not also potentially serving as a marital aid.[28]

In Chapter 5, in the context of netporn addiction, I discussed the idea of *time* being perceived differently when online; an idea with specific relevance to Internet-aided infidelity.

The Bonus Round

In my book *Cheating on the Sisterhood: Infidelity and Feminism*, I proposed the idea of the "bonus round" in affairs:

> An affair is distinguished from a committed relationship in numerous ways, most notably in its separation from reality and everydayness and its existence in a kind of bonus round ... The bonus round of infidelity means that, in most cases, participants frequently live outside of their affair, usually residing in their real worlds of commit[ment].[29]

As related to *online* relationships, psychologists Jo Lamble and Sue Morris present a similar idea:

> In Internet relationships the couple tend to stay in the bubble because the relationship cannot be incorporated into everyday life—it only occurs on the computer screen and in your heart and mind ... There's no opportunity for the bubble to burst because this can only happen in the normal chaos of daily living ... If you think about it, there really is not a lot of different between an e-relationship and a holiday romance.[30]

On screen this possibility of cybersex offering something exciting and existing in a different reality played out in *Little Children*. The narrator

(Will Lyman), for example, discussed Richard's relationship with the SluttyKay site, describing an occasion when he was in his office perusing the site but had to abruptly click out when approached by a colleague: "Casually, but with great haste, Richard banished SluttyKay from his screen ... and re-entered the flow of an ordinary day." Richard's time with SluttyKay existed *outside* of the parameters of normalcy in a kind of bonus round, outside of the flows of the ordinary. The concept of a bonus round—commonly used in computer gaming—has amplified relevance for other online behaviors. Any affair—regardless of where it is initiated or where it plays out—has properties such as it being secret, escapist and existing beyond the ordinary (a hallmark, after all, of romance), in turn making it seem special if not as, the sociologist Eva Illouz suggests, *sacred*, given that romantic love has replaced religion as the modern source of meaning and significance.[31] The Internet is able to bolster these feelings, something Ben-Ze'ev discussed:

> Cyberspace does not merely significantly increase the availability of desired alternatives, but it is in fact an alternative, available world which runs parallel to the actual one ... For many people, cyberspace is even better than the world they actually live in.[32]

In some examples, this desire to escape through Internet-aided intimacy, in fact, gets verbalized. In *Baram-pigi joheun nal* (*A Day for an Affair*), when Tweetie first meets her online date in person, some of her first words to him are, "let's go somewhere far." Tweetie seemingly wants the bubble of their courtship—and its separation from her real life—to continue in their physical interactions. Such feelings, in fact, can prove so tempting that cybersex and online affairs can become addictive, something psychologist Mark Schwartz and Stephen Southern addressed:

> Compulsive cybersex represents a courtship disorder in which the "high" of being wanted by someone for sex regulates affect and bolsters a fragile self. The fantasy world of cybersex is a dissociative experience in which a person escapes the demands of daily life, as well as the pain and shame of past trauma.[33]

As mentioned in Chapter 5, time in the context of cyberspace has high-level malleability. More than this, and an idea discussed in Chapter 2, is that the nature of online relationships—most notably, *online-exclusive* relationships—is the importance of imagination; something with amplified significance in the context of infidelity whereby an imagined life away from domesticity is crucial. The Internet-aided affair, therefore, exists in a safe bubble where it is perfect—because it is not subject to the same stressors as an in-person relationship—albeit as one with the capacity to be consuming, as it was for Richard in *Little Children*.

Blaming the Internet

In Chapter 1 I discussed the economic themes underpinning online dating and notably identified the *planned obsolescence* interpretation of such liaisons: that in a landscape where securing new relationships is easy—not to mention in a world where, as noted, love has more prominence than religious faith—little incentive exists to remain in a liaison that fails to fulfil needs. While a range of literature identifies the idea of the Internet as a source of temptation,[34] more specific is the connection made to infidelity. Dan Slater's book *Love in the Time of Algorithms* spends much time exploring the relationship between the Internet and infidelity and at one point the author asks:

> If dating through the Internet becomes more and more popular, and sites become more efficient, what do you think will happen to commitment when people discover how much easier it's become to find new relationships?[35]

Slater references research done with those working in the online dating industry and noted that a prominent perception was that "Internet dating may be partly responsible for a rise in divorce rates."[36] This idea is, in fact, repeated in a range of academic studies. Counsellors Christine Murray and Emily Campbell noted that while technology provides a range of positives for relationships including "communicating, sharing affection, planning, and learning about one another,"[37] that significant deficits exist including technology leading to more "superficial and inauthentic" forms of connectedness,[38] that technology can take time and energy away from a relationship and notably that technology can help people form relationships and have easy access to people *other* than their partners. Communications scholars Russell Clayton, Alexander Nagurney and Jessica Smith undertook a study on heavy users of Facebook, finding a correlation between use of the site and "negative relationship outcomes" including physical and emotional cheating and divorce.[39] Psychologists Jaclyn Cravens and Jason Whiting unearthed similar findings.[40] Clayton, in his study of heavy users of Twitter, also found a correlation between use of the microblogging site and negative relationship outcomes including infidelity, breakup and divorce.[41] More broadly, psychologists identify a burgeoning role for the Internet in modern infidelity and relationship breakdown.[42] Even aside from breakups, people feeling neglected over their partners' Internet use is often identified as an Internet-age relationship dilemma and one that was flagged in the earliest days of the technology: reference to the *Internet widow* for example, dates back at least as early as 1995 in Alice Woolley's article for the British newspaper *The Independent*:

> The politician's wife knows her husband is vulnerable to affairs. The golf widow doesn't see her man from dawn till dusk. But spare a thought for those of us who share our lives with a computer nerd: you see, no woman can compete with a Mac and a modem.[43]

In Chapter 5, I outlined the problem of the Internet keeping us connected to past partners via social media. This idea alludes to another way that the Internet serves to tempt by granting access to things—sensations as well as people— that in previous eras were more difficult to obtain. A key aspect of this is access to the past. While the capacity for infidelity to make participants feel younger is something I have examined elsewhere,[44] more specifically it can give users access to bygone relationships and emotions. In the documentary *Talhotblond* (2009), for example, one of Thomas's explanations for engaging in his cyber-affair was nostalgia: "It made me feel like a kid again. Back when I thought I was happier." This very idea is depicted visually in the 2012 television biopic of the same name when, during the height of his cyberaffair, middle-aged Thomas looked in the mirror and saw an image of a much younger man reflected back at him. Without leaving his home, Thomas could experience some of the positives of an offline affair. Nostalgia, of course, has heightened relevance in the world of social media where connection to past loves, classmates and acquaintances are mere clicks away. In the Christian-drama *Online* (2013), a social networking site enabled John (Morgan Ayres) to reconnect with his high school love, Adrianna (Esseri Holmes), and facilitated the beginnings of an affair: tracking down Adrianna prior to the Internet age would have involved substantially more work than just a couple of mouse clicks while sitting in his office. The social scientist Alexander Lambert explored such nostalgia in his book *Intimacy and Friendship on Facebook*:

> Connecting with a *strong* tie who has moved out of one's immediate life-world provides emotional rewards which cannot be overstated … Wrapped up with the prevention of loss, Facebook offers the seductive possibility of 'return' … For estranged ties in particular, the desire to 'return' is a powerful one, imbued with nostalgia.[45]

Ben-Ze'ev also discussed nostalgia in *Love Online*:

> Online distant relationships are often associated with nostalgia. Nostalgia is a longing for circumstances that no longer exist or have never existed. Nostalgia has a utopian dimension stemming from the considerable role imagination plays in it. Hence, nostalgia is often about virtual reality that cannot be actualized. In this sense, nostalgia is not always about the past; it can be directed towards the future or the present.[46]

Nostalgia is something intimately linked to infidelity, not just about connecting a person to their past or to past lovers, but simply to qualities that have waned in their existing intimate relationships; something Leiblum and Döring discuss:

> [W]omen who have felt sexually ignored or rejected by their real-life partner may go online and discover that they become sought-after sexual playmates and the recipient of gratifying comments and compliments.[47]

This same idea was discussed in Carol Parker's memoir *The Joy of Cybersex* as related to her online sexual experiences outside of her marriage.[48] For Nancy in *Downloading Nancy*, her husband was distracted, preoccupied by everything but her; she was left depressed and resentful. Going online enabled Nancy to feel a level of excitement that her committed relationship no longer offered. A similar dynamic was evident in *Men, Women & Children*: Helen and her husband were in a relationship without passion and excitement; Helen's AshleyMadison-aided affair gave her back some emotional highs.[49]

Regardless of whether the Internet is a cause for infidelity or simply a means to cater it, it certainly makes conducting an affair easy due to some of the specific attributes of the technology. The psychologist John Suler discussed this issue in the context of the Internet's facilitation of compartmentalization, spotlighting, for example, the technology's role in *disinhibition*:

> When people have the opportunity to separate their actions online from their in-person lifestyle and identity, they feel less vulnerable about self-disclosing and acting-out. Whatever they say or do can't be directly linked to the rest of their lives. In a process of dissociation, they don't have to own their behavior by acknowledging it within the full context of an integrated online/offline identity. The online self becomes a compartmentalized self. In the case of expressed hostilities or other deviant actions, the person can avert responsibility for those behaviors, almost as if superego restrictions and moral cognitive processes have been temporarily suspended from the online psyche. In fact, people might even convince themselves that those online behaviors "aren't me at all."[50]

Compartmentalization has extensive relevance to a discussion on infidelity where the idea of living multiple lives is a hallmark. In *Cheating on the Sisterhood*, I discussed how feelings of wrongdoing, love, lust and betrayal are often boxed away and separated from one's perception of self so that an affair is able to continue.[51] While this is common behavior in any clandestine activity, it has particular relevance to Internet activity whereby an online/offline life-split is standard behavior. A gamer in psychologist Sherry Turkle's book discussed this issue in the context of his online gameplay:

> I split my mind. I'm getting better at it. I can see myself as being two or three or more. And I just turn on one part of my mind and then another when I go from window to window ... And then I'll get a real-time message, and I guess that's RL [real-life]. It's just one more window.[52]

In Chapter 1 I discussed the idea that skills learnt through computing have the capacity to infiltrate our offline behavior, for example, online shopping for goods has influenced online shopping for intimacy. The capacity for offline and online lives to be split—that new *windows can be opened*—is a good example of this, whereby computing has skilled people up with some of the psychological tools useful in infidelity, thus at the very least partly implicating the Internet in the carrying out of affairs by making it both physically and psychologically easier.

In narratives with cybersex as a theme—for example, *Net Games* and *Web of Desire*—the Internet facilitated married people in experiencing a sexual life that was different from what they were used to but to do so from the comfort of their homes or offices and with less disruption to their primary relationships. Similarly, in the aforementioned *Looking* episode, while Kevin's continued browsing of Grindr was hurtful to Patrick, arguably it was *less so* than it would have been if Patrick had actually cheated on him: browsing was a way for Kevin to continue to feel he had options—to feel like he was still participating in the chase—without being a cheater.[53]

Looking centered on the lives of homosexual characters in San Francisco. The series provides a good segue into a discussion about the role of the Internet on screen as related to specifically catering to the needs of characters with same-sex sexual desires. Many of the appeals proffered by the technology for gay characters have relevance to other kinds of sexual deviations and are also explored in the following sections.

The Internet and Homosexuality

The Triple-A engine of the Internet—affordability, accessibility and, notably, *anonymity*[54]—has facilitated participation in a range of sexual practices whereby some of the traditional barriers like cost, supply and exposure have been rendered largely unimportant. The earliest research on the Internet identified a role in connecting the sexually marginalized. Communications theorist John Campbell, for example, noted that "gay men have been quick to employ computer-mediated communication technologies to expand their social networks."[55] Psychologists Michael Ross and Michael Kauth tackled the *why* of this dynamic:

> For men struggling with their sexuality, going to gay bars, bookstores, or support groups makes a public statement about self-identity that can be risky and frightening. However, accessing sexual images on the Internet or participating in male chatrooms entails less personal risk or stigma.[56]

The screen reflects the range of ways that the Internet has been useful for characters on a journey of sexual discovery: as part of quenching curiosities as well as enabling intimate socialization.

The idea of using netporn to explore arousal triggers makes sense: depictions of every imaginable sexual configuration can be found easily.

Therefore, it seems logical that for someone trying to understand his or her own sexuality, that the Internet—that netporn—might play a key role. On screen, putatively heterosexual characters, for example, Charlie (Evan Handler) in the "Dead Rock Stars" episode of the drama *Californication* (2007–14) or Dwight in the "Gay Witch Hunt" episode of the sitcom *The Office* (2005–13), both watch gay netporn. In both examples, however, their viewing was less about a journey of sexual discovery and more so about research: Charlie was trying to carve out a niche for himself as an agent for homosexual writers and Dwight was trying to conjure a gaydar. While in research on coming out stories gay porn is identified as playing a key role,[57] on screen this idea is alluded to in scenes where the type of material chosen for masturbation outs a character.[58] In the Australian drama *2:37* (2006), for example, when the teen jock Luke (Sam Harris) masturbates to gay porn it works to reveal his latent desires. On screen and another role for the Internet in a coming out journey centers on it serving as a tentative step in socialization for young men at the pre-gay stage.[59] The psychotherapist Michael Shernoff identified the process that a person might go through before embracing a gay identity, in turn spotlighting a role for the Internet:

> Psychologically, it may feel vastly safer for a man who is in a stage of pre-gay identity formation to test the waters chatting online with men either to homosocialize or to arrange a sexual liaison, rather than having to actually brave going into a gay bar, club, or community center or having real-life sexual or social encounters, which were the only available options in the days prior to the Internet.[60]

On screen and young gay people using the Internet for homosocializing before actually embracing a gay identity plays out in numerous examples. The comedy *Geography Club* (2013), for example, opened with the teenager RUS96/Russell (Cameron Deane Stewart) scheduling an in-person meeting in a gay chatroom:

72FINS: I have these sick shades. Orange frames. I'll wear those.
RUS96: Cool. I'll be wearing a green shirt with a cartoon lizard on it. Don't be jealous.
72FINS: Ha. Okay.
RUS96: Look ... it's really important you don't tell anyone.
72FINS: For sure. Same here.
RUS96: I mean, I'm not even sure I'm ... you know.
72FINS: Totally get it. I don't like labels either.

In the "Four to Tango" episode of the drama series *Dawson's Creek* (1998–2003), the gay teenager Jack (Kerr Smith) had been exchanging emails with a fellow gay teen, Ben (Tony Schnur), and eventually scheduled an offline meeting. In the "Versatile Toppings" episode of the mystery series *Veronica Mars* (2004–7), the titular teen (Kristen Bell) investigated the hacking of the Pirate's SHIP [Student Homosexual Internet Posting] website, a site established by the gay student Ryan (Bradford Anderson) for closeted Neptune High students to discreetly communicate. These three examples introduce, and also illustrate, several themes underpinning the Internet's relevance to homosexual intimacy seekers but, more so, nonvanilla intimacy seekers more broadly. In the following sections, the role of the Internet in facilitating intimacy for sexual outliers is explored in the areas of gentle entries into sexual subversion, discretion and dabbling.

A Gentle Entry

For teens like 72FINS in *Geography Club* and Jack in *Dawson's Creek*, the Internet allowed them a gentle entry to homosexual life; the technology gave characters who were not yet fully out in their real life the opportunity to socialize online as a homosexual. Most importantly, the technology allowed them to pace the emergence of their homosexual selves. 72FINS in fact, never turned up to the meeting in the park and Jack never went to meet Ben in the café: both characters were, seemingly, not quite ready to completely out themselves as homosexual—they didn't necessarily want to act on their homosexuality *physically* yet, even though homosocializing held great appeal. Ross and Kauth discussed this idea noting, "For many gay and bisexual men, the Internet is a 'safe' place to explore sexual feelings, discover others like them, and develop social and sexual relationships."[61]

The idea of the Internet as a safe place for socializing was also a theme in *Veronica Mars*: the entire reason that the Pirate's SHIP site existed—and also the reason why its hacking was such a concern to the users—was that these teens had not actually come out yet. For such characters there was still a cost to their homosexual identity and thus the Internet provided an opportunity to be discreet, to be anonymous, but to still homosocialize; ideas that Jack in *Dawson's Creek* articulated well in a conversation with his sister, Andie (Meredith Monroe), where he explained why he didn't meet up with Ben:

> Andie, this is different. This is a whole new level of my life that I don't even know if I'm ready for. When I walk through that door and I say hello to this guy my entire life is going to be different. I'm not just going to be telling the world that I'm gay, I'm actually going to *be* gay.

The homosocialization benefit of the Internet for Jack is an idea identifiable in academic discussions, for example, as apparent in the work of the sociologist C.J. Pascoe:

> The internet and new media have given a great gift to gay boys in terms of their ability to find a community of youth like themselves. Because there often are not enough out gay boys at school to form a

community, gay boys use social network sites to link to other teenagers like themselves who might not attend their school. In this way teens both expand their friendship circle and their dating pool.[62]

Jennifer Egan, in a *The New York Times* article from 2000, similarly identified the role of the Internet in helping teens to develop a support system. Her article centered on "Jeffrey" who claimed: "The Internet is the thing that has kept me sane ... the Internet is my refuge":

> For homosexual teenagers with computer access, the Internet has, quite simply, revolutionized the experience of growing up gay. Isolation and shame persist among gay teenagers, of course, but now, along with the inhospitable families and towns in which many find themselves marooned, there exists a parallel online community—real people like them in cyberspace with whom they can chat, exchange messages and even engage in (online) sex. What was most critical to the gay kids I spoke with was the simple, revelatory discovery that they were not alone.[63]

Certainly Pascoe and Egan's comments help illustrate the experiences of the gay characters in *Geography Club*, *Dawson's Creek* and *Veronica Mars* where a life, and identity, outside of their high school life was made possible by technology.

A Discreet Outlet

As apparent in the scenes discussed thus far, the Internet can enable characters to audition a homosexual identity; they can be gay online, digitally meet like-oriented people, and interact in a way that their offline life may not allow, or which they are undecided about whether to commit to it. One reason why the Internet has such a role here is privacy. For the teens in *Geography Club*, *Veronica Mars* and *Dawson's Creek*, discretion is a key theme, an idea depicted in a range of screen examples.

In the "Present Tense" episode of the drama series *Faking It* (2014–), the gay hook-up app "Stubble" is mentioned when Shane (Michael J. Willett) speculated that Duke (Skyler Maxon), a fellow teen in his mixed martial arts class, had a profile on the app. It turned out that Duke was indeed a Stubble-user but explained to Shane, "I'm not out yet so I have to keep things discreet."

The Internet also has a role in allowing adult characters who might still be closeted to discreetly participate in sexual interests that may be embarrassing, illegal or reputation-damaging. Russell (Marc Blucas) in the "The City That Never Sleeps" episode of the police-drama *Blue Bloods* (2010–), for example, was a famous actor who was shadowing officers in preparation for a role. While Russell was putatively heterosexual, during the episode he used the "Tryster" hook-up app to arrange a clandestine liaison with a man. Similar themes transpired in the drama *The Dying Gaul* (2005). Jeffrey (Campbell Scott), was married to Elaine (Patricia Clarkson), and has an affair with the male screenwriter Robert (Peter Sarsgaard). For Jeffrey, erotic email correspondence was part of the fuel, and then became a supplement, to his physical relationship with Robert: Jeffrey was able to use the privacy of the Internet to help him experience a part of his sexuality that was not yet public and which would—and eventually did—have negative consequences on his life if exposed. A closet-themed example at the other end of the sexuality spectrum transpired in the "Lifeline" episode of *The L Word*. Tina (Laurel Holloman) was in a relationship with Bette (Jennifer Beals) but used chatrooms to experience her attraction to men; it was a way for her to play with heterosexual desires—seemingly only a small part of her identity—while remaining in her lesbian dyad.

Social theorist Avi Shoshana investigated the capacity for the Internet to enable people to explore an alternate sexual-self online, notably married heterosexual men who sometimes had sexual encounters with other men. Tamar, for example, a 39-year-old man in the study, illustrated numerous themes discussed thus far in this book, notably the role of the Internet in helping him discreetly acquire—helping him discreetly *shop for* (Chapter 1)—homosexual liaisons while remaining in his marriage:

> This is exactly what I need. I don't need to live with a man or to have sex with only men. I really don't need that. It suits me to have sex with a man let's say once a month, or whenever I need to. There are months that I don't go into the website at all—it's this thing like "oops now I'm inside, oops now I'm outside" ... I am a straight married man who is sometimes also attracted to men. ... The thing is that it is exactly the amount that suits me. I go shopping sometimes [laughs]. Most of the time I don't need to go shopping. Most of the time it suits me to be as if I'm straight, with my wife and the children.[64]

While people like Tamar, as well as Russell in *Blue Bloods*, Jeffrey in *The Dying Gaul* and Tina in *The L Word*, could each be construed as being closeted in their sexuality, this isn't the only interpretation for their online activity; as explored in the next section such characters can be interpreted as *dabbling* in sexuality with the help of the Internet; that rather than thinking of sexuality in the context of fixed and immovable categories, rather, sexuality is something more fluid and categories are able to be moved between with the help of the technology.

Online Sexual Dabbles

Discussed in the context of *Blue Bloods*, *The Dying Gaul* and *The L Word*, were characters who used the Internet to dabble in sexual behaviors that were not reflective of their usual preferences. This idea, in fact, has relevance for Internet-aided participation in a range of nonvanilla sexual behaviors. The most common means by which this is done is netporn, where characters are able to experience their sexuality vicariously by looking at depictions of certain kinky acts and either act simply as a voyeur to the material, alternatively consume it by imagining themselves within it. In the drama *Middle Men* (2009), in one of the netporn entrepreneur Jack's (Luke Wilson) monologues he stated, "Whatever you want to see is there in your home or office, twenty-four hours a day, and it's ready when you are, discreetly, privately, and in whatever flavor you choose." The sociologist Phillip Vannini made a similar point:

> [A]ll I have to do is choose. Brunettes, construction works, redheads, well-hung firefighters, midget couples, bukkake aficionados, watersports buffs, German exhibitions, all await my choice on the virtual shelves of the mall of flesh known as Internet porn.[65]

This idea of *flavor* is detectable in a range of examples where netporn enables characters to dabble in nonvanilla sexuality. In *Men, Women & Children*, Chris uses pornography as an outlet for his dominance and submission themed sexual interests; in the drama *Afterschool* (2008), adolescent Robert (Ezra Miller) does the same thing. In the "Dex, Lies, and Videotape" episode of crime-drama *Dexter* (2006–13), police analyst Vince Masuka (C.S. Lee)—a character consistently presented as perverted[66]—commented to a superior, "So I hear a rumor you're tracking all our internet activity. So is it true? 'Cause I can explain all that she-male stuff." The Internet was used similarly in the "Screams of Silence: The Story of Brenda Q" episode of *Family Guy* (1999–), when Quagmire masturbated to clown netporn.

While thus far I have discussed the Internet aiding legal nonvanilla sexuality, worth noting is the technology used to participate in sex of the illegal variety. One of the biggest downsides of mainstreamed Internet access—one that has received extensive news media attention—is child porn. It is thus no surprise that television, particularly shows with a ripped-from-the-headlines remit, have storylines involving child porn production and distribution, in line with the screen's tendency to suffer from cyberphobia.[67] In a variety of examples, characters use the Internet to access child porn, something that transpires in the "Spankdaddy" episode of the Canadian crime-drama *Blue Murder* (2001–4), the "911," "Friending Emily," "Chat Room" and "Web" episodes of *Law & Order: Special Victims Unit* (1999–) and the "P911" episode of *Criminal Minds* (2005–). While such characters potentially rationalize their behavior as less egregious than child abuse—that watching sexual depictions of children is preferable to seeking physical intimacy from them—of course, their demand for such materials perpetuates to its production. Use of such porn, however, is identified in research as helping to curb desires for physical participation.[68]

In my book *Part-Time Perverts: Sex, Pop Culture and Kink Management* I discussed the concept of *dabbling* in nonmainstream sexuality: where perverse sex gets participated in only occasionally.[69] If we consider the possibilities for multiple identities to play out online, the idea of one of the selves being homosexual (or *heterosexual* as in the case for Tina in *The L Word*), alternatively, a sadomasochist or even a pedophile, makes sense: that despite the reality that sexual interests invariably come to define a person in our culture, in reality the time spent engaged is usually only a very small portion of a life. Certainly the idea of the Internet serving as an outlet to cater to compartmentalized identity[70] is apparent in a range of academic work. In psychologist Kimberly Young's research on online gaming, for example, a Doom-11 player referenced the idea of the Internet providing an outlet for a different self:

> By day, I am a mild-mannered husband and a dedicated worker ... but by night, with a click of the button, I turn into the most aggressive bastard you can imagine. And no one knows it's me doing this. I think it keeps me from actually hurting people—like beating my wife. It's scary to me. I need help with this.[71]

As Turkle summarized, "Experiences on the Internet extend the metaphor of windows—now RL itself ... can be 'just one more window.'"[72] For characters with nonsexual vanilla predilections which they might be titillated by but don't necessarily want to—or can't—participate in, these interests can be dabbled in voyeuristically or vicariously.

While thus far I have discussed *dabbling* in the context of netporn, in fact, the screen offers a range of other ways that characters engage in their favored deviations. This idea was illustrated well in dialogue from the "Mikado" episode of the sci-fi series *Millennium* (1996–99) in a conversation between protagonist Frank (Lance Henriksen), his colleague Peter (Terry O'Quinn) and the IT specialist Brian (Allan Zinyk) in the context of the online activity of a murder victim:

FRANK: Her pseudonym online was Queen Libido.
PETER: These [emails] are quite explicit. Doesn't sync with a librarian from the Sheboygan Conservatory of Music.
BRIAN: Some people feel liberated from their normal self when they adopt an Internet persona. In the anonymity of cyberspace people are free to experiment. Online I've changed my name, my appearance, sexual orientation. Even gender.
PETER: That's more personal information than I need, Brian.

Here, while the victim was clearly playing out different sexual identities online, so too, in fact was Brian. The idea of characters using the Internet—chatrooms, as well as virtual realities and Second Life–type platforms—to trial sexual personalities that differ from real life is widely identifiable. This idea, for example, has already been referenced in the context of heterosexuality in *The L Word*, sadomasochism in *American Horror Story*, and infidelity in *Net Games* and *Web of Desire*. In the sci-fi television series *VR.5* (1995), the shy, flannelette shirt–wearing Sidney (Lori Singer) used virtual reality to play out a seductive, sexually aggressive alter ego. In the sci-fi film *The Lawnmower Man* (1992), Jobe (Jeff Fahey) and his girlfriend Marnie (Jenny Wright) used virtual reality software to have sex: as Jobe said, before they began, "In here we can be anything we want to be." Jobe, in fact, used the software to play out a rape fantasy; a fantasy Marnie did not consent to. Rape is similarly a theme in the sci-fi film *Gamer* (2009). The speculative future narrative centered on the use of reality-simulation software that uses real people as avatars. In the film, the obese, disabled Gorge (Ramsey Moore) enacted numerous rape fantasies playing as a rapist as well as a rape victim. Rape also gets mentioned in *Chatroom* in dialogue between Mo and an unnamed older woman in a chatroom exchange which starts with him confessing his burgeoning interest in eleven-year-old Keisha:

MO: She's really lovely and she's into gymnastics. She's really clever. Um, but but I'm attracted to her and that's a bit weird.

OLDER WOMAN: Would you like me to be Keisha?

MO: No you're alright, thanks.

OLDER WOMAN: What you doing here if you like Keisha so much?

MO: Well, a friend gave me the idea. To go online, y'know, see what the older lady likes, yeah.

OLDER WOMAN: Get your mind off the kids?

MO: Yeah, that's the idea. Yeah.

OLDER WOMAN: Unless you're a pervert. In which case you take it any way you can. I'm into rape scenarios.

The Lawnmower Man scene alludes to another rationale for use of the Internet to experience nonvanilla sex: partner reluctance. Jobe, for example, likely wouldn't have been successful in convincing Marnie to play out an offline rape scenario and thus he did so in cyberspace where to him—even if not, seemingly, to Marnie—different rules apply. A similar idea played out in the "User Friendly" cybersex-themed episode of the sitcom *Married With Children* (1987–97). Bud (David Faustino) had volunteered for a cybersex experiment, and found the experience so satisfying that his interest in pursuing a real-life relationship with his love interest, Amber, had waned: "Look, Kelly," he explained to his sister (Christina Applegate), "I don't need Amber, I have her. Dr. Kessler introduced me to cybersex and I can create Amber anytime I want … She does what I want, whenever I want it." Akin to the appeal of cybersex for Jobe in *The Lawnmower Man*, Bud didn't need to convince Amber to go out with him, let alone sleep with him, nor did he need to bother negotiating sexual limits with her, he could simply "have" her in the fantasy world of cyberspace, akin to how Paul in *Mad About You* could *have* Christie Brinkley regardless of her interest or consent. These ideas were also a theme in the "Virtual Slide" episode of the sci-fi series *Sliders* (1995–2000): Quinn (Jerry O'Connell) used virtual reality technology to participate in a sexual fantasy involving his colleague Maggie (Kari Wuhrer). When the real Maggie discovered his use of the technology she reprimanded him: "You have sex with me without my consent? ... For God's sake, Quinn, you can't just go around using people's likenesses for your own twisted pleasure." With the use of the technology, Quinn didn't need to seduce or cajole or negotiate, he could simply have—on-demand—the sex he wanted. Similar rationales appeared to motivate Don's preference for netporn-aided masturbation in *Don Jon*, whereby in using porn, he didn't have to bother with pleasantries or reciprocity:

> Blowjob? Sure, it's fucking fantastic in person ... if she'll do it. But in real life, if you wanna get head, you gotta give head ... I know, some guys love eating pussy, but the thing about those guys is, they're fucking crazy. Don't get me wrong, I like a good pussy-eating clip. But, from down here, there's nothing good about this.

The "La Douleur Exquise!" episode of *Sex and the City* (1998–2004) offered a variation on the use of the Internet for intimacy, providing Stanford (Willie Garson) an outlet for his underwear fetish as well as later, an offline opportunity to physically participate, something discussed by the series narrator, Carrie (Sarah Jessica Parker):

> Meanwhile, at a fetish across town, Stanford Blanche had a secret sex life. A very active secret sex life on the Internet as "Rick9Plus." It all started innocently enough as a goof on a lonely Friday night. But pretty soon he was logging in hours and hours on his favorite website. It was a comfort to know that others shared his underwear fetish. Sometimes as many as 2,000 hits a day. No sooner had Rick9Plus entered the chatroom that he got a message from his favorite on-screen pal, "Bigtool4U." Some fetishes can only flourish behind closed doors in the very late night hours on a laptop ...

In *Part-Time Perverts* I identified that many people opt for "safer" ways to participate in their sexual deviations; for example, their fantasy might be illegal (like pedophilia), disruptive to relationships (like infidelity) or compromising to one's sense of self and identity (like sadomasochism).[73] While in *Part-Time Perverts* I discussed these safer ways in a more generic sense—about any kind of substitute erotic activity replacing the initial sexual fantasy—research indeed documents a specific role for the Internet in creating safer ways for nonvanilla sexualities to play out. As early as 1998, for example, communication theorists Malcolm Parks and Lynne

Roberts identified that MUDs "provide users with the perception of a safe environment for social interaction in which individuals can explore all types of relationships without fear of repercussions in their physical lives."[74] Leiblum and Döring similarly discussed this idea noting: "Personal inhibition levels, social controls, and the lack of willing partners and sexual scenes that may limit sexual activity in everyday contexts are obsolete in cyberspace."[75] As the authors argue, "It is easy for latent desires to be realized in cyberspace."[76] The sociologist Dennis Waskul also addressed these ideas, noting "the Internet makes possible, and even understandable, experiences that in any other context would be unusual or just plain bizarre."[77] In Cleo Odzer's reflections on her participation in cybersex, she similarly described her online sex life as about having "the freedom to be and do anything, I had sex with three men at once. I had sex with a woman. I had sex with three men and woman once. Posing as a man, I had sex with a woman. Posing as a gay man, I had sex with a man … I had all sorts of sex in every new way I could think of."[78]

While for many people fantasy will be restricted to role-play within the parameters of chatrooms or virtual or simulated environments, for others, the Internet actually helps them find people to play out their fantasies with in real life. Earlier, for example, I mentioned Stanford in *Sex and the City*: through his participation in chatrooms, he actually ended up meeting a community of men with underwear fetishes, in turn alluding to a key function of the Internet for people who want to make their fantasy more physical.

Network Expansion

In the thriller *Untraceable* (2008), after Arthur Elmer (Jesse Tyler Ferguson) was wrongly arrested as a suspect in a murder investigation, the investigator, Jennifer (Diane Lane), explained his release to her colleagues:

> Got our proof it wasn't Elmer. Starting Friday at 1pm, Elmer was logged into a chatroom for twelve consecutive hours. At the time Miller disappeared, Elmer was engaged in a steamy, private chat with the first tenor of the men's chorus of Greater Tacoma.

While Elmer is not a character developed well enough for audiences to know whether he was closeted, chatrooms were, nonetheless, an outlet for his homosexuality. Chatrooms were a way—potentially even the *only* way for him—to express his sexuality; it was a social space for him to be homosexual, in line with Campbell's research noting: "gay men have been quick to employ computer-mediated communication technologies to expand their social networks."[79]

The most obvious way that the Internet is presented on screen is by providing characters a means to experience their sexuality, most obviously through the arrangement of hook-ups.

The participation of gay males in online dating (which, invariably takes the form of online *hook-ups*), happens in the American gay-themed comedies like *Breaking the Cycle* (2002), *Eating Out 3: All You Can Eat* (2009), *Is It Just Me?* (2010) and *eCupid* (2011), along with the "Daddy Dearest (Sonny Boy)" episode of *Queer as Folk* (2000–2005), the Filipino drama *inter.m@tes* (2004) and the Argentinian Film *El tercero* (*The Third One*) (2014). Equally it is relevant for lesbian characters too: in lesbian drama series *The L Word* and *Lip Service* (2010–12) gay female characters date online; in the television drama *Murder Dot Com* (2008), the lesbian character, Lauren (Robyn Lively), does so, too. Equally, as discussed in Chapter 5, in a range of narratives—for example, *Looking, Blue Bloods, 2 Broke Girls* (2011–), *Please Like Me* (2013–), *Faking It* (2014–), *How to Get Away With Murder* (2014–), *Orphan Black* (2013–) and *Marry Me* (2014–15)—homosexual characters specifically use hook-up apps.

Discretion has already been discussed in this chapter. While on one hand this relates to problems that outing oneself might have, it also links more broadly to the idea of there existing a cost to being open about one's identity. For homosexuals, while prejudice and stereotyping are central costs to outing one's sexuality, another penalty centers on the possibility of misjudging the orientation of a crush. Just as online dating has its greatest use as a place where everyone is outing themselves as looking for intimacy, this has heightened relevance for gay characters. In gay chatrooms and on gay dating sites participants are relatively safe in the assumption that they are communicating with other homosexuals. In *Eating Out 3: All You Can Eat*, this benefit in fact gets verbalized when the elderly character, Harry (Leslie Jordan), commented: "Your generation," he says to young Casey (Daniel Skelton), "has it pretty easy when it comes to finding all the other fish in the sea." The same idea emerged in a conversation in *Breaking the Cycle*, between the gay characters Chad (Ryan White) and Sammy (Stephen Halliday):

SAMMY: Gay guys meeting on the net is the latest thing. Years ago gay people had to meet on a beach or cruised a parking lot or even a park.
CHAD: Yeah but they got caught by the cops—
SAMMY: People meeting on the Net that's the thing. You gotta admit, it's better than the park.

While the efficiency that Sammy refers to has equivalent relevance for heterosexual intimacy seekers (Chapter 1), it is of particular relevance to homosexual characters whose dating pool is not only smaller but navigating it has, traditionally, been riskier.

While network expansion has particular relevance for homosexual characters, it also enables characters with niche sexual interests to also find people to participate with. A good illustration of this transpired in the "Free Dental" episode of the legal-drama *The Practice* (1997–2004). At the beginning of this chapter I quoted Cindy's mention of bug fetishists in the *Orange is the New Black* episode: Henry (Henry Winkler) in *The Practice* in fact, had a *crush* fetish; he got sexually aroused by watching bugs get trampled on. He goes online to find a woman willing to do this for him; she did so in exchange for free teeth cleaning.[80] Cindy also mentioned cannibalism and— appearing to reference the real-life German Internet-themed cannibalism case involving Armin Meiwes—the Australian horror film *Feed* (2005) included an Internet-aided cannibalism liaison. The British comedy-drama *Dogging: A Love Story* (2009) centered on the fetish of having sex while being watched. Throughout the film the Internet provided the means by which opportunities to have sex in public, alternatively to watch such a display, were advertised via the Internet. Connecting people for fringe sexual behaviors—notably public sex—is widely documented in academic research. In legal scholar Chris Ashford's work on public sex he briefly discussed the role of the Internet both in educating people on, and popularizing the activity in netporn, but also in advertising opportunities for such sex.[81] Information technology theorist Paul Bocij addressed the same themes.[82] Media theorists Niall Richardson, Clarissa Smith and Angela Werndly also explored the interesting intersection between the Internet and nonvanilla sex such as dogging:

> Dogging websites are an interesting phenomenon because they straddle the divide between on- and offline selves. Dogging is an offline (i.e., real world) practice ... which takes place in car parks, beauty spots and other secluded public spaces ... It is also a feature of online spaces— there are sites dedicated to images and videos of dogging activities, but also community sites which suggest this is a thriving sexual subculture. On the community sites, members can find out about local, national and international dogging sites, arrange meetings, swap experiences/ images and information and communicate with other doggers.[83]

A variation on the idea of the Internet used to create networks is the idea of it being used to bridge geographic boundaries. While this idea was discussed in Chapter 5 where couples who were geographically separated were able to maintain intimacy even though they were in different locations, for people with nonmainstream sexual interests, finding someone sexually compatible in your local area might be difficult, if not impossible: the Internet can make this less of a problem.

Sex and Geography

The concept of a dating pool raises another issue disproportionately affecting homosexuals: geography. With less of the population sharing your sexual preferences, meeting a partner serendipitously in real life is difficult, and therefore the Internet can help overcome this problem. The backstory of the romantic-drama *Ciao* (2008), for example, centered on an online friendship between two gay men: Andrea (Alessandro Calza) from Italy and Mark (Chuck Blaum) from the US. Andrea had planned to visit Mark but the latter was killed in a car crash before he arrived. Andrea visits Mark's friends in the US anyhow, and in one scene has a conversation with Lauren (Ethel Lung) about why he was dating someone in the United States:

LAUREN: Is there no one in Italy you could date? People who live in Genoa?
ANDREA: There's not much of a scene there. It's not like Rome, you know. It's not easy to meet other guys. So my social outlet is quite limited and I end up meeting people online.

In the drama *On_Line* (2002) a similar theme emerges when a young gay man—Ed (Eric Millegan)—was in a suicide chatroom lamenting, "I'm the only queer in all of Ohio." In these two examples the Internet served to compensate for the lack of a physical gay community in characters' home towns. Certainly these ideas illustrate academic work in this area. In sociologist Keith Durkin's work on the Internet, he identified that, "One of the most sociologically significant aspects of the Internet is its capability to bring together geographically dispersed individuals."[84] The social theorist J. Dallas Dishman made a similar point, noting that, "In the virtual spaces that gay men create, they are not ... the 'odd man out in society.'"[85]

For the characters in *Dogging: A Love Story* discussed earlier—as with most people, in fact, regardless of their specific sexual interests—public sex constitutes only a small, invariably *compartmentalized*, part of their lives. The idea of the Internet aiding in dabbling in perverse sex is identifiable both on screen and in published work on technology and sexuality. For some sexual perversions the technology is essential; voyeurism and exhibitionism are two examples whereby the technology itself plays a pivotal role.

Voyeurism and Exhibitionism

In the "Attack of the Killer App" episode of the animated series *Futurama* (1999–2013), the following exchange transpires between Fry and Bender:

FRY: Since when is the Internet about robbing people of their privacy?
BENDER: August 6, 1991.

Bender references the date Tim Berners-Lee announced the World Wide Web project, and in this remark identifies how the Internet has changed perceptions of privacy. On screen and the idea of privacy gets played with narratives involving exhibitionism and voyeurism. While both of these sexual practices had a life, and also a screen presence, prior to the Internet, the Internet facilitates participation, if not, in fact, creates opportunities to *capitalize* on such behavior.

The production of for-profit erotic webcam footage is a theme in a range of screen narratives, for example, the "Voyeur's Web" episode of the crime-drama *NCIS* (2003–), the thriller *Look @ Me* (2006), the "Chinese Walls" episode of the British crime-drama *The Inspector Lynley Mysteries*

(2001–7), the Taiwanese drama *Ci qing* (*Spider Lilies*) (2007) and the television drama *Selling Innocence* (2005). While there exists the capacity for the female performers in each of these cam sites to be construed as doing so to cater to their exhibitionist fantasies, more explicitly, these sites are framed as a product of the sex industry that gets consumed by male voyeurs. While in the examples mentioned, the narrative focus was on the performers, in others the male consumption of such sites is spotlighted, for example, in the aforementioned dramas *Little Children*, *Shame* and *On_Line*, as well as the British mini-series *Killer Net* (1998) and the Canadian comedy *Control Alt Delete* (2008): in each, male characters watch female characters perform via webcams, consuming the material voyeuristically as they would any other kind of porn.[86] The feminist scholar Michele White discussed the gendered nature of such consumption, noting how "Internet settings often reproduce stereotyped ideas about bodies and support gendered ways of looking."[87] Certainly on screen the dynamic complies with the gendered standard: men watch women perform on webcam, in line with how commonly men watch women perform in porn, as well as in other media.[88]

In the scenes discussed thus far, a legal kind of voyeurism is participated in whereby users are allowed the illusion of peeping on the illicit; something discussed by media theorist Susanna Paasonen where she noted that in such sites "[v]iewers are aware of the performative nature of 'hidden camera' shots but decide to play along by orienting themselves in a particular way."[89] Worth noting, however, is that illicit and illegal voyeurism also transpires in a range of narratives where characters—invariably male—use the Internet to spy on women who are actually completely unaware that they are on display. A comic allusion to this idea was made in the "Oh Honey" episode of the sitcom *How I Met Your Mother* (2005–14) when, Honey (Katy Perry)—a character presented as highly gullible—revealed, "My apartment building is so safe. My landlord even installed a security camera in my shower." While this idea is joked about in this example, the idea of secretly installed cameras actually transpires in numerous other examples. In the "Home Invasions" episode of *The Practice*, unbeknownst to Lucy (Marla Sokoloff), she became the star of a live webcam show after her building superintendent surreptitiously installed cameras throughout her apartment. In the "Chinese Walls" episode of *The Inspector Lynley Mysteries*, a webcam star, Emily (Isabella Calthorpe), became the victim of such voyeurism when the tech support guy for her site, Darren (Joe Armstrong), installed cameras in her home to spy on her. In the "Eyes In" episode of the Canadian police-drama *Flashpoint* (2008–12), Stuart (Kris Lemche) was a tutor in love with his pupil Rebecca (Meaghan Rath) and hacked into her webcam to spy on her. In the television drama *The Husband She Met Online* (2013), a minor character—who solicits dates for the protagonist, Craig (Jason Gray-Stanford)—has a number of women he refers to as "slaves" who he, unbeknownst to them, regularly watches via hacked webcams. In the British drama *Cyberbully* (2015), Casey's webcam was similarly hacked to spy on her. Such scenes are indeed a type of digital peeping and also examples of cyberstalking; a topic I explore elsewhere.[90] While such scenes showcase the role of the Internet in catering to voyeurism, such presentations are also reflective of widespread fears in the zeitgeist about privacy cybersecurity, as Bender in *Futurama* alluded. The *The Husband She Met Online*, *Flashpoint* and *Cyberbully* examples specifically tap into the fears of hacked webcams which have received widespread media coverage, notably in the context of hacked baby monitors,[91] a theme, incidentally, at the heart of the "Kidnapping 2.0" episode of the crime-drama *CSI-Cyber* (2015–).

While Internet-aided *voyeurism* makes sense—after all, the Internet is already mainstreamed as a means to watch sexually explicit content—it also has a clear role in *exhibitionism*. In the comedy *Sex Tape* (2014), for example, the unnamed proprietor of YouPorn (Jack Black), explained to Annie and Jay why he would happily remove their sex tape from his site (which had been leaked to him without their permission):

> Do you have any idea how many people are makin' sex tapes out there? We get about a thousand new ones every day. I don't need to be puttin' up sex tapes from people who don't want their sex tapes up there.

While Jay (Jason Segel) and Annie (Cameron Diaz) in *Sex Tape* did record their sexual adventures, neither had any intention of making the material public and thus it isn't an example of exhibitionism so much as self-arousal.[92] In other examples, however, characters do display themselves sexually for their own gratification. In *On_Line* for example, Moe (Harold Perrineau) coerced his girlfriend Moira (Isabel Gillies) into having sex on webcam. In the thriller *Strangers Online* (2009), exhibitionists phone into an online video show; the first caller is Ruth (Crystal Craft) who flashed her breasts and later claimed to be fourteen-years-old; another was Marty who just wanted to expose his buttocks. Another caller wanted to publicly reveal—and confess—his fetish for dressing up in women's clothing. *Strangers Online* also alluded to another kind of exhibitionism/voyeurism where violent material is broadcast online for the enjoyment of the participants and an audience interested in the gruesome.[93]

Just as the Internet has made participating in voyeurism as easy as accessing netporn, equally so, it has made participating in this kink both simple and desirable; the latter tapping into the idea of the Internet creating the illusion of celebrity, something illustrated in an exchange between FBI colleagues Rossi (Joe Mantegna) and Morgan (Shemar Moore) in the "Elephant's Memory" episode of *Criminal Minds*:

ROSSI: Can somebody explain to me the appeal of these sites? Eating sushi tonight—yum! Boss is keeping me late at work—grrr! Whose life is so important that we'd be interested in this kind of detail?

MORGAN: I don't know, I guess that's the running joke, right? I mean, nobody is. But we'd all like to believe that there's actually an audience out there that wants to follow our every move.

The actor Alan Cumming in his memoir *Not My Father's Son* addressed this same issue:

> It's really hard to talk about being famous. We live in a society that is obsessed with it, that ranks it was the best thing you could possibly achieve in your life. I believe social media outlets like Facebook and Twitter are an absolute product of this obsession, as they partly manufacture how it feels to be famous for people who are not. You put personal information and images out into the world and the more friends or followers you obtain, the less knowledge you have of who is watching or keeping track. It's great to feel popular of course, but there is a downside.[94]

While the women in the webcam narratives mentioned earlier could be construed as exhibitionists given the nature of their work, in fact, with the exception of *Look @ Me*, most of the female participants seem to be participating for profit rather than to cater to any personal sexual interests. In *Look @ Me*, however, the cam performer, Tina (Elina Madison), explicitly outs herself as exhibitionist, both in the dialogue spoken to camera—"I feel desirable when you look at me"—but more so in her behavior *off*-cam; she is shown enjoying sex with the windows open as well as the feel of her office colleagues' eyes on her. Similar themes are apparent in a subplot of *Cyber Seduction: His Secret Life*: teenager Monica (Nicole Dicker) was presented as being so very into porn—so interested in *displaying* her sexuality—that she performed on an erotic webcam herself. In the Canadian comedy *Control Alt Delete*, by the end of the narrative it is discovered that Jane (Sonja Bennett) was the star of a webcam focused on her use of the bathroom: while not much is known about whether she was earning an income from the site, it seems clear that exhibitionism was a clear motive.

This chapter has examined the role of the Internet in helping people participate in nonmainstream forms of sexual intimacy such as homosexuality, exhibitionism and voyeurism. This role ranges from the provision of information, the capacity to network, access to explicit representations and even a means to orchestrate kinky hook-ups.

Notes

1. The link between computing cultures—including hacking—and fringe sexualities is something I discuss elsewhere (Lauren Rosewarne, *Cyberbullies, Cyberactivists, Cyberpredators: Film, TV, and Internet Stereotypes* [Santa Barbara, CA: Praeger, 2016]).
2. Yow-Juin Wang, "Internet Dating Sites as Heterotopias of Gender Performance: A Case Study of Taiwanese Heterosexual Male Daters," *International Journal of Cultural Studies*, 15, 5, (2011): 485–500, 486.
3. Gayle Rubin, "Thinking Sex: Notes for a Radical Theory of the Politics of Sexuality," in *The Lesbian and Gay Studies Reader*, ed. Henry Abelove (New York: Routledge, 1993): 3–44, 16.

4. Carsten Glöckner, *Sex 2.0: Pornography and Prostitution Influenced by the Internet Feminist Views on Pornography and Prostitution* (Munich: Verlag, 2009); Anthony Ferguson, *The Sex Doll: A History* (Jefferson, NC: McFarland & Co, 2010).

5. Feona Attwood, "The Sexualization of Culture," in *Mainstreaming Sex: The Sexualization of Western Culture*, ed. Feona Attwood (London: I.B. Tauris & Co, 2009): xiii–2; Brian McNair, *Porno? Chic! How Pornography Changed the World and Made It a Better Place* (New York: Routledge, 2013).

6. Lauren Rosewarne, "School of Shock, Film, Television and Anal Education," *Sex Education: Sexuality, Society and Learning*, 15, 4 (2015): 553–65.

7. Charles Edgley and Kenneth Kiser, "Polaroid Sex: Deviant Possibilities in a Technological Age," *Journal of American Culture* (1981): 59–64, 59.

8. Charles Edgley and Kenneth Kiser, "Polaroid Sex: Deviant Possibilities in a Technological Age," *Journal of American Culture* (1981): 59–64, 59.

9. Alan Hunter, "Review: Men, Women & Children Starring Jennifer Garner and Adam Sandler," *Express*, December 5, 2014. Accessed March 23, 2015, from http://www.express.co.uk/entertainment/films/543955/Men-Women-Children-review-starring-Jennifer-Garner-Adam-Sandler.

10. Rochelle Siemienowicz, "A Clumsy, Clammy Critique of Modern Web Culture," *SBS*, November 25, 2014. Accessed March 24, 2015, from http://www.sbs.com.au/movies/movie/men-women-children.

11. Betsy Sharkey, "'Men, Women & Children' Is Artificial Look at Internet World," *LA Times*, September 30, 2014. Accessed March 25, 2015, from http://www.latimes.com/entertainment/movies/la-et-mn-men-women-children-review-20141001-column.html.

12. John C. Bridges, *The Illusion of Intimacy: Problems in the World of Online Dating* (Santa Barbara, CA: Praeger, 2012), 7.

13. Robert E. Freeman-Longo, "Children, Teens, and Sex on the Internet," in *Cybersex: The Dark Side of the Force*, ed. Al Cooper (Philadelphia, PA: Brunner-Routledge, 2000): 75–90.

14. In Chris Hansen, *To Catch a Predator: Protecting Your Kids from Online Enemies Already in Your Home* (New York: Penguin Group, 2007), 191–92.

15. While in *Men, Women & Children* and *eCupid* characters are lured into infidelity because of television commercials, worth noting are two examples where television commercials similarly tempt single characters to date leading to *positive* outcomes. In the Christian-drama *Christian Mingle* (2014), for example, Gwyneth (Lacey Chabert) sees numerous television advertisements for the titular website before signing up. By the end of the film, she is successfully coupled with the first man she meets on the site. In the Canadian television drama *Perfect Romance* (2004), Peter (Henry Ian Cusick) was at home feeling sorry for himself when he sees a television commercial for PerfectMatch.com: "When you're tired of the bar scene, had enough of the head games, when you're ready to find true love, romance is as close as your computer and your dreams are just a few keystrokes away." Like Gwyneth, by the end of the film, Peter is successfully coupled with the first woman he met on the site.

16. Interestingly, while Jamie used the technology for a very brief exchange with tennis player Andre Agassi, ultimately she used it to hear her husband tell her—repeatedly—that he was wrong and she was right, providing a very gender-stereotypical presentation of how virtual reality technology would be used in practice.

17. Janet Reibstein and Martin Richards, *Sexual Arrangements* (London: Heinemann, 1992), 5.

18. Arthur G. Neal and Sara F. Collas, *Intimacy and Alienation* (New York: Garland, 2000), 134.

19. Christa Worthington, "Making Love in Cyberspace," *The Independent* (October 6, 1996). Accessed June 30, 2014, from http://www.independent.co.uk/arts-entertainment/making-love-in-cyberspace-1355874.html.

20. It is worth spotlighting that in both *Web of Desire* and *Net Games*, the characters who become attached and who attribute significance to online liaisons are women, in line with the stereotype of women's greater, and quicker, emotional investment in relationships.

21. Even though Derek knew that Cindy had not had any sexual contact with Stephen, his sense of betrayal likely stemmed from his sense of misdirected emotional energies, an idea discussed by the partner of a cybersex participant in psychologist Jennifer Schneider's research: "For me the issue has not been the difference between having e-mail sex or actual physical contact, it is that someone else is receiving his attention and I am not" (in Jennifer P. Schneider, "The New 'Elephant in the Living Room': Effects of Compulsive Cybersex Behaviors on the Spouse," in *Sex & The Internet: A Guidebook for Clinicians*, ed. Al Cooper (New York: Brunner-Routledge, 2002): 169–86, 178).

22. Aaron Ben-Ze'ev, *Love Online: Emotions on the Internet* (New York: Cambridge University Press, 2004), 4.

23. In Aaron Ben-Ze'ev, *Love Online: Emotions on the Internet* (New York: Cambridge University Press, 2004), 4.

24. Lauren Rosewarne, *Cheating on the Sisterhood: Infidelity and Feminism* (Santa Barbara, CA: Praeger, 2009).

25. In Aaron Ben-Ze'ev, *Love Online: Emotions on the Internet* (New York: Cambridge University Press, 2004), 240.

26. In Cathy Winks and Anne Semans, *The Woman's Guide to Sex on the Web* (San Francisco, CA: Harper Collins, 1999), 170.

27. Sandra Leiblum and Nicola Döring, "Internet Sexuality: Known Risks and Fresh Chances for Women," in *Sex and the Internet: A Guidebook for Clinicians*, ed. Al Cooper (New York: Brunner-Routledge, 2002): 19–45, 30.

28. This idea, in fact, was referenced in an unnamed episode of the lesbian-themed Scottish series *Lip Service* (2010–12) when Tess (Fiona Button) speculated that most of the women online are "hets after a free lezzie floorshow." One date that she goes on actually does end up in her inadvertently performing in a "free lezzie floorshow" when her date had a husband who wanted to watch. It turns out that Tess's date was trying to maintain the spark in her marriage.

29. Lauren Rosewarne, *Cheating on the Sisterhood: Infidelity and Feminism* (Santa Barbara, CA: Praeger, 2009), 17.

30. Jo Lamble and Sue Morris, *Online and Personal: The Reality of Internet Relationships* (Sydney: Finch Publishing, 2001), 26.

31. Eva Illouz, *Consuming the Romantic Utopia: Love and the Cultural Contradictions of Capitalism* (Berkeley, CA: University of California Press, 1997).

32. Aaron Ben-Ze'ev, *Love Online: Emotions on the Internet* (New York: Cambridge University Press, 2004), 61.

33. Mark F. Schwartz and Stephen Southern, "Compulsive Cybersex: The New Tea Room," in *Cybersex: The Dark Side of the Force*, ed. Al Cooper (Philadelphia, PA: Brunner-Routledge, 2000): 127–44, 127.

34. Lauren Rosewarne, *Part-Time Perverts: Sex, Pop Culture and Kink Management* (Santa Barbara, CA: Praeger, 2011); Daniel Akst, *Temptation: Finding Self-Control in an Age of Excess* (New York: Penguin Books, 2011).

35. Dan Slater, *Love in the Time of Algorithms* (New York: Current, 2013), 11.

36. Dan Slater, *Love in the Time of Algorithms* (New York: Current, 2013), 122.

37. Christine E. Murray and Emily C. Campbell, "The Pleasures and Perils of Technology in Intimate Relationships," *Journal of Couple & Relationship Therapy: Innovations in Clinical and Educational Interventions*, 14 (2015): 116–40, 116.

38. Christine E. Murray and Emily C. Campbell, "The Pleasures and Perils of Technology in Intimate Relationships," *Journal of Couple & Relationship Therapy: Innovations in Clinical and Educational Interventions*, 14 (2015): 116–40, 134.

39. Russell B. Clayton, Alexander Nagurney and Jessica R. Smith, "Cheating, Breakup, and Divorce: Is Facebook Use to Blame?" *Cyberpsychology, Behavior, and Social Networking*, 16, 10 (2013): 717–20.

40. Jaclyn D. Cravens and Jason B. Whiting, "Clinical Implications of Internet Infidelity: Where Facebook Fits In," *The American Journal of Family Therapy*, 42 (2014): 325–39.

41. Russell B. Clayton, "The Third Wheel: The Impact of Twitter Use on Relationship Infidelity and Divorce," *Cyberpsychology, Behavior, and Social Networking*, 17, 7 (2014): 425–30.

42. Monica T. Whitty and Laura-Lee Quigley, "Emotional and Sexual Infidelity Offline and in Cyberspace," *Journal of Marital and Family Therapy*, 34, 1 (2008): 461–68; Katherine M. Hertlein and Fred P. Piercy, "Essential Elements of Internet Infidelity Treatment," *Journal of Marital and Family Therapy*, 38 (2012): 257–70; Pieternel Dijkstra, Dick P. H. Barelds and Hinke A.K. Groothof, "Jealousy in Response to Online and Offline Infidelity: The Role of Sex and Sexual Orientation," *Scandinavian Journal of Psychology*, 54 (2013): 328–36.

43. Alice Woolley, "Confessions of an Internet Widow," *The Independent*, June 12, 1995. Accessed August 4, 2015, from http://www.independent.co.uk/life-style/confessions-of-an-internet-widow-1586108.html.

44. Lauren Rosewarne, *Cheating on the Sisterhood: Infidelity and Feminism* (Santa Barbara, CA: Praeger, 2009).

45. Alexander Lambert, *Intimacy and Friendship on Facebook* (New York: Palgrave Macmillan, 2013), 80–81.

46. Aaron Ben-Ze'ev, *Love Online: Emotions on the Internet* (New York: Cambridge University Press, 2004), 54–55.

47. Sandra Leiblum and Nicola Döring, "Internet Sexuality: Known Risks and Fresh Chances for Women," in *Sex and the Internet: A Guidebook for Clinicians* (New York: Brunner-Routledge, 2002): 19–45, 26.

48. Carol Parker, *The Joy of Cyber Sex* (Kew, Victoria: Mandarin, 1997), 52–53.

49. *Men, Women & Children*, despite being a highly conservative film insofar as the treatment of technology, in fact hints to the possibility that Helen and Don's extramarital transgressions in face *benefited* their marriage: the narrative appears to conclude with the couple trying to resurrect their union (Lauren

Rosewarne, *Cheating on the Sisterhood: Infidelity and Feminism* [Santa Barbara, CA: Praeger, 2009]).

50. John Suler, "The Online Disinhibition Effect," *CyberPsychology & Behavior*, 7 (2004): 321–26, 322.

51. Lauren Rosewarne, *Cheating on the Sisterhood: Infidelity and Feminism* (Santa Barbara, CA: Praeger, 2009).

52. In Sherry Turkle, *Life on the Screen: Identity in the Age of the Internet* (New York: Simon and Schuster, 1995), 13.

53. Dan Slater in his book *Love in the Time of Algorithms* discussed this idea of *having options* in the context of online dating, identifying some of the benefits: "The perception that one has options instills feelings of autonomy, which in turn contributes to psychological and physical health" (Dan Slater, *Love in the Time of Algorithms* [New York: Current, 2013], 119).

54. Al Cooper, "Sexuality and the Internet: Surfing into the New Millennium," *CyberPsychology & Behavior*, 1 (1998): 187–93.

55. John Edward Campbell, *Getting It On Online: Cyberspace, Gay Male Sexuality and Embodied Identity* (New York: Harrington Park Press, 2004), 7.

56. Michael W. Ross and Michael R. Kauth, "Men Who Have Sex with Men, and the Internet: Emerging Clinical Issues and Their Management," in *Sex and the Internet: A Guidebook for Clinicians*, ed. Al Cooper (New York: Brunner-Routledge, 2002): 47–69, 52.

57. Greg Miraglia, *Coming Out from Behind the Badge: Stories of Success and Advice from Police Officers "Out" on the Job* (Bloomington, IN: AuthorHouse, 2007); Michael C. LaSala, *Coming Out, Coming Home: Helping Families Adjust to a Gay or Lesbian Child* (New York: Columbia University Press, 2010); Cavan Sieczkowski, "Jesse Tyler Ferguson Came Out After He Was Caught Stealing Gay Porn," *Huffington Post*, September 26, 2014. Accessed July 28, 2015, from http://www.huffingtonpost.com/2014/09/26/jesse-tyler-ferguson-came-out-gay-porn_n_5887858.html.

58. Elsewhere I discuss a number of narratives—for example the British drama *Velvet Goldmine* (1998), the drama *American Girl* (2002), the biopic *The Runaways* (2010) and the thriller *Reflections in a Golden Eye* (1967)—whereby the masturbation material chosen worked to expose a character's homosexuality (Lauren Rosewarne, *Masturbation in Pop Culture: Screen, Society, Self* [Lanham, MD: Lexington Books, 2014]).

59. The psychologist Vivienne Cass identified *pre-gay* as the first in six common stages in homosexual identity formation (Vivienne C. Cass, "Homosexual Identity Formation: A Theoretical Model," *Journal of Homosexuality*, 4, 30 [1979]: 219–35).

60. Michael Shernoff, "Social Work Practice with Gay Individuals," in *Social Work Practice with Lesbian, Gay, Bisexual, and Transgender People*, ed. Gerald P. Mallon (New York: The Haworth Press, 1998): 141–78, 155.

61. Michael W. Ross and Michael R. Kauth, "Men Who Have Sex with Men, and the Internet: Emerging Clinical Issues and Their Management," in *Sex and the Internet: A Guidebook for Clinicians*, ed. Al Cooper (New York: Brunner-Routledge, 2002): 47–69, 66.

62. C.J. Pascoe, "Gay Boys," in *Boy Culture: An Encyclopedia*, v. 1, eds. Shirley R. Steinberg, Michael Kehler and Lindsay Cornish (Santa Barbara, CA: ABC-CLIO, 2010), 11.

63. Jennifer Egan, "Lonely Gay Teen Seeking Same," *New York Times Magazine*, December 10, 2000. Accessed February 18, 2015, from http://www.nytimes.com/2000/12/10/magazine/lonely-gay-teen-seeking-same.html.

64. In Avi Shoshana, "Symbolic Interaction and New Social Media Surfing to an Alternative Self: Internet Technology and Sexuality among 'Married Straight Homosexual Men,'" *Symbolic Interaction and New Media*, 43 (2014): 173–200, 185.

65. Phillip Vannini, "Così Fan Tutti: Foucault, Goffman, and the Pornographic Synopticon," in *Net.seXX: Readings on Sex, Pornography and the Internet*, ed. Dennis D. Waskul (New York: Peter Lang, 2004): 75–89, 75–76.

66. Communications scholar Ashley Donnelly for example, described Masuka as "charmingly perverted" (Ashley M. Donnelly, *Renegade Hero or Faux Rogue: The Secret Traditionalism of Television Bad Boys* [Jefferson, NC: McFarland and Company, 2014], 49).

67. Barry Sandywell, "Monsters in Cyberspace Cyberphobia and Cultural Panic in the Information Age," *Information, Communication & Society*, 9, 1 (2006): 39–61.

68. Lauren Rosewarne, *Masturbation in Pop Culture: Screen, Society, Self* (Lanham, MD: Lexington Books, 2014).

69. Lauren Rosewarne, *Part-Time Perverts: Sex, Pop Culture and Kink Management* (Santa Barbara, CA: Praeger, 2011).

70. I discuss the idea of compartmentalization as related to sexual behavior elsewhere. (See Lauren Rosewarne, *Part-Time Perverts: Sex, Pop Culture and Kink Management* [Santa Barbara, CA: Praeger, 2011].).

71. In Kimberly S. Young, *Caught in the Net: How to Recognize the Signs of Internet Addiction—And a Winning Strategy for Recovery* (New York: John Wiley & Sons, 1998), 15.

72. Sherry Turkle, *Life on the Screen: Identity in the Age of the Internet* (New York: Simon and Schuster, 1995), 14.

73. Lauren Rosewarne, *Part-Time Perverts: Sex, Pop Culture and Kink Management* (Santa Barbara, CA: Praeger, 2011).

74. Malcolm R. Parks and Lynne D. Roberts, "Making Moosic: The Development of Personal Relationships on Line and a Comparison to Their Off-Line Counterparts," *Journal of Social and Personal Relationships*, 15 (1998): 517–37, 531.

75. Sandra Leiblum and Nicola Döring, "Internet Sexuality: Known Risks and Fresh Chances for Women," in *Sex and the Internet: A Guidebook for Clinicians*, ed. Al Cooper (New York: Brunner-Routledge, 2002): 19–45, 29.

76. Sandra Leiblum and Nicola Döring, "Internet Sexuality: Known Risks and Fresh Chances for Women," in *Sex and the Internet: A Guidebook for Clinicians*, ed. Al Cooper (New York: Brunner-Routledge, 2002): 19–45, 29.

77. Dennis D. Waskul, *Self-Games and Body-Play: Personhood in Online Chat and Cyberspace* (New York: Peter Lang, 2003), 10.

78. Cleo Ozder, *Virtual Spaces: Sex and the Cyber Citizen* (New York: Berkley Books, 1997), 43.

79. John Edward Campbell, *Getting It on Online: Cyberspace, Gay Male Sexuality and Embodied Identity* (New York: Harrington Park Press, 2004), 7.

80. While not a sexual fetish, nonetheless, going online in pursuit of someone to share an obsessive interest in bugs transpires in the "Bugged" episode of the sitcom *Family Matters* (1989–98): Steve (Jaleel White) used the Internet to connect

with Agnes (Amy Hunt), a fellow bug enthusiast whom he chatted to online and then met in person.

81. Chris Ashford, "From Cruising to Dogging: The Surveillance and Consumption of Public Sex," in *Out of the Ordinary: Representations of LGBT Lives*, eds. Ian Rivers and Richard Ward (Newcastle: Cambridge Scholars Publishing, 2012): 77–92.

82. Paul Bocij, *The Dark Side of the Internet: Protecting Yourself and Your Family from Online Criminals* (Westport, CT: Praeger, 2006).

83. Niall Richardson, Clarissa Smith and Angela Werndly, *Studying Sexualities: Theories, Representations, Cultures* (London: Palgrave Macmillan, 2013), ebook.

84. Keith F. Durkin, "The Internet as a Milieu for the Management of a Stigmatized Sexual Identity," in *Net.seXX: Readings on Sex, Pornography and the Internet*, ed. Dennis D. Waskul (New York: Peter Lang, 2004): 131–47, 131.

85. J. Dallas Dishman, "Ecologies of Cyberspace: Gay Communities on the Internet," in *From Chicago to L.A.: Making Sense of Urban Theory*, ed. Michael Dear (Thousand Oaks, CA: Sage Publications 2002): 293–318, 310.

86. In *Cyberbullies, Cyberactivists, Cyberpredators* I discuss in greater detail the capacity to consider netporn consumption as an act of voyeurism (Lauren Rosewarne, *Cyberbullies, Cyberactivists, Cyberpredators: Film, TV, and Internet Stereotypes* [Santa Barbara, CA: Praeger, 2016]).

87. Michele White, *The Body and the Screen: Theories of Internet Spectatorship* (Cambridge, MA: MIT Press, 2006), 57.

88. Worth noting, while this section has explored female webcam performers, it is also worth briefly acknowledging the existence of male performers, too. In the "P911" episode of *Criminal Minds* (2005–), the teen Kevin (Daryl Sabara) performed on a webcam site. This also transpired in the "Web" episode of *Law & Order: Special Victims Unit* (1999–) and was a subplot in *Disconnect* (2012), where male and female teens produced sexual webcam content. While voyeurism is of course, a theme in these examples, they also allude to the perversion of pedophilia.

89. Susanna Paasonen, *Carnal Resonance: Affect and Online Pornography* (Cambridge, MA: MIT Press, 2011), 179.

90. Lauren Rosewarne, *Cyberbullies, Cyberactivists, Cyberpredators: Film, TV, and Internet Stereotypes* (Santa Barbara, CA: Praeger, 2016).

91. Dan Massoglia, "The Webcam Hacking Epidemic," *The Atlantic*, December 23, 2014. Accessed August 27, 2015, from http://www.theatlantic.com/technology/archive/2014/12/the-webcam-hacking-epidemic/383998/; Matthew Sparkes, "Is Your Webcam Allowing Hackers to Peer into Your Home?" *The Telegraph*, November 20, 2014. Accessed August 27, 2015, from http://www.telegraph.co.uk/technology/news/11242650/Is-your-webcam-allowing-hackers-to-peer-into-your-home.html.

92. In my book *Masturbation in Pop Culture*, I discussed the capacity for characters to become aroused by looking at themselves naked in the mirror and then masturbating (Lauren Rosewarne, *Masturbation in Pop Culture: Screen, Society, Self* [Lanham, MD: Lexington Books, 2014]).

93. In *Cyberbullies, Cyberactivists, Cyberpredators*, I discuss a range of narratives— for example, the "Mikado" episode *Millennium* (1996–99), the "Killer Chat"

episode of the crime-drama *Numb3rs* (2005–10), the horror films *FearDotCom* (2002), *Satsujin Douga Sit* (*Death Tube: Broadcast Murder Show*) (2010) and the thrillers *Untraceable* (2008), *The Card Player* (2004) and *Dot.Kill* (2005)—where violent material is broadcast for the viewing pleasure of gore voyeurs (Lauren Rosewarne, *Cyberbullies, Cyberactivists, Cyberpredators: Film, TV, and Internet Stereotypes* [Santa Barbara, CA: Praeger, 2016]).

94. Alan Cumming, *Not My Father's Son: A Memoir* (New York: HarperCollins, 2014), 242–43.

Conclusion

Online dating, the use of hook-up apps and netporn, have each become not merely common but are now the default methods of finding intimacy with others, with the self.

The screen, of course, has not caught up with this off-screen mainstreaming. Whereas in reality most online activity is thoroughly perfunctory and seldom eventful—getting catfished, encountering human traffickers or being introduced to a rapist or an organ thief are by no means the real-life norm—the screen tells a very different story. *Over and over and over again.* To self-stimulate to netporn marks a person as an addict, as a pervert; to date online frames us as a failure, as unfuckable. To use a hook-up app is tantamount to soliciting destiny with a serial killer.

Intimacy on the Internet: Media Representations of Online Connections is a convergence of my previous work on sexuality, on technology and on popular media. This book contributes to our understanding of the screen's role in educating us, prejudicing us, frightening us, misinforming us and very occasionally even *mirroring* our off-screen experiences. As shown across my research, there exists a substantial gap between our lived experiences of sex, gender and those depictions found in film and television.

This volume spotlights how on one hand, the screen accurately reflects that we are using the Internet ever more in our private, intimate lives, but on the other—and more troublingly—it frames this role as problematic: that "Internet people" are more likely to be liars, con artists and villains; that the love and sex experienced (or merely *instigated*) online is somehow less authentic and that the bonds forged online are tenuous at best. Such demonization, however, should not be surprising: the screen has a long history of seizing on new technology—of voraciously incorporating it into narratives[1]—and portraying it as ultimately dangerous, uncivilizing and threatening to social order. This is, of course, a complex situation. While popular media generally has no vested interest in social engineering our perceptions of technology,[2] it does have a remit to entertain. And the Internet particularly—as a place, as a tool—provides infinite opportunities for exciting and dramatic screen fiction. Film and television make online-aided intimacy worth watching by focusing on the dangerous (or farcical) possibilities; ones that already have entrenched salience in the minds of the audience because they are in sync with those tech-themed news stories that have already garnered disproportionate attention and framed cyberspace as a badlands in the popular imaginary.

While such depictions may not be surprising, their role in perpetuating stigma and fears decades on from the inception of the technology is a reminder that amid screen fiction's fervent interest in showcasing new technology, there exists no responsibility to do so with any fairness or accuracy. As the long history of techno- and cyberphobia-themed narratives highlight, audiences are apparently eager to consume tech-themed narratives so long as they cater to our established prejudices and provide us further fuel for our tech-based angst.

Just as love and sex are topics that fascinate, bewilder and often terrify in real life, such anxieties are common undercurrents in our popular culture. The addition of technology stirs in other ingredients highlighting new ways to do the things we have been doing offline since the beginning of time, and presenting new challenges for those who pursue such methods. For my purposes, despite the trend toward negativity, screen representations of online intimacy-seeking exist as entertaining excuses to have some necessary scholarly conversations about the role we want technology to have in our lives.

One of my central rationales for academic work in popular culture is the analysis of screen narratives as a vehicle for discussing social issues: after all—and particularly in relation to matters of sex and gender—popular media is where we solicit far more information than we ever will from textbooks.[3] As examined throughout this book, these screen examples put on our agenda questions about what constitutes intimacy, closeness and sex in the Internet age. They force us to examine how we think about betrayal, about the veracity of relationships and about the relevance, endurance and accuracy of the stigma surrounding such topics. Through the "spoonful of sugar"—by the pleasurable medium of film and television[4]—audiences get an informal education about the Internet and intimacy. Invariably, however, this education is marred by hyperbole, stereotype and scare-mongering.

Notes

1. Daniel, Dinello, *Technophobia! Science Fiction Visions of Posthuman Technology* (Austin, TX: University of Texas Press, 2005); Lauren Rosewarne, *Cyberbullies, Cyberactivists, Cyberpredators: Film, TV, and Internet Stereotypes* (Santa Barbara, CA: Praeger, 2016).
2. Christian-drama exists as a media with a specific barrow to push.
3. Lauren Rosewarne, "School of Shock, Film, Television and Anal Education," *Sex Education: Sexuality, Society and Learning*, 15, 4 (2015): 553–65.
4. Lauren Rosewarne, "School of Shock, Film, Television and Anal Education," *Sex Education: Sexuality, Society and Learning*, 15, 4 (2015): 553–65.

Media References

Movies

2:37 (2006)
40-Year-Old Virgin, The (2005)
A.I. Artificial Intelligence (2001)
Adoration (2008)
Afterschool (2008)
All About Christmas Eve (2012)
All I Want For Christmas (2013)
Alleluia (2014)
American Girl (2002)
American Reunion (2012)
Annie Claus is Coming to Town (2011)
Baram-pigi joheun nal (A Day for an Affair) (2007)
Be with Me (2005)
Because I Said So (2007)
Bicentennial Man (1999)
Big Hero 7 (2014)
Birthday Girl (2001)
Blind Marriage (1914)
Boy She Met Online, The (2010)
Breaking the Cycle (2002)
Bride He Bought Online, The (2015)
Bringing Down the House (2003)
Burn After Reading (2008)
Can't Hardly Wait (1998)
Card Player, The (2004)
Carry On Loving (1970)
Case of You, A (2013)
Catfish (2010)
Catfish: Meeting the Girl in the Pictures (2010)
Celebrity Sex Tape (2012)
Center of the World, The (2001)
Chatroom (2010)
Chloe (2009)
Christian Mingle (2014)
Christmas Bounty (2013)
Christmas Song, A (2012)

Ci qing (Spider Lilies) (2007)
Ciao (2008)
Cinderella Story, A (2004)
Clerks II (2006)
Closer (2004)
Control Alt Delete (2008)
Copycat (1995)
Craigslist Killer, The (2011)
Crossing Delancey (1988)
Cyber Seduction: His Secret Life (2005)
Cyberbully (2015)
Cyberstalker (2012)
Da Kath and Kim Code (2005)
Dangerous Love (1988)
Deadly Messages (1985)
Demolition Man (1993)
Diario de una ninfómana (Diary of a Nymphomaniac) (2008)
Disconnect (2012)
Dogging: A Love Story (2009)
Don Jon (2013)
Dot.Kill (2005)
Downloading Nancy (2008)
Dying Gaul, The (2005)
Easier With Practice (2000)
Eating Out 3: All You Can Eat (2009)
eCupid (2011)
El tercero (The Third One) (2014)
EuroTrip (2004)
Every Mother's Worst Fear (1998)
Ex Machina (2015)
FearDotCom (2002)
Feed (2005)
Fetish (Make Yourself At Home) (2008)
Finding Faith (2013)
Fireproof (2008)
Frenzy (1972)
Gamer (2009)
Geography Club (2013)
Get Carter (1971)
Gigante (Giant) (2009)
Girl 6 (1996)
Girl He Met Online, The (2014)
Girl with No Number, The (2011)
Girl$ (2010)
Going the Distance (2012)
Good Luck Chuck (2007)
Hard Candy (2005)
Hello, Dolly! (1969)
Her (2013)

Hitch (2005)
Honeymoon Killers, The (1969)
Hooked (2003)
Hot Tub Time Machine (2010)
*How a French Nobleman Got a Wife Through the 'New York Herald' Personal
   Columns* (1904)
Husband She Met Online, The (2013)
I Love You, Man (2009)
I Origins (2014)
In Search of a Midnight Kiss (2007)
Inbetweeners 2, The (2014)
inter.m@tes (2004)
Internet Dating (2008)
Is It Just Me? (2010)
Jack and Jill (2011)
Jay and Silent Bob Strike Back (2001)
Jobs (2013)
Johnny Mnemonic (1995)
Kairo (Pulse) (2001)
Karmina (1996)
L'amore in città (Love in the City) (1953)
Landru (Bluebeard) (1963)
Lawnmower Man, The (1992)
Lil Bub & Friendz (2013)
Little Children (2006)
Lonely Hearts (2006)
Look @ Me (2006)
Love, Sex and Eating the Bones (2003)
Lured (1947)
Maniac (2012)
Matchmaker, The (1958)
Matchmaker, The (1997)
Matrix, The (1999)
Me and You and Everyone We Know (2005)
Medianeras (Sidewalls) (2011)
Meet Prince Charming (2002)
Megan is Missing (2011)
Men, Women & Children (2014)
Metropolis (1927)
Middle Men (2009)
Miss Kicki (2009)
Miss Match (2003)
Model and the Marriage Broker, The (1951)
Mojave Phone Booth (2006)
Monsieur Verdoux (1947)
Murder Dot Com (2008)
Must Love Dogs (2005)
Napoleon Dynamite (2004)
Net Games (2003)

Net, The (1995)
NetForce (1999)
Next Stop Wonderland (1998)
Occident (2002)
On_Line (2002)
One Chance (2013)
Online (2013)
Pairan (Failan) (2001)
Parenthood (1989)
Paul Blart: Mall Cop (2009)
Perfect Couple, A (1979)
Perfect Man, The (2005)
Perfect Romance (2004)
Perfect Stranger (2007)
Personal (1904)
Personals, The (1982)
Pièges (Personal Column) (1939)
Profundo Carmesí (Deep Crimson) (1996)
Pulse 2: The Afterlife (2008)
Red State (2011)
Reflections in a Golden Eye (1967)
Riri Shushu no subete (All About Lily Chou-Chou) (2001)
Runaways, The (2010)
Saber, The (2007)
Satsujin Douga Sit (Death Tube: Broadcast Murder Show) (2010)
Sea of Love (1989)
Selling Innocence (2005)
Sex Drive (2008)
Sex Tape (2014)
Sexting in Suburbia (2012)
Shadow of a Doubt (1943)
Shame (2011)
Shop Around the Corner, The (1940)
Singles (1992)
Smiley (2012)
Snow Globe Christmas, A (2013)
Something's Gotta Give (2003)
Somewhere Tonight (2011)
Steve Jobs (2015)
Strange Days (1995)
Strangeland (1998)
Strangers Online (2009)
Sum of Us, The (1994)
Surrogates (2009)
Talhotblond (2009)
Talhotblond (2012)
Temptation: Confessions of a Marriage Counselor (2013)
Ten Inch Hero (2007)
Thanks for Sharing (2012)

Thomas est amoureux (Thomas in Love) (2000)
Trainwreck (2015)
Transcendence (2014)
Trust (2010)
Truth (2013)
Truth About Cats and Dogs, The (1996)
Untraceable (2008)
Uphill Battle (2013)
UWantMe2KillHim? (2013)
Velvet Goldmine (1998)
Very Harold & Kumar 3D Christmas, A (2011)
Very Merry Mix-Up, A (2013)
Virginity Hit, The (2010)
Virtuosity (1995)
Web of Desire (2009)
Weird Science (1985)
Wife He Met Online, The (2012)
Wish I Was Here (2014)
You and I (2011)
You Can't Hurry Love (1988)
You've Got Mail (1998)
Zheng hun qi shi (The Personals) (1998)

Television Shows

2 Broke Girls (2011–)
3rd Rock from the Sun (1996–2001)
A to Z (2014–15)
Absolutely Fabulous (1992–2012)
Ally McBeal (1997–2002)
Alpha House (2013–)
American Dad! (2005–)
American Horror Story (2011–)
Arrested Development (2003–14)
Baby Daddy (2012–)
Being Erica (2009–11)
Betas (2014)
Big Bang Theory, The (2007–)
Big C, The (2010–13)
Black Box (2014)
Blue Bloods (2010–)
Blue Murder (2001–4)
Bones (2005–)
Boondocks, The (2005–)
Bosom Buddies (1980–82)
Boston Legal (2004–8)
Brotherly Love (1995–97)
Buffy the Vampire Slayer (1997–2003)
Burn It (2003)

Californication (2007–14)
Criminal Minds (2005–)
CSI (2000–2015)
CSI: Cyber (2015–)
Dateline (1992–)
Dates (2013)
Dawson's Creek (1998–2003)
DCI Banks (2010–)
Degrassi: The Next Generation (2001–)
Dexter (2006–13)
District, The (2000–2004)
Doc Martin (2004–)
Drew Carey Show, The (1995–2004)
Elementary (2012–)
Escape Artist, The (2013)
Exes, The (2011–)
Faking It (2014–)
Fall, The (2013–)
Family Guy (1999–)
Family Matters (1989–98)
Fargo (2014–)
Flashpoint (2008–12)
Fresh Prince of Bel-Air, The (1990–96)
Friends (1994–2004)
Futurama (1999–2013)
Gates, The (2010)
Ghostwriter (1992–95)
Girls (2012–)
Glee (2009–15)
Good Wife, The (2009–)
Grace and Frankie (2015–)
Grey's Anatomy (2005–)
Ground Floor (2013–15)
Hart of Dixie (2011–15)
Homeland (2011–)
Hot in Cleveland (2010–)
Hot Properties (2005)
House (2004–12)
House of Cards (2013–)
How I Met Your Mother (2005–14)
How to Get Away With Murder (2014–)
Inbetweeners, The (2008–10)
Inspector Lynley Mysteries, The (2001–7)
Intelligence (2014)
It's Always Sunny in Philadelphia (2005–)
Jacob: The Series (2015)
Jane By Design (2012)
Joey (2004–6)
Johnny Bravo (1997–2004)

jPod (2008) *Killer Net* (1998)
L Word, The (2004–9)
Law & Order: Special Victims Unit (1999–)
League, The (2009–)
Lewis (2006–)
Lip Service (2010–12)
Looking (2014–15)
Love at Risk (2013)
Lovespring International (2006)
Mad About You (1992–99)
Make It or Break It (2009–12)
Manhattan Love Story (2014)
Marble Hornets (2009–14)
Married With Children (1987–97)
Marry Me (2014–15)
Mentalist, The (2008–15)
Millennium (1996–99)
Millers, The (2013–15)
Mindy Project, The (2012–)
Modern Family (2009–)
Mr. Robot (2015–)
My Family (2000–2011)
My Three Sons (1960–72)
Nanny, The (1993–99)
Nash Bridges (1996–2001)
NCIS (2003–)
Neighbours (1985–)
New Girl (2011–)
New Tricks (2003–)
No Ordinary Family (2010–11)
Numb3rs (2005–10)
Nurse Jackie (2009–)
Odd Couple, The (1970–75)
Office, The (2005–13)
Orange is the New Black (2013–)
Orphan Black (2013–)
Parks and Recreation (2009–15)
Please Like Me (2013–)
Practice, The (1997–2004)
Psych (2006–14)
Queer as Folk (2000–2005)
Real McCoys, The (1957–63)
Red Green Show, The (1991–2006)
Saturday Night Live (1975–)
Scandal (2012–)
Scott & Bailey (2011–)
Scrubs (2001–10)
Selfie (2014)
Sex and the City (1998–2004)

Silicon Valley (2014–)
Simpsons, The (1989–)
Skins (2007–13)
Sliders (1995–2000)
Smallville (2001–11)
Sons of Anarchy (2008–14)
South Park (1997–)
Stalker (2014–15)
Starlings (2012–13)
State of Affairs (2014–)
Suddenly Susan (1996–2000)
Suits (2011–)
Super Fun Night (2013–14),
Supernatural (2005–)
Tell Me You Love Me (2007)
The Simpsons (1989–)
Three's Company (1977–84)
Trophy Wife (2013–14)
Two and a Half Men (2003–)
Ugly Betty (2006–10),
Veronica Mars (2004–7)
VR.5 (1995)
Web Therapy (2011–)
Wild Palms (1993)
Winter (2015–)
Without a Trace (2002–9)
X-Files, The (1993–2002)

Songs

The Beatles, "Can't Buy Me Love" (1964)
Kenny Loggins, "Danny's Song" (1971)
The Little River Band, "Lonesome loser" (1979)

Bibliography

"Baby Found Alive; Woman Arrested". *CNN*, December 18, 2004. Accessed July 15, 2015, from http://www.cnn.com/2004/US/12/18/fetus.found.alive/index.html?eref=sitesearch.

"Internet Is Rife with Fraud and as Lawless as Wild West, Warn Peers". *The Times* (London), August 10, 2007, 5.

"Online Dating No Longer Loser Central". *Corpus Christi Caller-Times*, June 29, 2003. Accessed July 11, 2015, from LexisNexis.

Agger, Ben. *Oversharing: Presentations of Self in the Internet Age*. New York: Routledge, 2012.

Akst, Daniel. *Temptation: Finding Self-Control in an Age of Excess*. New York: Penguin, 2011.

Albright, Julie M. and Eddie Simmens. "Flirting, Cheating, Dating and Mating in a Virtual World". In *The Oxford Handbook of Virtuality*. Edited by Mark Grimshaw. New York: Oxford University Press, 2014, 284–303.

Allweiss, David. "Copyright Infringement on the Internet: Can the Wild, Wild West Be Tamed". *Touro Law Review*, 15, 3, 1999, 1005–52.

Amichai-Hamburger, Yair and Elisheva Ben-Artzi. "Loneliness and Internet Use". *Computers in Human Behavior*, 19, 2003, 71–80.

Anderegg, David. *Nerds: How Dorks, Dweebs, Techies and Trekkies Can Save America*. New York: Penguin, 2011.

Ansari, Aziz and Eric Klinenberg. "How to Make Online Dating Work". *New York Times*, June 13, 2015. Accessed June 27, 2015, from http://www.nytimes.com/2015/06/14/opinion/sunday/how-to-make-online-dating-work.html.

Ansari, Aziz and Eric Klinenberg. *Modern Dating*. New York: Penguin, 2015.

Arquilla, John and David Ronfeldt. *In Athena's Camp: Preparing for Conflict in the Information Age*. Santa Monica, CA: RAND, 1997.

Ashford, Chris. "From Cruising to Dogging: The Surveillance and Consumption of Public Sex". In *Out of the Ordinary: Representations of LGBT Lives*. Edited by Ian Rivers and Richard Ward. Newcastle: Cambridge Scholars, 2012, 77–92.

Attwood, Feona. "The Sexualization of Culture". In *Mainstreaming Sex: The Sexualization of Western Culture*. Edited by Feona Attwood. London: I.B. Tauris, 2009, xiii–2.

Barkho, Gabriela. "Have Hookup Apps Killed Digital Dating Stigma?" *The Daily Dot*. September 17, 2014. Accessed August 23, 2015, from http://www.dailydot.com/lifestyle/online-dating-stigma/.

Barlow, John Perry. "Crime and Puzzlement". *Whole Earth Review*, Fall, 1990, 44–47.

Barraket, Jo and Millsom S. Henry-Waring. "Getting It On(line) Sociological Perspectives on E-dating". *Journal of Sociology*, 44, 2008, 149–165.

Batteau, Allen W. *Technology and Culture*. Long Grove, IL: Waveland Press, 2010.

Bauman, Zygmunt. *Liquid Love: On the Frailty of Human Bonds*. Malden, MA: Polity Press, 2003.

Beamon, Nika C. *I Didn't Work This Hard Just to Get Married: Successful Single Black Women Speak Out*. Chicago, IL: Lawrence Hill, 2009.

Ben-Ze'ev, Aaron. *Love Online: Emotions on the Internet*. New York: Cambridge University Press, 2004.

Bercovici, Jeff. "Love on the Run: The Next Revolution in Online Dating". *Forbes*, February 14, 2014. Accessed July 11, 2015, from http://www.forbes.com/sites/jeffbercovici/2014/02/14/love-on-the-run-the-next-revolution-in-online-dating/.

Black, Claudia. *Deceived: Facing Sexual Betrayal Lies and Secrets*. Center City, MN: Hazelden, 2009.

Block, Joel D. and Kimberly Dawn Neumann. *The Real Reasons Men Commit: Why He Will—or Won't—Love, Honor and Marry You*. Avon, MA: Adams Media, 2009.

Bocij, Paul. *The Dark Side of the Internet: Protecting Yourself and Your Family from Online Criminals*. Westport, CT: Praeger, 2006.

Boris, Eileen. *Intimate Labors: Cultures, Technologies, and the Politics of Care*. Stanford, CA: Stanford University Press, 2010.

Brett, Samantha. *The Catch: How to Be Found by the Man of Your Dreams*. Sydney: Allen and Unwin, 2012.

Bridges, John C. *The Illusion of Intimacy: Problems in the World of Online Dating*. Santa Barbara, CA: Praeger, 2012.

Bruce, Michael. "The Virtual Bra Clasp: Navigating Technology in College Courtship". In *College Sex—Philosophy for Everyone*. Edited by Michael Bruce and Robert M. Stewart. Malden, MA: John Wiley & Sons, 2010, 40–50.

Busby, Amy. "Online Dating Not for Losers". *Pearland Journal*, March 26, 2009, A2.

Cacioppo, John T., James H. Fowler and Nicholas A. Christakis. "Alone in the Crowd: The Structure and Spread of Loneliness in a Large Social Network". *Journal of Personality and Social Psychology*, 97, 7, 2009, 977–91.

Cacioppo, John T., Stephanie Cacioppo, Gian C. Gonzaga, Elizabeth L. Ogburn, and Tyler J. VanderWeele. "Marital Satisfaction and Break-ups Differ Across On-line and Off-line Meeting Venues". *Psychological & Cognitive Sciences*, 110, 2013, 10135–40.

Campbell, John Edward. *Getting It On Online: Cyberspace, Gay Male Sexuality and Embodied Identity*. New York: Harrington Park Press, 2004.

Carnes, Patrick. *Out of the Shadows: Understanding Sexual Addiction*. Center City, MN: Hazelden, 2001.

Cass, Vivienne C. "Homosexual Identity Formation: A Theoretical Model". *Journal of Homosexuality*, 4, 30, 1979, 219–35.

Chen, Brian X. *Always On*. Philadelphia, PA: Da Capo Press, 2012.

Chen, Wenhong. "Internet Use, Online Communication, and Ties in Americans' Networks". *Social Science Computer Review*, 31, 4 (2013): 404–23.

Cheok, Adrian David. *Art and Technology of Entertainment Computing and Communication*. New York: Springer, 2010.

Childress, Natalye. *Aftermath of Forever: How I Loved, Lost, and Found Myself*. Portland, OR: Microcosm, 2014.

Chin, Yann-Ling. "'Platonic Relationships' in China's Online Social Milieu: A Lubricant for Banal Everyday Life?" *Chinese Journal of Communication*, 4, 4, 2011, 400–416.

Clayton, Russell B. "The Third Wheel: The Impact of Twitter Use on Relationship Infidelity and Divorce". *Cyberpsychology, Behavior, and Social Networking*, 17, 7, 2014, 425–30.

Clayton, Russell B., Alexander Nagurney and Jessica R. Smith. "Cheating, Breakup, and Divorce: Is Facebook Use to Blame?" *Cyberpsychology, Behavior, and Social Networking*, 16, 10, 2013, 717–20.

Cocks, Harry. *Classified: The Secret History of the Personal Column*. London: Random House, 2009.

Connell, Claudia. "Single White Female Seeks Anyone Other Than These Losers". *Daily Mail (London)*, January 20, 2011, 56.

Cooper, Al. "Sexuality and the Internet: Surfing into the New Millennium". *CyberPsychology & Behavior*, 1, 1998, 187–93.

Cooper, Al, Coralie Scherer and I. David Marcus. "Harnessing the Power of the Internet to Improve Sexual Relationships". In *Sex and the Internet: A Guidebook for Clinicians*. Edited by Al Cooper. New York: Brunner-Routledge, 2002, 209–30.

Cooper, Al and Eric Griffin-Shelley. "Introduction. The Internet: The Next Sexual Revolution". In *Sex and the Internet: A Guidebook for Clinicians*. Edited by Al Cooper and Eric Griffin-Shelley. New York: Brunner-Routledge, 2002, 1–15.

Cornwell, Benjamin and David C. Lundgren. "Love on the Internet: Involvement and Misrepresentation in Romantic Relationships in Cyberspace vs. Realspace". *Computers in Human Behavior*, 17, 2001, 197–211.

Couch, Danielle, Pranee Liamputtong and Marian Pitts. "What Are the Real and Perceived Risks and Dangers of Online Dating? Perspectives from Online Daters". *Health, Risk & Society*, 14, 7–8, 2012, 697–714.

Cravens, Jaclyn D. and Jason B. Whiting. "Clinical Implications of Internet Infidelity: Where Facebook Fits In". *American Journal of Family Therapy*, 42, 2014, 325–39.

Cumming, Alan. *Not My Father's Son: A Memoir*. New York: HarperCollins, 2014.

Darné, Kevin. "Online Dating: Is Everyone a Catfish, Conman, Liar, Cheater, Predator or Loser?". *Chicago Examiner*, March 4, 2013. Accessed July 11, 2015, from http://www.examiner.com/article/online-dating-is-everyone-a-catfish-conman-liar-cheater-predator-or-loser.

Davis, Laurie. *Love at First Click: The Ultimate Guide to Online Dating*. New York: Simon and Schuster, 2013.

Daynes, Kerry. "Is There a Psychopath in Your Inbox?". *The Telegraph*, February 2, 2012. Accessed July 15, 2015, from http://www.telegraph.co.uk/lifestyle/9064008/Is-there-a-psychopath-in-your-inbox.html.

Delaney, Brigid. *This Restless Life: Churning Through Love, Work and Travel*. Carlton: Melbourne University Press, 2009.

DeMasi, Sophia. "Shopping for Love: Online Dating and the Making of a Cyber Culture of Romance". In *Handbook of the New Sexuality Studies*. Edited by Steven Seidman, Nancy Fischer and Chet Meeks. New York: Routledge, 2006, 223–32.

Dembling, Sophia. *Introverts in Love: The Quiet Way to Happily Ever After*. New York: Perigee Books, 2015.

Dewey, Caitlin. "The Complete, Terrifying History of 'Slender Man,' the Internet Meme That Compelled Two 12-Year-Olds to Stab Their Friend". *The Washington Post*, June 3, 2014. Accessed July 15, 2015, from http://www.washingtonpost.com/news/the-intersect/wp/2014/06/03/the-complete-terrifying-history-of-slender-man-the-internet-meme-that-compelled-two-12-year-olds-to-stab-their-friend/.

DeZellar, Amy. *Dating Amy: 50 True Confessions of a Serial Dater*. New York: Hachette, 2006.

Dijkstra, Pieternel, Dick P. H. Barelds and Hinke A.K. Groothof, "Jealousy in Response to Online and Offline Infidelity: The Role of Sex and Sexual Orientation", *Scandinavian Journal of Psychology*, 54, 2013, 328–36.

Dinello, Daniel. *Technophobia! Science Fiction Visions of Posthuman Technology*. Austin: University of Texas Press, 2005.

Dines, Gail, Robert J. Jensen and Ann Russo. *Pornography: The Production and Consumption of Inequality*. New York: Routledge, 1998.

Dishman, J. Dallas. "Ecologies of Cyberspace: Gay Communities on the Internet". In *From Chicago to L.A.: Making Sense of Urban Theory*. Edited by Michael Dear. Thousand Oaks, CA: Sage, 2002, 293–318.

Dixon, Wheeler W. *The Charm of Evil: The Life and Films of Terence Fisher*. Metuchen, NJ: Scarecrow Press, 1991.

Donn, Jessica E. and Richard C. Sherman. "Attitudes and Practices Regarding the Formation of Romantic Relationships on the Internet". *CyberPsychology & Behavior*, 5, 2, 2002, 107–23.

Donnelly, Ashley M. *Renegade Hero or Faux Rogue: The Secret Traditionalism of Television Bad Boys*. Jefferson, NC: McFarland, 2014.

Dunham, Lena. *Not That Kind of Girl: A Young Woman Tells You What She's Learned*. New York: Random House, 2014.

Dunn, Michael J., Stacey Brinton and Lara Clark. "Universal Sex Differences in Online Advertisers Age Preferences: Comparing Data from 14 Cultures and 2 Religion Groups". *Evolution and Human Behavior*, 31, 6, 2010, 383–93.

Durkin, Keith F. "The Internet as a Milieu for the Management of a Stigmatized Sexual Identity". In *Net.seXX: Readings on Sex, Pornography and the Internet*. Edited by Dennis D. Waskul. New York: Peter Lang, 2004, 131–47.

Dvorak, John, Chris Pirillo and Wendy Taylor, *Online! The Book*. Upper Saddle River, NJ: Pearson Education, 2004.

Eckel, Sara. *It's Not You: 27 (Wrong) Reasons You're Single*. New York: Penguin, 2014.

Edgley, Charles and Kenneth Kiser. "Polaroid Sex: Deviant Possibilities in a Technological Age". *Journal of American Culture*, 5, 1, 1981, 59–64.

Edwards, Rosy. *Confessions of a Tinderella*. New York: Cornerstone, 2015.

Eerikäinen, Hannu. "Cybersex: A Desire for Disembodiment. On the Meaning of the Human Being in Cyber Discourse". In *Mediapolis: Aspects of Texts, Hypertexts, and Multimedial Communication*. Edited by Sam Inkinen. Berlin: Walter de Gruyter, 1998, 203–42.

Egan, Jennifer. "Lonely Gay Teen Seeking Same". *New York Times Magazine*, December 10, 2000. Accessed February 18, 2015, from http://www.nytimes.com/2000/12/10/magazine/lonely-gay-teen-seeking-same.html.

Eggers, Dave. *The Circle*. New York: Vintage Books, 2013.

Fallik, Dawn. "Online Losers Are Easy to Spot; Danger Signs in Internet Dating". *The Philadelphia Inquirer*, November 19, 2006, F02.

Fein, Ellen and Sherrie Schneider. *The Rules for Online Dating: Capturing the Heart of Mr. Right in Cyberspace*. New York: Pocket Books, 2002.

Ferguson, Anthony. *The Sex Doll: A History*. Jefferson, NC: McFarland, 2010.

Fertik, Michael and David Thompson. *Wild West 2.0.: How to Protect and Restore Your Online Reputation on the Untamed Social Frontier*. New York: American Management Association, 2010.

Finkel, Eli J., Paul W. Eastwick, Benjamin R. Karney, Harry T. Reis and Susan Sprecher. "Online Dating: a Critical Analysis from the Perspective of Psychological Science". *Psychological Science in the Public Interest*, 13, 1, 2012, 3–66.

Foxton, Willard. "Online Dating: How Devious Companies Make Money Out of Heartache". *The Telegraph*, February 14, 2013. Accessed June 27, 2015, from http://blogs.telegraph.co.uk/technology/willardfoxton2/100008824/online-dating-how-devious-companies-make-money-out-of-heartache/.

Franek, Mark. "Foiling Cyberbullies in the New Wild West". *Educational Leadership*, 63, 4, 2005, 39–43.

Freeman-Longo, Robert E. "Children, Teens, and Sex on the Internet". In *Cybersex: The Dark Side of the Force*. Edited by Al Cooper. Philadelphia: Brunner-Routledge, 2000, 75–90.

Gartland, Fiona. "Graham Dwyer and Elaine O'Hara: The Master-Slave Relationship". *The Irish Times*, March 30, 2015. Accessed July 15, 2015, from http://www.irishtimes.com/news/crime-and-law/graham-dwyer-and-elaine-o-hara-the-master-slave-relationship-1.2156173.

Gaylin, Willard. *The Male Ego*. New York: Viking, 1992.

Geraci, Ron. *The Bachelor Chronicles*. New York: Kensington Books, 2006.

Gerbner, George. "Toward 'Cultural Indicators': The Analysis of Mass Mediated Message Systems". In *The Analysis of Communication Content: Developments in Scientific Theories and Computer Techniques*. Edited by George Gerbner, Ole R. Holsti, Klaus Krippendorf, William J. Paisley, and Philip J. Stone. New York: John Wiley, 1969, 123–132.

Gerbner, George and Larry Gross. "Living with Television: The Violence Profile". *Journal of Communication*, 26, 2, 1976, 173–99.

Gershon, Ilana. *The Breakup 2.0: Disconnecting Over New Media*. Ithaca, NY: Cornell University Press, 2010.

Gershon, Ilana. "The Samoan Roots of the Manti Te'o Hoax". *The Atlantic*, January 24, 2013. Accessed August 20, 2015, from http://www.theatlantic.com/entertainment/archive/2013/01/the-samoan-roots-of-the-manti-teo-hoax/272486/.

Gibbs, Jennifer L., Nicole B. Ellison, and Rebecca D. Heino. "Self-Presentation in Online Personals: The Role of Anticipated Future Interaction, Self-Disclosure, and Perceived Success in Internet Dating". *Communication Research*, 33, 2, 2006, 152–77.

Gilbey, Ryan. "Trust Me, I'm a Film-Maker: The Men Behind Catfish Come Clean". *The Guardian*, November 19, 2010. Accessed July 7, 2015, from http://www.theguardian.com/film/2010/nov/20/catfish-fact-or-fiction-film.

Glöckner, Carsten. *Sex 2.0: Pornography and Prostitution Influenced by the Internet Feminist Views on Pornography and Prostitution*. Munich: Verlag, 2009.

Gonzaga, Gian. *eHarmony Guide to Dating the Second Time Around*. London: Hachette, 2011.

Greenfield, David and Maressa Orzack. "The Electronic Bedroom: Clinical Assessment of Online Problems and Internet-Enabled Sexual Behavior". In *Sex and the Internet:*

A Guidebook for Clinicians. Edited by Al Cooper. New York: Brunner-Routledge, 2002, 129–45.

Greenspan, Sam. *11 Points Guide to Hooking Up.* New York: Skyhorse, 2011.

Griscom, Rufus. "Why Are Online Personals So Hot?" *Wired*, November 2002. Accessed July 16, 2015, from http://archive.wired.com/wired/archive/10.11/view.html?pg=2.

Grish, Kristina. *The Joy of Text: Mating, Dating, and Techno-Relating.* New York: Simon Spotlight Entertainment, 2006.

Guadagno, Rosanna E., Bradley M. Okdie and Sara A. Kruse. "Dating Deception: Gender, Online Dating, and Exaggerated Self-Presentation". *Computers in Human Behavior*, 28, 2012, 642–47.

Gwinnell, Esther. *Online Seductions: Falling in Love with Strangers on the Net.* New York: Kodansha International, 1998.

Hall, Jeffrey A. "First Comes Social Networking, Then Comes Marriage? Characteristics of Americans Married 2005–2012 Who Met Through Social Networking Sites". *Cyberpsychology, Behavior and Social Networking*, 17, 5, 2014, 322–26.

Hall, Paula. *Understanding and Treating Sex Addiction.* New York: Routledge, 2013.

Hancock, Jeffrey T. "Digital Deception: Why, When and How People Lie Online". In *Oxford Handbook of Internet Psychology.* Edited by Adam Joinson, Katelyn McKenna, Tom Postmes and Ulf-Dietrich Reips. New York: Oxford University Press, 2009, 289–302.

Hancock, Jeffrey T., Catalina Toma and Nicole Ellison. "Separating Fact from Fiction: An Examination of Deceptive Self-Presentation in Online Dating Profiles". *Personality and Social Psychology Bulletin*, 34, 8, 2008, 1023–36.

Hancock, Jeffrey T., Catalina Toma and Nicole Ellison. "The Truth about Lying in Online Dating Profiles". *CHI 2007 Proceedings*, 2007, 449–52. Accessed July 25, 2015, from https://msu.edu/~nellison/hancock_et_al_2007.pdf.

Hansen, Chris. *To Catch a Predator: Protecting Your Kids from Online Enemies Already in Your Home.* New York: Penguin, 2007.

Harmon, Amy. "Online Dating Not Just for Lovable Losers". *Lexington Herald-Leader*, June 29, 2003. Accessed July 11, 2015, from LexisNexis.

Hertlein, Katherine M. "The Integration of Technology into Sex Therapy". *Journal of Family Psychotherapy*, 21, 2010, 117–31.

Hertlein, Katherine M. and Fred P. Piercy. "Essential Elements of Internet Infidelity Treatment". *Journal of Marital and Family Therapy*, 38, 2012, 257–70.

Hess, Amanda. "Online Dating Will Soon Be Obsolete". *Slate*, October 21, 2013. Accessed August 21, 2015, from http://www.slate.com/blogs/xx_factor/2013/10/21/pew_study_on_internet_romance_online_dating_is_more_normal_than_ever_but.html.

Hitsch, Günter J., Ali Hortaçsu and Dan Ariely. "What Makes You Click: Mate Preferences in Online Dating". *Quantitative Marketing and Economics*, 8, 4, 2010, 393–427.

Hod, Itay. "Why Hollywood Is Hooking Up with Tinder, Grindr for Movie, TV and Music Projects". *The Wrap*, June 3, 2015. Accessed August 1, 2015, from http://www.thewrap.com/hollywood-swipes-right-for-tinder-grindr-to-market-movies-tv-and-music/.

Hollander, Dore. "Among Young Adults, Use of the Internet to Find Sexual Partners Is Rising". *Perspectives on Sexual and Reproductive Health*, 34, 6, 2002, 134–46.

Howitt, Dennis and Kerry Sheldon. *Sex Offenders and the Internet*. Hoboken, NJ: John Wiley & Sons, 2007.

Hunter, Alan. "Review: Men, Women & Children Starring Jennifer Garner and Adam Sandler". *Express*, December 5, 2014. Accessed March 23, 2015, from http://www.express.co.uk/entertainment/films/543955/Men-Women-Children-review-starring-Jennifer-Garner-Adam-Sandler.

Illouz, Eva. *Consuming the Romantic Utopia: Love and the Cultural Contradictions of Capitalism*. Berkeley: University of California Press, 1997.

Illouz, Eva. *Why Love Hurts: A Sociological Explanation*. Malden, MA: Polity, 2012.

Jacobson, Bonnie. *The Shy Single: A Bold Guide to Dating for the Less-Than-Bold Dater*. Emmaus, PA: Rodale, 2004.

Jensen, John B. *The Marriage MBA: The 7 Things You Need to Know about Dating and Relationships*. Victoria, BC: Friesen Press, 2014.

Johnson, Ida M. and Robert T Sigler. *Forced Sexual Intercourse in Intimate Relationships*. Brookfield, VT: Ashgate, 1997.

Johnson, Nicola F. *The Multiplicities of Internet Addiction: The Misrecognition of Leisure and Learning*. Burlington, VT: Ashgate, 2009.

Joinson, Adam N. "Self-Esteem, Interpersonal Risk and Preference for E-mail to Face-to-Face Communication". *CyberPsychology*, 7, 2004, 472–78.

Kapsis, Robert E. *Jonathan Demme: Interviews*. Jackson: University Press of Mississippi, 2009.

Kasperkevic, Jana. "Cord Cutters on Net Neutrality". *The Guardian*, February 22, 2015. Accessed July 25, 2015, from http://www.theguardian.com/technology/2015/feb/22/cord-cutters-net-neutrality-end-wild-wild-west-nternet.

Katz, Evan Marc. *I Can't Believe I'm Buying This Book: A Commonsense Guide to Successful Internet Dating*. Berkeley, CA: Ten Speed Press, 2003.

Katz, James E. and Ronald E. Rice. *Social Consequences of Internet Use: Access, Involvement and Interaction*. Cambridge, MA: MIT Press, 2002.

Kaufmann, Jean-Claude. *Love Online*. Malden, MA: Polity, 2012.

Kay, Russell. "DeepWeb". *Computerworld*, December 19, 2005, 28.

Keats, Jonathon. *Control + Alt + Delete: A Dictionary of Cyberslang*. Guilford, CT: Lyons Press, 2007.

Kember, Sarah. "Feminist Figuration and the Question of Origin". In *Futurenatural: Nature, Science, Culture*. Edited by Jon Bird, Barry Curtis, Melinda Mash, George Robertson, Tim Putnam and Lisa Tickner. New York: Routledge, 1996, 253–66.

Kimmel, Michael S. "Masculinity as Homophobia: Fear, Shame and Silence in the Construction of Gender Identity". In *Gender Relations in Global Perspective: Essential Readings*. Edited by Nancy Cook. Toronto: Canadian Scholars' Press, 2007, 73–82.

Klesse, Christian. *The Spectre of Promiscuity: Gay Male and Bisexual Non-monogamies and Polyamories*. Burlington, VT: Ashgate, 2007.

Knoblock, Leanne K. and Kelly G. McAninch. "Uncertainty Management". In *Interpersonal Communication*. Edited by Charles R. Berger. Berlin: Walter de Gruyter, 2014, 297–320.

Kotsko, Adam. *Creepiness*. Alresford, Hants: Zero Books, 2015.

Kowalski, Robin M., Sue Limber and Patricia W. Agatston. *Cyberbullying: Bullying in the Digital Age*. Malden, MA: Wiley-Blackwell, 2012.

Kramer, Mette and Torben Grodal. "Partner Selection and Hollywood Films". In *The Psychology of Love*, volume 2. Edited by Michele A. Paludi. Santa Barbara, CA: ABC-CLIO, 2012, 3–22.

Kraut, Robert, Michael Patterson, Vicki Lundmark, Sara Kiesler, Tridas Mukopadhyay and William Scherlis. "Internet Paradox: A Social Technology That Reduces Social Involvement and Psychological Well-Being?" *American Psychologist*, 53, 9, 1998, 1017–31.

Krulos, Tea. *Monster Hunters: On the Trail with Ghost Hunters, Bigfooters, Ufologists, and Other Paranormal Investigators*. Chicago: Chicago Review Press, 2015.

Lambert, Alexander. *Intimacy and Friendship on Facebook*. New York: Palgrave Macmillan, 2013.

Lamble, Jo and Sue Morris. *Online and Personal: The Reality of Internet Relationships*. Sydney: Finch, 2001.

LaSala, Michael C. *Coming Out, Coming Home: Helping Families Adjust to a Gay or Lesbian Child*. New York: Columbia University Press, 2010.

Lawson, Helene M. and Kira Leck. "Dynamics of Internet Dating". *Social Science Computer Review*, 24, 2, 2006: 189–208.

Lea, Martin and Russell Spears. "Love at First Byte? Building Personal Relationships Over Computer Networks". In *Understudied Relationships: Off the Beaten Track*. Edited by Julia T. Wood and Steve Duck. Thousand Oaks, CA: Sage, 1995, 197–233.

Leiblum, Sandra and Nicola Döring. "Internet Sexuality: Known Risks and Fresh Chances for Women". *Sex and the Internet: A Guidebook for Clinicians*. Edited by Al Cooper. New York: Brunner-Routledge, 2002, 19–45.

Ley, David J. *The Myth of Sex Addiction*. Lanham, MD: Rowman and Littlefield, 2012.

Lieberman, Janice and Bonnie Teller. *How to Shop for a Husband: A Consumer Guide to Getting a Great Buy on a Guy*. New York: St. Martin's Press, 2009.

Lloyd, Sally A. and Beth C. Emery. *The Dark Side of Courtship: Physical and Sexual Aggression*. Thousand Oaks, CA: Sage, 2000.

Luscombe, Belinda. "Facebook and Divorce: Airing the Dirty Laundry". *Time*, June 22, 2009. Accessed August 3, 2015, from http://content.time.com/time/magazine/article/0,9171,1904147,00.html.

Madden, Mary and Amanda Lenhart. "Online Dating". Washington: Pew Internet, 2006. Accessed January 18, 2015, from http://www.pewinternet.org/2006/03/05/online-dating/.

Manjikian, Mary. *Threat Talk: The Comparative Politics of Internet Addiction*. Burlington, VT: Ashgate, 2012.

Mapes, Diane. *How to Date in a Post-Dating World*. Seattle, WA: Sasquatch Books, 2006.

Markham, Annette N. "Internet Communication as a Tool for Qualitative Research", In *Qualitative Research: Theory, Method and Practice*. Edited by David Silverman. London: Sage, 2011, 95–124.

Markowitz, Sidney L. *What You Should Know about Jewish Religion, History, Ethics and Culture*. New York: First Carol, 1992.

Martinez, Michelle. "Dating Web Sites". In *The Social History of the American Family: An Encyclopedia*. Edited by Marilyn J. Coleman and Lawrence H. Ganong. Thousand Oaks, CA: Sage, 2014, 320–22.

Masciotra, David. *Mellencamp: American Troubadour*. Lexington: University Press of Kentucky, 2015.

Massoglia, Dan. "The Webcam Hacking Epidemic". *The Atlantic*, December 23, 2014. Accessed August 27, 2015, from http://www.theatlantic.com/technology/archive/2014/12/the-webcam-hacking-epidemic/383998/.

McHugh, Molly. "Facebook Breakups Just Got a Little Less Depressing". *Wired*, November 19, 2015. Accessed December 15, 2015, from http://www.wired.com/2015/11/facebook-breakup-tools/.

McKenna, Katelyn Y.A. and John A. Bargh. "Plan 9 from Cyberspace: The Implications of the Internet for Personality and Social Psychology". *Personality and Social Psychology Review*, 4, 1, 2000, 57–75.

McNair, Brian. *Porno? Chic! How Pornography Changed the World and Made It a Better Place*. New York: Routledge, 2013.

Miraglia, Greg. *Coming Out from Behind the Badge: Stories of Success and Advice from Police Officers "Out" on the Job*. Bloomington, IN: AuthorHouse, 2007.

Mitchael, Anna. *Just Don't Call Me Ma'am: How I Ditched the South, Forgot My Manners, and Managed to Survive My Twenties with (Most of) My Dignity Still Intact*. Berkeley, CA: Seal Press, 2010.

Mokyr, Joel. *The Gifts of Athena: Historical Origins of the Knowledge Economy*. Princeton, NJ: Princeton University Press, 2002.

Mondimore, Francis Mark. *A Natural History of Homosexuality*. Baltimore: John Hopkins University Press, 1996.

Morahan-Martin, Janet and Phyllis Schumacher. "Loneliness and Social Uses of the Internet". *Computers in Human Behavior*, 19, 2003, 659–71.

Morrissey, Tracie Egan. "Satan, Rape and Murder: The Life of Miranda Barbour, Craigslist Killer". *Jezebel*, February 21, 2014. Accessed July 15, 2015, from http://jezebel.com/satan-rape-and-murder-the-life-of-miranda-barbour-cr-1526169756.

Murray, Christine E. and Emily C. Campbell. "The Pleasures and Perils of Technology in Intimate Relationships". *Journal of Couple & Relationship Therapy: Innovations in Clinical and Educational Interventions*, 14, 2015, 116–40.

Muskat, Hedda. *Dating Confidential: A Singles Guide to a Fun, Flirtatious and Possibly Meaningful Social Life*. Naperville, IL: Sourcebooks, 2004.

Nakamoto, Steve. *Men Are Like Fish: What Every Woman Needs to Know about Catching a Man*. Hunting Beach, CA: Java Books, 2010.

Neal, Arthur G. and Sara F. Collas. *Intimacy and Alienation*. New York: Garland, 2000.

Neves, Barbara Barbosa. "Does the Internet Matter for Strong Ties? Bonding Social Capital, Internet Use, and Age-Based Inequality". *International Review of Sociology*, 24 July (2015): 1–19.

Nie, Norman H. "Sociability, Interpersonal Relations, and the Internet: Reconciling Conflicting Findings". *American Behavioral Scientist*, 45, 3, 2001, 420–35.

O'Hehir, Andrew. "Untangling the "Catfish" Hoax Rumors". *Salon*, October 14, 2010. Accessed July 7, 2015, from http://www.salon.com/2010/10/14/catfish/.

Olds, Jacqueline and Richard S. Schwartz. *The Lonely American: Drifting Apart in the Twenty-First Century*. Boston MA: Beacon Press, 2009.

Orth, Maureen. "Killer@Craigslist". *Vanity Fair*, October 2009. Accessed July 15, 2015, from http://www.vanityfair.com/culture/2009/10/craigslist-murder200910.

Oyer, Paul. *Everything I Needed to Know about Economics I Learned from Online Dating*. Boston, MA: Harvard Business Review Press, 2014.

Ozder, Cleo. *Virtual Spaces: Sex and the Cyber Citizen*. New York: Berkley Books, 1990.

Paasonen, Susanna. *Carnal Resonance: Affect and Online Pornography*. Cambridge, MA: MIT Press, 2011.

Parker, Carol. *The Joy of Cyber Sex*. Kew, Victoria: Mandarin, 1997.

Parks, Malcolm R. and Lynne D. Roberts. "Making Moosic: The Development of Personal Relationships on Line and a Comparison to Their Off-Line Counterparts". *Journal of Social and Personal Relationships*, 15, 1998, 517–37.

Pascoe, C.J. "Gay Boys", in *Boy Culture: An Encyclopedia*, v. 1. Edited by Shirley R. Steinberg, Michael Kehler and Lindsay Cornish. Santa Barbara, CA: ABC-CLIO, 2010, 11–15.

Paul, Pamela. *Pornified: How Pornography Is Transforming Our Lives, Our Relationships, and Our Families*. New York: Times Books, 2005.

Paumgarten, Nick. "Looking for Someone". *The New Yorker*, July 4, 2011. Accessed July 26, 2015, from http://www.newyorker.com/magazine/2011/07/04/looking-for-someone.

Payne, Robert. *The Promiscuity of Network Culture: Queer Theory and Digital Media*. New York: Routledge, 2015.

Pearce, Robert W. and Cherie W. Blackburn. "'Wild, Wild West' of the Internet Collides with Trademark Law". *South Carolina Business Journal*, 19, 3, 2000, 7–10.

Penn, Mark and E. Kinney Zalesne. *Microtrends: The Small Forces Behind Tomorrow's Big Changes*. New York: Twelve, 2007.

Perlroth, Nicole and David E. Sanger. "Obama Calls for New Cooperation to Wrangle the 'Wild West' Internet". *The New York Times*, February 13, 2015. Accessed July 25, 2015, from http://www.nytimes.com/2015/02/14/business/obama-urges-tech-companies-to-cooperate-on-internet-security.html?_r=0.

Phillips, Kendall R. *Projected Fears: Horror Films and American Culture*. Westport, CT: Praeger, 2005.

Pomerance, Murray. *City That Never Sleeps: New York and the Filmic Imagination*. Piscataway, NJ: Rutgers University Press, 2007.

Putnam, Robert D. *Bowling Alone: The Collapse and Revival of American Community*. New York: Simon and Schuster, 2000.

Quayle, Ethel and Max Taylor. *Child Pornography: An Internet Crime*. New York: Routledge, 2003.

Reibstein, Janet and Martin Richards. *Sexual Arrangements*. London: Heinemann, 1992.

Reis, Elizabeth. "Impossible Hermaphrodites: Intersex in America, 1620–1960". *Journal of American History*, 92, 2, 2005, 411–41.

Richardson, Niall, Clarissa Smith and Angela Werndly. *Studying Sexualities: Theories, Representations, Cultures*. London: Palgrave Macmillan, 2013.

Roche, Mary M. Doyle. *Children, Consumerism, and the Common Good*. Lanham, MD: Lexington Books, 2009.

Rosewarne, Lauren. "Don't Blame Stephanie Scott's Murder on the Internet". *ABC The Drum*, April 15, 2015. Accessed April 30, 2015, from http://www.abc.net.au/news/2015-04-15/rosewarne-dont-blame-stephanie-scotts-murder-on-the-internet/6394560.

Rosewarne, Lauren. "Happily, Willingly Manipulated". *The Conversation*, April 23, 2015. Accessed July 29, 2015, from https://theconversation.com/happily-willingly-manipulated-40710.

Rosewarne, Lauren. "Her, Hungry Ghosts and Rethinking Intimacy". *The Conversation*, February 11, 2014. Accessed July 9, 2015, from http://theconversation.com/her-hungry-ghosts-and-rethinking-intimacy-22757.

Rosewarne, Lauren. "Love Is a (Regulatory) Battlefield: The ACCC Takes on Dating Website Scammers". *The Conversation*, February 20, 2012. Accessed July 26,

2015, from https://theconversation.com/love-is-a-regulatory-battlefield-the-accc-takes-on-dating-website-scammers-5377.

Rosewarne, Lauren. "School of Shock, Film, Television and Anal Education". *Sex Education: Sexuality, Society and Learning*, 15, 4, 2015, 553–65.

Rosewarne, Lauren. "The Euphemisms Chapter". In *American Taboo: The Forbidden Words, Unspoken Rules, and Secret Morality of Popular Culture*. Santa Barbara, CA: Praeger, 2013, 67–86.

Rosewarne, Lauren. "The Fat Ugly Truth about Dating". *The Conversation*, July 10, 2015. Accessed July 12, 2015, from https://theconversation.com/the-fat-ugly-truth-about-dating-44515.

Rosewarne, Lauren. "The Hacking of Ashley Madison and the Fantasy of Infidelity". *The Drum*, July 23, 2015. Accessed July 25, 2015, from http://www.abc.net.au/news/2015-07-23/rosewarne-ashley-madison-and-the-fantasy-of-infidelity/6641742.

Rosewarne, Lauren. *Cheating on the Sisterhood: Infidelity and Feminism*. Santa Barbara, CA: Praeger, 2009.

Rosewarne, Lauren. *Cyberbullies, Cyberactivists, Cyberpredators: Film, TV, and Internet Stereotypes*. Santa Barbara, CA: Praeger, 2016.

Rosewarne, Lauren. *Masturbation in Pop Culture: Screen, Society, Self*. Lanham, MD: Lexington Books, 2014.

Rosewarne, Lauren. *Part-Time Perverts: Sex, Pop Culture and Kink Management*. Santa Barbara, CA: Praeger, 2011.

Rosewarne, Lauren. *Periods in Pop Culture: Menstruation in Film and Television*. Lanham, MD: Lexington Books, 2012.

Rosewarne, Lauren. *Sex in Public: Women, Outdoor Advertising and Public Policy*. Newcastle: Cambridge Scholars, 2007.

Ross, Jeffrey Ian. *Encyclopedia of Street Crime in America*. Thousand Oaks, CA: Sage, 2013.

Ross, Michael W. and Michael R. Kauth. "Men Who Have Sex with Men, and the Internet: Emerging Clinical Issues and Their Management". In *Sex and the Internet: A Guidebook for Clinicians*. Edited by Al Cooper. New York: Brunner-Routledge, 2002, 47–69.

Rubin, Gayle. "Thinking Sex: Notes for a Radical Theory of the Politics of Sexuality". In *The Lesbian and Gay Studies Reader*. Edited by Henry Abelove. New York: Routledge, 1993, 3–44.

Russell, Mark. "Rapist Jason John Dinsley on Parole When He Beat Sharon Siermans to Death with Cricket Bat". *The Age*, December 20, 2013. Accessed July 15, 2015, from http://www.theage.com.au/victoria/rapist-jason-john-dinsley-on-parole-when-he-beat-sharon-siermans-to-death-with-cricket-bat-20131219-2zoqq.html.

Sandywell, Barry. "Monsters in Cyberspace Cyberphobia and Cultural Panic in the Information Age". *Information, Communication & Society*, 9, 1, 2006, 39–61.

Schmitz, Andreas, Jan Skopek, Florian Schulz, Doreen Klein and Hans-Peter Blossfeld. "Indicating Mate Preferences by Mixing Survey and Process-Generated Data: The Case of Attitudes and Behaviour in Online Mate Search". *Historical Social Research*, 34, 1, 2009, 77–93.

Schneider, Jennifer P. "The New 'Elephant in the Living Room': Effects of Compulsive Cybersex Behaviors on the Spouse". In *Sex and the Internet: A Guidebook for Clinicians*. Edited by Al Cooper. New York: Brunner-Routledge, 2002, 169–86.

Schneiderman, Eric T. "Taming the Digital Wild West". *Westchester County Business Journal*, May 5, 2015. Accessed July 25, 2015, from LexisNexis.

Schreiber, Michele. *American Postfeminist Cinema: Women, Romance and Contemporary Culture*. Edinburgh: Edinburgh University Press, 2015.

Schroeder, Audra. "Mindy Kaling Wants Tinder Users to Hook Up with Her TV Show". *The Daily Dot*, January 2, 2014. Accessed August 1, 2015, from http://www.dailydot.com/entertainment/mindy-project-characters-fake-tinder-profiles/.

Schwartz, Mark F. and Stephen Southern. "Compulsive Cybersex: The New Tea Room". *Cybersex: The Dark Side of the Force*. Edited by Al Cooper. Philadelphia: Brunner-Routledge, 2000, 127–44.

Senechal, Diana. *Republic of Noise: The Loss of Solitude in Schools and Culture*. Lanham, MD: Rowman and Littlefield, 2011.

Seto, Michael C. *Internet Sex Offenders*. Washington DC: American Psychological Association, 2013.

Sharkey, Betsy. "'Men, Women & Children Is Artificial Look at Internet World". *LA Times*, September 30, 2014. Accessed March 25, 2015, from http://www.latimes.com/entertainment/movies/la-et-mn-men-women-children-review-20141001-column.html.

Shechtman, Anna. "What's Missing from Her". *Slate*, January 3, 2014. Accessed July 9, 2015, from http://www.slate.com/blogs/browbeat/2014/01/03/her_movie_by_spike_jonze_with_joaquin_phoenix_and_scarlett_johansson_lacks.html.

Shernoff, Michael. "Social Work Practice with Gay Individuals". In *Social Work Practice with Lesbian, Gay, Bisexual, and Transgender People*. Edited by Gerald P. Mallon. New York: Haworth Press, 1998, 141–78.

Shoshana, Avi. "Symbolic Interaction and New Social Media Surfing to an Alternative Self: Internet Technology and Sexuality among 'Married Straight Homosexual Men'". *Symbolic Interaction and New Media*, 43, 2014, 173–200.

Sieczkowski, Cavan. "Jesse Tyler Ferguson Came Out After He Was Caught Stealing Gay Porn". *Huffington Post*, September 26, 2014. Accessed July 28, 2015, from http://www.huffingtonpost.com/2014/09/26/jesse-tyler-ferguson-came-out-gay-porn_n_5887858.html.

Siemienowicz, Rochelle. "A Clumsy, Clammy Critique of Modern Web Culture", *SBS*, November 25, 2014. Accessed March 24, 2015, from http://www.sbs.com.au/movies/movie/men-women-children.

Silber, Dan. "How to Be Yourself in an Online World". In *Dating—Philosophy for Everyone: Flirting with Big Ideas*. Edited by Kristie Miller and Marlene Clark. Malden, MA: John Wiley & Sons, 2010, 180–94.

Silva, Kristian. "Gable Tostee Granted Bail but Banned from Tinder". *Brisbane Times*, November 19, 2014. Accessed July 27, 2015, from http://www.brisbanetimes.com.au/queensland/gable-tostee-granted-bail-but-banned-from-tinder-20141119-11po6s.html.

Silverstein, Judith and Michael Lasky. *Online Dating for Dummies*. Hoboken, NJ: Wiley, 2004.

Simmel, Georg and Kurt H. Wolff. *The Sociology of Georg Simmel*. Glencoe, IL: Free Press, 1950.

Simsion, Graeme. *The Rosie Effect: A Novel*. New York: Simon and Schuster, 2014.

Singh, Sunny. "Fear of Meeting Mr. Right". In *Single Woman of a Certain Age: Romantic Escapades, Shifting Shapes, and Serene Independence*. Edited by Jane Ganahl. Maui, HI: Inner Ocean, 2005, 113–20.

Skopek, Jan. Andreas Schmitz and Hans-Peter Blossfeld. "The Gendered Dynamics of Age Preferences: Empirical Evidence from Online Dating". *Journal of Family Research*, 3, 2011, 267–90.

Slater, Dan. "A Million First Dates: How Online Dating Is Threatening Monogamy". *The Atlantic*, 311, 1, 2013, 40–46.

Slater, Dan. *Love in the Time of Algorithms*. New York: Current, 2013.

Sledge, Kaffie. "Psychos Lurk Online". *Columbus Ledger-Enquirer*. March 13, 2003. Accessed July 15, 2015, from LexisNexis.

Smith, Brian R. *Soft Words for a Hard Technology: Humane Computerization*. Englewood Cliffs, NJ: Prentice Hall, 1984.

Smolen, Ann G. "The Multiple Meanings of the Electrified Mind". In *The Electrified Mind: Development, Psychopathology, and Treatment in the Era of Cell Phones and the Internet*. Edited by Salman Akhtar. Lanham, MD: Roman & Littlefield, 2011, 129–40.

Solomon, Steven D. and Lorie J. Teagno. *Intimacy After Infidelity: How to Rebuild and Affair-Proof Your Marriage*. Oakland, CA: New Harbinger, 2006.

Spangler, Todd. "USA's 'Suits' Gets Down and Flirty with Tinder App". *Variety*, July 12, 2013. Accessed August 1, 2015, from http://variety.com/2013/digital/news/usas-suits-gets-down-and-flirty-with-tinder-app-1200562019/.

Sparkes, Matthew. "Is Your Webcam Allowing Hackers to Peer into Your Home?" *The Telegraph*, November 20, 2014. Accessed August 27, 2015, from http://www.telegraph.co.uk/technology/news/11242650/Is-your-webcam-allowing-hackers-to-peer-into-your-home.html.

Sprecher, Susan, Amy Wenzel and John H. Harvey. *Handbook of Relationship Initiation*. New York: Psychology Press, 2008.

Stahler, Kelsea. "Is Tinder Sexist? Why I Deleted Tinder on Principle, Even Though I Used to Love It". *Bustle*, July 10, 2014. Accessed August 22, 2015, from http://www.bustle.com/articles/30917-is-tinder-sexist-why-i-deleted-tinder-on-principle-even-though-i-used-to-love-it.

Stapleton, Christine. "Online Dating Preferences Not Subject to Debate". *Palm Beach Post* (Florida), July 12, 2009, 3D.

Stark, Jill and Laura Banks. "Love Me Tinder: Is the Hook-up Culture about Liberation or Exploitation". *Sydney Morning Herald*, December 15, 2013. Accessed August 4, 2015, from http://www.smh.com.au/lifestyle/life/love-me-tinder-is-the-hookup-culture-about-liberation-or-exploitation-20131214-2ze9k.html.

Steers, Mai-Ly N., Robert E. Wickham and Linda K. Acitelli. "Seeing Everyone Else's Highlight Reels: How Facebook Usage Is Linked to Depressive Symptoms". *Journal of Social and Clinical Psychology*, 33, 8, 2014, 701–31.

Stieger, Stefan, Tina Eichinger and Britta Honeder. "Can Mate Choice Strategies Explain Sex Differences? The Deceived Persons' Feelings in Reaction to Revealed Online Deception of Sex, Age, and Appearance". *Social Psychology*, 40, 1, 2009, 16–25.

Stollak, Kayli. *Granny Is My Wingman*. New York: Houghton Mifflin Harcourt, 2013.

Strupeck, Margo. *Seven Deadly Clicks: Essential Lessons for Online Safety and Success*. San Francisco, CA: Zest Books, 2013.

Subotky, Julie. *Consider It Done: Accomplish 228 of Life's Trickiest Tasks*. New York: Random House, 2011.

Suler, John. "The Online Disinhibition Effect", *Cyber Psychology and Behavior*, 7, 2004, 321–26.

Sutton, Ted. "Project Flame". *Slate*, March 4, 2014. Accessed June 25, 2015, from http://www.slate.com/articles/technology/technology/2014/03/before_okcupid_and_match_com_there_was_project_flame_what_happened_when.html.

Thomas, Jim. "Cyberpoaching Behind the Keyboard: Uncoupling the Ethics of 'Virtual Infidelity'". In *Net.seXX: Readings on Sex, Pornography and the Internet*. Edited by Dennis D. Waskul. New York: Peter Lang, 2004, 149–77.

Thomsen, Michael. *Levitate the Primate: Handjobs, Internet Dating and Other Issues for Men*. Alresford, Hants: Zero Books, 2012.

Tsunokai, Glenn T., Allison R. McGrath and Jillian K. Kavanagh. "Online Dating Preferences of Asian Americans". *Journal of Social and Personal Relationships*, 31, 6, 2014, 796–814.

Turkle, Sherry. *Alone Together: Why We Expect More from Technology and Less from Each Other*. New York: Basic Books, 2011.

Turkle, Sherry. *Life on the Screen: Identity in the Age of the Internet*. New York: Simon and Schuster, 1995.

Van Gelder, Lindsy. "The Strange Case of the Electronic Lover". In *Computerization and Controversy: Value Conflicts and Social Choices*. Edited by Charles Dunlop and Rob Kling. New York: Academic Press, 1991, 533–46.

Vannini, Phillip. "Così Fan Tutti: Foucault, Goffman, and the Pornographic Synopticon". In *Net.seXX: Readings on Sex, Pornography and the Internet*. Edited by Dennis D. Waskul. New York: Peter Lang, 2004, 75–89.

Volney, Patrick Gay. *Freud on Sublimation: Reconsiderations*. Albany: State University of New York Press, 1992.

Wallace, Patricia. *The Psychology of the Internet*. New York: Cambridge University Press, 1999.

Wang, Yow-Juin. "Internet Dating Sites as Heterotopias of Gender Performance: A Case Study of Taiwanese Heterosexual Male Daters". *International Journal of Cultural Studies*, 15, 5, 2011, 485–500.

Waskul, Dennis D. *Self-Games and Body-Play: Personhood in Online Chat and Cyberspace*. New York: Peter Lang, 2003.

Webb, Amy. *Data, A Love Story: How I Cracked the Online Dating Code to Meet My Match*. London: Dutton, 2013.

Webb, William. *The HTTP Murders: 15 Cyber Killers You Never Want to Meet Online*. Anaheim, CA: Absolute Crime Books, 2013.

White, Michele. *The Body and the Screen: Theories of Internet Spectatorship*. Cambridge, MA: MIT Press, 2006.

Whitty, Monica and Jeff Gavin. "Age/Sex/Location: Uncovering Social Cues in the Development of Online Relationships". *CyberPsychology and Behavior*, 4, 2001, 623–30.

Whitty, Monica T. "Liar, Liar! An Examination of How Open, Supportive, and Honest People Are in Chat Rooms". *Computers in Human Behavior*, 18, 2002, 343–52.

Whitty, Monica T. and Adam N. Joinson. *Truth, Lies and Trust on the Internet*. New York: Routledge, 2009.

Whitty, Monica T. and Adrian N. Carr. *Cyberspace Romance: The Psychology of Online Relationships*. New York: Palgrave Macmillan, 2006.

Whitty, Monica T. and Laura-Lee Quigley. "Emotional and Sexual Infidelity Offline and in Cyberspace". *Journal of Marital and Family Therapy*, 34, 1, 2008, 461–68.

Wilde, Liz. *A Girl's Guide to Dating*. New York: Ryland Peters & Small, 2005.

Williams, Nanci. *Fishtails: Men Who Bite, Dates That Suck, and Other Cautionary Tales from a Mid-Life Fishing Expedition*. Cork: BookBaby, 2012.

Wilson, Bruce. "Weirdos Are Online and Out of Control". *The Daily Telegraph*, January 20, 2001. Accessed July 15, 2015, from LexisNexis.

Winks, Cathy and Anne Semans. *The Woman's Guide to Sex on the Web*. San Francisco, CA: Harper Collins, 1999.

Woolley, Alice. "Confessions of an Internet Widow". *The Independent*, June 12, 1995. Accessed August 4, 2015, from http://www.independent.co.uk/life-style/confessions-of-an-internet-widow-1586108.html.

Worthington, Christa. "Making Love in Cyberspace". *The Independent*, October 6, 1996. Accessed June 30, 2014, from http://www.independent.co.uk/arts-entertainment/making-love-in-cyberspace-1355874.html.

Wortley, Richard and Stephen Smallbone. *Internet Child Pornography: Causes, Investigation, and Prevention*. Santa Barbara, CA: Praeger, 2012.

Yarrow, Kit and Jayne O'Donnell. *Gen BuY: How Tweens, Teens and Twenty-Somethings Are Revolutionizing Retail*. San Francisco, CA: Wiley, 2009.

Young, Kimberly S. *Caught in the Net: How to Recognize the Signs of Internet Addiction—And a Winning Strategy for Recovery*. New York: John Wiley & Sons, 1998.

Young, Kimberly S. "Internet Addiction: The Emergence of a New Clinical Disorder". Paper presented at the 104th Annual Meeting of the American Psychological Association, August 16 (1996).

Young, Kimberly S. and Cristiano Nabuco de Abreu. *Internet Addiction: A Handbook and Guide to Evaluation and Treatment*. Hoboken, NJ: John Wiley & Sons, 2011.

Zeman, Ned. "The Boy Who Cried Dead Girlfriend". *Vanity Fair*, June 2013. Accessed August 20, 2015, from http://www.vanityfair.com/culture/2013/06/manti-teo-girlfriend-nfl-draft.

Zimmer, Ben. "Catfish: How Manti Te'o's Imaginary Romance Got Its Name". *The Boston Globe*, January 27, 2013. Accessed August 20, 2015, from https://www.bostonglobe.com/ideas/2013/01/27/catfish-how-manti-imaginary-romance-got-its-name/inqu9zV8RQ7j19BRGQkH7H/story.html.

Index

Printed in the United States
By Bookmasters